Cambodia

Nick Ray

KU-160-078

LONELY PLANET PUBLICATIONS
Melbourne • Oakland • London • Paris

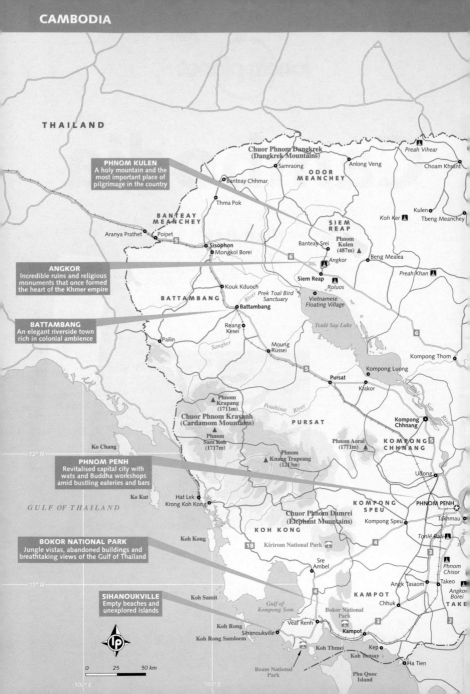

CAMBODIA

THAILAND

PHNOM KULEN
A holy mountain and the most important place of pilgrimage in the country

ANGKOR
Incredible ruins and religious monuments that once formed the heart of the Khmer empire

BATTAMBANG
An elegant riverside town rich in colonial ambience

PHNOM PENH
Revitalised capital city with wats and Buddha workshops amid bustling eateries and bars

BOKOR NATIONAL PARK
Jungle vistas, abandoned buildings and breathtaking views of the Gulf of Thailand

SIHANOUKVILLE
Empty beaches and unexplored islands

Chuor Phnom Dangrek
(Dangkrek Mountains)

Samraong

Preah Vihear

Anlong Veng

Choam Khsant

ODOR
MEANCHEY

Banteay Chhmar

Thma Pok

BANTEAY
MEANCHEY

Aranya Prathet

Poipet

Sisophon

Mongkol Borei

Kouk Kduoch

BATTAMBANG

Battambang

Reang
Kesei

Pailin

Sangker

Moung
Russei

SIEM
REAP

Koh Ker

Kulen

Tbeng Meanchey

Banteay Srei

Phnom
Kulen
(487m)

Angkor

Siem Reap

Roluos

Prek Toal Bird
Sanctuary

Vietnamese
Floating Village

Beng Mealea

Preah Khan

Tonlé Sap Lake

Kompong Thom

Ko Chang

GULF OF THAILAND

Ko Kut

Hat Lek
Krong Koh Kong

Koh Kong

Phnom
Krapang
(1711m)

Chuor Phnom Krayanh
(Cardamom Mountains)

Phnom
Sam Koh
(1717m)

Phnom
Knang Trapeang
(1213m)

Pursat

Krakor

Kompong Luong

Pouthisat River

PURSAT

Phnom Aoral
(1771m)

Kompong
Chhnang

KOMPONG
CHHNANG

Udong

KOMPONG
SPEU

Chuor Phnom Damrei
(Elephant Mountains)

KOH KONG

Koh Kong

Kirirom National Park

Sre
Ambel

Kompong Speu

PHNOM PENH

Takhmau

Tonlé Bati

Phnom
Chisor

Angk Tasaom

Takeo

KAMPOT

Chhuk

Angkor
Borei

TAKE

Koh Samit

Koh Rong

Sihanoukville

Koh Rong Samloem

Gulf of
Kompong Som

Veal Renh

Bokor
National
Park

Kampot

Kep

Koh Thmei

Ream National
Park

Koh Tonsay

Phu Quoc
Island

Ha Tien

12° N

11° N

102° E

103° E

0   25   50 km

LP

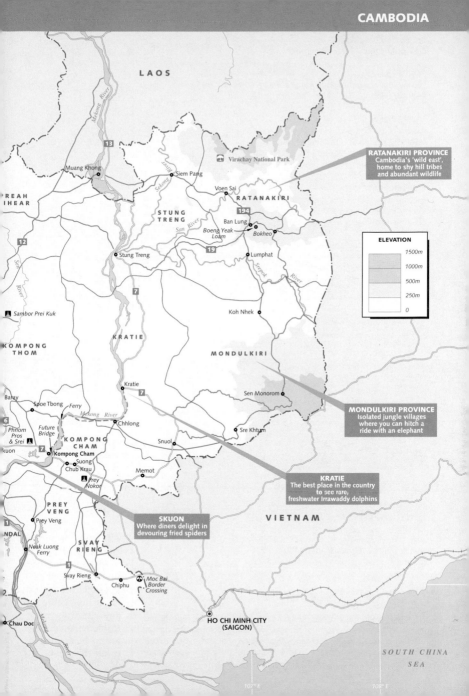

LAOS

Muang Khong

13

Siem Pang

Voen Sai

RATANAKIRI PROVINCE
Cambodia's 'wild east',
home to shy hill tribes
and abundant wildlife

Virachay National Park

REAH
IHEAR

12

STUNG
TRENG

RATANAKIRI

194

Ban Lung

Boeng Yeak
Loam

Bokheo

Stung Treng

19

Lumphat

Sambor Prei Kuk

7

Koh Nhek

KOMPONG
THOM

KRATIE

MONDULKIRI

ELEVATION

	1500m
	1000m
	500m
	250m
	0

Baray

Kratie

Spoe Tbong Ferry

7

Sen Monorom

Mekong River

Chhlong

Future
Bridge

Phnom
Pros
& Srei

MONDULKIRI PROVINCE
Isolated jungle villages
where you can hitch a
ride with an elephant

7

KOMPONG
CHAM

Snuol

Sre Khtum

kuon

Kompong Cham

Suong
Chub Krau

Memot

Prey
Nokor

KRATIE
The best place in the country
to see rare,
freshwater Irrawaddy dolphins

PREY
VENG

Prey Veng

VIETNAM

1

NDAL

SKUON
Where diners delight in
devouring fried spiders

Neak Luong
Ferry

SVAY
RIENG

Svay Rieng

Chiphu

Moc Bai
Border
Crossing

Chau Doc

**HO CHI MINH CITY
(SAIGON)**

102° E

108° E

SOUTH CHINA
SEA

Cambodia
3rd edition – April 2000
First published – September 1992

Published by
Lonely Planet Publications Pty Ltd A.C.N. 005 607 983
192 Burwood Rd, Hawthorn, Victoria 3122, Australia

Lonely Planet Offices
Australia PO Box 617, Hawthorn, Victoria 3122
USA 150 Linden St, Oakland, CA 94607
UK 10a Spring Place, London NW5 3BH
France 1 rue du Dahomey, 75011 Paris

Photographs
All of the images in this guide are available for licensing from
Lonely Planet Images.
email: lpi@lonelyplanet.com.au

Front cover photograph
A Cambodian monk diverts his attention from more earthly demands
to view a solar eclipse. (Mick Elmore)

ISBN 0 86442 670 4

text & maps © Lonely Planet 2000
photos © photographers as indicated 2000

Printed by Craft Print Pte Ltd, Singapore

All rights reserved. No part of this publication may be reproduced,
stored in a retrieval system or transmitted in any form by any means,
electronic, mechanical, photocopying, recording or otherwise, except
brief extracts for the purpose of review, without the written permission
of the publisher and copyright owner.

Although the authors and Lonely Planet try to make the information as accurate as possible, we accept no responsibility for any loss, injury or inconvenience sustained by anyone using this book.

Contents – Text

TEMPLES OF ANGKOR

SIEM REAP

AROUND CAMBODIA

LANGUAGE

GLOSSARY

ACKNOWLEDGMENTS

INDEX

MAP LEGEND

METRIC CONVERSION

Contents – Maps

MAP INDEX

A table of contents listing all the maps in this book appears on page 3 and a full colour map of Cambodia is at the front of the book

0   25   50 km

THAILAND

LAOS

Ban Lung p220

Angkor (see list at bottom)
Siem Reap p178

Battambang p201

Tonlé Sap

Kratie p218

Sen Monorom p223

Kompong Cham p208

River

Mekong

VIETNAM

Phnom Penh Maps
Phnom Penh p100
Central Phnom Penh p104
The Royal Palace &
The Silver Pagoda p113

Ta Prohm, Tonlé Bati p133

Sihanoukville p188   Kampot p193

GULF OF THAILAND

Angkor Maps
Temples of Angkor p138
Angkor Wat 149
Central Structure of Angkor Wat p151
Central Area of Angkor Thom p154
Bayon p155
Baphuon p158
Phnom Bakheng p162
Ta Prohm p164
Ta Keo p165
Preah Khan p167
Preah Neak Pean p168
Pre Rup p169
Preah Ko p170
Bakong p171
Banteay Srei p173

The Author

Nick Ray

A Londoner of sorts, Nick comes from Watford, the sort of town that makes you want to travel. He studied history and politics at the University of Warwick and staggered out a few years later, dazed and confused, clutching a piece of paper that said he knew stuff about things. After a stint as a journalist in London, he decided the bind and grind of office hours was not for him and headed overseas. During this time he found himself leading people astray on adventure tours in countries from Morocco to Vietnam. But Cambodia was the one country that really got under his skin and he likes to think of it as something of a base these days. If you spend enough time in the Heart of Darkness bar in Phnom Penh you'll probably run into him.

FROM THE AUTHOR

This book is the sum of many parts and many people have helped me in many ways, some without even realising it. First and foremost my heartfelt thanks go out to the people of Cambodia: their spirit and stoicism, their humour and humility have brought me back to this country time and time again. If it wasn't for their welcome I never would have fallen in love with the place. Two Cambodians in particular assisted with this book. Kulikar Sotho helped make this book easier to write for reasons both personal and professional and has taught me more about strength in the face of adversity than I would have believed possible. She will hold a place in my heart forever. Paul Im, sometimes of the UN, sometimes professionally unemployed, lent me his computer when mine was in terminal decline, enabling me to get the book finished on time. If only a few Cambodian politicians cared about their country as much as he does, it would be a better place.

Next up a big thanks to my mum and dad for making the effort to visit Cambodia. It was the kind of place that used to send shock waves down my mum's spine a few years ago, so I am glad you loved it and are coming back. Quite a number of old friends helped along the way, although hindered might be a better word. Many thanks to Chris 'Rincon' Johnson for being there when I was robbed and helping out with everything. Andrew 'De Beers' Dear has made it twice, and it has been great to see him even if he hasn't done much to help the books. Andrew 'I'm dark about that' Burke put a journalist's sheen of objectivity on some of my wilder observations. Thanks to Andy Johnson for making three visits and Liam Moore, Jack Ladd, Tara Burke and Fiona Thompson for making the long haul for a short time; it was appreciated. Thanks too to John McGeoghan, who is helping the teachers of Siem Reap educate the children of the province. Cambodia needs

5

more people like him and I thank him from the bottom of my heart for his regular hospitality.

A lot of people helped with information and statistics. Firstly, thanks to His Excellency Veng Sereyvuth, Minister of Tourism for the Kingdom of Cambodia. He used to use Lonely Planet guides back in the early 80s; quite a trailblazer, he has a good idea of where he wants to take the Cambodian tourism industry and helped me out whenever I asked. Further thanks to many of his staff in the provincial offices who tried their best to help. Helene Valentin at Diethelm Travel filled in some gaps during my first days back in the country, and Phillippa Thomas from Voluntary Service Overseas assisted in getting hold of background information on some of the more out of the way places that volunteers operate from.

The Mennonite Central Committee deserves a big thank you for providing me with a banquet lunch at Bokor and taking the bags down the mountain in the rain. Rudolf and Abbas at the Angkor Swiss Centre in Siem Reap kept me up to date on a developing town during my many visits. Davide at the Marco Polo Restaurant in Kampot showed me the finer side of Kep and its nearby islands; surely it is due a revival. Many other people helped out, including Chris at Thai Airways, Anthony at the Foreign Correspondents' Club, William and Masaki at the Angkor Hotel, Laurent Holdener for showing me the road to Beng Mealea, Frederic for protecting the birds of Tonlé Sap lake, and Benito of Krousar Thmey and La Casa for running a restaurant that benefits the people of Cambodia.

Many tourists, expats and locals hung out with me in various parts of the country, sharing Angkor and adventures in equal measure. In no particular order a big hello to Alan Morgan, Zeman, Craig, George Beach, Smiley and all the many members of the Narin family, Chom, Mac, John 'Ronnie' Barker, Jason, Tay, Richie, Andrea, Josh, Emma, Sylvan, Brian, Jack S, Mark Mitcheltree, Jane, Alice, Pia, Elle, Dougal and the Mondulkiri motorcyclists, Phil, Ross, Steve, Ben, Larni and Simon: you survived, even with only one day's experience! A thought for Lindsaye from Scotland who was last seen walking from Mondulkiri to Ratanakiri: I hope you aren't drinking puddles.

And no thanks whatsoever to the bastard who robbed me!

This Book

Author Nick Ray immersed himself in Cambodian culture to update and significantly expand *Cambodia* for this 3rd edition. He built upon the efforts of Tony Wheeler and Daniel Robinson, who wrote the original work, and Chris Taylor, who updated the book for its 2nd edition.

From the Publisher

This book was produced at Lonely Planet's Melbourne office. Cherry Prior coordinated the editing, with plenty of help from proofers Kate Daly, Joanne Newell and Kristin Odijk. Meredith Mail arrived just in time to coordinate mapping and design. Chris Love, Tim Fitzgerald, Jack Gavran, Chris Thomas and Neb Milic assisted with the mapping. Quentin Frayne organised the Language chapter and Shahara Ahmed cast an eye over all health matters. Tim Uden provided Quark support, Maria Vallianos designed the cover and Valerie Tellini from LPI provided the photographs. Matt King coordinated the illustrations and Kusnandar organised the climate chart.

Special thanks to Glenn Beanland and Kristin for invaluable advice and patience and, of course, to author Nick Ray, for his hard work and commitment to Cambodia.

THANKS
Many thanks to the travellers who used the last edition and wrote to us with helpful hints, advice and interesting anecdotes. Your names appear in the back of this book.

Foreword

ABOUT LONELY PLANET GUIDEBOOKS

The story begins with a classic travel adventure: Tony and Maureen Wheeler's 1972 journey across Europe and Asia to Australia. Useful information about the overland trail did not exist at that time, so Tony and Maureen published the first Lonely Planet guidebook to meet a growing need.

From a kitchen table, then from a tiny office in Melbourne (Australia), Lonely Planet has become the largest independent travel publisher in the world, an international company with offices in Melbourne, Oakland (USA), London (UK) and Paris (France).

Today Lonely Planet guidebooks cover the globe. There is an ever-growing list of books and there's information in a variety of forms and media. Some things haven't changed. The main aim is still to help make it possible for adventurous travellers to get out there – to explore and better understand the world.

At Lonely Planet we believe travellers can make a positive contribution to the countries they visit – if they respect their host communities and spend their money wisely. Since 1986 a percentage of the income from each book has been donated to aid projects and human rights campaigns.

Updates Lonely Planet thoroughly updates each guidebook as often as possible. This usually means there are around two years between editions, although for more unusual or more stable destinations the gap can be longer. Check the imprint page (following the colour map at the beginning of the book) for publication dates.

Between editions up-to-date information is available in two free newsletters – the paper *Planet Talk* and email *Comet* (to subscribe, contact any Lonely Planet office) – and on our Web site at www.lonelyplanet.com. The *Upgrades* section of the Web site covers a number of important and volatile destinations and is regularly updated by Lonely Planet authors. *Scoop* covers news and current affairs relevant to travellers. And, lastly, the *Thorn Tree* bulletin board and *Postcards* section of the site carry unverified, but fascinating, reports from travellers.

Correspondence The process of creating new editions begins with the letters, postcards and emails received from travellers. This correspondence often includes suggestions, criticisms and comments about the current editions. Interesting excerpts are immediately passed on via newsletters and the Web site, and everything goes to our authors to be verified when they're researching on the road. We're keen to get more feedback from organisations or individuals who represent communities visited by travellers.

Lonely Planet gathers information for everyone who's curious about the planet – and especially for those who explore it first-hand. Through guidebooks, phrasebooks, activity guides, maps, literature, newsletters, image library, TV series and Web site we act as an information exchange for a worldwide community of travellers.

Research Authors aim to gather sufficient practical information to enable travellers to make informed choices and to make the mechanics of a journey run smoothly. They also research historical and cultural background to help enrich the travel experience and allow travellers to understand and respond appropriately to cultural and environmental issues.

Authors don't stay in every hotel because that would mean spending a couple of months in each medium-sized city and, no, they don't eat at every restaurant because that would mean stretching belts beyond capacity. They do visit hotels and restaurants to check standards and prices, but feedback based on readers' direct experiences can be very helpful.

Many of our authors work undercover, others aren't so secretive. None of them accept freebies in exchange for positive write-ups. And none of our guidebooks contain any advertising.

Production Authors submit their raw manuscripts and maps to offices in Australia, USA, UK or France. Editors and cartographers – all experienced travellers themselves – then begin the process of assembling the pieces. When the book finally hits the shops, some things are already out of date, we start getting feedback from readers and the process begins again ...

WARNING & REQUEST

Things change – prices go up, schedules change, good places go bad and bad places go bankrupt – nothing stays the same. So, if you find things better or worse, recently opened or long since closed, please tell us and help make the next edition even more accurate and useful. We genuinely value all the feedback we receive. Julie Young coordinates a well travelled team that reads and acknowledges every letter, postcard and email and ensures that every morsel of information finds its way to the appropriate authors, editors and cartographers for verification.

Everyone who writes to us will find their name in the next edition of the appropriate guidebook. They will also receive the latest issue of *Planet Talk*, our quarterly printed newsletter, or *Comet*, our monthly email newsletter. Subscriptions to both newsletters are free. The very best contributions will be rewarded with a free guidebook.

Excerpts from your correspondence may appear in new editions of Lonely Planet guidebooks, the Lonely Planet Web site, *Planet Talk* or *Comet*, so please let us know if you *don't* want your letter published or your name acknowledged.

Send all correspondence to the Lonely Planet office closest to you:

Australia: PO Box 617, Hawthorn, Victoria 3122
USA: 150 Linden St, Oakland, CA 94607
UK: 10A Spring Place, London NW5 3BH
France: 1 rue du Dahomey, 75011 Paris

Or email us at: talk2us@lonelyplanet.com.au

For news, views and updates see our Web site: www.lonelyplanet.com

HOW TO USE A LONELY PLANET GUIDEBOOK

The best way to use a Lonely Planet guidebook is any way you choose. At Lonely Planet we believe the most memorable travel experiences are often those that are unexpected, and the finest discoveries are those you make yourself. Guidebooks are not intended to be used as if they provide a detailed set of infallible instructions!

Contents All Lonely Planet guidebooks follow roughly the same format. The Facts about the Destination chapters or sections give background information ranging from history to weather. Facts for the Visitor gives practical information on issues like visas and health. Getting There & Away gives a brief starting point for researching travel to and from the destination. Getting Around gives an overview of the transport options when you arrive.

The peculiar demands of each destination determine how subsequent chapters are broken up, but some things remain constant. We always start with background, then proceed to sights, places to stay, places to eat, entertainment, getting there and away, and getting around information – in that order.

Heading Hierarchy Lonely Planet headings are used in a strict hierarchical structure that can be visualised as a set of Russian dolls. Each heading (and its following text) is encompassed by any preceding heading that is higher on the hierarchical ladder.

Entry Points We do not assume guidebooks will be read from beginning to end, but that people will dip into them. The traditional entry points are the list of contents and the index. In addition, however, some books have a complete list of maps and an index map illustrating map coverage.

There may also be a colour map that shows highlights. These highlights are dealt with in greater detail in the Facts for the Visitor chapter, along with planning questions and suggested itineraries. Each chapter covering a geographical region usually begins with a locator map and another list of highlights. Once you find something of interest in a list of highlights, turn to the index.

Maps Maps play a crucial role in Lonely Planet guidebooks and include a huge amount of information. A legend is printed on the back page. We seek to have complete consistency between maps and text, and to have every important place in the text captured on a map. Map key numbers usually start in the top left corner.

Although inclusion in a guidebook usually implies a recommendation we cannot list every good place. Exclusion does not necessarily imply criticism. In fact there are a number of reasons why we might exclude a place – sometimes it is simply inappropriate to encourage an influx of travellers.

Introduction

For two decades, war and a vast communist-inspired 'experiment' removed Cambodia from the traveller's map. The very word Cambodia came to be associated with atrocities, poverty and refugees. The tragedy of it all belonged to the Cambodians, but it has also been a great loss to travellers in Asia.

During much of the 1990s Cambodia remained a difficult country in which to travel due to the presence of Khmer Rouge guerrillas in many of the provinces. If that wasn't enough to scare people away, then the politicians in Phnom Penh usually managed to cook up a crisis that would deter those considering a visit to the country's highlights. However, the long and bloody civil war is finally over and the Khmer Rouge is no longer terrorizing the people of Cambodia. This is good news, not just for the stoical people of Cambodia, but also for tourists planning to visit the country, as many more areas are now opening up that simply could not be visited a few years ago. However, it is a young peace and land mines remain a widespread problem, so it pays to check the latest security situation before heading off into more isolated rural areas.

Cambodia lies at the heart of Indochina, bordered by Thailand to the west, Laos and Thailand to the north and Vietnam to the east. It is a fascinating place that, despite its tiny size and its large, powerful neighbours, has managed to remain uniquely Khmer. Its cultural traditions predate those of Thailand, and unlike Vietnam, which was always influenced by China, its dominant influences stem from the Indian subcontinent.

Modern-day Cambodia is the successor-state of the mighty Khmer empire, which during the Angkorian period (9th to 14th centuries) was the cultural heartland of South-East Asia. It ruled over much of what is now Vietnam, Laos and Thailand, and its legacy is one of the wonders of the world. The ruins of Angkor are in a category of their own: there is no other historical site in South-East Asia that matches their grandeur.

The traveller's first glimpse of Angkor Wat, which represents the full flowering of Khmer genius, is a breathtaking experience, matched only by sights such as the Potala Palace of Lhasa or the Forbidden City of Beijing.

Cambodia has enormous potential as a travel destination, and investors are moving in with an eye to the day when tourists arrive in the numbers that nearby Vietnam enjoys. The land borders with Thailand are now open to foreigners and there is talk of direct flights between Siem Reap and Phuket. Cambodia is now well and truly back on the travel map of South-East Asia. To talk in terms of millions may sound fanciful, but with the temples of Angkor, Cambodia has something to offer that none of its neighbours can rival. It also has empty beaches and islands along the south coast of the country, and national parks that are just starting to see visitors. The meandering Mekong River holds the promise of boat trips through Cambodia, Laos and even into China. Its mighty waters also provide a habitat for some of the last remaining freshwater dolphins in Asia. In the northeast of the country are wild and mountainous landscapes, home to Cambodia's ethnic minorities and much of the country's diminishing wildlife and forest.

Finally there are the people. Cambodians have weathered years of bloodshed, poverty and political instability. Somehow they have come through the experience with smiles still intact. Admittedly Cambodia needs the money that tourism brings, but there is an air of genuine enthusiasm and warmth towards foreign visitors. Nobody comes away from Cambodia without a measure of admiration and affection for the inhabitants of this beautiful yet troubled country.

Facts about Cambodia

HISTORY
Early Beginnings

Cambodia came into being, so the legend goes, through the union of a princess and a foreigner. The foreigner was an Indian Brahman named Kaundinya. The princess was the daughter of a dragon king who ruled over a watery place. One day, as Kaundinya sailed by, the princess paddled out in a boat to greet him. Kaundinya shot an arrow from his magic bow into her boat, causing the princess to fearfully agree to marriage. In need of a dowry, her father drank up the waters of his land and presented them to Kaundinya to rule over. The new kingdom was named Kambuja.

Like many legends, this one is historically opaque, but it does say something about the cultural forces that brought Cambodia into existence; in particular its relationship with its great subcontinental neighbour, India. Cambodia's religious, royal and written traditions stemmed from India and began to coalesce as a cultural tradition in their own right from around the 1st century AD.

Very little is known about prehistoric Cambodia. Evidence of cave dwellers has been found in the north-west of Cambodia. Carbon dating on ceramic pots found in the area shows they were made around 4200 BC. But it is difficult to say whether there is a direct relationship between these cave-dwelling pot makers and contemporary Khmers. Examinations of bones dating back to around 1500 BC, however, suggest that the people living in Cambodia at that time resembled Cambodians of today.

Archaeological evidence shows that Cambodians prior to 1000 BC lived in houses on stilts (as they do today), and subsisted on a diet that included large quantities of fish and cultivated rice. Early Chinese records report that the Cambodians were 'ugly' and 'dark' and went about naked; a pinch of salt is always required when reading the culturally chauvinistic reports of imperial China concerning its 'barbarian' neighbours.

Indianisation & Funan

The early Indianisation of Cambodia probably occurred via trading settlements that sprang up from the 1st century AD on the coastline of what is now southern Vietnam. Such settlements served as ports of call for boats following the trading route from the Bay of Bengal to the southern provinces of China. The largest of these was known as Funan, close to contemporary Oc-Eo in Kien Giang Province of southern Vietnam.

Funan is a Chinese name, and it may be a transliteration of the ancient Khmer name for mountain: *bnam*. Although very little is known about Funan, much has been made of its importance as an early South-East Asian centre of power despite there being little evidence to support this.

It is most likely that between the 1st and 8th centuries Cambodia was a collection of small states, each with its own elites that sometimes strategically intermarried and sometimes went to war with one another. Funan was no doubt one of these states, and as a major sea port was undoubtedly pivotal in the transmission of Indian culture into the interior of Cambodia.

What historians do know about Funan they have mostly gleaned from Chinese sources. These report that Funan-period Cambodia (1st to 6th centuries AD) embraced the worship of the Hindu deities Shiva and Vishnu and at the same time Buddhism. The *lingam*, a phallic totem, appears to have been the focus of ritual and an emblem of kingly might, a feature that was to evolve further in the Angkorian cult of the god king. The people practised primitive irrigation, which enabled the cultivation of rice, and traded raw commodities such as spices with China and India.

Chenla Period

From the 6th century Funan's importance as a port declined, and Cambodia's population gradually concentrated along the Mekong and Tonlé Sap rivers (as is the case today). The move may be related to the development of wet-rice agriculture. From the 6th to the 8th centuries Cambodia was probably a collection of competing kingdoms, ruled by autocratic kings who legitimised their absolute rule through hierarchical social concepts borrowed from India.

This period is generally referred to as the Chenla. Again, as is the case with Funan, it is a Chinese term and there is little to support the idea that the Chenla was a unified kingdom that held sway over all Cambodia. Indeed, the Chinese themselves referred to the 'water Chenla' and the 'land Chenla', the former probably located in the Mekong Delta, the latter in the upper reaches of the Mekong River.

Still, the people of Cambodia were known at least to the Chinese, and gradually the region was becoming more cohesive. Before long the fractured kingdoms of Cambodia would merge to become the greatest kingdom of South-East Asia.

Angkorian Period

An inscription at the sacred mountain of Phnom Kulen, to the north of Angkor, reads that in the year 802 Jayavarman II participated in a ritual that proclaimed him a 'universal monarch', or a *devaraja* (god king). Who was Jayavarman II and what was he doing before this? It is thought he may have resided in the Buddhist Shailendras' court in Java as a young man. One of the first things he did when he returned to Cambodia was to hold a ritual that made it impossible for Java to control the lands of Cambodia. From this point, Jayavarman II brought the lands of Cambodia under his control through alliances, proclaiming himself king in the process.

Jayavarman II was the first of a long succession of kings who presided over the rise and fall of the South-East Asian empire that was to leave behind the stunning legacy of Angkor. The first records of the massive irrigation works that supported the population of Angkor begin in the reign of Indravarman I (reigned 877-889). His rule also marks the beginning of Angkorian art, with the building of temples in the Roluos area, notably the Bakong. His son, Yasovarman I (reigned 889-910), moved the royal court to Angkor proper, establishing a temple mountain on Phnom Bakheng.

By the turn of the 11th century the kingdom of Angkor was losing control of its territories. Suryavarman I (1002-1049), an usurper, moved into the power vacuum and, like Jayavarman II two centuries before, reunified the kingdom through war and alliances. He annexed the kingdom of Lopburi in Thailand and extended his control of Cambodia. A pattern was beginning to emerge, which can be seen throughout the Angkor period: dislocation and turmoil, followed by reunification and further expansion under a powerful king. The most productive periods architecturally occurred after periods of turmoil, indicating that newly incumbent monarchs felt the need to celebrate and perhaps legitimise their rule with massive building projects.

From around 1066 Angkor was again riven by conflict, becoming the focus of rival bids for power. It was not until 1112, with the accession of Suryavarman II, that the kingdom was again unified. Suryavarman II embarked on another phase of expansion, waging wars in Vietnam and the region of southern Vietnam known as Champa. He also established links with China. But Suryavarman II will mostly be remembered as the king who, in his devotion to the Hindu deity Vishnu, commissioned Angkor Wat.

Suryavarman II had brought Champa to heel and reduced it to vassal status. In 1177, however, the Chams struck back in a naval expedition up the Mekong and into the Tonlé Sap (Great Lake). They took the city of Angkor by surprise and put its king to death. A year later a cousin of Suryavarman gathered forces about him and defeated the Chams in another naval battle. The new leader was crowned in 1181 as Jayavarman VII.

A devout follower of Mahayana Buddhism, Jayavarman VII built the city of Angkor Thom and many other monuments. Indeed most of the monuments visited by tourists in Angkor today were constructed during Jayavarman VII's reign. He also commissioned a vast array of public works. But as David Chandler points out in his *History of Cambodia*, Jayavarman VII is a figure of many contradictions. The bas-reliefs of the Bayon, for example, depict him presiding over battles of terrible ferocity, while statues of the king show him in a meditative, otherworldly aspect. His program of temple construction and other public works were carried out in great haste, no doubt bringing enormous hardship to the labourers who provided the muscle.

Decline & Fall

Some scholars maintain that decline was hovering in the wings at the time Angkor Wat was built, when the Angkorian empire was at the height of its remarkable productivity. There are indications that the irrigation network was overworked, and massive construction projects such as Angkor Wat and Angkor Thom no doubt put an enormous strain on the royal coffers and on the common people who subsidised them in taxes and hard work. Certainly, after the reign of Jayavarman VII, temple construction effectively came to a halt, in large part because Jayavarman VII's public works quarried local sandstone into oblivion.

Another important aspect of this period was the decline of Cambodian political influence on the peripheries of its empire. The Thai kingdom of Ayuthaya, on the other hand, grew in strength and made repeated incursions into Angkor, sacking the city in 1431. During this period, perhaps drawn by the opportunities for sea trade with China, the Khmer elite began to migrate to the Phnom Penh area.

The next 150 years of Khmer history was dominated by dynastic rivalries and almost continuous warfare with the Thais. Although the Khmers once pushed westward all the way to the Thai capital of Ayuthaya (only to find it occupied by the Burmese), the Thais recovered and dealt a crushing blow to the Khmers by capturing their capital in 1594.

Shortly before the Khmer defeat, the Cambodian king, Satha, requested the assistance of the Spanish and Portuguese, who had recently become active in the region. In 1596 a Spanish expedition arrived in Cambodia to assist Satha only to find that he had been deposed by an usurper, Chung Prei. After a series of disagreements and the sacking of the Chinese quarter of Phnom Penh by the Spanish forces, the Spanish attacked the palace and killed Chung Prei. The Spanish then decided to return to Manila, but while marching through Laos, they changed their minds and returned to Phnom Penh, installing one of Satha's sons on the throne. Resentment of the power wielded by the Spanish grew among court officials until 1599, when the Spanish garrison at Phnom Penh was massacred. Shortly thereafter, Satha's brother ascended the throne with the help of the Thais.

From about 1600 until the arrival of the French in 1863, Cambodia was ruled by a series of weak kings who, because of continual challenges by dissident members of the royal family, were forced to seek the protection – granted, of course, at a price – of either Thailand or Vietnam. In the 17th century, assistance from the Nguyen Lords of southern Vietnam was given on the condition that Vietnamese be allowed to settle in what is now the southern region of Vietnam, at that time part of Cambodia and today still referred to by the Khmers as 'lower Cambodia'. In the west, the Thais established dominion over the provinces of Battambang and Siem Reap; by the late 18th century they had firm control of the Cambodian royal family. Indeed, one king was crowned in Bangkok and placed on the throne at Udong with the help of the Thai army. That Cambodia survived through the 18th century as a distinct entity is due to the preoccupations of its neighbours: while the Thais were expending their energy and resources in fighting the Burmese, the Vietnamese were wholly absorbed by internal strife, including the rivalry between the Trinh Lords and the Nguyen Lords, and the Tay Son Rebellion.

French Rule

Cambodia's dual Thai and Vietnamese suzerainty ended in 1864, when French gunboats intimidated King Norodom (reigned 1860-1904) into signing a treaty of protectorate. French control of Cambodia, which developed as an adjunct to French colonial interests in Vietnam, at first involved relatively little direct interference in Cambodia's affairs of state. However, the French presence did prevent Cambodia's expansionist neighbours from annexing any more Khmer territory and helped keep Norodom on the throne despite the ambitions of his rebellious half-brothers.

By the 1870s French officials in Cambodia began pressing for greater control over internal affairs. In 1884 Norodom was forced into signing a treaty that turned his country into a virtual colony. This sparked a two year rebellion that constituted the only major anti-French movement in Cambodia until after WWII. This uprising ended when the king was persuaded to call upon the rebel fighters to lay down their weapons in exchange for a return to the pre-treaty arrangement.

During the next two decades senior Cambodian officials, who saw certain advantages in acquiescing to French power, opened the door to direct French control over the day-to-day administration of the country. At the same time the French maintained Norodom's court in a splendour probably unequalled since the Angkorian period, thereby greatly enhancing the symbolic position of the monarchy. The king's increased stature served to legitimise the Cambodian state, thereby pre-empting the growth of any sort of broad-based nationalist movement; a situation in marked contrast to that in Vietnam. Indeed, the only large-scale popular protest of any kind between the 1880s and the 1940s was an essentially peaceful peasant uprising in 1916, which ended when the king agreed to consider their grievances.

King Norodom was succeeded by King Sisowath (reigned 1904-27), who was followed on the throne by King Monivong (reigned 1927-41). Upon the death of King Monivong, the French governor general of Japanese-occupied Indochina, Admiral Jean Decoux, placed 19-year-old Prince Norodom Sihanouk on the Cambodian throne. The choice was based on the assumption that Sihanouk would prove pliable; this proved to be a major miscalculation.

During WWII, Japanese forces occupied much of Asia, and Cambodia was no exception. However, with many in France collaborating with the occupying forces in mainland Europe, the Japanese were happy to let these French allies control affairs in Cambodia. However, with the fall of Paris in 1944, and coordinated French policy in disarray, the Japanese were forced to take direct control of the territory. After WWII the French returned, making Cambodia an 'autonomous state within the French Union', but retaining de facto control. The years after 1945 were marked by strife among the country's various political groupings, a situation made more unstable by the Franco-Viet Minh War then raging in Vietnam and Laos.

Independence

In January 1953 King Sihanouk, who had been at odds with the dominant Democratic Party, took decisive action, dissolving the parliament, declaring martial law and embarking on what became known as the 'royal crusade': his travelling campaign to drum up international support for his country's independence.

Independence was proclaimed on 9 November 1953 and recognised by the Geneva Conference of May 1954, which ended French control of Indochina. However, internal political turmoil continued, much of it the result of conflicts between Sihanouk and his domestic opponents. In March 1955 Sihanouk abdicated in favour of his father Norodom Suramarit to pursue a career as a politician. His newly established party, Sangkum Reastr Niyum (the People's Socialist Community), won every seat in parliament in the September 1955 elections. Sihanouk dominated Cambodian politics for the next 15 years, serving as prime minister until his father's death in 1960, when no new king was named and he became chief of state.

Although he feared the Vietnamese communists, during the early 1960s Sihanouk considered South Vietnam and Thailand, both allies of the USA (which he mistrusted), the greatest threats to Cambodia's security and even survival. He was particularly shaken by the overthrow and subsequent murder of President Ngo Diem of South Vietnam in an American-backed coup in 1963. Diem had been a staunch ally of Washington, so what hope was there for an unreliable Sihanouk? In an attempt to fend off these many dangers, he declared Cambodia neutral in international affairs. In May 1965 Sihanouk, convinced that the USA had been plotting against him and his family, broke diplomatic relations with Washington and tilted towards North Vietnam, the Viet Cong and China. In addition, he accepted that the North Vietnamese army and the Viet Cong would use Cambodian territory in their battle against South Vietnam and the US.

These moves and his socialist economic policies alienated right-leaning elements in Cambodian society, including the officer corps of the army and the urban elite. At the same time, left-wing Cambodians, many of them educated abroad, deeply resented his internal policies, which did not allow for political dissent. Compounding Sihanouk's problems was the fact that all classes were fed up with the pervasive corruption in government ranks. Although most peasants – the vast majority of the population – revered Sihanouk as a semidivine figure, a rural-based rebellion broke out in 1967, leading him to conclude that the greatest threat to his regime came from the left. Bowing to pressure from the army, he implemented a policy of harsh repression against left-wingers.

In 1969 the USA began a secret program of bombing suspected communist base camps in Cambodia. For the next four years, until bombing was halted by the US Congress in August 1973, huge areas of the eastern half of the country were carpet bombed by US B-52s, killing uncounted

thousands of civilians and turning hundreds of thousands more into refugees.

Lon Nol Regime

By 1969 the conflict between the army and leftist rebels had become more serious and Sihanouk's political position had greatly deteriorated. In March 1970, while Sihanouk was on a trip to France, General Lon Nol and Prince Sisowath Matak, Sihanouk's cousin, deposed him as chief of state, apparently with US consent. Pogroms against ethnic Vietnamese living in Cambodia soon broke out, prompting many to flee. Sihanouk took up residence in Beijing, where he set up a government-in-exile nominally in control of an indigenous Cambodian revolutionary movement that Sihanouk had nicknamed the Khmer Rouge (French for Red Khmer). This was a definitive moment in contemporary Cambodian history as the Khmer Rouge exploited its partnership with Sihanouk to draw new recruits into the small organisation. Many former Khmer Rouge fighters argue that they 'went to the hills', a euphemism for joining the Khmer Rouge, to fight for their king.

On 30 April 1970 US and South Vietnamese forces invaded Cambodia in an effort to rout some 40,000 Viet Cong and North Vietnamese troops who were using Cambodian bases in their war to overthrow the South Vietnamese government. As a result of the invasion, the Vietnamese communists withdrew deeper into Cambodia, thus posing an even greater threat to the Lon Nol government. At the same time, the new government was becoming very unpopular as a result of unprecedented greed and corruption in its ranks. Savage fighting quickly engulfed the entire country, bringing misery to millions of Cambodians; many fled rural areas for the relative safety of Phnom Penh and provincial capitals. Between 1970 and 1975 several hundred thousand people died in the fighting.

During the next few years the Khmer Rouge came to play a dominant role in trying to overthrow the Lon Nol regime. It was strengthened by the support of the Vietnamese, although the Khmer Rouge

King Sihanouk

Norodom Sihanouk has been a constant presence in the topsy-turvy world of Cambodian politics. A colourful man of many enthusiasms and shifting political positions, his amatory exploits tended to dominate his early reputation. Later he became the prince who stage-managed the close of French colonialism, autocratically led an independent Cambodia, was imprisoned by the Khmer Rouge and, from privileged exile, finally returned triumphant as king. Whatever else he may be, he is certainly a survivor.

Sihanouk was born in 1922, the only son of Prince Norodom Suramarit, grandson of King Norodom (1860-1904), and Princess Sisowath Kossamak, daughter of King Sisowath Monivong (1927-41). He was not an obvious contender for the throne. The French saw the young prince as a pliant monarch. He was crowned in 1941, at just 19 years old, with his education incomplete. And in the four years before the Japanese arrived and presented Cambodia briefly with the gift of liberation, he was all the French had hoped he would be.

With the French colonial masters removed, however, Sihanouk promptly abolished two French laws: the first was the compulsory romanisation of the Khmer alphabet; the second was the enforcement of the Gregorian calendar over the traditional lunar one. This was, it must be said, his only act of defiance in five months of de facto independence, but it marks the cautious beginning of Sihanouk's involvement in politics.

Sihanouk acquiesced quietly to the return of French rule in August 1945. But by 1952 he had embarked on his self-styled 'royal crusade' for independence. He began it by dismissing an elected government and appointing himself prime minister, announcing that within three years Cambodia would be independent. He embarked on a lobbying and publicity campaign in France and the USA, a brief defiant exile in Thailand, and sponsored a civil militia that attracted some 100,000 volunteers. The French backed out of Cambodia in late 1953.

A year after achieving independence, Sihanouk made one of his characteristically unpredictable decisions: he would abdicate. Thwarted in his attempts to revise the constitution and provide the throne with far-reaching political powers, he was probably afraid of being marginalised to the pomp of royal ceremony. The 'royal crusader' became 'citizen Sihanouk'. He vowed never again to return to the throne. Meanwhile his father became king. It was a masterstroke that offered Sihanouk both royal authority and supreme political power.

Elections were held in 1955. They were marred by intimidatory violence and voting fraud. Sihanouk's Sangkum Reastr Niyum (People's Socialist Community party) won 83% of the vote. By this time he was in full political swing and had discovered a passion for rhetoric. On one occasion, in 1957, he summoned his political opposition to a palace debate before a huge audience and demolished them in three hours of impassioned oratory. His opponents were beaten by the palace guards as they slunk away.

By the mid-1960s Sihanouk had been supreme commander of Cambodia for a decade. After innumerable love affairs, he had finally settled on Monique Izzi, the daughter of a Franco-Italian father and a Cambodian mother, as his consort. As war raged in Vietnam and leftist discontent with right-wing politics blossomed at home, Sihanouk launched his movie career. Between 1966 and 1969 he directed, produced and starred in nine movies.

The conventional wisdom was that 'Sihanouk is Cambodia' – his leadership was unassailable. But as the cinema took more and more of his time, Cambodia was being drawn

King Sihanouk

inexorably into the Vietnam War. Government troops battled with a leftist insurgency in the countryside; the economy was in tatters; and Sihanouk came to be regarded as a liability. His involvement in the film industry and his announcements that Cambodia was 'an oasis of peace' suggested a man who had not only abdicated from the throne but also from reality.

In early 1970 with forces gathering against him, Sihanouk briefly flirted with the idea of reclaiming the throne. Instead, he departed for France. On 18 March the National Assembly voted to remove Sihanouk from office. Not long after, Cambodia was declared a republic and Sihanouk was sentenced to death *in absentia*.

Sihanouk went into exile in Beijing and threw in his lot with the communists. It was a practical step. The communists aimed to topple the Lon Nol government, and this suited Sihanouk. In 1973 he and his consort, Monique, joined Pol Pot and other communist leaders on a trip to Khmer Rouge-controlled Siem Reap. Photographs and film record the royal couple sightseeing in the black peasant garb preferred by the Khmer Rouge. When the Khmer Rouge marched into Phnom Penh on 17 April 1975, Sihanouk issued a statement in Beijing heralding the event as a great victory against imperialism.

In a deserted Phnom Penh, Sihanouk was confined to the Royal Palace as a prisoner of the Khmer Rouge. He remained there until early 1979 when, on the eve of the Vietnamese invasion, he was flown to Beijing. The Khmer Rouge killed many of Sihanouk's children, grandchildren and relatives, but curiously they spared the patriarch's life.

It was to be a decade before Sihanouk finally returned to Cambodia. Meanwhile, against all odds, he was back at centre stage again, calling the shots, forming alliances with the Khmer Rouge, breaking them off. He clearly hadn't learned much from his first disastrous association with the Khmer Rouge. After the May 1993 elections, Sihanouk suddenly announced that he was forming a coalition government with himself starring as president, prime minister and military leader. He failed.

Sihanouk has never quite given up wanting to be everything for Cambodia: international statesman, general, president, film director, man of the people. On 24 September 1993, after 38 years in politics, he settled once again for the role of king.

King Sihanouk remains a popular monarch in the countryside, but many urban Cambodians have less time for him, feeling he has allowed himself to be consistently outwitted by first the Khmer Rouge and later Hun Sen and the Cambodian People's Party (CPP). It is hard for him to detach himself from the political arena in Cambodia as his son Prince Norodom Ranariddh leads the National United Front for an Independent, Peaceful and Cooperative Cambodia (FUNCINPEC), the country's second largest party. More is the pity, as his final years as the King of Cambodia could have been better used as an apolitical role model. However, he did use his clout to broker the latest coalition between the CPP and FUNCINPEC, which broke the deadlock that followed the 1998 elections.

The most important question regarding King Sihanouk and one that has yet to be answered is: who will succeed him? It has yet to be decided by a committee that has yet to be formed, and should the King pass away in the meantime, it could once again plunge the country into chaos as the politicians argue over who succeeds to the throne. One thing is certain: if the monarchy continues to exist in Cambodia, the new monarch, whoever it may be, will never match the presence of Sihanouk – the last in a long line of Angkor's god kings.

leadership would vehemently deny this from 1975 onwards. The Vietnamese had much more combat experience than their Khmer Rouge counterparts; and it was the North Vietnamese that routed Lon Nol's forces in 1973 after the Khmer Rouge very nearly had been overrun in Siem Reap Province. So decisive was the Vietnamese victory that it almost allowed the Khmer Rouge to take Phnom Penh in 1973, two years before it eventually marched into the capital. The leadership of the Khmer Rouge, including Paris-educated Pol Pot (formerly Saloth Sar) and Khieu Samphan, had fled into the countryside in the 1960s to escape the summary justice then being meted out to suspected leftists by Sihanouk's security forces.

Despite massive US military and economic aid, Lon Nol never succeeded in gaining the initiative against the Khmer Rouge, which pursued a strategy of attrition. Large parts of the countryside fell to the rebels and many provincial capitals were cut off from Phnom Penh. On 17 April 1975 – two weeks before the fall of Saigon (now Ho Chi Minh City) – Phnom Penh surrendered to the Khmer Rouge.

Khmer Rouge Regime

Upon taking Phnom Penh, the Khmer Rouge implemented one of the most radical and brutal restructurings of a society ever attempted; its goal was to transform Cambodia into a Maoist, peasant-dominated agrarian cooperative. Within two weeks of coming to power the entire population of the capital and provincial towns, including everyone in the hospitals, was forced to march out to the countryside and placed in mobile work teams to do slave labour – preparing the fields, digging irrigation canals – for 12 to 15 hours a day. Disobedience of any sort often brought immediate execution. The advent of Khmer Rouge rule was proclaimed 'Year Zero'. Currency was abolished and postal services were halted. Except for one fortnightly flight to Beijing (China was providing aid and advisers to the Khmer Rouge), the country was cut off from the outside world.

It is still not known how many Cambodians died at the hands of the Khmer Rouge over the next four years. The Vietnamese claimed three million deaths, while foreign experts long considered the number closer to one million. Yale University researchers undertaking ongoing investigations concluded in early 1996 that the figure is at least two million, and may even end up being higher.

Sihanouk returned to Phnom Penh in September 1975 as titular chief of state but resigned three months later. He remained in Phnom Penh, imprisoned in his palace and kept alive only at the insistence of the Chinese, who considered him useful. During the Vietnamese invasion of Cambodia in December 1978, Sihanouk was flown to Beijing to prevent him falling into the hands of the new government.

Vietnamese Intervention

From 1976 to 1978, the xenophobic government in Phnom Penh instigated a series of border clashes with Vietnam, whose southern region – once part of the Khmer empire – it claimed. Khmer Rouge incursions into Vietnamese border provinces left hundreds of Vietnamese civilians dead. On 25 December 1978 Vietnam launched a full scale invasion of Cambodia, toppling the Pol Pot government two weeks later (on 7 January 1979). As Vietnamese tanks neared Phnom Penh, the Khmer Rouge fled westward with as many civilians as it could seize, taking refuge in the jungles and mountains on both sides of the border with Thailand. The Vietnamese installed a new government led by two former Khmer Rouge officers, Hun Sen, who had defected to Vietnam in 1977, and Heng Samrin, who had done the same in 1978. The official version of events is that the Heng Samrin government came to power in a revolutionary uprising against the Pol Pot regime. The Khmer Rouge's patrons, the Chinese communists, launched a massive reprisal raid across Vietnam's northernmost border in early 1979 in an attempt to buy their allies time. It failed, and after 17 days the Chinese withdrew, their fingers badly burnt by their Vietnamese enemies.

The social and economic dislocation that accompanied the Vietnamese invasion – along with the destruction of rice stocks and unharvested fields by both sides (to prevent their use by the enemy) – resulted in a vastly reduced rice harvest in early 1979. The chaotic situation led to very little rice being planted in the summer of 1979. By the middle of that year the country was suffering from a widespread famine. As hundreds of thousands of Cambodians fled to Thailand, a massive international famine relief effort, sponsored by the United Nations (UN), was launched.

In June 1982 Sihanouk agreed, under pressure from China, to head a military and political front opposed to the Phnom Penh government and the 170,000 Vietnamese troops defending it. The Sihanouk-led resistance coalition brought together – on paper, at least – FUNCINPEC (the French acronym for the National United Front for an Independent, Neutral, Peaceful and Co-operative Cambodia), which comprised a royalist group loyal to Sihanouk; the Khmer People's National Liberation Front, a non-communist grouping formed by former prime minister and banker Son Sann; and the Khmer Rouge, officially known as the Party of Democratic Kampuchea and by far the largest and most powerful of the three.

For much of the 1980s Cambodia remained closed to the western world, save for the presence of some aid groups. Government policy was effectively under the control of the Vietnamese so Cambodia found itself very much in the eastern bloc camp. Students were made to learn Russian and a number of Cambodians found themselves studying in cities like Moscow, Prague and Warsaw. Chinese Khmers found life hard under the Vietnamese occupation as they were often singled out for ill-treatment, and for a time at least the Vietnamese had a plan to repatriate them to China. The economy was in tatters for much of this period as Cambodia, like Vietnam, suffered from the effects of a US sponsored embargo. However, with the advent of Mikhail Gorbachev in the former USSR and the Vietnamese embrace of their own form

of *perestroika*, known as *doi moi*, Cambodia became something of a laboratory for their economic experiments.

In 1985 the Vietnamese overran all the major rebel camps inside Cambodia, forcing the Khmer Rouge and its allies to retreat into Thailand. From that time the Khmer Rouge – and, to a much more limited extent, the other two factions – engaged in guerrilla warfare aimed at demoralising its opponents. Tactics used by the Khmer Rouge included shelling government-controlled garrison towns, planting thousands of mines along roads and in rice fields, attacking road transport, blowing up bridges, kidnapping village chiefs and killing local administrators and school teachers. The Khmer Rouge also forced thousands of men, women and children living in the refugee camps it controlled to work as porters, ferrying ammunition and other supplies into Cambodia across heavily mined sections of the border.

Throughout the 1980s Thailand actively supported the Khmer Rouge and the other resistance factions, seeing them as a counterweight to Vietnamese power in the region. In fact, in 1979 Thailand demanded that, as a condition for allowing international food aid for Cambodia to pass through its territory, food had to be supplied to the Khmer Rouge forces encamped in the Thai border region as well. Along with weaponry supplied by China (and delivered by the Thai army), this international assistance was essential in enabling the Khmer Rouge to rebuild its military strength.

At the same time Malaysia and Singapore supplied weapons to the two smaller factions of the coalition. During the mid-1980s the British government dispatched the Special Air Service (SAS) to a Malaysian jungle camp to train guerrilla fighters in land mine-laying techniques. Although officially assisting the smaller factions, it is certain the Khmer Rouge benefited from this experience and enhanced its mine-laying capabilities. It then used these new-found skills to intimidate and terrorise the Cambodian people. As part of its campaign to harass and isolate Hanoi (capital of Vietnam), the USA gave more than

US$15 million a year in aid to the noncommunist factions of the Khmer Rouge-dominated coalition and helped it to retain its seat at the UN assembly in New York.

By the late 1980s the military wing of FUNCINPEC, the Armée Nationale Sihanoukiste, had 12,000 troops; Son Sann's faction, plagued by internal divisions, could field some 8000 soldiers; and the Khmer Rouge's National Army of Democratic Kampuchea was believed to have 40,000 troops. The army of the Phnom Penh government, the Kampuchean People's Revolutionary Armed Forces, had 50,000 regular soldiers and another 100,000 men and women serving in local militia forces.

UNTAC at the Helm

In September 1989 Vietnam, suffering from economic woes and eager to end its international isolation, announced that it had withdrawn all of its troops from Cambodia; however, evidence suggests that Vietnamese soldiers wearing Cambodian uniforms remained in the country well into 1990. With most of the Vietnamese gone, the opposition coalition, still dominated by the Khmer Rouge, launched a series of offensives, bringing the number of refugees inside the country to over 150,000 by the autumn of 1990. In the first eight months of 1990 over 2000 Cambodians lost their lives in the fighting between the Khmer Rouge dominated coalition and government forces.

Diplomatic efforts to end the civil war began to bear fruit in September 1990, when a plan agreed upon in Paris by the five permanent members of the UN Security Council (the USA, the former USSR, China, France and Britain) was accepted by both the Phnom Penh government and the three factions of the resistance coalition.

According to the plan, the Supreme National Council (SNC), a coalition of all factions, was to be formed under the presidency of Sihanouk. Meanwhile the United Nations Transitional Authority in Cambodia (UNTAC) was to supervise the administration of the country and to create an atmosphere in which free elections could take place.

UNTAC was successful in achieving SNC agreement to most international human rights covenants; a large number of non-governmental organisations (NGOs) were established in Cambodia; and most importantly, on 25 May 1993, elections were held with a 89.6% turnout. The results were far from decisive, however, with FUNCINPEC, led by Prince Norodom Ranariddh, taking 58 seats in the National Assembly, the Cambodian People's Party (CPP), which represented the previous communist government, taking 51 seats, and the Buddhist Liberal Democratic Party (BLDP) taking 10 seats. As a result, Cambodia ended up with two prime ministers: Norodom Ranariddh as first prime minister, and Hun Sen as second prime minister. Control of the various ministries was also spread among the three contending parties.

Within months of the elections taking place, local diplomats and reporters were complaining that the diffusion of central authority had led to a situation where real power lay in the hands of provincial leaders, whose loyalties lay with the CPP and communist-style power structures.

UNTAC was quick to pack up and go home, patting itself on the back for a job well done. Even today, it is heralded as one of the UN's success stories. The reality is that it was an ill-conceived and poorly executed peace because so many of the powers involved in brokering the deal had their own agendas to advance. It was a travesty that the Khmer Rouge was allowed to play a part in the process after the barbarities it had inflicted on its people. It must have seemed like a cruel joke to the many Cambodians who had lost countless family members under its rule, and very rapidly it became far more than a cruel joke, as the UN's half-botched disarmament program took weapons away from rural militias who for so long provided the backbone of the government's provincial defence network against the Khmer Rouge. This left communities throughout the country unprotected, while the Khmer Rouge used the veil of legitimacy conferred upon it by the peace process to re-establish a guerrilla network throughout the country. It is not an exaggeration to say that by 1994, when it was finally outlawed by the government, the Khmer Rouge was probably a greater threat to the stability of Cambodia than at any time since 1979.

If that wasn't bad enough, the UN presence also kick-started Cambodia's AIDS epidemic, with well-paid overseas soldiers boosting the prostitution industry. Cambodia's AIDS problem is now among the worst in Asia, and all this was done with taxpayers' money in the name of progress.

Machiavellian Times

As early as 1995 there were two major political incidents that boded ill for democratic politics. The first of these was the ouster of Sam Rainsy, a Paris-educated accountant, from FUNCINPEC. Rainsy lost his position as finance minister in mid-1994, a job he had excelled at, largely, it was surmised, because of his outspoken criticisms concerning corruption and government policy. In May 1995 his party membership was rescinded and one month later he was sacked from the National Assembly. He formed the Khmer Nation Party (now called the Sam Rainsy Party) and found himself the country's leading dissident in no time at all. Even his former FUNCINPEC allies turned against him; Prince Ranariddh was famously heard to remark in early 1995 that foremost among the prospects for Rainsy's wife was widowhood.

The other political headliner of 1995 was the arrest and exile of Prince Norodom Sirivudh, secretary general of FUNCINPEC, former foreign minister and half-brother of King Sihanouk. He had allegedly plotted to kill Hun Sen. Prince Sirivudh has been described as a good-humoured man, always quick with an off-the-cuff joke, but the only one laughing at his so-called quip about assassinating Hun Sen was Hun Sen, who found himself with the perfect excuse to clear another political adversary from his path.

Dealing with the Khmer Rouge

When the Vietnamese toppled the Pol Pot government in 1979, the Khmer Rouge disappeared into the jungle. The regime boycotted the 1993 elections and later rejected peace talks aimed at creating a ceasefire. Although it was a signatory to the Paris peace accords, the alliance collapsed over the role the CPP should play in the political process: to the Khmer Rouge it was anathema to deal with anyone so close to the Vietnamese.

Defections of some 2000 troops from the Khmer Rouge army in the months following the elections offered some hope that the long-running insurrection would fizzle out. Government-sponsored amnesty programs, however, initially turned out to be ill-conceived: the policy of reconscripting Khmer Rouge troops and returning them to fight their former comrades with poor pay and conditions provided little incentive to desert.

The problem was not just the poorly equipped and frequently unpaid Cambodian army. Evidence pointed to military cooperation with the Khmer Rouge. Leaked Khmer Rouge documents in mid-1994 revealed that large quantities of arms were sold to it by the Cambodian military, and that such arms sales were continuing even as those conducting the sales were attacking Khmer Rouge positions.

In 1994 the Khmer Rouge resorted to a new tactic of targeting tourists, with horrendous results for a number of foreigners in Cambodia. During 1994 three people were taken from a taxi on the road to Sihanoukville and subsequently shot. A few months later another three foreigners were seized from a train bound for Sihanoukville and in the ransom drama that followed they were executed, probably some time in September, as the army closed in.

The government changed its course during the middle of the 1990s, opting for more carrot and less stick in a bid to end the war. The defection program was stepped up a gear and slowly but surely isolated Khmer Rouge units began coming over to the government side in return for amnesties and an army uniform. Another important development was that the Thai government, a longtime supporter of the rebels, finally began to clamp down on Khmer Rouge border movements, an act that theoretically severed the

Blood Brother No 1

Pol Pot, Brother No 1 in the Khmer Rouge regime, is a name that sends shivers down the spines of most Cambodians and foreigners alike. It was Pol Pot who was most associated with the bloody madness of the regime he led between 1975 and 1979; and his policies heaped misery, suffering and death on millions of Cambodians. Even after his overthrow in 1979 he cast a long shadow over the Cambodian people: for many of them just knowing he was still alive was traumatic and unjust. He died on 15 April 1998.

Pol Pot was born Saloth Sar in a small village near Kompong Thom in 1925. He had a relatively privileged upbringing and his education included, ironically, some time in a wat. As a young man he won a scholarship to study in Paris and spent several years there with Ieng Sary, who would later become foreign minister. It is here that he is believed to have developed his radical Marxist thought, later to transform into the politics of extreme Maoist agrarianism. Back in Cambodia, Saloth Sar became a school teacher, entering politics in the late 1950s. Very little is known about his early political career.

During the 1960s Sihanouk switched from friend to foe of the left and back again, but in 1963 his repressive policies sent Saloth Sar and comrades fleeing to the jungles of Ratanakiri. It was from this time that he began to call him himself Pol Pot, although it was not for a number of years that anyone would make the connection between the one-time teacher and the leader of Democratic Kampuchea. Once the Khmer Rouge was allied with Sihanouk, following his overthrow by Lon Nol in 1970 and subsequent exile in Beijing, its support soared and the faces of the leadership became familiar. However, Pol Pot remained a shadowy figure in the hierarchy leaving the public duties to Khieu Samphan and Ieng Sary.

When the Khmer Rouge marched into Phnom Penh on 17 April 1975, few people could have anticipated the hell that was to come. Pol Pot, with the help of others, was the architect of one of the most radical and brutal revolutions in the history of mankind. Proclaimed as Year Zero, Cambodia was on a self-destructive course to sever all ties with the past.

Pol Pot was not to emerge as the public face of the revolution until the end of 1976, after returning from a trip to his mentors in Beijing. During his leadership he spent much of his time living in Phnom Penh, moving from residence to residence, paranoid about his security. He granted almost no interviews to foreign media and was seen only on propaganda movies

Khmer Rouge lines of revenue: gems and timber transported into Thailand for sale.

The defection program certainly advanced government control in certain provinces, but countrywide the situation smacked of stalemate with neither side advancing significantly. The breakthrough came in August 1996 when Ieng Sary, Brother No 3 in the Khmer Rouge hierarchy and foreign minister during its rule, was denounced by Pol Pot for corruption. He subsequently led a mass defection of fighters and their dependents from the Pailin area, and this effectively sealed the fate of the remaining Khmer Rouge. Pailin, rich in gems and timber, had long been the economic

springboard from which the Khmer Rouge could launch counter-offensives against the government. The severing of this income, coupled with the fact that government forces now had only one front on which to concentrate their resources, suggested that the days of civil war were numbered.

By 1997 cracks were appearing in the paper-thin coalition and the fledgling democracy once again found itself under siege. On 31 March 1997 a grenade was thrown into a group of Sam Rainsy supporters demonstrating peacefully outside the National Assembly. Many were killed and Sam Rainsy narrowly escaped injury. He fled into self-imposed exile, blaming

Blood Brother No 1

produced by government television or on the occasional broadcast by Yugoslav journalists. Curiously enough, however, those who did meet Pol Pot during this period described him as a genial and charismatic man. Such was his aura and reputation that by the last year of the regime, a cult of personality was developing around him and busts of him were produced.

He was fervently anti-Vietnamese, a sentiment fuelled by the pivotal role the Vietnamese played in arming and advising the Khmer Rouge during its jungle years. It was the Vietnamese that called the shots in the early days of the guerrilla war, something that rankled a fiercely patriotic Pol Pot. He was never to forget that the Vietnamese considered the Cambodian revolution of secondary importance to their own. Ironically, it was indeed the Vietnamese that turned out to be his greatest enemy, invading Cambodia on 25 December 1978 and overthrowing the Khmer Rouge government on 7 January 1979. Pol Pot and his supporters were sent fleeing to the jungle near the Thai border, from where they spent the next decade launching attacks on government positions in Cambodia.

Pol Pot spent much of the 1980s living in an armed compound in Thailand, and with the connivance of both China and the west was able to rebuild his shattered forces and once again threaten the stability of Cambodia. It is thought he stepped down as nominal head of the Khmer Rouge in 1985, but no doubt continued to call the shots from behind the scenes as he had done in the earliest days of the revolution. Throughout the 1980s and 90s his enigma increased as the international media speculated as to the real fate of Pol Pot. His demise was reported so often that when he finally passed away on 15 April 1998 many Cambodians refused to believe it until they had seen his body on television or in newspapers. Even then many were skeptical.

Pol Pot is a name known throughout the world, yet little is known about the man himself. Even the author of his biography *Brother Number One*, Cambodia expert David Chandler, could not find more than 200 pages to write about the man. He granted an interview to journalist Nate Thayer in 1997, but this was far from revealing as he disclaimed all responsibility for the excesses of his regime. It would be equally misleading to put together a portrait of the man from Khmer Rouge sources now living in Pailin as it is all too easy to blame a dead man for the horror of his rule. The truth about many episodes in his life will now never be known: he has carried his secrets to the grave.

Hun Sen and the CPP for the attack. However, it was the Khmer Rouge that again grabbed the headlines. As the politicians in Phnom Penh vied to draw the remaining Khmer Rouge out of their northern bases, Pol Pot ordered the execution of Son Sen, former defence minister during the Khmer Rouge regime, and many of his family members. This provoked a putsch within the Khmer Rouge leadership, as the one-legged hardline general Ta Mok seized control of the movement and put Pol Pot on 'trial'. This was widely seen as a cosmetic exercise carried out in an attempt to shift the collective responsibility of the mass killings onto the shoulders of one man. Ru-

mours flew about Phnom Penh that Pol Pot would soon be brought there to face international justice, but it was never to happen. July saw the focus shift back to Phnom Penh as the brittle government coalition fell apart amid scenes of heavy fighting.

The Coup

The events of July 1997, as they are euphemistically referred to in Cambodia, were preceded by a lengthy courting period in which both FUNCINPEC and the CPP attempted to win the trust of the remaining Khmer Rouge hardliners in northern Cambodia. First Prime Minister Norodom Ranariddh was close to forging a deal with the jungle fighters and was keen to get it sewn up before Cambodia's accession to the Association of Southeast Asian Nations (ASEAN), as nothing would provide a better entry fanfare than the ending of Cambodia's long civil war. In his haste, he didn't pay enough attention to detail and was outflanked and subsequently outgunned by Second Prime Minister Hun Sen. On 5 July 1997 fighting again erupted on the streets of Phnom Penh as troops loyal to the CPP clashed with those loyal to FUNCINPEC. The heaviest exchanges were around Pochentong airport and key government buildings, but before long the dust had settled and the CPP once again effectively controlled Cambodia. Hun Sen accused Prince Ranariddh of illegally attempting to ship arms into Cambodia via the port of Sihanoukville and of colluding with the Khmer Rouge. They were pretty spurious charges and they led many in the international community to roundly condemn Hun Sen's actions. The strongman had finally flexed his muscles and there was to be no doubt as to which party commanded the support of the military.

The international reaction was swift and decisive. ASEAN suspended Cambodia's imminent membership of the regional organisation, the Cambodian seat at the UN was declared vacant and the donor community put a freeze on all new aid money. This was to have a serious impact on the Cambodian economy over the next two years.

Following the coup, the remnants of FUNCINPEC forces on the Thai border around O Smach formed an alliance with the last of the Khmer Rouge under Ta Mok's control. The fighting may have ended, but the deaths did not: several prominent FUNCINPEC politicians and military leaders were murdered in extrajudicial executions, and even today no-one has been brought to justice for these crimes. Many of FUNCINPEC's leading politicians fled abroad, while the leading generals camped out in the jungle near the Thai border, leading a resistance struggle, together with the Khmer Rouge, against forces loyal to the CPP. Hun Sen quickly appointed Ung

Huot, a FUNCINPEC parliamentarian, as first prime minister, although real power now lay firmly in the misleadingly named second prime minister's hands.

As 1998 began the CPP announced an all-out offensive against its enemies in the north. By April it was closing in on the Khmer strongholds of Anlong Veng and Preah Vihear, and amid this heavy fighting Pol Pot managed to evade justice – he died in the Khmer Rouge's captivity on April 15. He was cremated soon after without an official autopsy, breeding rumours and gossip in Phnom Penh for a few weeks. The fall of Anlong Veng in April was followed by the fall in May of Preah Vihear; and the big three, Ta Mok, Khieu Samphan and Nuon Chea, were forced to flee into the jungle near the Thai border with their remaining troops. It was around this time that the strategically important Hill 200 fell to government forces and here they found the so-called 'KR papers', all the notes from high level meetings that had taken place over the preceding year. In them were details of how the organisation planned to betray Prince Norodom Ranariddh, after using an alliance with FUNCINPEC to secure a foothold in Cambodian politics once more. The plan was ambitious, if not absurd, but more importantly highlighted the risk Ranariddh took in dealing with the devil. Hun Sen was to ably exploit these papers to defend his coup.

Election Time Again

Much of 1998 was dominated by election fever. It was to be the country's second election and many observers were pessimistic about the chances for democracy after the tumultuous events of 1997. At the start of 1998 FUNCINPEC leader, Prince Norodom Ranariddh, had still not returned to the country as he faced a variety of charges amounting to treason. FUNCINPEC's provincial network was also in tatters as many of its representatives had either left the country, been murdered or switched allegiances in a bid for political survival. However, Sam Rainsy was back: he returned to Cambodia at the end of 1997 after many months of self-imposed exile.

Ranariddh was tried in absentia during March and found guilty on charges of both arms smuggling and collusion with the Khmer Rouge. He subsequently received a pardon on 21 March from King Sihanouk at Hun Sen's request, and returned to Cambodia at the end of the month. The run-up to the election was remarkably quiet by Cambodian standards. The opposition formed an alliance to contest the elections called the National United Front (NUF), which brought together FUNCINPEC and the Sam Rainsy Party, plus a couple of smaller parties. They were never exactly united, but the alliance gave the parties a stronger voice against the government. The Khmer Rouge was roundly ignored and fortunately its threats to destabilise the election were reduced to a single deadly attack near the polling station in Anlong Veng.

The election took place on 26 July amid opposition charges of voter intimidation. Numerous election observers had flown into Cambodia some months earlier to ensure the process was free and fair, and they hastily declared the ballot a success. The opposition cried foul and the subsequent standoff again plunged Cambodia into a crisis of confidence. The results gave the CPP 64 seats, FUNCINPEC 43 seats and the Sam Rainsy Party 15 seats. The CPP was now the dominant force in Cambodian politics, but lacked the two-thirds majority required to govern alone. As the opposition escalated its campaign for democracy in August, mass demonstrations began in the capital, which soon descended into rioting, fighting and repression. The country looked set for yet another period of instability.

King Sihanouk added his voice to the post-electoral debate, offering to act as a mediator in the formation of a coalition. He was able to bring the squabbling leaders to a table at his residence in Siem Reap and, eventually, after much posturing on all sides, a coalition was announced on 23 November. It was business as usual, with a much-weakened FUNCINPEC agreeing to govern with a now dominant CPP. Part of the coalition deal ensured amnesties for those FUNCINPEC supporters still facing charges, including exiled princes Sirivudh and Chakrapong, and General Neak Bun Chhay.

The formation of a new coalition government allowed the politicians to once more concentrate on bringing an end to the civil war. In December 1998 almost all the remaining Khmer Rouge guerrillas turned themselves over to government forces in return for amnesty and the Khmer Rouge effectively ceased to exist as a military organisation. However, the big three continued to remain at large with an increasingly small number of soldiers, numbering perhaps only several hundred.

On 25 December Hun Sen received the Christmas present he had been waiting for: telephoning from Pailin, Khieu Samphan requested that he and Nuon Chea be permitted to defect to the government side. Hun Sen had long been an advocate of a trial for these remaining leaders, but he appeared to do an about turn and treated them to a lavish VIP reception, talking of the need for reconciliation. At a press conference in Phnom Penh, Nuon Chea, former Brother No 2 in the Khmer Rouge hierarchy, made a pathetic apology to the Cambodian people for their suffering, and so lame was it that even Ieng Sary (foreign minister during the Khmer Rouge's rule) later rebuked him. The international community began to pile on the pressure for the establishment of some sort of war crimes tribunal to try the remaining Khmer Rouge leadership, while Hun Sen fired off contradictory salvos about who should be tried and for what.

Many Cambodians would no doubt like to see the Khmer Rouge leadership put on trial over the mass killings, but this will possibly never take place as the Chinese may move to block any such proceedings. The Chinese were staunch allies of the Democratic Kampuchea regime between 1975 and 1979 and many Khmer Rouge policies had their origins in Beijing. There is also the delicate issue of national reconciliation to consider, as Cambodia is now at peace for the first time in more then 30 years. A trial of senior leaders could send a message to former Khmer Rouge fighters around the country –

Naming Rights

Cambodia has changed its name so many times over the last few decades that there are understandable grounds for confusion. For the Cambodians, their country is Kampuchea. The name is derived from the word Kambu-ja, meaning 'those born of Kambu', the mythical founder of the country. It dates back as far as the 10th century. The Portuguese 'Camboxa' and the French 'Cambodge', from which the English name 'Cambodia' is derived, are adaptations of 'Kambu-ja'.

Since gaining independence in 1953, the country has been known in English as many things before coming full circle:

- The Kingdom of Cambodia (in French, Le Royaume du Cambodge).
- The Khmer Republic (under Lon Nol, who ruled from 1970 to 1975).
- Democratic Kampuchea (under the Khmer Rouge, the communist party which controlled the country from 1975 to 1979).
- The People's Republic of Kampuchea (under the Vietnamese-backed Phnom Penh government from 1979 to 1989).
- The State of Cambodia (in French, L'État du Cambodge; in Khmer, Roët Kampuchea) from mid-1989.
- The Kingdom of Cambodia (from the May 1993 elections).

It was the Khmer Rouge that insisted the outside world use the name Kampuchea. Changing the country's official English name back to Cambodia (which has been used by the US State Department all along) was intended as a symbolic move to distance the present government in Phnom Penh from the bitter connotations of the name Kampuchea, which westerners and overseas Khmer alike associate with the murderous Khmer Rouge regime.

when will they come for us – and lead to a resumption of unrest. The Cambodian people deserve justice after so much suffering, but it could be argued that the nation would be better served by a truth commission that cleanses the nation's soul without seeking revenge. For senior leaders, all blame resides with a dead Pol Pot, but if lower ranking cadres are encouraged to come forward the full truth may emerge. There is an awful lot of pent up anger in Cambodia and knowing the truth could be more cathartic to the average Cambodian than seeing pathetic old men on trial.

Cambodia Today

Both politically and economically, Cambodia is in a shaky position as donor countries tire of the rampant corruption and bad government that blights the country. Politically, the country is plagued by the divisions of its past. Politicians were either with the Vietnamese or against them, members of the CPP or FUNCINPEC – and this can have a considerable effect on career chances in any walk of life in Cambodia. Many observers are pessimistic about the future of democracy in Cambodia as the CPP continues to tighten its grip on power. FUNCINPEC's provincial hierarchy was decimated in the aftermath of July 1997's fighting, and the party remains divided over the strategy pursued by its leader Prince Norodom Ranariddh in the months that followed. Although a popular party due to the royal connection, it lacks the muscle to seriously challenge the CPP, and Ranariddh has allowed himself to be somewhat sidelined as President of the National Assembly. Sam Rainsy remains the perceived voice of democracy in Cambodia, but lacks the rural support and following among the military so crucial for success. He also lost some credibility in the run up to the elections by relying heavily on anti-Vietnamese rhetoric in his campaign speeches.

The press continues to enjoy the sort of freedom of speech that is unthinkable in many of the neighbouring ASEAN countries, but the intimidation and murder of opposition journalists is sadly not uncommon, and state television is now firmly under the control of the CPP – dishing out a daily diet of propaganda about Hun Sen's achievements between karaoke videos and soap operas.

The CPP is in effective control of Cambodia today, but the party is not as united as it might at first appear. Politics in Cambodia has always been somewhat feudal, with allegiances only as permanent as the money or weaponry that buys them. Hun Sen is no one-man-show and owes some of his success to figures in the business world and the military: he is only guaranteed to stay in power as long as he cooperates with their agendas. However, he does command the respect of the most important elements of the military and this should help satisfy his political ambitions for several years to come.

Hun Sen, the master chess player from Takhmau, has a political guile and cunning unrivalled in Cambodia. He has slowly but surely divided and conquered the opposition, isolating opponents before destroying them: first Rainsy, then Sirivudh and finally Ranariddh. The events of the first parliament read like a script, and there are now few politicians left to challenge him, as they have learned that to do so is folly indeed. He is often perceived as the bad guy of Cambodian politics and, while it is true that his democratic credentials are far from impressive, it is hardly the case that Ranariddh, often hailed as the good guy overseas, is without his flaws.

Love him or hate him, Hun Sen is at least a force for stability in Cambodia and a wily politician who has shown himself consistently able to outflank the opposition. He has proved himself a survivor, personally as well as politically, for he lost an eye during his youth. With the opposition down if not out, a shortage of clean and able politicians in Cambodia and a poorly educated electorate, it appears, for the time at least, that 'in the kingdom of the blind the one-eyed man is king'.

GEOGRAPHY & GEOLOGY

Cambodia covers 181,035 sq km, or a little over half the size of Vietnam. The country's maximum extent is about 580km (east-west) and 450km (north-south). It is bounded on the west by Thailand, on the north by Thailand and Laos, on the east by Vietnam and to the south by the Gulf of Thailand.

Cambodia's two dominant topographical features are the Mekong River, which is almost 5km wide in places, and the Tonlé Sap lake. The Mekong, which rises in Tibet, flows about 486km through Cambodia before continuing, via southern Vietnam, to the South China Sea. At Phnom Penh, it splits into the Upper River (called simply the Mekong or, in Vietnamese, the Tien Giang) and the Lower River (the Bassac River; in Vietnamese, the Hau Giang). The rich sediment deposited during the Mekong's annual wet-season flooding has made for very fertile agricultural land. Most of Cambodia's streams and rivers flow into the Mekong-Tonlé Sap basin.

The Tonlé Sap lake is linked to the Mekong at Phnom Penh by a 100km-long channel known as the Tonlé Sap river. From mid-May to early October (the rainy season) the level of the Mekong rises, backing up the Tonlé Sap river and causing it to flow north-west into the Tonlé Sap lake. During this period, the Tonlé Sap lake swells from 3000 sq km to over 7500 sq km; its maximum depth increases from about 2.2m to more than 10m. As the water level of the Mekong falls during the dry season, the Tonlé Sap river reverses its flow, draining the waters of the lake back into the Mekong. This extraordinary process makes the Tonlé Sap lake one of the world's richest sources of freshwater fish. It is estimated that the lake provides a livelihood for about 40% of the Cambodian population and its fish provide almost 60% of the country's fish protein intake.

In the centre of Cambodia, around the Tonlé Sap lake and the upper Mekong Delta, is a low-lying alluvial plain where the vast majority of Cambodians live. Extending outward from this plain are thinly forested transitional plains with elevations of no more than about 100m above sea level.

In the south-west, much of the area between the Gulf of Thailand and the Tonlé Sap lake is covered by a highland region formed by two distinct upland blocks: the Chuor Phnom Kravanh (Cardamom Mountains) in south-western Battambang Province and Pursat Province, and the Chuor Phnom Damrei (Elephant Mountains) in the provinces of Kompong Speu, Koh Kong and Kampot. Along the southern coast is a heavily forested lowland strip isolated from the rest of the country by the mountains to the north. Cambodia's highest peak is Phnom Aoral (1813m), in Pursat Province.

Along Cambodia's northern border with Thailand, the plains abut an east-west oriented sandstone escarpment, more than 300km long and 180m to 550m in height, that marks the southern limit of the Chuor Phnom Dangkrek (Dangkrek Mountains). In the north-eastern corner of the country (the provinces of Ratanakiri and Mondulkiri), the transitional plains give way to the Eastern Highlands, a remote region of densely forested mountains and high plateaus that extends eastward into Vietnam's Central Highlands and northward into Laos.

Cambodia can be neatly divided into two geomorphological regions: the central plains of the Mekong-Tonlé Sap basin, which formed from an ancient marine gulf and later filled with alluvium and colluvium (rock fragments from the base of cliffs) from the Mekong River; and the basin periphery of mountain ranges, which include a variety of mineral and soil types. Cambodia's main mineral resources include basalt in Kompong Cham Province, granite in Kompong Chhnang Province, limestone in the west and north-west, quartz in Takeo Province, marble in Stung Treng Province, and gems in Pailin and to a lesser extent Ratanakiri Province. There are also thought to be extensive natural gas deposits off the coast of Cambodia and sufficient oil, if recoverable, to make Cambodia energy self-sufficient.

CLIMATE

The climate of Cambodia is governed by two monsoons, which set the rhythm of rural life. The cool, dry, north-eastern mon-

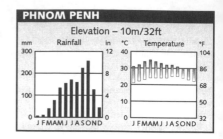

PHNOM PENH
Elevation – 10m/32ft
Rainfall / Temperature

soon, which carries little rain, blows from about November to February. From May to October, the south-western monsoon brings strong winds, high humidity and heavy rains. Even during the wet season it rarely rains in the morning: most precipitation comes in the afternoon, and even then only sporadically.

Maximum daily temperatures range from more than 40°C in April, the hottest month, to the high 20s during January, the coolest month. Daily minimum temperatures are usually no more than 10°C below the maximums.

Annual rainfall varies considerably from area to area. Whereas the seaward slopes of the south-west highlands receive more than 5000mm of rain per annum, the central lowlands average only about 1400mm. Between 70% and 80% of the annual rainfall is brought by the south-western monsoon.

ECOLOGY & ENVIRONMENT
Logging

The biggest threat to the environment in Cambodia is logging. In the mid-1960s Cambodia was reckoned to have around 75% rainforest coverage. Surveys carried out in mid-1993 concluded this had been reduced to 49%, around half of which was primary forest. Worse still, reports today also conclude that the wholesale shift from a command economy to a market economy has led to an asset-stripping bonanza by the cash-strapped government and military, and that virtually all of Cambodia's primary resources are under some kind of unaccountable control.

The problem is not just the parlous state of the Cambodian economy but the international demand for timber and the fact that neighbouring countries like Thailand and Laos enforce much tougher logging regulations, while at the same time helping to flout Cambodia's lax restrictions. It's small wonder then that foreign logging companies have been flocking to Cambodia. By late 1995, 27 companies had licences or applications to log Cambodia's rainforests. By the end of 1997 just under seven million hectares of the country's land area had been allocated as concessions, amounting to almost all of Cambodia's forest except national parks and protected areas; however, even in these supposed havens, illegal logging continues and no tree in Cambodia is safe.

Logging deals are controversial for many reasons, not least the destruction of Cambodia's natural habitat. Deals have been made by the prime ministers without reference to forestry officials and are usually confidential, and stipulations on how the logging should be carried out are hazy. The involvement of senior figures is crucial to the success of this trade as it confers legitimacy on actions that may possibly contravene Cambodian law. In late 1998 British environmental group Global Witness obtained official papers in Laos that included both former first prime minister Ung Huot and current prime minister and then second prime minister Hun Sen's signatures authorising illegal timber exports. With collusion at the most senior level, what hope is there for Cambodia's disappearing forest and its fauna.

Travelling around the provinces, it is impossible to believe the government's rhetoric about clampdowns and enforcement of law, as in many parts of the country the rape of natural resources seems to be worsening rather then improving. The Royal Cambodian Armed Forces (RCAF) is the driving force behind much of the logging in Cambodia: it assists in logging legal concessions under the guise of providing security and logs illegally elsewhere. The proceeds from these operations contribute towards the army's grey (undeclared) budget, with its nominal budget already taking up more than half the government's cash. The long-term implications could be far more damaging than simply deforestation. Without trees to cloak the hills, the rains will inevitably carry away large amounts of topsoil during future monsoons. There can be no doubt that in time this will have a catastrophic effect on the Tonlé Sap lake, as the shallow waters recede from prolonged siltation as occurred with the Aral Sea of Central Asia. Combined with overfishing and pollution, this vital organ in the lives of so many Cambodians may eventually be destroyed – an unmitigated disaster for future generations.

The tragedy is that the money generated from all this illegal activity could easily be raised for the treasury's coffers, and with the loss of far fewer trees, from controlled logging. In 1997 the government officially made about US$12.8 million from the forests, but illegal operations over the same period generated an estimated US$184.2 million. This is money such a poor country can ill-afford to lose, but with the endemic culture of corruption in Cambodia it is difficult to be optimistic for the future of the forests, especially when few in the international community are willing or able to do much about it. Every time the subject is brought up at international donor meetings, action against illegal logging is taken until the cheques are signed, and then it is business as usual until the next round of handouts.

Pollution

Cambodia has a pollution problem, but it is not of the same nature as the carbon monoxide crises in neighbouring capitals such as Bangkok and Jakarta: Phnom Penh is the only city that suffers from air pollution. The country does, however, suffer the ill-effects of an extremely primitive sanitation system in urban areas, and in rural areas sanitary facilities are nonexistent, with only 4% of the population having access to proper facilities. These conditions breed and spread disease with people being forced to defecate on open ground and urinate in rivers. Epidemics of diarrhoea are not uncommon and among young children it is the number one killer in Cambodia. This type of biological pollution may not be as immediately apparent as smog over a city, but in the shorter term it is far more hazardous to the average Cambodian.

The other pollution crisis that erupted at the end of 1998 was Sihanoukville's toxic-waste dumping scandal. Formosa Plastics, a Taiwanese company, deposited a large amount of mercury-contaminated waste about 20km from town. Tests later showed that the waste had a far higher level of toxicity than permitted and a number of dock workers who handled the material subsequently died. It is said that customs officials were implicated in a bribery deal that had allowed the waste into the country. Formosa Plastics eventually agreed to collect the waste, but not before Sihanoukville's reputation as Cambodia's leading beach resort had taken a battering.

The worry for Cambodia is not so much that one dump has been uncovered, but how many dumps have gone unnoticed? Cambodia has a long coast, so for an unscrupulous company to enter its waters and dump waste at sea would not be difficult, particularly given the diminutive status of the country's navy. For the sake of Cambodia's marine life, it must be hoped this is just conjecture, but with world waste increasing daily, it is quite possible the mercury contamination will be the first rather than last pollution crisis to hit this beautiful but blighted country.

Damming the Mekong

With a meandering length of around 4200km, the Mekong is the longest river in South-East Asia, and some 50 million people depend on it for their livelihoods. In terms of fish biodiversity, the Mekong is second only to the Amazon; but with energy needs ever spiralling in Thailand and Vietnam, it is very tempting for a poor country like Cambodia to dam the river and make money from hydro-electric power. Even more tempting for Cambodia is the fact that the United Nations Development Programme (UNDP) and the Asia Development Bank would pay for much of the construction costs. Environmental groups are already calling foul.

Overseeing development plans for the river is the Mekong River Commission (MRC), formed by the UNDP and comprising Cambodia, Thailand, Laos and Vietnam.

The odd one out is China, which has around 20% of the Mekong but calls it the Lancang and feels it can do what it wants with the river without reference to its neighbours. China is already at work on a number of dam projects on the upper reaches of the Mekong, and many environmentalists fear that such projects will have an adverse effect down river.

China's dam projects are shrouded in secrecy, but there are thought to be 15 projects planned, with three operational by the year 2009. Meanwhile, the MRC has plans for 11 dams for the Mekong in Laos and Cambodia.

Environmental concerns focus on a number of issues. For a start, even though the MRC dams planned for the Mekong will be small, it is thought they will flood some 1900 sq km and displace around 60,000 people. Secondly, there are worries about how the dams will affect fish migration – some environmentalists claim that the dams might halve the fish population of the Mekong and perhaps even Tonlé Sap lake. Finally, and perhaps of most concern, is the importance of the annual monsoon flooding of the Mekong, which deposits nutrient-rich silt across vast tracts of land used for agriculture. Environmentalists say even a drop of 1m in Mekong water levels would result in around 2000 sq km less flood area around Tonlé Sap lake, a result with potentially disastrous consequences for Cambodia's farmers.

The Mekong is a huge untapped resource. It is probably inevitable that it be harnessed to make much needed power for the region. Local environmentalists hope that this can be done in the context of open discussion and with foresight. Many fear, however, that long-term interests will be scrapped in favour of short-term profits.

Dams are planned for a few other rivers around Cambodia, although if you were to believe some of the ministry maps you would think the government was going to dam every bit of water in the country. The most realistic project is the damming of the San River, which flows into the Mekong near Stung Treng. This major river, together with the Sekong and Srepok rivers, contributes an estimated 10% to 20% of the

JULIA WILKINSON

JULIA WILKINSON

NICK RAY

GLENN BEANLAND

NICK RAY

Cambodia's people are remarkably warm and enthusiastic, despite poverty and decades of political instability.

RICHARD I'ANSON

ANDERS BLOMQVIST

RICHARD I'ANSON

BERNARD NAPTHINE

Religion and religious rituals are part of daily life, with most people following the Buddhist faith.

Mekong's total flow at Kratie. If the dam goes ahead it could be a major earner, with exports of power to Thailand and Vietnam. However, the effects on the local indigenous population, Virachay National Park and fish stocks have not been considered in any detail yet – and perhaps never will be.

Meanwhile, Down on the Shrimp Farm

Thai shrimp farmers have descended on Cambodia, mainly in the coastal areas of Koh Kong Province. Mangroves make ideal grounds for the commercial farming of the tiger prawn, a seafood with phenomenal money-making powers throughout Asia. To farm tiger prawns, however, it is necessary to clear the mangroves and create artificial ponds. Fertilisers and chemical feeds are required, and it is also necessary to pump out polluted water and replenish it with clean water, creating damage to the surrounding environment. Within two or three years a pool will have to be abandoned and the farming relocated to another area, leaving a trail of environmental destruction.

There is very little in it for Cambodia. Generally the shrimp farms are established with big-business bucks, unskilled Khmer labour is used for the menial work and 90% of the product that is produced is shipped to Thailand. The pity of it is that mangroves foster remarkably diverse ecosystems and have an integral relationship with oceanic fish populations, serving as spawning grounds for many species that are commercially fished. The government is looking at ways in which it can regulate commercial shrimp farming in its mangroves, but underfunding and ignorance on the part of the locals living in mangrove areas is making the job very difficult.

Most of the shrimp farms have begun to fail, the shrimps dying from disease and poorly maintained habitat. This has meant many Cambodians who were encouraged to invest in shrimp farms as a lucrative money earner are now financially ruined. The mangrove swamps are unlikely to return soon either as many people in the province are chopping them down for charcoal produc-

tion. All in all the shrimp farming saga has been a pretty sorry experience for the Cambodian environment.

FLORA

The central lowland consists of rice paddies, fields of dry crops such as corn and tobacco, tracts of reeds and tall grass, and thinly wooded areas. The transitional plains are mostly covered with savanna grasses, which grow to a height of 1.5m.

In the south-west, virgin rainforests grow to heights of 50m or more on the rainy seaward slopes of the mountains. Nearby, higher elevations support pine forests. Vegetation in the coastal strip includes both evergreen and mangrove forests. In the northern mountains there are broadleaf evergreen forests with trees soaring 30m above the thick undergrowth of vines, bamboos, palms and assorted woody and herbaceous ground plants. The Eastern Highlands are covered with grassland and deciduous forests. Forested upland areas support many varieties of orchid.

In the past two decades, a great deal of deforestation has taken place, and the pace has been quickening over the past five years. Both the Malaysians and the Indonesians have bought major timber concessions and illegal logging is widespread.

The symbol of Cambodia is the sugar palm tree, which is used in construction (for roofs and walls) and in the production of medicine, wine and vinegar. Because of the way sugar palms grow (over the years, the tree keeps getting taller but the trunk, which lacks a normal bark, does not grow thicker), their trunks retain shrapnel marks from every battle that ever raged around them. Some sugar palms have been shot clear through the trunk.

FAUNA

Cambodia's larger wild animals include bears, elephants, rhinoceroses, leopards, tigers and oxen. The lion, although often incorporated into Angkorian heraldic devices, has never been seen here. Among the country's more common birds are cormorants, cranes, egrets, grouse, herons, pelicans, pheasants and wild ducks. These and some rarer species can be seen at the Prek Toal Bird Sanctuary near Siem Reap. There is also a great variety of butterflies. Four types of snake are especially dangerous: the cobra, the king cobra, the banded krait and Russell's viper.

Endangered Species

Cambodia is home to a number of diminishing species including elephants, rhinoceroses, leopards and tigers, but very little is known about numbers as their habitats are extremely remote.

In 1995 the World Wildlife Fund (WWF) announced a fundraising campaign to save the tigers of Indochina. There are thought to be tigers in Virachay National Park and remote parts of Mondulkiri, but they are threatened by poachers. Magical powers of potency (sexual, mainly) are ascribed to tiger parts throughout Asia, especially by the Chinese.

Given that much of the country has been off limits for such a long time, some suggest Cambodia harbours animals that have become extinct elsewhere in the region. For the moment it remains conjecture, but as the national park system becomes more effective it is hoped that whatever is out there will at least be protected.

Sightings of rare storks last seen in Laos in 1993 were reported in early 1995. Meanwhile, the kouprey (wild ox), adopted by Sihanouk as the national animal in 1963, is thought to linger on in very small numbers in the north-east of Cambodia. The discovery of an isolated herd of Javan rhinoceroses in south-west Vietnam in 1998 suggests that there may be more in nearby Mondulkiri.

Swimming in the rivers of Cambodia are some of the last remaining freshwater Irrawaddy dolphins. These inhabit stretches of the Mekong between Kratie and the Lao border. There are fewer remaining here than in Laos, but it is still possible to see them near Kratie, particularly in the dry season when the river level is low. The giant catfish, known to reach up to 5m in length, is also threatened due to its popularity on menus from Hong Kong to Tokyo.

Other creatures on the endangered species list include the marbled cat, the pileated gibbon, the brown-antlered deer, Marshall's horseshoe bat, the giant ibis and the Siamese crocodile.

NATIONAL PARKS

For much of the 1990s the country's national park system was little more than lines drawn on a map, but this is fast changing with assistance from the UNDP and assorted NGOs. The most important national parks in the country include: Bokor, which occupies a 1000m plateau on the south coast overlooking Kampot; Ream, which includes a marine reserve and is just a short distance from Sihanoukville; Kirirom, 675m above sea level in the Chuor Phnom Damrei, 112km south-west of Phnom Penh; and Virachay, the kingdom's largest park nestled against the border with Laos and Vietnam in north-east Cambodia. Bokor is home to wild elephants and there is now accommodation available at the summit. Ream has developed a visitor program, which includes a boat trip and guided walks, while Kirirom has a basic guesthouse and is popular with Khmers at weekends. There is little in the way of facilities at Virachay, but rangers are keen to welcome visitors and have centres in Voen Sai and Siem Pang.

Other protected areas in the country include biospheres and a bird sanctuary on the Tonlé Sap lake and a small park in the vicinity of Kep.

GOVERNMENT & POLITICS

At the May 1993 elections Cambodia became a constitutional monarchy. Prince Sihanouk, who abdicated in 1955, accepted the crown and rules as king. The constitution of September 1993 theoretically allows for separation of powers between the executive, legislative and judicial branches of government. In practice it rarely works this way, however. Decades of war and one-party rule have made Cambodia's administrative and legal structures slow to respond to the challenge of neutrality.

Cambodia's second election in July 1998 took place amid charges of voter intimidation and human rights abuses. The CPP was declared the victor, taking 64 seats in the assembly, while FUNCINPEC took 43 and the Sam Rainsy Party 15. It took several months for a government to form itself and this was not to happen before a series of protests, riots and deaths. Eventually King Sihanouk brokered a coalition deal that saw the some time allies and some time enemies in FUNCINPEC and the CPP again engage in an uneasy political embrace. The CPP holds 16 of the ministries while FUNCINPEC controls 15; the CPP controls most of the important financial ministries, while FUNCINPEC has the poisoned chalice of the social ministries.

Hun Sen is the country's sole prime minister, while Ranariddh has had to settle for the less influential position of president of the National Assembly. Part of the electoral deal was also the formation of a Senate to check the legislative power of the assembly, but most observers see this as little more than an indulgence for Chea Sim, CPP president and acting head of state in the king's absence. The CPP effectively controls the country today as the party is now in firm control of the Royal Cambodian Armed Forces. Despite his popularity in Phnom Penh, Sam Rainsy and his eponymously named party have no role in the government and are the only effective opposition in the country.

ECONOMY

Badly shaken by decades of internal conflict, Cambodia's economy is gradually improving but is still in very poor shape. For a long time rubber was Cambodia's primary export, but the plantations in the north and east of the country produce very little compared with colonial days. Rubber has been eclipsed in recent years by timber exports, which in 1994 accounted for US$194 million, nearly half the country's export earnings. Such figures, of course, disguise illegal exports of timber such as those carried out by the military or the Vietnamese. The 1997 figures suggest that the Cambodian government made only US$12.7 million in forestry revenues, while illegal logging was estimated to have raised US$184.2 million for the protagonists.

Curiously, Cambodia's second biggest export earner is the transshipment of cigarettes and consumer goods. These come from Singapore, Malaysia and China. Cambodia has low import tariffs, and imports can thus be lucratively shipped on to more restrictive regional markets such as Vietnam.

Cambodia is one of the poorest countries in Asia, although you could be forgiven for not realising this should you visit only Phnom Penh and Siem Reap. Cambodia's economic statistics are low by international standards, with average salaries less than US$300 a year and about 40% of the population classified as poor. The figures look worse when you consider that Cambodia's principal sources of foreign exchange are unsustainable: foreign aid and timber sales. Foreign aid has far and away been Cambodia's chief money-spinner over recent years, contributing to more than half the government's annual budget. It accounts for most of the signs of affluence that the visitor sees in Phnom Penh – foreign cars, European restaurants and mobile phones. It also explains why many government workers were paid late or not at all during 1998; with aid frozen in the aftermath of July 1997's fighting, there simply wasn't enough money left in the coffers.

Out in the countryside, where 85% of the population lives, Cambodia remains a very poor place where most people's livelihoods are agriculturally based and reliant on the vagaries of the annual south-west monsoon. A shortage of rain resulted in bad harvests in 1994 and 1995. International relief efforts and government assistance only narrowly staved off famine in some areas.

The regional economic crisis that engulfed much of Asia during 1997 and 1998 had fewer repercussions for Cambodia than some of its larger neighbours because Cambodia's economy is so undeveloped in the first place. However, investment by countries such as Malaysia, which poured money into Cambodia during the 1990s, has nosedived. Some of the tourism projects being touted were dubious, such as a Disney like light show at Angkor, so their cancellation is probably a good thing for Cambodia.

Bulging Pockets of Corruption

Cambodians have a proverb for every walk of life and the rampant problem of corruption is no exception. The saying goes, 'Small people take small bribes, big people take big bribes' and this aptly sums up the situation in Cambodia today. *Puk roluy* is Khmer for corruption and translates literally as 'something that is rotten and should be thrown away'. And indeed, in a survey carried out by the Centre for Social Development, the results of which were published in August 1998, 98% of the Cambodians questioned said it was very important to end corruption in the country.

The current outbreak of corruption is by no means a new trend in Cambodia – the problem was so widespread by the 19th century that many Cambodians had virtually enslaved themselves to their protectors. Yet another proverb summed up the situation succinctly: 'The rich must protect the poor, just as clothing protects the body'.

Following Cambodia's independence, the word government become synonymous with corruption. It is alleged that in almost any matter that required government involvement, money had to change hands. By the late 1960s a Sangkum Reastr Niyum party membership card, which was required for any government job, was selling for 1000r, the equivalent of a week's salary for the average low-ranking civil servant. The situation worsened when the US moved in to prop up the Lon Nol government; non-existent soldiers were added to the payroll and deaths and desertions went unreported. It is thought that by 1972 the military was pocketing the pay of about 100,000 of these phantom fighters. More seriously perhaps, many of those in the military and government sold weapons and supplies to the highest bidder, no matter for which side they fought.

Corruption faded during the Pol Pot era, but for many Cambodians the stakes involved in bribery were much higher as often they were buying their lives in gold. Following the overthrow of the Khmer Rouge by the Vietnamese, survival was often the daily challenge and there was little or no scope for widespread corruption. However, certain sections of the government managed to accumulate personal fortunes during this period, and in the Thai border camps small-scale corruption was rampant as unscrupulous characters bartered and sold aid supplies.

However, it was the arrival of the free market and later the United Nations (UN) that really sent corruption spiralling out of control. The arrival of the United Nations Transitional

The factional fighting of July 1997 had a much bigger impact on the economy than the regional crisis. Donors suspended lucrative aid packages, which just about kept the government's head above water, and this led to a budgetary crisis for much of 1998. Many government workers including teachers, soldiers and police were forced to go without their meagre salaries for months at a time; needless to say there were those in the military and police who found other ways to make money, including illegal logging and armed robbery. The teachers stuck to more legitimate and less lucrative means of survival and went on strike. However, happy days are here again: the international community approved a three year package worth more than US$1 billion in Tokyo in February 1999. This will subsidise almost half of Cambodia's government spending during the next five years and hopefully go some way towards demobilising the vastly inflated armed forces.

The government must act to raise revenue – currently little or no tax is paid in many parts of the country. A 10% sales tax was introduced at the start of 1999, but this alone is not enough to fund the sort of social programs Cambodia needs. Some observers suggest the key to Cambodia's future lies in scaling down aid money to demonstrate clearly to the Cambodian people just who is responsible for their plight and force the

Bulging Pockets of Corruption

Authority in Cambodia (UNTAC) heralded the injection of more than US$2 billion into the country's tiny economy and created a bonanza of opportunity. The situation was so bad that it was estimated by 1995 that corruption was costing the government about US$100 million a year in lost revenue. The figure today is much higher as the revenue lost to illegal logging alone is more than US$100 million. The saddest part of the saga is that the majority of Cambodians are extremely honest and their struggle to survive is already hard enough without widespread corruption.

The average Cambodian encounters corruption from an early age – even some doctors and nurses are known to demand money before administering crucial treatment. In education, it is not uncommon for students to bribe teachers to see the exam papers in advance or for well-connected pupils to buy someone else's results after the test, thus depriving an able student of the chance for a scholarship. Teachers are also known to sell text books donated from overseas to make some money, and many teachers levy a charge for pupils to attend class.

The other vocations that can be particularly lucrative are in the police force and army, and for the tourist at least, this is usually the only time you will encounter corruption. Traffic police in Phnom Penh are visible all over the city, but certain patches are more desirable than others because they offer the opportunity for a shakedown or two. Officers often bribe supervisors to work a junction on a busy road, as during the course of the day they can make more than US$20 in payments from 'traffic violators'. The military earns a steady income on checkpoints in more remote parts of the country. Although this is a shrinking business since the end of the war against the Khmer Rouge, it can still make soldiers a lot of money if the road is perceived to be insecure – and the easiest way to facilitate this perception is to carry out 'bandit' attacks every once in a while, by leaving your uniform at home, but not your B-40 grenade launcher.

Corruption needs to be eradicated in Cambodia before the country can realistically travel the road to development. However, with low salaries and little action, it would appear Cambodia is set for many more years of puk roluy. If you are a tourist you'll probably be forced to part with a few thousand riel, but if you're on business, then you better come with a briefcase stuffed full of cash – that's dollars, not riel.

government to get its act together. However, it is just as feasible that the country would collapse if aid money was to be permanently withdrawn.

Tacit membership of ASEAN is a step forward for the country, both economically and politically. It means that Cambodia's neighbours have a vested interest in peace and prosperity in the future: full membership will no doubt lead to a greater exploitation of Cambodia's economy by these partners, but at the same time should bring in some aid money for social welfare, health care and infrastructure projects.

The challenge for Cambodia is to create an environment in which sustainable economic development can take place. At present, the signs indicate that the government is all too willing to encourage foreign investment in projects that generate short-term wealth for a few, but offer few long-term benefits for the many. Deforestation is an obvious example of this, but the endemic culture of corruption means that any investment in Cambodia is likely to do the same.

POPULATION & PEOPLE

Cambodia's first population census in decades, carried out in 1998, put the population of the country at 11,426,223. Phnom Penh is the largest city with a population of about one million. The most populated province is also the largest – Kompong Cham, where 14.1% of Cambodians live. The most sparsely populated is Mondulkiri, where 0.3% of the population lives, though it is one of the country's larger provinces. Krong Kep and Krong Pailin have the smallest populations of about 25,000 each, although the latter is bound to grow rapidly with an influx of former Khmer Rouge fighters and their dependents.

Infant mortality rates in Cambodia are the highest in the South-East Asia at 115 per 1000. Due to poverty, poor sanitation and disease, it is estimated that nearly one child in five dies before the age of five. Malnutrition and the effects of a mono-nutritional (single-staple) diet are also serious, with about half the children under five either stunted or underweight. Maternal mortality rates are also high at 650 per 100,000 live births, and many women experience health complications after birth. These figures are hardly surprising when you consider that in rural areas only 26% of the population has access to safe water and only 6% has access to proper sanitation. Diarrhoea is the biggest killer among young children.

Life expectancy is also low, with an average of 51.6 years. The much discussed imbalance of women to men due to years of conflict is not as serious as is sometimes suggested, but it is still significant: there are 93.1 males to every 100 females, up from 86.1 to 100 in 1980. There is, however, a marked imbalance in age groups as about 50% of the population is under the age of 15. The rapidly expanding population is projected to reach 20 million by 2020.

Women

The status of women in Cambodia is somewhat ambiguous. While up to 20% of women head the household, and in many families women are the sole breadwinners, men have a monopoly on all the most important positions of power at a governmental level and at a domestic level are able, should they wish, to control the purse strings through intimidation.

While women are certainly not discriminated against as a political or religious pol-

icy in Cambodia, they are rarely afforded the same opportunities as males. In recent years laws have been passed on abortion, domestic violence and trafficking that have improved the legal position of women, but they have had little effect on the overall picture. Even in the circumstances of a failing marriage, women have little room for manoeuvre, as it is only the husband who can grant a divorce.

As young children, females are treated fairly equally, but as they get older their access to education becomes more restricted, particularly in rural areas, where the majority of the population lives, as there is not the option of staying in wats (Buddhist temples) to continue studies as there is for boys.

Many women set up simple businesses in their town or village, but should they want to progress further, it is not an easy path. As of 1998, there were only seven female legislators in Parliament from a total of 122, even though women made up 56% of the voters; there were no women of ministerial rank; there were no female provincial governors; there were only eight female judges among 110 and no prosecutors; and only 13% of administrative and management positions and 28% of professional positions are held by women nationally.

Other issues of concern for women in Cambodia are those of domestic violence, prostitution and the spread of sexually transmitted infections (STIs). Domestic violence is quite widespread, but exactly how serious a problem is not known because of the fear and shame involved. There is a high incidence of child prostitution in the country and illegal trafficking of prostitutes within Cambodia and in and out of Thailand and Vietnam. The number of cases of human immunodeficiency virus (HIV) is increasing at an alarming rate, in fact the highest rate of increase in Asia. World Health Organization (WHO) figures show the rate of infection among Cambodian sex workers and pregnant women is high.

Ethnic Khmers

According to official statistics, around 96% of the people who live in Cambodia are ethnic

Khmers (ethnic Cambodians), making the country the most homogeneous in South-East Asia. In reality, there are probably much higher numbers of Vietnamese and Chinese than such statistics account for.

The Khmers have inhabited Cambodia since the beginning of recorded history (around the 2nd century AD), many centuries before the Thais and Vietnamese migrated to the region. During the next six centuries, Khmer culture and religion were Indianised by contact with the civilisations of India and Java. Over the centuries, the Khmers have mixed with other groups resident in Cambodia, including the Javanese (8th century), Thai (10th to 15th centuries), Vietnamese (from the early 17th century) and Chinese (since the 18th century).

Ethnic Vietnamese

The Vietnamese are probably the largest non-Khmer ethnic group in Cambodia. According to government figures published in March 1995, Cambodia is host to around 100,000 Vietnamese. Unofficial observers claim that the real figure may be as high as one million. The official Khmer Rouge position was that there are four million Vietnamese in Cambodia. The truth is, no-one knows. There is a great deal of mutual dislike and distrust between the Cambodians and the Vietnamese, even those who have been living in Cambodia for generations. While the Khmers refer to the Vietnamese as *yuon*, a derogatory term that means 'barbarians', the Vietnamese look down on the Khmers and consider them lazy for not farming every available bit of land, an absolute necessity in densely populated Vietnam. Historic antagonisms between the Vietnamese and the Khmers are exacerbated by the prominence of ethnic Vietnamese among shopowners.

For the Khmers the mistrust of the Vietnamese has a historical basis. The Vietnamese appropriated the lands of the Mekong Delta from the Khmers in the 16th and 17th centuries and now govern the people and area known as Kampuchea Krom. With Vietnamese encroachments on Cambodian territory continuing to be a major concern in Cambodia, and with the border between them still not satisfactorily demarcated, it is unlikely that such prejudice will disappear in the near future.

Ethnic Chinese

Officially, the government claims there are around 50,000 ethnic Chinese in Cambodia. This is another unrealistic figure. Other informed observers say there are more likely to be as many as half a million of them.

Until 1975 the ethnic Chinese controlled the country's economic life. In recent years they have re-emerged as a powerful economic force, mainly due to investment by overseas Chinese from other parts of Asia. Although intermarriage with Khmers is not infrequent, the Chinese have managed to retain a significant degree of cultural distinctiveness.

Cham Muslims

Cambodia's Cham Muslims (known locally as the Khmer Islam) officially number around 203,000. Unofficial counts put the figure at around half a million. They live in villages on the banks of the Mekong and the Tonlé Sap rivers, mostly in Kompong Cham and Kompong Chhnang provinces. The Cham Muslims suffered particularly vicious persecution between 1975 and 1979, when a large part of their community was exterminated. Many Cham mosques that were destroyed under the Khmer Rouge are now being rebuilt.

Ethno-Linguistic Minorities

Cambodia's diverse *chunchiet* (ethno-linguistic minorities, or hill tribes), who live in the country's mountainous regions, probably number from 60,000 to 70,000. Collectively, they are known as *Khmer loeu*, literally the 'upper Khmer'.

The majority of the hill tribes are in the north-east of Cambodia, in the provinces of Ratanakiri, Mondulkiri, Stung Treng and Kratie. The largest group is known as the Tumpoun (many other spellings are used), who number around 15,000. Other groups include the Kreung, Kra Chok, Kavet, Brao and Jorai.

Khmer Krom

The Khmer Krom people of southern Vietnam are ethnic Khmer separated from Cambodia by historical deals and Vietnamese encroachment on what was once Cambodian territory. Nobody is sure just how many of them there are – estimates vary from one million to seven million, depending on who is doing the counting; but however many Khmer Krom there are, the issue of their treatment in Vietnam is gaining increasing attention. Local representatives of these displaced Khmer point to Bosnia as an example of how ethnic frustration can erupt into violence if left to simmer for too long.

The history of Vietnamese expansion into Khmer territory has long been a staple of Khmer schoolbooks. King Chey Chetha II of Cambodia, in keeping with the wishes of his Vietnamese queen, first allowed Vietnamese to settle in the Cambodian town of Prey Nokor in 1620. It was obviously the thin edge of the wedge. Prey Nokor is now better known as Ho Chi Minh City (Saigon).

Representatives of the Khmer Krom claim that although they dress as Vietnamese and carry Vietnamese identity cards, they remain culturally Khmer. Vietnamese attempts to quash Khmer Krom language and religion (the Khmer are Hinayana Buddhists, while the Vietnamese practise Mahayana Buddhism), have for the most part failed. Even assimilation through inter-marriage has failed to take place on a large scale.

Many Khmer Krom would like to see Cambodia act as a mediator in the quest for greater autonomy and ethnic representation in Vietnam. The Cambodian government, for its part. is more concerned with the vast numbers of illegal Vietnamese inside its borders, as well as reports of encroachments by the Vietnamese into the west of Cambodia.

The hill tribes of Cambodia have long been isolated from mainstream Khmer society and there is little in the way of mutual understanding. They practise shifting cultivation, rarely staying in one place for more than four or five years. Finding a new location for a village requires the mediation of a village elder with the spirit world. Very few of the minorities wear the sort of colourful traditional costumes you see in Thailand, Laos and Vietnam. While this may not make for interesting photographs, it takes away that depressing human safari park feel there is to visiting tribal villages in other countries.

Little research has been done on Cambodia's hill tribes and tourism in the northeast is still in its infancy. A seminar held in 1995 entitled 'Ethnic Communities and Sustainable Development in North-East Cambodia' was given over almost entirely to reports on the fate of hill tribes in Thailand and Laos. Given the plight of the Thai hill tribes, the seminar found much to be concerned about regarding the impact of tourism, development and logging on Cambodia's even more isolated hill tribes.

Repatriation Programs

Since 1992 the United Nations High Commissioner for Refugees (UNHCR) has repatriated more than 370,000 Cambodians, most of whom had sought refuge in Thailand. The first returnees crossed the border at Poipet (Poay Pet) on 30 March 1992. The following year, hundreds of thousands more were resettled and able to take part in their country's elections. Dozens of nongovernment aid agencies provided support for the program, one of the largest and most complex ever undertaken.

Even today there are significant numbers of internally displaced people in the country who fled heavy fighting in the north and north-west of the country during 1998. During the first half of 1999, many internally displaced Cambodians were returned to the original areas they inhabited. This included the return of a number of chunchiet, who were originally recruited by the Khmer Rouge during the late 1960s, to their homes in Mondulkiri and Ratanakiri.

EDUCATION

King Sihanouk took a lively interest in education early in his reign. Between 1953 and 1968 the number of primary students rocketed from 300,000 to one million. Even more spectacularly, the number of secondary students increased from 5000 to around one million. Nine universities were also established in this period. Unfortunately, despite its good intentions, the program has been widely criticised for creating uniformly poor educational levels and unrealistic employment expectations – there were not enough highly skilled jobs to go around.

The Pol Pot regime of the 1970s put a stop to educational development. Indeed, as far as the Khmer Rouge was concerned, education was an evil. Many qualified teachers perished at this time, so that by 1979 Cambodia only had around 3000 qualified secondary teachers left.

Through the 1980s and 1990s the situation has been improving gradually. Adult literacy rates are approximately 65%, but vary wildly between provinces. It is generally thought that overall education standards are higher than they have ever been. Four technical institutions and two universities have been established. In Phnom Penh and in regional centres, private schools have also blossomed, offering courses in English, French, computer literacy and accounting, among other subjects.

Sadly, there is a disparity between the number of males and females remaining within the education system. This can be partly accounted for by the opportunity for males to continue their education within the environment of a wat, thus lessening the cost burden on the family, but must also come down to a certain degree of inequality between the sexes (see Women under the Population & People section earlier in this chapter).

ARTS

The Khmer Rouge's assault on the past and on artists and intellectuals was a terrible blow to Cambodian culture. Indeed for many years the common consensus among many Khmers was that their culture had been irrevocably lost. The Khmer Rouge not only did away with living bearers of Khmer culture, it also destroyed cultural artefacts, statues, musical instruments, books and anything that served as a reminder of a past it wished to efface (strangely, the temples of Angkor survived). Despite this, Cambodia today is witnessing a resurgence of traditional arts and a limited amount of experimentation in modern arts. A trip to the School of Fine Arts in Phnom Penh is evidence of the extent to which Khmer culture has bounced back.

Dance

More than any of the other traditional arts, Cambodia's royal ballet is a tangible link with the glory of Angkor. Early in his reign, King Sihanouk released the traditional harem of royal *apsara* (heavenly nymphs) that went with the crown. Nevertheless, prior to the Pol Pot regime, classical ballet was still taught at the palace. Its traditions stretched long into the past, when the art of the apsara redounded to the glory of the divine king.

Cambodian court dance is related to the dance of Thailand, Java and India. They all share the same cultural sources, and many of the dances enact scenes from the Hindu Ramayana.

Dance fared particularly badly during the Pol Pot years. Very few dancers and teachers survived, and only one old woman survived who knew how to make the elaborate costumes that are sewn piece by piece onto the dancers before a performance. In 1981, with a handful of teachers, the School of Fine Arts was reopened and the training of dance students resumed. For the first intake of students, preference was given to orphans.

At a performance of royal dance, you will see much that resembles Thai dance (unless you are expert in such things): the same stylised hand movements; the same sequined, lamé costumes; the same opulent stupa-like head wear. Though many popular dances staged nowadays also mix elements of more lively folk dance into the performance. Where traditionally royal dance was an all-female affair (with the exception of the role of the monkey), often there are now more male dancers featured.

Another interesting dance tradition is *lkhaon khaol*, Cambodia's masked theatre. Traditionally all the roles are played by men, like kabuki in Japan and some of the regional opera styles in China. In times past it was a popular form of entertainment, with troupes touring the country presenting performances of the Ramayana over several evenings. A narrator presides over the performance, providing dialogue and instructions to the small accompanying orchestra. Short performances of masked theatre are sometimes included in shows put on for foreign tourists.

Music
The bas-reliefs on some of the monuments in the Angkor region depict musicians and apsara holding instruments. The instruments that are depicted are similar to the traditional Khmer instruments of today, which suggests that Cambodia has a long musical tradition all its own.

Traditionally the music of Cambodia was an accompaniment to a ritual or performance that had religious significance. Musicologists have identified six types of musical ensemble, each used in different settings. The most traditional of these is the *areak ka*. This is an ensemble that performs music at weddings. The instruments used include a *tro khmae* (three-stringed fiddle), a *khsae muoy* (singled-stringed bowed instrument) and *skor areak* (drums), among others.

Instruments used in performances of dance are naturally more percussive. If you see a dance performance in Cambodia you will probably see a reduced ensemble of musicians performing, though sometimes the dances are performed to taped music. The instruments generally include at least one stringed instrument, a *roneat* (xylophone) and sets of drums and cymbals.

Much of Cambodia's traditional music was lost during the Pol Pot era. During this time many Khmers settled in the USA, where a lively Khmer pop industry developed. Influenced by US music and later exported back to Cambodia, it has been enormously popular. Phnom Penh too has a burgeoning pop industry, and it is easy to join in the fun by visiting one of the innumerable karaoke bars around the country.

Architecture
Khmer architecture reached its period of greatest magnificence during the Angkorian era (the 9th to 14th centuries). Some of the finest examples of architecture from this period are Angkor Wat and the structures of Angkor Thom. See the Temples of Angkor special section for more information on the architectural styles of the Angkor era.

Today, most rural Cambodian houses are built on high wood pilings (if the family can afford it) and have thatch roofs, walls made of palm mats and floors of woven bamboo strips resting on bamboo joists. The shady space underneath is used for storage and for people to relax at midday.

Sculpture
Even in the pre-Angkor era, in the periods generally referred to as Funan and Chenla, the people of Cambodia were producing masterfully sensuous sculpture that was no simple copy of the Indian forms it was modelled on. Some scholars maintain that the Cambodian forms are unrivalled in India itself.

The earliest surviving Cambodian sculpture dates from the 6th century. Most of it depicts Vishnu with four or eight arms. Generally Vishnu has acquired Indochinese facial characteristics and is more muscular than similar Indian sculpture, in which divinities tend towards rounded flabbiness. A large eight-armed Vishnu from this period is displayed at the National Museum in Phnom Penh.

Also on display at the National Museum is a statue of Harihara, a divinity who combines aspects of both Vishnu and Shiva. The statue dates from the end of the 7th century,

Sihanouk & the Silver Screen

Between 1966 and 1969 Sihanouk wrote, directed and produced nine feature films, a figure that would put the average workaholic Hollywood director to shame. Sihanouk took the business of making films very seriously, and family and officials were called upon to do their bit – the minister of foreign affairs played the male lead in Sihanouk's first feature, *Apsara* (Heavenly Nymph). When, in the same movie, a show of military hardware was required, the air force was brought into action, as was the army's fleet of helicopters.

The world premiere of *Apsara* was something of a flop, the foreign community failing to patronise the movie. Although, as Milton Osbourne says in his biography *Sihanouk – Prince of Light, Prince of Darkness*, the Chinese embassy staff did at least have the good manners to excuse themselves on the pretext of pressing business elsewhere – 'because of the Cultural Revolution'.

Not that this put the royal film maker off. On the contrary, Sihanouk continued to make movies, often taking on the leading role himself. Notable performances saw him as a spirit of the forest and as a victorious general. Perhaps it was no surprise, given the king's apparent addiction to the world of celluloid dreams, that Cambodia should challenge Cannes and Berlin with its Phnom Penh International Film Festival. The festival was held twice, in 1968 and 1969. Sihanouk won the grand prize on both occasions.

and the sensuous plasticity of the musculature prefigures the technical accomplishment of Angkor era art.

The sculpture of the pre-Angkor period is not restricted to the depiction of Hindu deities. This period also features much Buddhist-inspired sculpture, mainly in the form of Bodhisattva. By the 9th century and the beginning of the Angkor era proper, however, the sculptures become exclusively Hindu-inspired.

Innovations of the early Angkor era include free-standing sculpture that dispenses with the stone aureole that in earlier works supported the multiple arms of Hindu deities. The faces assume an air of tranquillity, and the overall effect is less animated. In the National Museum, look for the statue of Shiva from the Bakong, Roluos, for an example of early Angkorian sculpture: the sculpture depicts a stocky frame and a smiling face that is characteristic of this period.

The Banteay Srei style of the late 10th century is commonly regarded as a high point in the evolution of South-East Asian art. The National Museum has a splendid piece from this period: a sandstone statue of Shiva holding Uma, his wife, on his knee.

The Baphuon style of the 11th century was inspired to a certain extent by the sculpture of Banteay Srei, producing some of the finest works to have survived into the 20th century. In the National Museum, look for the life-size *Vishnu Reclining*, which is featured in the bronze display hall. Only the head, shoulders and two right arms have survived; it was once inlaid with precious metal and gems that would have brought the statue to life.

The statuary of the Angkor Wat period is felt to be conservative and stilted, lacking the grace of much earlier work. The genius of this period manifests itself more clearly in the architecture and fabulous bas-reliefs of Angkor Wat itself.

The final high point in Angkorian sculpture is the Bayon period from the end of the 12th century to the beginning of the 13th. In the National Museum in Phnom Penh, look for the superb representation of Jayavarman VII, an image that simultaneously projects great power and sublime tranquillity. Also represented from this period is the simple image of Jayarajadevi from Preah Khan in central Cambodia.

Sculpture in Cambodia went into decline from the end of the Angkor era.

Cinema

Cambodians complain that their film industry is all but dead. In 1989 some 200 film companies were registered with the Cinema Department. By mid-1995 only six were left. Local directors point to low cinema audience numbers and the popularity of foreign videos as the main problem. Even Prime Minister Hun Sen has weighed in on the issue, claiming that local scriptwriters should 'write more happy endings' if they want to revive Cambodian film.

At least one Cambodian director has had success in recent years, though. Rithy Panh's *People of the Rice Fields* was nominated for the Palme d'Or at the Cannes Film Festival in May 1995. The film touches only fleetingly on the Khmer Rouge, depicting the lives of a family eking out an arduous existence in the rice fields. Rithy Panh has been active in encouraging other young Cambodians to take up film making, holding screenwriting seminars in Phnom Penh. He has plans to make another feature film.

SOCIETY & CONDUCT

Greetings

Like the Thais, who have their *wai*, the Cambodians traditionally greet each other with the *sompiah*, which involves pressing the hands together in prayer and bowing. In general the higher the hands and the lower the bow the more respect is shown. In recent decades this custom has been partially replaced by the western practice of shaking hands. But, although men tend to shake hands with each other, women usually use the traditional greeting with both men and women. It is considered acceptable (or perhaps excusable) for foreigners to shake hands with Cambodians of both sexes.

Visiting Khmers

As is the case throughout Asia, a small token of gratitude in the form of a gift is always appreciated when you visit someone. Gifts should always be offered with the right hand. If you want to be particularly polite, support your right elbow with the fingers of your left hand as you do so. Before entering a Khmer home, always remove your shoes.

Dress

Both men and women often wear sarongs (made of cotton, a cotton-synthetic blend or silk), especially at home. Men who can afford it usually prefer to wear silk sarongs. Most urban Khmer men dress in trousers and many women dress in western-style clothing.

On formal occasions such as religious festivals and family celebrations, women often wear *hols* (a type of shirt) during the day. At night they change into single-colour silk dresses called *phamuongs*, which are decorated along the hems. If the celebration is a wedding, the colours of such garments are stipulated by the day of the week on which the wedding is held.

Modesty

The women of Cambodia are very modest in their dress – much more so than the Vietnamese. When eating at home, they sit on floor mats with their feet to the side rather than in the lotus position, as do the men. As in Thailand, nude bathing is unacceptable.

Visiting Pagodas

The Khmer are tolerant and may choose not to point out improper behaviour to their foreign guests, but you should dress and act with the utmost respect when visiting wats or other religious sites (such as some of the temples of Angkor). This is all the more important given the vital role Buddhism has played in the lives of many Cambodians in the aftermath of the Khmer Rouge holocaust. Proper etiquette in pagodas is mostly a matter of common sense.

Unlike Thailand, a woman may accept something from a monk, but she should be careful not to touch him as she does so. A few other tips include:

- Don't wear shorts or tank tops.
- Take off your hat when entering the grounds of the wat.
- Take off your shoes before going into the *vihara* (sanctuary).
- If you sit down in front of the dais (the platform on which the Buddhas are placed), sit with your feet to the side rather than in the lotus position.

- Never point your finger – or, nirvana forbid, the soles of your feet – towards a person or a figure of the Buddha.

Dos & Don'ts

There are some other rules that are worth remembering while you are in the country:

- Getting angry and showing it by shouting or becoming abusive is impolite and a poor reflection on you; in addition, it is unlikely to accomplish much. If things aren't being done as they should, remember that there is a critical shortage of trained people in the country because the vast majority of educated Cambodians either fled the country or were killed between 1975 and 1979.
- As in Thailand, it is improper to pat children on the head.
- If you would like someone to come over to you, motion with your whole hand held palm down – signalling with your index finger and your palm pointed skyward may be interpreted as being sexually suggestive.
- When using a toothpick, it is considered polite to hold it in one hand and to cover your open mouth with the other.
- When handing things to other people, use both hands or your right hand only, never your left hand (reserved for toilet ablutions).

RELIGION
Hinduism

Hinduism flourished alongside Buddhism from the 1st century until the 14th century. In Funan and during the pre-Angkorian period, Hinduism was represented by the worship of Harihara (Shiva and Vishnu embodied in a single deity). During the time of Angkor, Shiva was the deity most in favour with the royal family, although in the 12th century he seems to have been superseded by Vishnu.

Buddhism

The majority of the people of Cambodia are followers of Theravada, or Hinayana, Buddhism. Buddhism was introduced to Cambodia between the 13th and 14th centuries and was the state religion until 1975.

The Theravada (Teaching of the Elders) school of Buddhism is an earlier and, according to its followers, less corrupted form of Buddhism than the Mahayana schools found in east Asia or in the Himalayan lands. The Theravada school is also called the 'southern' school as it took the southern route from India, its place of origin, through South-East Asia – in this case Myanmar (Burma), Thailand, Laos and Cambodia – while the 'northern' school proceeded north into Nepal, Tibet, China, Korea, Mongolia, Vietnam and Japan. Because the southern school tried to preserve or limit the Buddhist doctrines to only those canons codified in the early Buddhist era, the northern school gave Theravada Buddhism the name Hinayana, meaning the 'Lesser Vehicle'. The northern school considered itself Mahayana, the 'Great Vehicle', because it built upon the earlier teachings, 'expanding' the doctrine to respond more to the needs of lay people, or so it claimed.

Theravada doctrine stresses the three principal aspects of existence: *dukkha* (suffering, unsatisfactoriness, disease), *anicca* (impermanency, transience of all things) and *anatta* (nonsubstantiality or nonessentiality of reality: no permanent 'soul'). These concepts, when 'discovered' by Siddhartha Gautama in the 6th century BC, were in direct contrast to the Hindu belief in an eternal, blissful Self, or Paramatman, hence Buddhism was originally a 'heresy' against India's Brahmanic religion.

Gautama, an Indian prince turned ascetic, subjected himself to many years of severe austerities to arrive at this vision of the world and was given the title Buddha, 'the Enlightened' or 'the Awakened'. Gautama Buddha spoke of four noble truths, which had the power to liberate any human being who could realise them. These four noble truths are:

- The truth of suffering – 'Existence is suffering'.
- The truth of the cause of suffering – 'Suffering is caused by desire'.
- The truth of the cessation of suffering – 'Eliminate the cause of suffering (desire) and suffering will cease to arise'.
- The truth of the path – 'The eight fold path is the way to eliminate desire/extinguish suffering'.

The eight fold path *(atthangika-magga)* consists of:

- Right understanding.
- Right-mindedness (or 'right thought').
- Right speech.
- Right bodily conduct.
- Right livelihood.
- Right effort.
- Right attentiveness.
- Right concentration.

The eight fold path is also known as the Middle Way since it avoids both extreme austerity and extreme sensuality.

The ultimate goal of Theravada Buddhism is *nibbana* (or in the ancient Indian-language Sanskrit, *nirvana*), which literally means the 'blowing out' or 'extinction' of all causes of dukkha. Effectively it means elimination of all desire and suffering, reaching a blessed state – the final stage of reincarnation. In reality, most Buddhists aim for rebirth in a 'better' existence rather than the supramundane goal of nibbana, which is highly misunderstood by Asians as well as westerners. Many Buddhists express the feeling that they are somehow unworthy of nibbana. By feeding monks, giving donations to temples and performing regular worship at the local wat they hope to improve their lot, acquiring enough merit to prevent or at least lessen the number of rebirths. The making of merit is an important social as well as religious activity. The concept of reincarnation is almost universally accepted by Cambodian Buddhists, and to some extent even by non-Buddhists.

The Trilatna (Triratna), or Triple Gems of Buddhism, are the Buddha, the Dharma (the teachings) and the Sangha (the Buddhist Brotherhood). The Buddha in his sculptural form is found on high shelves or altars in homes and shops as well as in temples. The Dharma is chanted morning and evening in every wat. The Sangha is represented by the street presence of orange-robed monks, especially in the early morning hours when they perform their alms rounds, in what almost has become a travel-guide cliche in motion.

Socially, every Buddhist male is expected to become a monk for a short period in his life, optimally between the time he finishes school and starts a career or marries. Men or boys under 20 years of age may enter the Sangha as novices and this is not unusual since a family earns great merit when one of its sons takes robe and bowl. Traditionally, the time spent in the wat is three months during the Buddhist Lent *(phansaa* or *watsa)*, which begins in July and coincides with the rainy season. However, nowadays men may spend as little as a week or 15 days to accrue merit as monks.

Monks must follow 227 vows or precepts and many monks ordain for a lifetime. Of these, a large percentage become scholars and teachers, while some specialise in healing and/or folk magic. There is no similar hermit-like order for nuns, but women are welcome to reside in temples as lay nuns, with shaved heads and white robes.

The women have to follow only eight precepts. Because discipline for these

Buddhism has been reinstated as the official religion and young men are again being encouraged to become monks.

'nuns' is much less arduous, they don't attain quite as high a social status as do monks. However, despite not performing ceremonies on behalf of other lay persons, they engage in the same basic religious activities (meditation and study of dharma) as monks. The reality is that wats that draw sizeable contingents of nuns are highly respected because women don't choose temples for reasons of clerical status – when more than a few reside at one temple it's because the teachings there are considered particularly strong.

Archaeologists have determined that before the 9th century, a period during which Sanskrit was used in ritual inscriptions, the Theravada school constituted the prevalent form of Buddhism in Cambodia. Inscriptions and images indicate that Mahayana Buddhism was in favour after the 9th century, but was replaced in the 13th century by a form of Theravada Buddhism, which arrived, along with the Pali language, from Sri Lanka via Thailand.

Between 1975 and 1979 the vast majority of Cambodia's Buddhist monks were murdered by the Khmer Rouge and virtually all of the country's more than 3000 wats were damaged or destroyed. In the late 1980s Buddhism was again made the state religion. At that time, Cambodia had about 6000 monks, who by law had to be at least 60 years old. The age requirements have been relaxed and young monks are once again a normal sight.

Islam

Cambodia's Muslims are descendants of Chams who migrated from what is now central Vietnam after the final defeat of the kingdom of Champa by the Vietnamese in 1471. Whereas their compatriots who remained in Vietnam were only partly Islamicised, the Cambodian Chams adopted a fairly orthodox version of Sunni Islam and maintained links with other Muslim communities in the region. Like their Buddhist neighbours, however, the Cham Muslims call the faithful to prayer by banging on a drum, rather than with the call of the *muezzin*, as in most Muslim lands.

Today, the Muslim community of Phnom Penh includes the descendants of people who emigrated from Pakistan and Afghanistan several generations ago, and a neighbourhood near Psar Tuol Tom Pong is still known as the Arab Village. However, there are only about half a dozen Muslims fluent in Arabic, the language of the Koran, in all of Cambodia. In 1989, 20 Cambodian Muslims made the *hajj* (pilgrimage) to Mecca. Halal meat (killed according to Islamic law) is available in Phnom Penh in the Psar O Russei, Psar Tuol Tom Pong and Psar Char markets.

A small heretical community known as the Zahidin follows traditions similar to those of the Muslim Chams of Vietnam, praying once a week (on Friday) and observing Ramadan (a month of dawn-to-dusk fasting) only on the first, middle and last days of the month.

The Khmer Rouge seems to have made a concerted effort to annihilate Cambodia's Cham Muslim community.

Vietnamese Religions

During the 1920s quite a few ordinary Cambodians became interested in Caodaism, a colourful syncretic religion founded in Vietnam.

Facts for the Visitor

THE BEST & WORST

Until the recent ending of the long civil war, Cambodia was a very difficult country in which to travel. Security was a perennial concern for visitors and many people found it simpler and safer to restrict their trips to Phnom Penh and Angkor. This was sensible behaviour as for much of the 1990s the kidnap and murder of foreigners was a very real possibility and, indeed, several westerners died at the hands of the Khmer Rouge. Those that did venture off the trail, however, found themselves in a beautiful country of friendly people, untainted by the advent of mass tourism. Cambodia looks set for big changes as word spreads that peace has broken out. If the politicians can keep their bickering to words, not weapons, the country can expect a vast increase in tourist arrivals.

Cambodia has relied heavily on Angkor when promoting itself as a tourist destination, and not without good reason: it really is one of the most impressive sights on earth. Few can fail to be moved by the sheer grace and majesty of Angkor Wat: the sublime unity of its five towers; the delicate and intricate sculpture that decorates the lower walls; and the sheer size of the temple complex, the world's largest religious building.

Angkor is much more than one temple. There are many more religious buildings scattered across a wide area around Siem Reap and visitors will discover a wealth of architecture as they explore: the enigmatic and intimidating faces watching over the Bayon; the devouring might of the jungle eating its way through Ta Prohm; and the demure beauty of Banteay Srei, host to some of the finest carving that the Angkor period produced.

However, just as Angkor is more than its wat, Cambodia is more than Angkor, although you could be forgiven for not realising this from the promotional material available in the country. As the country opens up to travel by road, many more places can be visited now that were long kept off the map by conflict or cost. Sihanoukville has long attracted visitors, but, now that Kampot Province has opened its arms to tourism, you can visit the abandoned seaside town of Kep or the wilds of Bokor National Park and its eerie, abandoned mountain-top town, with its beautiful views. The north-east, one of the remotest areas in the country, is home to all of Cambodia's *chunchiet* (minorities), much of its vanishing wildlife and forest, and some landscapes of outstanding natural beauty.

Elsewhere in the provinces, the numerous sleepy provincial capitals make interesting and economical transit stops as you journey through the country. They all tend to offer the same steady diet of colonial architecture, riverside location and some very friendly locals. Perhaps the best of the bunch are Battambang, with its well-preserved architecture and nearby temples, and Kompong Thom, helpfully located between Phnom Penh and Siem Reap, and a base from which to explore the pre-Angkorian 7th century capital of Sambor Prei Kuk.

There aren't many bad places in Cambodia, as the locals help to make even the most boring town in the country lively. However, there are two obvious exceptions and unfortunately they are the first places many overland travellers see when they arrive in Cambodia: Poipet and Koh Kong. They are unattractive border towns, with little history, and after too long in either you could be forgiven for asking yourself why you have come to Cambodia. And there are still some badlands in parts of the country: check local conditions carefully if planning to travel on the road between Kratie and Stung Treng, to areas around Snuol or to the central part of northern Cambodia.

Cambodia's road system is undeniably one of the worst in Asia. The words national highway might conjure up dreams of tarmac and top speed, but forget it: most roads could be confused with BMX tracks. See the Getting Around chapter for more bile on Cambodia's roads. On a more serious note, Cambodia's political history has been extremely ugly and Cambodia's politicians have a habit of messing things up for their people, so don't assume you can go anywhere and do anything just because you have read about a place in this guide. There is no substitute for checking out the latest situation in Cambodia on the ground, either in local newspapers, from non-governmental organisations (NGOs) or people in the know, or on guesthouse verandas.

SUGGESTED ITINERARIES

Cambodia is a relatively small country, but travelling around is complicated by the complete lack of infrastructure in the provinces. As ever, what you can expect to see in Cambodia depends mainly on how much time and money you have available and, if travelling by road, a little bit of luck – breakdowns are pretty common and they can wipe a day or so out of a schedule. Don't forget that the season can have an effect on your mobility within Cambodia. During the wet season, many roads become much harder to navigate and this can slow you down considerably.

Visitors with only a week to spare in the country will realistically find themselves restricted to seeing the temples of Angkor and the capital, Phnom Penh. Those with 10 days might like to include more time at the temples and attempt a visit to the holy mountain of Phnom Kulen, make a trip to the beaches at Sihanoukville or take a boat journey up the Mekong River to Kratie or Kompong Cham.

Two weeks allows the visitor to consider a more ambitious trip into the provinces. It is possible to do a loop around the attractions of the south coast, taking in Sihanoukville, Kampot, Kep, Bokor National Park, the ruined temples around Takeo and the other attractions along National Hwy 2, including Phnom Chisor, the zoo at Phnom Tamao, or Tonlé Bati. Another option would be to stop in some of the provincial towns around the Tonlé Sap (Great Lake) between Phnom Penh and Siem Reap. Battambang has a relaxed atmosphere and Kompong

Thom offers a chance to break the long and uncomfortable journey on National Hwy 6. Some of the remoter parts of the country in the north-east are more difficult to include on an itinerary as transport is not always as reliable as elsewhere in the country. By road, it is relatively straightforward to get to Mondulkiri and back in just one week with enough time to get a feel for the lifestyle in the meantime. However, Ratanakiri can only be considered as part of a two week trip if you are willing to factor in a return flight as it is generally a three day journey in each direction.

Those with three weeks in Cambodia can see much of the country, including Phnom Penh, Angkor, the south coast and one of the other destinations listed as an option for a two week trip. If you decide to stay for one month, as many travellers end up doing, you can see almost all of the country's attractions, although in the wet season road conditions may limit access to one or two places. It is not unrealistic to include all the places listed above, although you may find yourself choosing between Mondulkiri and Ratanakiri, unless you want to shell out on a flight to the latter. The adventurous might want to try an overland trip to the mountain temple of Preah Vihear on the Thai border, although for the foreseeable future this will remain a whole lot more accessible from the Thai side.

PLANNING
When to Go

Cambodia can be visited at any time of year. You might want to coordinate your trip, however, with one of the annual festivals – see the Public Holidays & Special Events section later in this chapter.

The ideal months to be in Cambodia are December and January, when humidity levels are relatively low and there is little likelihood of rain. From early February temperatures start to rise until the hottest month, April, in which temperatures often exceed 40°C. Some time in May the south-west monsoon brings rain and cooler weather. The wet season, which lasts from May to October, need not be a bad time to visit as it doesn't tend to rain for that long each day, just very hard. Angkor is surrounded by lush foliage and the moats are full of water at this time of year. If you are planning to visit the hill-tribe regions of the north-east, however, the wet season makes travel pretty tough on some of the more remote tracks.

Maps

Tourist maps of Cambodia and Phnom Penh are available in Phnom Penh and Siem Reap, though they are of fairly poor quality. The Periplus *Cambodia Travel Map* at 1:1,100,000 scale is probably the best around and is available in Phnom Penh and Bangkok bookshops. The Nelles Verlag *Vietnam, Laos & Cambodia* map at 1:1,500,000 scale is another good map.

Point Maps & Guides produces some nice 3-D maps of both Phnom Penh and Siem Reap.

For serious map buffs or cartographers the Psar Thmei (New Market) in Phnom Penh is well stocked with Vietnamese and Khmer-produced maps of towns and provinces.

What to Bring

The usual rule applies: bring as little as possible. Phnom Penh is surprisingly well stocked with travel provisions, so if you have forgotten or lost anything it should be possible to replace it there. Nevertheless, it is always best to be prepared.

A good backpack is one outlay you will never regret. Look into buying a frameless or internal-frame pack – these are generally easier to deal with in crowded travel conditions and more comfortable to walk with. Also consider buying a pack that converts into a carry bag – it is less likely to be damaged on airport carousels and is more presentable if you ever need to discard the backpacker image.

A day-pack is essential and a belt-pack is OK for maps, extra film and other bits and pieces, but don't use it for valuables such as your travellers cheques and passport.

You will need few clothes as Cambodia is blessed with year-round warm to steaming-hot weather. As is the case almost everywhere else in South-East Asia, you will not need a sleeping bag: again it will be too hot

most of the time unless you stay in an air-con room. Those staying in guesthouses might like to come prepared with a 'sheet sleeping bag' (two sheets sewn together), but the bedding provided in Cambodia is generally reasonable.

Almost any essentials you forget can be picked up in Phnom Penh, though prices are generally higher than in Bangkok or Ho Chi Minh City (Saigon).

Absolutely essential is a good pair of sunglasses and sunscreen (UV) lotion. The latter can be bought at the Lucky Supermarket in Phnom Penh. An alarm clock is important for getting up on time to catch your flight, bus or whatever – make sure yours is lightweight, and bring extra batteries or a battery charger (size AA rechargeable batteries can be bought in most towns in Cambodia).

The following is a check list of things you might consider packing:

- Photocopy of passport, documents including vaccination certificate, diplomas, photocopy of marriage licence and student identification (ID) card, and visa photos (about 20).
- Money belt or vest, padlock, day-pack.
- Long pants, short pants, long-sleeved shirt, T-shirts, nylon jacket, socks, thongs or sandals, swimwear.
- Umbrella or rain poncho, rain cover for backpack
- Sunglasses, contact-lens solution.
- Deodorant, shampoo, soap, razor, razor blades, shaving cream, sewing kit, spoon, sunhat, tampons, toothbrush, toothpaste, comb, nail clippers, tweezers.
- Compass, Swiss army knife, leak-proof water bottle, alarm clock, camera and accessories, extra camera battery, short-wave radio, Walkman, address book, pens, notepad, torch (flashlight) with batteries and bulbs.
- Mosquito repellent, sunscreen, vitamins, laxatives, condoms, contraceptives, medical kit (see the boxed text 'Medical Kit Check List' later in this chapter).

TOURIST OFFICES

Cambodia has only a handful of tourist offices, and those encountered by the independent traveller in Phnom Penh and Siem Reap are generally unhelpful unless you look like you're going to spend money.

However, in the provinces it is a different story as the staff are often shocked and excited to see visitors. They may have to drag the director out of a nearby karaoke bar, even at 10 am, but once it is made clear that you are a genuine tourist they will usually tell you everything there is to know about places of interest. More and more towns are ambitiously opening tourist offices, but they have nothing in the way of brochures or maps yet.

Cambodia has no tourist offices abroad and it is unlikely that Cambodian embassies will be of much assistance in planning a trip, besides providing visas.

VISAS & DOCUMENTS
Passport

Not only is a passport essential but you also need to make sure that it's valid for at least six months beyond the *end* of your trip – most countries will not issue a visa if you have less than six months validity left on your passport.

It's also important to make sure that there is plenty of space left in your passport. Do not set off on a six month trek across Asia with only two blank pages left – a Cambodian visa alone takes up one page. It is sometimes possible to have extra pages added to your passport, but most people will be required to get a new passport. This is possible for most foreign nationals in Cambodia, but it can be time consuming and costly, as many embassies process new passports in Bangkok.

Losing a passport is not the end of the world, but it is a serious inconvenience. To expedite the issuance of a new passport, make sure that you have the information on your data pages written down somewhere, or better still make a photocopy of these pages, and keep these records separate from your passport.

Visas

Most nationalities receive a one month visa on arrival at Pochentong and Siem Reap airports. The cost is US$20 for a tourist visa and US$25 for a business visa and you require one passport photo. If you intend to find work in Cambodia then opt for the business visa as it is easily extendable for long periods officially and, unofficially, indefinitely. A tourist visa can be extended only once.

If you are coming overland from Thailand through Poipet or Koh Kong, you will need to obtain a visa in Bangkok in advance. Likewise, travellers arriving overland from Vietnam will have to obtain a visa before they reach the Moc Bai border crossing, and this can be done either at the embassy in Hanoi or the consulate in Ho Chi Minh City. You must have Moc Bai as an exit point on your Vietnamese visa to use this route, although if you do not have this on the original visa it can be arranged in Ho Chi Minh City for a hefty fee of US$20.

The land border with Laos will most likely open during the lifetime of this book and, should you enter Cambodia this way, it will doubtless be necessary to arrange a Cambodian visa in Vientiane or Bangkok in advance.

Visa Extensions Visa extensions are granted in Phnom Penh by the Direction des Etrangers, an office of the Ministry of Information located on Phlauv (Ph) 200, just off Norodom Blvd. Tourist visas can be extended only once for one or three months whereas business visas can be extended indefinitely as long as you come with bulging pockets. You can probably even arrange citizenship if you bring enough of the old greenbacks.

There are two ways of getting an extension, one official and one unofficial, and unsurprisingly the time and money involved differ greatly. Officially a one week extension costs US$20, one month US$30, three months US$60, six months US$100, and one year US$150; using this route they will hold your passport for 25 days and, for a business extension, will require more paperwork than even a communist bureaucrat could drool over. This is fine if your employer offers to make the arrangements for you, but if not you really need to go unofficial. They don't call it corruption in Cambodia but 'under the table', and you can have your passport back the next day for inflated prices of US$45 for one month, US$80 for three months, US$150 for six months and US$250 for one year. Once you join the 'unofficials' you can pretty much extend your visa ad infinitum.

One passport photograph is required for visa extensions and there is a US$1 charge for the application form.

Travel Permits
The Cambodian government no longer requires that foreign travellers obtain travel permits for those destinations that are outside Phnom Penh.

Onward Tickets
Customs officials at Pochentong airport are not in the habit of checking air tickets and onward tickets are not required.

Travel Insurance
A travel insurance policy that covers theft, property loss and medical expenses is more essential for Cambodia than for most other parts of South-East Asia. Theft is less a problem in Cambodia than you might imagine, but in the event of serious medical problems or an accident you will probably need to be airlifted to Bangkok, an expense that stretches beyond the average traveller's budget.

There are a wide variety of travel insurance policies available, and it is wise to check with a reliable travel agent about which will best suit you in Cambodia. The policies handled by STA Travel (which has branches in Bangkok) are usually good value.

When you buy your travel insurance *always* check the small print:

• Some policies specifically exclude 'dangerous activities' such as scuba diving and motorcycling. If you are going to be riding a motorbike in Cambodia, check that you will be covered.
• Check whether your medical coverage requires you to pay first and claim later; if this is the case you will need to keep all documents relating to your medical treatment.
• In the case of Cambodia, it is essential that you check to see that your medical coverage includes the cost of emergency evacuation.

Driving Licence
For obvious reasons, car hire is not available in Cambodia and it is very unlikely you will find any use for a driving licence. Motorbikes are available for hire in Phnom Penh, but licences are never checked.

Student & Youth Cards
Student and youth cards won't get you anywhere in Cambodia, though they may be useful in Thailand. In general, the availability of cheap counterfeit student cards in places like Bangkok has done much to rob the student card of whatever value it once had.

International Health Card
There are no direct flights from areas where infection with yellow fever is a possibility, but it's worth carrying an International Health Card, or International Certificate of Vaccination. See Immunisations under Predeparture Planning in the Health section later in this chapter for recommended vaccinations.

Copies
All important documents (passport data page and visa page, credit cards, travel insurance policy, air tickets, driving licence etc) should be photocopied before you leave home. Leave one copy with someone at home and keep another with you, separate from the originals.

It's also a good idea to store details of your vital travel documents in Lonely Planet's free online Travel Vault in case you lose the photocopies or can't be bothered with them. Your password-protected Travel Vault is accessible online anywhere in the world – create it at www.ekno.lonelyplanet.com.

EMBASSIES & CONSULATES
Cambodian Embassies & Consulates
Cambodian diplomatic representation abroad is still thin on the ground, though the situation is gradually improving.

Australia
  Embassy:
  (☎ 02-6273 1259, fax 6273 1053)
  5 Canterbury Court, Deakin, Canberra, Australian Capital Territory (ACT) 2600

China
    Embassy:
    (☎ 01-6532 1889, fax 6532 3507)
    9 Dongzhimenwai Dajie, 100600, Beijing
France
    Embassy:
    (☎ 01-45 03 47 20, fax 45 03 47 40)
    4 Rue Adolphe Yvon, 75016 Paris
Germany
    Embassy:
    (☎/fax 0228-328 572)
    Grüner Weg 8, 53343 Wachtberg Pech, Bonn
India
    Embassy:
    (☎/fax 011-642 3782)
    B47 Soami Nagar, New Delhi, 110017
Indonesia
    Embassy:
    (☎ 021-548 3716, fax 548 3684)
    4th floor, Panin Bank Plaza, Jalan 52 Palmerah Utara, Jakarta 11480
Japan
    Embassy:
    (☎ 03-3478 0861, fax 3478 0865)
    8-6-9 Akasaka, Minato-ku, 107 Tokyo
Laos
    Embassy:
    (☎/fax 21-314952)
    Tha Deau, Bon That Khao, Vientiane
Russia
    Embassy:
    (☎/fax 095-956 6573)
    Strarokonyushenny Per 16, Moscow
Thailand
    Embassy:
    (☎ 02-254 6630, fax 253 9859)
    185 Rajadamri Rd, Bangkok 10330
USA
    Embassy:
    (☎ 202-726 7742, fax 726 8381)
    4500 16th St, NW, Washington, DC 20011
Vietnam
    Embassy:
    (☎ 04-825 3788, fax 826 5225)
    71 Tran Hung Dao St, Hanoi
    Consulate:
    (☎ 08-829 2751, fax 829 2744)
    41 Phung Khac Khoan St, Ho Chi Minh City

Cambodia also has embassies in Bulgaria, Cuba, the Czech Republic, Hungary and North Korea.

Embassies & Consulates in Cambodia

These are all based in Phnom Penh. There is quite a number of them nowadays, though some travellers will find that their nearest embassy is in Bangkok. Most embassies in Phnom Penh will happily provide information to their nationals about the current security situation in Cambodia and can replace your passport in the event that it is lost or stolen. Embassies will not, however, provide funds for onward travel, though some will contact your relatives at home to enable them to send money.

Those intending to visit Laos should note that Lao visas are available in Phnom Penh for US$35 and take one working day. For Vietnam, one-month single-entry visas cost US$50 and take five working days, rising in steady increments to US$80 for a processing time of one working day. There is no surcharge for Moc Bai as a valid entry point.

Embassies and consulates in Cambodia include:

Australia
    Embassy:
    (☎ 426000/1, fax 426003)
    11, Ph 254
Bulgaria
    Embassy:
    (☎ 723181/2, fax 726491)
    227 Norodom Blvd
Canada
    see Australia
China
    Embassy:
    (☎ 426271, fax 426972)
    256 Mao Tse Toung Blvd
Cuba
    Embassy:
    (☎ 724181)
    98, Ph 214
France
    Embassy:
    (☎ 430020)
    1 Monivong Blvd
    Consulate:
    Contact Colonel Billaut, PO Box 17, Siem Reap, 20 Wat Bo Village
Germany
    Embassy:
    (☎ 426381, fax 427746)
    76-78, Ph 214
Hungary
    Embassy:
    (☎ 722781, fax 426216)
    463 Monivong Blvd
India
    Embassy:
    (☎ 722981)
    777 Monivong Blvd

Indonesia
   Embassy:
   (☎ 426148, fax 426571)
   179, Ph 51
Japan
   Embassy:
   (☎ 427161, fax 426162)
   75 Norodom Blvd
Laos
   Embassy:
   (☎ 426441, fax 427454)
   15-17 Mao Tse Toung Blvd
Malaysia
   Embassy:
   (☎ 426176, fax 426004)
   161, Ph 51
Philippines
   Embassy:
   (☎ 280048)
   33, Ph 294
Poland
   Embassy:
   (☎ 426250)
   767 Monivong Blvd
Russia
   Embassy:
   (☎ 723081, fax 426776)
   213 Samdech Sothearos Blvd
Thailand
   Embassy:
   (☎ 426124)
   4 Monivong Blvd
UK
   Embassy:
   (☎ 427124, fax 428295)
   27-29, Ph 75
USA
   Embassy:
   (☎ 426436, fax 426437)
   27, Ph 240
Vietnam
   Embassy:
   (☎ 018-810694)
   436 Monivong Blvd

There are also Vietnamese consulates in Sihanoukville and Battambang.

Your Own Embassy

It's important to realise what your own embassy – the embassy of the country of which you are a citizen – can and can't do to help you if you get into trouble.

Generally speaking, it won't be much help in emergencies if the trouble you're in is remotely your own fault. Remember that you are bound by the laws of the country you are in. Your embassy will not be sympathetic if you end up in jail after committing a crime locally, even if such actions are legal in your own country.

In genuine emergencies you might get some assistance, but only if other channels have been exhausted. For example, if you need to get home urgently, a free ticket home is exceedingly unlikely – the embassy would expect you to have insurance. If you have all your money and documents stolen, it might assist with getting a new passport, but a loan for onward travel is out of the question.

Some embassies used to keep letters for travellers or have a small reading room with home newspapers, but these days the mail holding service usually has been stopped and even newspapers tend to be out of date.

CUSTOMS

If Cambodia has customs allowances, it is keeping close-lipped about them. A 'reasonable amount' of duty free items are allowed into the country. Travellers arriving by air might bear in mind that alcohol and cigarettes sell at duty free (and lower) prices on the streets of Phnom Penh – a carton of Marlboro costs just US$8!

Like any other country, Cambodia does not allow travellers to import weapons, explosives or narcotics – some would say there are enough in the country already.

MONEY
Currency

Cambodia's currency is the riel, abbreviated in this guide by a lower-case 'r' written after the sum. From around 200r to the US dollar in mid-1989 the riel plummeted in value, settling at around 2600r to the US dollar for a few years before the regional economic crisis weakened it further, dragging it down to the current level of about 3800r.

Cambodia's second currency, some would say its first, is the US dollar, which is accepted everywhere and by everyone, though your change may arrive in riel. In the west of the country, the Thai baht (B) is also commonplace. If three currencies seem a little excessive, perhaps the Cambodians are making up for lost time: during the Pol Pot era, the country had *no* currency. The Khmer Rouge abolished money and blew up the National Bank building in Phnom Penh.

The sinking fortunes of the riel meant that, until recently, it was hardly worth the paper it was printed on. The government has responded by creating new higher-value denominations, although notes of 20,000r and upwards are still a fairly rare sight. The riel comes in notes of the following denominations: 100, 200, 500, 1000, 2000, 5000, 10,000, 20,000, 50,000 and 100,000.

Exchange Rates

country	unit		riel
Australia	A$1	=	2459r
Canada	C$1	=	2639r
euro	€1	=	3934r
France	1FF	=	600r
Germany	DM1	=	2011r
Japan	¥100	=	3779r
Laos	1000 kip	=	414r
New Zealand	NZ$1	=	1981r
Spain	100pta	=	2364r
Thailand	10B	=	997r
UK	UK£1	=	6221r
USA	US$1	=	3873r
Vietnam	10,000d	=	2764r

Exchanging Money

Cash Cambodia is one country where US dollars are extremely useful. Indeed, if you have enough cash, you will never have to use the bank because you can change small amounts of foreign currency for riel with jewellers and traders. Hardened travellers argue that your trip ends up being slightly more expensive if you rely on US dollars rather than riel, but in reality there's very little in it. It is worth always having about US$10 worth of riel kicking about as it is good for *motos* (motorbike taxis) and markets. If you pay for something cheap in US dollars you will always get change in riel, and gradually enough riel will accumulate in your wallet to pay for small items anyway. In remote areas such as Ratanakiri and Mondulkiri, locals often prefer riel.

The only other cash currency that can be useful is Thai baht in the west of the country. Prices in towns such as Koh Kong, Poipet and Sisophon are often quoted in baht and even in Battambang it is as commonly seen as the dollar. Any other currency will have to be changed at banks or moneychangers into US dollars or riel.

In the interests of making life as simple as possible, organise a supply of US dollars before you arrive in Cambodia. If you have cash in another major currency, you will be able to change it without any hassle at banks or markets in Phnom Penh or Siem Reap. Most banks tend to offer a punitive rate for any nondollar transaction so it can be better to use moneychangers, which are found in and around every major market.

Travellers Cheques Travellers cheques can be changed only at a limited number of banks in Phnom Penh, Siem Reap, Sihanoukville, Battambang and Kompong Cham. If you are travelling upcountry, you should change enough money before you go. It is best to have cheques in US dollars in Cambodia, though it is also possible to change most major currencies at branches of Canadia Bank and Cambodian Commercial Bank (CCB). Generally you will pay a minimum of 2% commission to change travellers cheques, although the Foreign Trade Bank on Norodom Blvd in Phnom Penh charges only 1%.

Credit Cards Except for top-end hotels and major purchases such as air tickets, credit cards are not particularly worthwhile.

Cash advances on credit cards are available in Phnom Penh, Siem Reap, Sihanoukville and Battambang, but charges are high, with most banks in the capital advertising a minimum charge of US$10 and often a percentage charge on top of that. If you want an advance of US$250 or under, try the Foreign Trade Bank in Phnom Penh as it charges a flat 4%. For more than US$250, CCB is the best option and the only option beyond Phnom Penh.

Several travel agents and hotels near the Psar Thmei also arrange cash advances for about 5% commission and this can be particularly useful if you get caught short at the weekend.

There are no automated teller machines (ATMs) in Cambodia.

International Transfers The Foreign Trade Bank can arrange transfers and has correspondent banks in the US, Europe, Asia and Australia, with relevant addresses and account details helpfully listed on a free handout. CCB also arranges reliable money transfers. The money will probably be routed through the Siam Commercial Bank in Bangkok, CCB's owner. Ideally, you should organise telegraphic transfers in Bangkok rather than Phnom Penh – it will be quicker this way.

Black Market There is no longer a black market in Cambodia. Exchange rates on the street are the same as those offered by the banks.

Security

A lightweight moneybelt that can be worn comfortably and discreetly inside your clothes is the best bet for carrying the bulk of your travel savings. A pair of nylon stockings with one leg folded inside the other can hold a lot of travellers cheques and other documents. It can be tied inconspicuously around your waist under your clothes without any discomfort. Some travellers use a pouch around the neck that rests inside their shirts, though this is usually fairly conspicuous. Bum-bags are not so sensible as they offer too tempting a target to any would-be thief.

Costs

For the most part, Cambodia is an inexpensive country in which to travel. Budget travellers who have arrived from Vietnam will find that accommodation rates are cheaper in Cambodia, but food costs are slightly higher. Prices for food and entertainment are higher in Phnom Penh and Siem Reap, thanks to a hangover from United Nations Transitional Authority in Cambodia (UNTAC) days and a large well-paid expat crowd.

Budget travellers can probably manage Phnom Penh on around US$10 a day, though there's not a great deal to be said for travelling this way – there is much that you will have to miss out on. Accommodation can be as cheap as US$2 to US$3 in Phnom Penh and Siem Reap (elsewhere, you will be looking at a minimum of US$5). It is generally possible to eat fairly well for US$2 to US$3, less if you go native and live off inexpensive soups and noodles from local markets.

Transportation can be a major expense if you are carefully watching your finances. However, with the opening up of land borders with Thailand and the advent of pickup trucks between Phnom Penh and Siem Reap, it is now a lot cheaper to get around by road than by plane or boat as in the old days. Travelling by train is almost free at 15r 'per' kilometre, but is painfully slow. There are regular, cheap bus services to Sihanoukville and provincial towns around the capital, and there is a regular bus to Ho Chi Minh City, although this takes a lot longer than using share taxis.

Visitors to Angkor will have to factor in the cost of entrance fees, which have finally settled down to US$20 for one day, US$40 for three days and US$60 for one week. An additional expense is the government ruling that travellers visiting the ruins must use a guide. A guide with a motorbike will cost a minimum of US$6 per day, although some guesthouses are now renting out motorbikes to guests so the rules may change. It's almost impossible to visit Angkor for less than US$20 per day.

Mid-range travellers are probably the best served in Cambodia. In Phnom Penh and Siem Reap there is an excellent range of accommodation from US$15 to US$25, and if you are happy spending US$5 or slightly more on meals, Phnom Penh in particular can be quite a gourmet experience. Having a little extra money also allows you the luxury of flying one-way or return to Siem Reap, and perhaps renting a taxi to visit sights around Phnom Penh.

At the top end of the scale, Cambodia now has several international-standard hotels to make one's stay more than comfortable.

However, should you stray beyond Phnom Penh and Siem Reap, you are not going to find anything other than budget and mid-range places.

Tipping & Bargaining

Tipping is not expected in Cambodia but, as is the case anywhere, if you meet with exceptional service or kindness, a tip is always greatly appreciated. Salaries remain extremely low in Cambodia and service is often superb thanks to a Khmer commitment to hospitality.

Bargaining is the rule in markets, when hiring vehicles and sometimes even when taking a room. The Khmers are not the ruthless hagglers that Thais and Vietnamese can be, so care should be taken not to come on too strong. A persuasive smile and a little friendly quibbling is usually enough to get a good price. Do try to remember that the aim is not to get the lowest possible price, but a price that is acceptable to both you and the seller. Back home, we pay astronomical sums for items like clothing that have been made in poorer countries for next to nothing, and don't even get the chance to bargain, just the opportunity to contribute to a corporate director's retirement fund. At least you get your say in Cambodia, so try not to abuse it. And remember, in many cases a few hundred riel is more important to the Cambodian with a family to support than to you on an extended vacation.

POST & COMMUNICATIONS

Post is now routed by air through Bangkok, which makes Cambodia a much more reliable place from which to send mail and parcels. Telephone connections with the outside world have also improved immensely, though they are not cheap.

Postal Rates

Postal rates are listed in the Phnom Penh general post office (GPO). Postcards cost 1400r to 1900r internationally. A 10g airmail letter to anywhere in the world costs 1800r to 2300r, while a 100g letter costs 6760r to anywhere in Asia, 7700r to Australia and Europe, and 9800r to the USA.

Parcel rates are 23,800r for 500g within Asia, 29,000r to Australia and Europe, and 39,500r to the USA. There is a 7000r fee for registered mail, but for larger items it is worth it.

Letters and parcels sent further afield than Asia can take up to two or three weeks to reach their destination.

Receiving Mail

The Phnom Penh GPO has a poste restante box at the far left-hand end of the post counter. Basically anybody can pick up your mail, so it's not a good idea to have anything valuable sent there. It costs 100r per item received.

Telephone

Domestic Most hotels in Phnom Penh will allow you to make local calls free of charge. Numbers starting with 011, 012, 015, 017 or 018 are mobile phone numbers. If you need to get connected to a mobile network, see the

Domestic Telephone Codes

Banteay Meanchey	☎ 054
Battambang	☎ 053
Kampot	☎ 033
Kandal	☎ 024
Kep	☎ 036
Koh Kong	☎ 035
Kompong Cham	☎ 042
Kompong Chhnang	☎ 026
Kompong Speu	☎ 025
Kompong Thom	☎ 062
Kratie	☎ 072
Mondulkiri	☎ 073
Odor Meanchey	☎ 065
Phnom Penh	☎ 023
Preah Vihear	☎ 064
Prey Veng	☎ 043
Pursat	☎ 052
Ratanakiri	☎ 075
Siem Reap	☎ 063
Sihanoukville	☎ 034
Stung Treng	☎ 074
Svay Rieng	☎ 044
Takeo	☎ 032

Information section in the Phnom Penh chapter for details. Local phone calls can also be made on the Ministry of Post & Telecommunications (MPTC) and Camintel public payphones, which are common in Phnom Penh, Siem Reap, Sihanoukville and Kompong Cham. It can sometimes be difficult to get through to numbers outside Phnom Penh, and there is no directory inquiries service. Some hotels have telephone directories for the capital if you need to track down a number. The other option is to get a copy of the *Phnom Penh City Guide* produced by Point Guides, which has pretty comprehensive coverage of business, services and government offices.

International It is easy to place an international call from MPTC or Camintel phone booths. You will need to get a phonecard, which in Phnom Penh can be bought at hotels, restaurants, the post office and shops displaying a sign, usually found near one of the booths. Phonecards come in denominations of US$2, US$5, US$10, US$20, US$50 and US$100.

International calls are expensive in Cambodia. To keep expenses to a minimum, ring on a Saturday or Sunday, when a discount of 20% prevails. It works out at a minimum of US$3 a minute even at the cheap rate, and to some countries more than US$4.

Before inserting your card into a public phone, always check that there is a readout on the liquid crystal display (LCD) unit. If there isn't, it probably means there is a power cut – inserting your card during a power cut can wipe the value off the card.

Telephoning from Battambang is cheaper as the Interphone offices route calls via Thailand. Calls to Thailand are only 10B a minute and calls to the rest of the world work out at about US$2 a minute.

To make international calls from Cambodia, the international access code is ☎ 00. To call Cambodia from outside the country, the country code is ☎ 855.

Home Country Direct Making reverse-charge (collect) calls in Cambodia is a hassle, but a home country direct service has been set up for some countries (for more information

ring Telstra on ☎ 426022 in Phnom Penh). Home country direct calls allow you to either reverse the charges or have the call charged to a Telstra or AT&T telecard. For the USA ring ☎ 1 800 881 001, for Australia ring ☎ 1 800 881 061, for the UK ring ☎ 1 800 881 044 and for France ring ☎ 1 800 881 033. No telephone card is required for these numbers.

Fax

If possible, save your faxes for somewhere else. They cost about US$4 to US$6 a page in Cambodia. Some of the more popular mid-range hotels in Phnom Penh have reliable business centres that can send and receive faxes. The best are the Golden Gate Hotel, the Goldiana Hotel and the Cathay Hotel. Phnom Penh's top-end hotels all have expensive business centres. The Foreign Correspondents' Club (FCC) in Phnom Penh is another good place to send and receive faxes.

Email & Internet Access

Business centres in Phnom Penh and Siem Reap offer monthly email accounts with unlimited usage for about US$20, although the National English Teaching Resource Centre of Cambodia (NETREC) is easily the cheapest at US$10. This is good value if you are intending to stay in Phnom Penh for a long period.

Internet access is now available in Phnom Penh and Siem Reap – see the Information sections in the Phnom Penh and Siem Reap chapters for details. In Phnom Penh costs average US$10 per hour, but with per second billing you can be online for as short a time as you like. Costs are exorbitant in Siem Reap as there is no provider there as yet, meaning connection requires a domestic call to the capital. No doubt a connection will soon be established with Thailand, which should make prices reasonable.

If you are carrying a portable computer and want your own connection to a server, Camnet operates out of a building in the post office complex in Phnom Penh, and BigPond, run by Telstra of Australia, is on Norodom Blvd. Prices are expensive by international standards and if you are using a mobile phone from remote areas the connection is poor.

INTERNET RESOURCES

The World Wide Web (WWW) is a rich resource for travellers. You can research your trip, hunt down bargain air fares, book hotels, check on weather conditions or chat with locals and other travellers about the best places to visit (or avoid!).

There's no better place to start your Web explorations than the Lonely Planet Web site (www.lonelyplanet.com). Here you'll find succinct summaries on travelling to most places on earth, postcards from other travellers and the Thorn Tree bulletin board, where you can ask questions before you go or dispense advice when you get back. You can also find travel news and updates to many of our most popular guidebooks, and the sub-WWWay section links you to the most useful travel resources elsewhere on the Web.

Some useful Web sites include:

The Internet Travel Guide
www.datacomm.ch/pmgeiser/Cambodia
(provides a good introduction to Cambodia for travellers)
The Cambodia Information Center
www.Cambodia.org
(lives up to its name with a comprehensive list of sites relating to Cambodia)
Beauty and Darkness: Cambodia, The Odyssey of the Khmer People
members.aol.com/Cambodia/index.htm
(concentrates on the Khmer Rouge period and more recent events)

BOOKS

There has been a lot of ink spilled over Cambodia, particularly regarding the horrendous events of the 1970s, but a lot of the books are quite hard to get hold of outside Cambodia. Phnom Penh is the best place for picking up books as there are quite a few stores, and Caltex petrol stations also have a good selection. See the Information section in the Phnom Penh chapter for details. Bangkok and Ho Chi Minh City bookshops are also worth checking out.

Most books are published in different editions by different publishers in different countries. As a result, a book might be a hardcover rarity in one country while it's readily available in paperback in another. Fortu-

nately, bookshops and libraries search by title or author, so your local bookshop or library is best placed to advise you on the availability of the following recommendations.

Lonely Planet

Lonely Planet publishes *South-East Asia,* an overall guide to travel on the South-East Asian trail, and *Read This First: Asia & India,* aimed at first-time travellers. Also available are the country guides *Vietnam, Laos, Myanmar (Burma)* and *Thailand,* as well as phrasebooks for the languages of those countries, and *Thailand, Vietnam* and *Laos* travel atlases.

Guidebooks

One of the best guidebooks to Cambodia for the visitor wanting to find some quiet corners of the country is *Cambodia Less Travelled* by Ray Zepp. He taught for a time at Phnom Penh University and spent his weekends and holidays travelling Cambodia eventually producing this book, which is part guide, part travel diary. During 1997 he produced a series of supplements on other parts of the country not fully covered in *Cambodia Less Travelled.* These include the *Northwest* (Battambang, Sisophon and Pursat), the *Northeast* (Ratanakiri and Mondulkiri), the *South Coast* (Kampot, Kep, Bokor and Svay Rieng) and *Day Trips Around Phnom Penh on the Ho Wah Genting Bus. Cambodia Less Travelled* is becoming harder to find, but the supplements are available for about US$2 in Phnom Penh's Psar Thmei.

Roland Neveu has produced a *Cambodia* guidebook, which is packed with solid information and nice photos, although it doesn't go into as much detail as Lonely Planet.

Another useful book, especially for anyone planning to spend a length of time in Phnom Penh, is the *Guide to Phnom Penh,* compiled by the Women's International Group. All proceeds from the book are donated to Cambodian charities, and it is packed with useful tips on living in Phnom Penh.

Travellers with an earnest archaeological bent heading out to Angkor are advised to pick up a copy of *Angkor – An Introduction* to the *Temples* by Dawn Rooney. This book is packed with illustrations and fascinating reading on Angkor. Also recommended is the pocket-size *Angkor – Heart of an Asian Empire* by Bruno Dagens. The emphasis in this book is more on the discovery and restoration of the ruins of Angkor, but it is lavishly illustrated and dripping with interesting asides.

Travel

There are not a lot of travel books about Cambodia around. The classic is Norman Lewis' *A Dragon Apparent*, an account of a 1950 foray into an Indochina that was soon to disappear. In the course of his travels, Lewis makes a circuit from Phnom Penh around the Tonlé Sap lake with a pause in Angkor. The book has been reissued as part of *The Norman Lewis Omnibus*. If Lewis' account is just a little outdated for you, then Lucretia Stewart's *Tiger Balm* covers similar territory 40 years later, at the start of the 1990s.

Another elusive book is the quaintly titled *Mistapim in Cambodia*, an entertaining account of a year spent travelling and living in Cambodia in the late 1950s by Christopher Pym.

On a more scholarly note, *To Angkor* (Société d'Éditions Géographiques, Maritimes et Coloniales, or SEGMC, Paris, 1939) is the English version of the French work *Vers Angkor* (Librairie Hachette, Paris, 1925). *Indochina* (SEGMC, Paris, 1939), an English-language condensation of the two volume set *Indochine du Nord* and *Indochine du Sud*, has the same spread on Cambodia as *To Angkor*. The most comprehensive section on Cambodia is to be found in the augmented and excellent 2nd edition of *Indochine du Sud* (SEGMC, Paris, 1939).

Francophone fans of antiquarian books may want to track down *Voyage au Cambodge* by Louis Delaporte (Librairie C Delgrave, Paris, 1880).

A more recent account of travels in Cambodia is *Gecko Tails* by Carol Livingstone, which deftly covers her time in the country during and after the UNTAC period. It is an easy-going read that introduces some interesting characters she encountered while living in Cambodia.

The latest book on the scene, which has ruffled a few feathers among the expat community in Phnom Penh and is certain to attract even more suspicious characters to the capital, is the candidly named *Off the Rails in Phnom Penh – Guns, Girls and Ganja* by Amit Gilboa. He lived here for a while and used his time delving head first into such murky subjects as prostitution and drugs. It is lively enough, but you can't help feeling that some of the expats he writes about could have done a better job themselves.

History & Politics

The best widely available history of Cambodia is David Chandler's *History of Cambodia*. It is available in Cambodia and Bangkok. Chandler has also documented recent Cambodian history in two more excellent titles: *The Tragedy of Cambodian History – Politics, War & Revolution since 1945* and *Brother Number One – A Political Biography of Pol Pot*.

Look out for Milton Osbourne's *Sihanouk – Prince of Light, Prince of Darkness*. This superbly written book provides a no-holds-barred look at the man who has played such a crucial role in the shifting fortunes of Cambodia's modern history. Besides providing a fascinating glimpse into the life of Sihanouk, the book also works well as a history of modern Cambodia.

The expansion of the Vietnam War into Cambodian territory and events through the mid-1970s are superbly documented by William Shawcross in his award-winning book *Sideshow: Kissinger, Nixon & the Destruction of Cambodia*.

Cambodia: Year Zero by François Ponchaud (originally published in French as *Cambodge: Année Zéro*) is an account of life in Cambodia under the Khmer Rouge. Other works on this period include: *The Stones Cry Out: A Cambodian Childhood, 1975-1980* by Molyda Szymusiak, originally published in French as *Les Pierres Crieront: Une Enfance Cambodgienne, 1975-1980*; *The Cambodian Agony* by David Ablin; and *The Murderous Revolution* by Martin Stuart-Fox.

Ben Kiernan, one of the foremost scholars on the Khmer Rouge, has written two detailed accounts of how the group came to power and what it did once in power. *How Pol Pot Came to Power* and *The Pol Pot Regime* are quite esoteric as they are primarily aimed at students of Cambodia, but if you are keen to read further on this subject, they offer unparalleled insights.

The atrocities of the Khmer Rouge are documented by *Kampuchea, Decade of Genocide: Report of the Finnish Enquiry Commission* edited by Kimmo Kiljunen. *Brother Enemy* is an excellent work by Nayan Chanda and offers an incredible insight into how Cambodia and Vietnam descended into war with a little help from their 'friends' in China, the former USSR and the USA.

William Shawcross' work *The Quality of Mercy: Cambodia, Holocaust and Modern Conscience* looks at the contradictions inherent in the massive international famine-relief operation mounted in 1979 and 1980. This still highly relevant title is available in Thailand in a paperback edition.

The Australian journalist Jon Pilger has written many articles on the tragedy of Cambodia and most have been published in collected works, including *Heroes, Distant Voices* and *Hidden Agendas.*

Jon Swain's *River of Time* and Tim Page's *Derailed in Uncle Ho's Victory Garden* take the reader back to an old Indochina, partly lost to the madness of war. Tim Page's quest for the truth behind the disappearance of photojournalist Sean Flynn in Kompong Cham Province in 1971 is compelling. Tim Page has also produced a photographic testament to the horrors of war called *Requiem*. It is dedicated to correspondents of all sides who died covering the Indochina conflict and includes many images from Cambodia.

Finally, Christopher J Koch's *Highways to a War* is a powerful fictional insight into life as a war correspondent during the civil war.

Angkor

The guidebooks *Angkor – An Introduction to the Temples* by Dawn Rooney and *Angkor –*

Heart of an Asian Empire by Bruno Dagens are two first-rate introductions to Angkor that make good supplemental guides.

Angkor: An Introduction by George Coedes gives excellent background information on Angkorian Khmer civilisation. You might also look for Malcolm MacDonald's *Angkor & the Khmers*; *Arts & Civilization of Angkor* by Bernard Groslier & Jacques Arthaud; and, in French, *Histoire d'Angkor* by Madeleine Giteau.

The Art of Southeast Asia by Philip Rawson has recently been reprinted in Thailand and has excellent chapters on Angkor. *Angkor* by Michael Freeman & Roger Warner is a big, glossy, coffee-table book on Angkor.

A recent coffee-table release is *Passage Through Angkor* by Mark Standen. Standen, a newcomer to photography, has come up with some of the most striking images ever produced of Angkor. If you want a photographic memento of Angkor, this is the best there is.

National Geographic has run some memorable features on Cambodia and Angkor. Some of the relevant issues are available in Phnom Penh. In particular, look out for 'The Temples of Angkor' and 'Kampuchea Wakens from a Nightmare' (May 1982). The temples feature contains a fine fold-out map of the Angkor region as it must have been at the height of its power.

FILMS

There have been a couple of definitive films made by Hollywood that deal with the conflict in Cambodia. *The Killing Fields* tells the story of American journalist Sydney Schanberg and his Cambodian assistant Dith Pran during and after the war. As the Khmer Rouge closes in on Phnom Penh, Dith Pran decides to stay and help Schanberg cover the takeover. As the new regime clears out Phnom Penh, most journalists seek refuge in the French embassy. Eventually, Dith Pran is forced to join the rest of Phnom Penh's citizens on the long march into the countryside. The remainder of the film deals with his attempts to survive the horror that engulfs the country. Most of the footage was actually shot in Thailand, not Cambodia: it was filmed in 1984 and at that time it would have been impossible to organise.

The other definitive movie about Cambodia is Francis Ford Coppola's *Apocalypse Now*, which tells the story of a renegade colonel, played by Marlon Brando, who goes AWOL (absent without leave) upstream in Cambodia. Martin Sheen plays a young soldier sent to bring him back, and the ensuing encounter makes for one of the most powerful indictments of war ever made. The story has some base in historical fact: a number of soldiers did disappear into the bush to train hill tribes in the art of war, including one notorious case in northern Laos. However, no single soldier or story forms the basis of the film, although it draws heavily from the novel *Heart of Darkness* by Joseph Conrad and the exploits of famous Vietnam-era soldiers such as Colonel John Paul Vann and Lieutenant-Colonel David Hackett. The film was shot in the Philippines, but the river depicted is thought to be the Srepok in Ratanakiri Province, north-east Cambodia.

For information about the Cambodian film industry, see the Arts section in the Facts about Cambodia chapter.

NEWSPAPERS & MAGAZINES

Despite occasional tirades by the government about foreign press interference in the country's 'internal affairs', Cambodia has a lively local English-language press. Bookshops in Phnom Penh have a wide range of English- and French-language newspapers and magazines.

Local Publications

The *Cambodia Daily* nearly lives up to its name, appearing at newsstands and restaurants daily on weekdays. It also has a weekend issue that usually includes a special feature report. It is an excellent overview of international agency stories with some local input, and also has Khmer and Japanese supplements. It costs just 1200r. The Friday edition has a useful 'This Week's Calendar' section.

The *Cambodge Soir* is a French paper that comes out on weekday evenings. It is

available in bookshops and most of the restaurants frequented by French patrons around Phnom Penh.

The *Phnom Penh Post* provides a very good overview of events in Cambodia. As well as informative feature stories, it has a lift-out map of Phnom Penh with restaurants and business services. It costs 3500r, but is worth it for its detail.

For the lighter side of life in Cambodia, the free monthly *Bayon Pearnik* combines humorous stories with human interest features from around the country and offers a refreshing counterbalance to the darker subjects dealt with by the mainstream press. The staff are also known for hosting regular parties so look out for posters in Phnom Penh guesthouses and adverts in the magazine.

International Publications

The Bangkok Post and the *Nation* are Thai English-language dailies that are widely available in Phnom Penh, usually by mid-afternoon on the day of publication, as is *The Straits Times* from Singapore. The FCC has copies you can read free-of-charge if you pop in for a coffee, a snack or a meal.

Monument Books and the bookshops at Hotel Le Royal and the Sofitel Cambodiana Hotel are the best stocked in Phnom Penh when it comes to newspapers; the French newspaper sections are especially comprehensive. Several-days-old copies of *The Australian* are usually also on sale. Other English-language newspapers on sale include the *Asia Times*, *International Herald Tribune* and *The Guardian Weekly*.

On the magazine front, the aforementioned bookshops have current copies of *The Economist*, *Far Eastern Economic Review*, *Asiaweek*, *Time*, *Newsweek* and a host of European titles in French, German and Italian.

RADIO & TV

The British Broadcasting Corporation (BBC) has broadcasts in Khmer and English at 100MHz FM in the capital. There are also one or two tourist stations playing tunes in the evening around 98 and 99MHz FM on the dial. The Cambodian radio station in Phnom Penh has an English-language news broadcast at 9 pm every evening. French speakers should tune in to Radio France International, which is relayed from Paris.

If you have a short-wave radio, it is possible to pick up the BBC World Service, Radio Australia and so on.

Most of the mid-range hotels in Phnom Penh have satellite TV reception, which means that you should have access to BBC World, Cable News Network (CNN), Star TV, Music Television (MTV), Cartoon Network, TV5 and the Australian Broadcasting Corporation (ABC). Without satellite reception, you are restricted to Channel 2 (which is French).

Khmer television has a couple of channels including Apsara and KTV, but most of the time the programs seem to involve forlorn people singing to each other or savage gunfight dramas imported from Hong Kong and China.

PHOTOGRAPHY & VIDEO
Film & Equipment
Print film and processing are cheap in Cambodia. A roll of ASA 100 Kodak or Fuji film (36 exposures) costs US$2, or US$3.50 for 400 ASA. Konika film is cheaper again. Printing is also cheap in Cambodia and most laboratories charge about US$4 for a roll of 36. The Fuji labs are the best quality, but the Konika ones are sometimes a little cheaper.

Slide film is also available cheaply in Phnom Penh. It costs US$5 for a roll of Kodak Elite or Fuji Sensia and US$6 for Fuji's Velvia or Provia range. Purchase as much as you need in Phnom Penh as it is pretty hard to come by elsewhere in the country. Do not have slide film processed in Cambodia unless it is really urgent. Many shops claim to be able to process slide film, but you'll more likely end up with black and white X-ray-style shots. City Colour Photo on Monivong Blvd, just north of the Psar Thmei, is the best bet in the capital.

General camera-supply needs can be satisfied in Phnom Penh. Camera batteries are easy to replace providing you don't require anything too obscure, but don't forget to carry a spare if you are heading off the trail.

If you take a video camera, make sure you keep the batteries charged and have the necessary charger, plugs and transformer for Cambodia (see Electricity later in this chapter). Take care with some of the electrical wiring in guesthouses around the country as it can be pretty amateurish. In Phnom Penh, it is possible to obtain video tapes for most formats, but elsewhere around the country you are unlikely to find anything you need. It is often worth buying a few tapes duty-free before you start your trip.

Technical Tips
The best light conditions in Cambodia begin around 20 minutes after sunrise and last for just one to two hours. The same applies for the late afternoon light, which begins to assume a radiant warm quality around an hour before sunset. From 10 am to around 3.30 pm you can expect the light to be harsh and bleaching – there's not much you can do with it unless you have a polarizer. Bear in mind that you have much more leeway with exposures in print film than you do in slide film. Snaps taken in poor light conditions often turn out OK in the printing process; with slides you either get it right or you don't.

Properly used, a video camera offers a fascinating record of your holiday. As well as videoing the obvious things – sunsets or spectacular views – remember to record some of the everyday details of life that you see around you. Often the most interesting things occur when you are actually filming something else. Remember too that, unlike photography, video flows so you can shoot scenes of countryside rolling past a car window to give an overall impression that isn't possible with a still camera. Video cameras have amazingly sensitive microphones and you might be surprised how much sound will be picked up. This can be a problem if there is a lot of ambient noise around – filming on the side of a busy road might seem OK when you do it, but viewing it back home might simply give you a deafening cacophony of traffic noise. One good rule for beginners is to try to film in long takes. Also, try not to move the camera around too much, otherwise you'll end up making your viewers seasick! And remember you are on holiday – don't let the video take over your life and turn your trip into a production.

Restrictions

The Cambodian armed forces don't seem too concerned about foreigners photographing bridges and so on, but most of these were built by foreigners using foreign aid anyway. It would still be sensible to exercise some restraint. Charging up to an armed convoy and snapping away might result in unpleasant consequences.

Photographing People

The usual rules apply: be polite about photographing and video taping people; don't push cameras into their faces; and have some respect for monks and people at prayer. It shouldn't be necessary to say this, but unfortunately there are a lot of amateur photographers out there who think that they're on assignment for *National Geographic*. In general, the Khmers are remarkably courteous people and if you ask nicely they'll agree to have their photograph taken. The same goes for video taping – ask permission first, although in rural areas you will often find children desperate to get in front of the lens and astonished to see themselves played back on a LCD screen. It is the closest most of them will get to being on television.

Airport Security

The X-ray machines at Pochentong airport are safe to put your film through. If you are carrying 1000 ASA or higher film, you should store it separately and ask to have it inspected by hand. Some professional photographers refuse to put any film through any x-ray machine. This is an unnecessary precaution, but then it is their livelihood.

TIME

Cambodia, like Vietnam, Thailand and Laos, is seven hours ahead of Greenwich Mean Time or Universal Time Coordinated

(GMT/UTC). When it is midday in Cambodia it is 10 pm the previous evening in San Francisco, 1 am in New York, 5 am in London and 3 pm in Sydney.

ELECTRICITY

Electricity in Phnom Penh and most of Cambodia is 220V, 50Hz. Power is in short supply in Cambodia and power cuts are frequent. Most hotels and restaurants have their own generators, but in rural areas you can expect to be without electricity for long periods every day.

Electric power sockets are generally of the round two-pin variety. Three-pin plug adaptors can be bought at the markets in Phnom Penh.

WEIGHTS & MEASURES

Cambodia uses the metric system. For those unaccustomed to this system, there is a metric/imperial conversion chart on the inside back cover of this guide.

LAUNDRY

Laundry is never a problem in Cambodia. All hotels provide a laundry service and, unless you are holed up in some top-end joint where they charge you to switch on the lights, it is either free or very cheap.

TOILETS

Although the occasional squat toilet turns up here and there, the general rule (particularly in hotels) is the sit-down variety. If you get out into the sticks, you will find that hygiene conditions deteriorate somewhat, but Cambodia is still a cleaner country than say China or India.

Public toilets are rare indeed, the only ones in the country being located near some of Angkor's more important temples. Should you find nature calling in rural areas, don't let modesty drive you into the bushes: *there may be land mines not far from the road or track*. Stay on the side of the road or grin and bear it.

HEALTH

Your health is more at risk in Cambodia than most other parts of South-East Asia

MICK ELMORE

MICK ELMORE

ANDERS BLOMQVIST

Traditional dance, more than any of the arts a link with the Angkor period, has undergone a revival since 1981.

Colonial architecture, Battambang.

Wat, Kompong Thom.

Wat Ek Phnom, Battambang.

Bas-relief at Wat Phnom.

Angkor Wat's central structure.

due to poor sanitation and a lack of effective medical treatment facilities. Once you venture into rural areas you should consider yourself very much on your own, as even where pharmacies and hospitals are available you may have trouble making yourself understood.

If you feel particularly unwell try to see a doctor rather than visit a hospital as the latter are pretty primitive and diagnosis can be erratic. If you fall seriously ill in Cambodia you should return to Phnom Penh as it is the only place in the country with decent emergency treatment. Pharmacies in the larger towns are remarkably well stocked and you don't need a prescription to get your hands on anything from antibiotics to antimalarials. Prices are very reasonable, but do check the expiry date as some medicine may have been on the shelves for a long time.

Don't let this make you overparanoid. Travel health depends on your predeparture preparations, your daily health care while travelling and how you handle any medical problem that does develop. While the potential dangers can seem quite frightening, in reality few travellers experience anything more than upset stomachs.

Predeparture Planning

Immunisations Plan ahead for getting your vaccinations: some of them require more than one injection, while some vaccinations should not be given together. Note that some vaccinations should not be given during pregnancy or to people with allergies – discuss these issues with your doctor.

It is recommended you seek medical advice at least six weeks before travel. Be aware that there is often a greater risk of disease among children and during pregnancy.

Record all vaccinations on an International Certificate of Vaccination, available from your doctor or government health department. You will need to carry proof of your vaccinations, especially yellow fever, as this is needed to enter Cambodia.

Discuss your requirements with your doctor, but vaccinations you should definitely consider for this trip include the following (for more details about the diseases themselves, see the individual entries later in this section).

Diphtheria & Tetanus Vaccinations for these two diseases are usually combined and are recommended for everyone. After an initial course of three injections (usually given in childhood), boosters are necessary every 10 years.

Polio Everyone should keep up to date with this vaccination, which is normally given in childhood. A booster every 10 years maintains immunity.

Hepatitis A Hepatitis A vaccine (eg Avaxim, Havrix 1440 or VAQTA) provides long-term immunity (possibly more than 10 years) after an initial injection and a booster at six to 12 months. Alternatively, an injection of gamma globulin can provide short-term protection against hepatitis A – two to six months, depending on the dose given. It is not a vaccine, but is ready-made antibody collected from blood donations. It is reasonably effective and, unlike the vaccine, it is protective immediately, but because it is a blood product, there are current concerns about its long-term safety. Hepatitis A vaccine is also available in a combined form, Twinrix, with hepatitis B vaccine. Three injections over a six-month period are required, the first two providing substantial protection against hepatitis A.

Typhoid Vaccination against typhoid may be required if you are travelling for more than a couple of weeks in Cambodia. It is now available either as an injection or as capsules to be taken orally. A combined hepatitis/typhoid vaccine has recently been developed, although its availability is limited – check with your doctor to find out its status in your country.

Hepatitis B Travellers who should consider vaccination against hepatitis B include those on a long trip, as well as those visiting countries where there are high levels of hepatitis B infection, where blood transfusions may not be adequately screened or where sexual contact or needle sharing is a possibility. Vaccination involves three injections, with a booster at 12 months. More rapid courses are available if necessary.

Yellow Fever A yellow fever vaccine is now the only vaccine that is a legal requirement for entry into Cambodia when coming from an infected area.

Rabies Vaccination should be considered by those who will spend a month or longer in Cambodia, especially if they are cycling, handling animals,

Everyday Health

Normal body temperature is up to 37°C (98.6°F); more than 2°C (4°F) higher indicates a high fever. The normal adult pulse rate is 60 to 100 per minute (children 80 to 100, babies 100 to 140). As a general rule the pulse increases about 20 beats per minute for each 1°C (2°F) rise in fever.

Respiration (breathing) rate is also an indicator of illness. Count the number of breaths per minute: Between 12 and 20 is normal for adults and older children (up to 30 for younger children, 40 for babies). People with a high fever or serious respiratory illness breathe more quickly than normal. More than 40 shallow breaths a minute may indicate pneumonia.

caving or travelling to remote areas, and for children (who may not report a bite). Vaccination involves having three injections over 21 to 28 days. If someone who has been vaccinated is bitten or scratched by an animal, they will require two booster injections of vaccine; those not vaccinated require more.

Japanese B Encephalitis Consider vaccination against this disease if spending a month or longer in Cambodia, making repeated trips or visiting during an epidemic. It involves three injections over 30 days.

Tuberculosis The risk of TB to travellers is usually very low, unless you will be living with or closely associated with local people. Vaccination against TB (BCG) is recommended for children and young adults living in high risk areas, including Asia, for three months or more.

Malaria Medication Antimalarial drugs do not prevent you from being infected but kill the malaria parasites during a stage in their development and significantly reduce the risk of becoming very ill or dying. Expert advice on medication should be sought, as there are many factors to consider, including the area to be visited, the risk of exposure to malaria-carrying mosquitoes, the side effects of medication, your medical history and whether you are a child or an adult or pregnant. Travellers heading to isolated areas in Cambodia should carry a treatment

dose of medication for use if symptoms occur. A combination of Cotexcin and Fansidar, which are cheaply and readily available in Cambodia, will do the trick. See the Insect-Borne Diseases entry later in this section for more details.

Health Insurance Make sure that you have adequate health insurance. See Travel Insurance under Visas & Documents earlier in this chapter for details.

Travel Health Guides If you are planning to be away or travelling in remote areas for a long period of time, you may like to consider taking a more detailed health guide. Lonely Planet's *Healthy Travel: Asia & India* is a handy pocket-size and is packed with useful information including pretrip planning, emergency first aid, immunisation and disease information and what to do if you get sick on the road. *Where There Is No Doctor*, by David Werner, is a very detailed guide intended for someone, such as a Peace Corps worker, going to work in an underdeveloped country.

Travel with Children from Lonely Planet also includes advice on travel health for younger children.

There are also a number of excellent travel health sites on the Internet. From the Lonely Planet home page there are links at www.lonelyplanet.com/weblinks/wlprep.htm #heal to the World Health Organization (WHO) and the US Centers for Disease Control & Prevention.

Other Preparations Make sure you're healthy before you start travelling. If you're going on a long trip make sure your teeth are in reasonable condition. If you wear glasses take a spare pair and your prescription.

If you require a particular medication take an adequate supply, as it may not be available locally. Take part of the packaging showing the generic name rather than the brand, which will make getting replacements easier. It's a good idea to have a legible prescription or letter from your doctor to show that you legally use the medication to avoid any problems.

Basic Rules

Food There is an old colonial adage which says 'If you can cook it, boil it or peel it you can eat it ... otherwise forget it'. Vegetables and fruit should be washed with purified water or peeled where possible. Beware of ice cream that is sold in the street or anywhere it might have been melted and refrozen; if there's any doubt (eg a power cut in the last day or two), steer well clear. Shellfish such as mussels, oysters and clams should be avoided as well as undercooked meat, particularly in the form of mince. Steaming does not make shellfish safe for eating.

If a place looks clean and well run and the vendor also looks clean and healthy, then the food is probably safe. In general, places that are packed with travellers or locals will be fine, while empty restaurants are questionable. The food in busy restaurants is cooked and eaten quite quickly with little standing around and is probably not reheated.

Water The number one rule is *be careful of the water* and especially ice. If you don't know for certain that the water is safe, assume the worst. Reputable brands of bottled water or soft drinks are generally fine, although in some places bottles may be refilled with tap water. Only use water from containers with a serrated seal – not tops or corks. Take care with fruit juice, particularly if water may have been added. Milk should be treated with suspicion as it is often unpasteurised, though boiled milk is fine if it is kept hygienically. Tea or coffee should also be OK, since the water should have been boiled.

Water Purification The simplest way of purifying water is to boil it thoroughly. Vigorous boiling should be satisfactory; however, at high altitude water boils at a lower temperature, so germs are less likely to be killed. Make sure you boil it for longer in these environments.

Consider purchasing a water filter for a long trip. There are two main kinds of filter. Total filters take out all parasites, bacteria and viruses and make water safe to drink. They are often expensive, but they can be more cost effective than buying bottled water. Simple filters (which can even be a nylon mesh bag) take out dirt and larger foreign bodies from the water so that chemical solutions work much more effectively; if water is dirty, chemical solutions may not work at all. It's very important when buying a filter to read the specifications, so that you know exactly what it removes from the water and what it doesn't.

Nutrition

If your diet is poor or limited in variety, if you're travelling hard and fast and therefore missing meals or if you simply lose your appetite, you can soon start to lose weight and place your health at risk.

Make sure your diet is well balanced. Cooked eggs, tofu, beans, lentils (dhal in India) and nuts are all safe ways to get protein. Fruit you can peel (bananas, oranges or mandarins, for example) is usually safe and a good source of vitamins. Melons can harbour bacteria in their flesh and are best avoided. Try to eat plenty of grains (including rice) and bread. Remember that although food is generally safer if it is cooked well, overcooked food loses much of its nutritional value. If your diet isn't well balanced or if your food intake is insufficient, it's a good idea to take vitamin and iron pills.

In hot climates make sure you drink enough – don't rely on feeling thirsty to indicate when you should drink. Not needing to urinate or voiding small amounts of very dark yellow urine is a danger sign. Always carry a water bottle with you on long trips. Excessive sweating can lead to loss of salt and therefore muscle cramping. Salt tablets are not a good idea as a preventative, but in places where salt is not used much, adding salt to food can help.

Simple filtering will not remove all dangerous organisms, so if you cannot boil water it should be treated chemically. Chlorine tablets (Puritabs, Steritabs or other brand names) will kill many pathogens, but not some parasites like giardia and amoebic cysts. Iodine is more effective in purifying water and is available in tablet form (such as Potable Aqua). Follow the directions carefully and remember that too much iodine can be harmful.

Medical Problems & Treatment

Self-diagnosis and treatment of health problems can be risky, so you should always seek professional medical help. Although we do give drug dosages in this section, they are for emergency use only. Correct diagnosis is vital.

An embassy, consulate or five-star hotel can usually recommend a local doctor or clinic. Antibiotics should ideally be administered only under medical supervision. Take only the recommended dose at the prescribed intervals and use the whole course, even if the illness seems to be cured earlier. Stop immediately if there are any serious reactions and don't use the antibiotic at all if you are unsure that you have the correct one. Some people are allergic to commonly prescribed antibiotics such as penicillin or sulpha drugs; carry this information (eg on a bracelet) when travelling.

Environmental Hazards

Heat Exhaustion Dehydration and salt deficiency can cause heat exhaustion. Take time to acclimatise to high temperatures, drink sufficient liquids and do not do anything too physically demanding.

Salt deficiency is characterised by fatigue, lethargy, headaches, giddiness and muscle cramps; salt tablets may help, but adding extra salt to your food is better.

Anhidrotic heat exhaustion is a rare form of heat exhaustion that is caused by an inability to sweat. It tends to affect people who have been in a hot climate for some time, rather than newcomers. It can progress to heatstroke. Treatment involves removal to a cooler climate.

Heatstroke This serious, occasionally fatal condition can occur if the body's heat-regulating mechanism breaks down and the body temperature rises to dangerous levels. Long, continuous periods of exposure to high temperatures and insufficient fluids can leave you vulnerable to heatstroke.

The symptoms are feeling unwell, not sweating very much (or at all) and a high body temperature (39° to 41°C or 102° to 106°F). Where sweating has ceased, the skin becomes flushed and red. Severe, throbbing headaches and lack of coordination will also occur, and the sufferer may be confused or aggressive. Eventually the victim will become delirious or convulse. Hospitalisation is essential, but in the interim get victims out of the sun, remove their clothing, cover them with a wet sheet or towel and then fan continually. Give fluids if they are conscious.

Jet Lag Jet lag is experienced when a person travels by air across more than three time zones (each time zone usually represents a one hour time difference). It occurs because many of the functions of the human body (such as temperature, pulse rate and emptying of the bladder and bowels) are regulated by internal 24-hour cycles. When we travel long distances rapidly, our bodies take time to adjust to the 'new time' of our destination, and we may experience fatigue, disorientation, insomnia, anxiety, impaired concentration and loss of appetite. These effects will usually be gone within three days of arrival, but to minimise the impact of jet lag:

- Rest for a couple of days prior to departure.
- Try to select flight schedules that minimise sleep deprivation; arriving late in the day means you can go to sleep soon after you arrive. For very long flights, try to organise a stopover.
- Avoid excessive eating (which bloats the stomach) and alcohol (which causes dehydration) during the flight. Instead, drink plenty of noncarbonated, nonalcoholic drinks such as fruit juice or water.
- Avoid smoking.
- Make yourself comfortable by wearing loose-fitting clothes and perhaps bringing an eye mask and ear plugs to help you sleep.
- Try to sleep at the appropriate time for the time zone you are travelling to.

Motion Sickness Eating lightly before and during a trip will reduce the chances of motion sickness. If you are prone to motion sickness try to find a place that minimises movement – near the wing on aircraft, close to midships on boats, near the centre on buses. Fresh air usually helps; reading and cigarette smoke don't. Commercial motion-sickness preparations, which can cause drowsiness, have to be taken before the trip commences. Ginger (available in capsule form) and peppermint (including mint-flavoured sweets) are natural preventatives of motion sickness.

Prickly Heat Prickly heat is an itchy rash caused by excessive perspiration trapped under the skin. It usually strikes people who have just arrived in a hot climate. Keeping cool, bathing often, drying the skin and using a mild talcum or prickly heat powder, or resorting to the use of air-conditioning may help.

Sunburn You can get sunburnt surprisingly quickly, even through cloud. Use a sunscreen, a hat, and a barrier cream for your nose and lips. Calamine lotion or Stingose are good for mild sunburn. Protect your eyes with good quality sunglasses.

Infectious Diseases

Diarrhoea Simple things like a change of water, food or climate can all cause a mild bout of diarrhoea, but a few rushed toilet trips with no other symptoms are not indicative of a major problem.

Dehydration is the main danger with diarrhoea, particularly in children or the elderly as dehydration can occur quite quickly. Under all circumstances *fluid replacement* (at least equal to the volume being lost) is the most important thing to remember. Weak black tea with a little sugar, soda water, or soft drinks allowed to go flat and diluted 50% with clean water are all good. With severe diarrhoea, a rehydrating solution is preferable to replace minerals and salts lost. Commercially available oral rehydration salts (ORS) are very useful; add them to boiled or bottled water. In an emergency you can make up a solution of six teaspoons of sugar and a half teaspoon of salt to a litre of boiled or bottled water. You need to drink at least the same volume of fluid that you are losing in bowel movements and vomiting. Urine is the best guide to the adequacy of replacement – if you have small amounts of concentrated urine, you need to drink more. Keep drinking small amounts often. Stick to a bland diet as you recover.

Gut-paralysing drugs such as Lomotil or Imodium can be used to bring relief from the symptoms of diarrhoea, although they do not actually cure the problem. Only use these drugs if you do not have access to toilets, eg if you *must* travel. For children under 12 years the use of Lomotil and Imodium is not recommended. Do not use these drugs if the person has a high fever or is severely dehydrated.

In certain situations antibiotics may be required: diarrhoea with blood or mucus (dysentery), any diarrhoea with fever, profuse watery diarrhoea, persistent diarrhoea not improving after 48 hours and severe diarrhoea. These suggest a more serious cause of diarrhoea and in these situations gut-paralysing drugs should be avoided.

In these situations, a stool test may be necessary to diagnose what bug is causing your diarrhoea, so you should seek medical help urgently. Where this is not possible the recommended drugs for bacterial diarrhoea (the most likely cause of severe diarrhoea in travellers) are norfloxacin 400mg twice daily for three days or ciprofloxacin 500mg twice daily for five days. These are not recommended for children or pregnant women. The drug of choice for children would be co-trimoxazole (Bactrim, Septrin or Resprim) with dosage dependent on weight. A five day course is given. Ampicillin or amoxycillin may be given in pregnancy, but medical care is necessary.

Two other causes of persistent diarrhoea in travellers are giardiasis and amoebic dysentery.

Giardiasis is caused by a common parasite, *Giardia lamblia*. Symptoms include stomach cramps, nausea, a bloated stomach, watery, foul-smelling diarrhoea and frequent gas. Giardiasis can appear several weeks after you have been exposed to the parasite. The symptoms may disappear for a few days and then return; this can go on for several weeks.

Amoebic dysentery, caused by the protozoan *Entamoeba histolytica*, is characterised by a gradual onset of low-grade diarrhoea, often with blood and mucus. Cramping abdominal pain and vomiting are less likely than in other types of diarrhoea, and fever may not be present. It will persist until treated and can recur and cause other health problems.

You should seek medical advice if you think you have giardiasis or amoebic dysentery, but where this is not possible, Tinidazole (Fasigyn) or metronidazole (Flagyl) are the recommended drugs. Treatment is a 2g single dose of Fasigyn or 250mg of Flagyl three times daily for five to 10 days.

Fungal Infections Fungal infections occur more commonly in hot weather and are usually found on the scalp, between the toes (athlete's foot) or fingers, in the groin and on the body (ringworm). You get ringworm (which is a fungal infection, not a worm) from infected animals or other people. Moisture encourages these infections.

To prevent fungal infections wear loose, comfortable clothes, avoid artificial fibres, wash frequently and dry yourself carefully. If you do get an infection, wash the infected area at least daily with a disinfectant or medicated soap and water, and rinse and dry well. Apply an antifungal cream or powder like tolnaftate (Tinaderm). Try to expose the infected area to air or sunlight as much as possible and wash all towels and underwear in hot water, change them often and let them dry in the sun.

Hepatitis Hepatitis is a general term for inflammation of the liver. It is a common disease worldwide. There are several different viruses that cause hepatitis, and they differ in the way that they are transmitted. The symptoms are similar in all forms of the illness, and include fever, chills, headache, fatigue, feelings of weakness and aches and

pains, followed by loss of appetite, nausea, vomiting, abdominal pain, dark urine, light-coloured faeces, jaundiced (yellow) skin and yellowing of the whites of the eyes. People who have had hepatitis should avoid alcohol for some time after the illness, as the liver needs time to recover.

Hepatitis A is transmitted by contaminated food and drinking water. You should seek medical advice, but there is not much you can do apart from resting, drinking lots of fluids, eating lightly and avoiding fatty foods. Hepatitis E is transmitted in the same way as hepatitis A; it can be particularly serious in pregnant women.

There are almost 300 million chronic carriers of **Hepatitis B** in the world. It is spread through contact with infected blood, blood products or body fluids, for example through sexual contact, unsterilised needles and blood transfusions, or contact with blood via small breaks in the skin. Other risk situations include having a shave, tattoo or body piercing with contaminated equipment. The symptoms of hepatitis B may be more severe than type A and the disease can lead to long term problems such as chronic liver damage, liver cancer or a long term carrier state. Hepatitis C and D are spread in the same way as hepatitis B and can also lead to long term complications.

There are vaccines against hepatitis A and B, but there are currently no vaccines against the other types of hepatitis. Following the basic rules about food and water (hepatitis A and E) and avoiding risk situations (hepatitis B, C and D) are important preventative measures.

HIV & AIDS Infection with the human immunodeficiency virus (HIV) may lead to acquired immune deficiency syndrome (AIDS), which is a fatal disease. Any exposure to blood, blood products or body fluids may put the individual at risk. The disease is often transmitted through sexual contact or dirty needles – vaccinations, acupuncture, tattooing and body piercing can be potentially as dangerous as intravenous drug use. HIV/AIDS can also be spread through infected-blood transfusions; some developing countries cannot afford to screen blood used for transfusions, and while the blood centre in Phnom Penh does screen, it is unlikely it is done in many of the provinces.

If you do need an injection, ask to see the syringe unwrapped in front of you, or take a needle and syringe pack with you.

Fear of HIV infection should never preclude any treatment for serious medical conditions.

According to WHO figures, rates of infection are highest amongst sex workers in Phnom Penh. The group's HIV prevalence increased from 10% in 1992 to over 40% in 1996. Rates are also at a similar level outside Phnom Penh. Other groups with high prevalence rates include the military (recorded at 7.1% in 1997) and pregnant women.

Intestinal Worms These parasites are most common in rural, tropical Cambodia. The different worms have different ways of infecting people. Some may be ingested on food such as undercooked meat (eg tapeworms) and some enter through your skin (eg hookworms). Infestations may not show up for some time, and although they are generally not serious, if left untreated some can cause severe health problems later. Consider having a stool test when you return home to check for these and determine the appropriate treatment.

Schistosomiasis Also known as bilharzia, this disease is transmitted by minute worms. They infect certain varieties of freshwater snails found in rivers, streams, lakes and particularly dams. The worms multiply and are eventually discharged into the water.

The worm enters through the skin and attaches itself to the intestines or bladder. The first symptom may be feeling unwell generally, or a tingling and sometimes a light rash around the area where it entered. Weeks later a high fever may develop. Once the disease is established abdominal pain and blood in the urine are other signs. The infection often causes no symptoms until the disease is well established (several months to years after exposure), when damage to internal organs is irreversible.

Avoiding swimming or bathing in fresh water where bilharzia is present is the main method of preventing the disease. Even deep water can be infected. If you do get wet, dry off quickly and dry your clothes as well.

A blood test is the most reliable way to diagnose the disease, but the test will not show positive until a number of weeks after exposure.

Sexually Transmitted Infections (STIs)
Gonorrhoea, herpes and syphilis are among these infections; sores, blisters or rashes around the genitals and discharges or pain when urinating are common symptoms. With some STIs, such as wart virus or chlamydia, symptoms may be less marked or not observed at all, especially in women. Syphilis symptoms eventually disappear completely, but the disease continues and can cause severe problems in later years. While abstinence from sexual contact is the only 100% effective prevention, using condoms is also effective. The treatment of gonorrhoea and syphilis is with antibiotics. The different STIs each require specific antibiotics. There is no cure for herpes or AIDS.

Typhoid Typhoid fever is a dangerous gut infection caused by contaminated water and food. Medical help must be sought.

In its early stages sufferers may feel they have a bad cold or flu on the way, as early symptoms are a headache, body aches and a fever that rises a little each day until it is around 40°C (104°F) or more. The victim's pulse is often slow relative to the degree of fever present – unlike a normal fever where the pulse increases. There may also be vomiting, abdominal pain, diarrhoea or constipation.

In the second week the high fever and slow pulse continue, and a few pink spots may appear on the body; trembling, delirium, weakness, weight loss and dehydration may occur. Complications such as pneumonia, perforated bowel or meningitis may occur.

Insect-Borne Diseases
Malaria This serious and potentially fatal disease is spread by mosquitoes. If you are

travelling in endemic areas it is extremely important to avoid mosquito bites and to take tablets to prevent this disease. Symptoms range from fever, chills and sweating, headache, aching joints, diarrhoea and abdominal pains, usually preceded by a vague feeling of ill-health. Seek medical help immediately if malaria is suspected. Without treatment malaria can rapidly become more serious and can be fatal.

If medical care is not available, malaria tablets can be used for treatment. You need to use a malaria tablet that is different from the one you were taking when you contracted malaria. If travelling widely in rural areas of Cambodia, it is worth visiting a pharmacy to purchase a treatment dose to save yourself complications in the event of an emergency. Cotexcin is one brand of the artesunate family of antimalarials from China that acts quickly to quell the symptoms of malaria. This drug has not been approved yet for use in the west, but is widely available in Cambodia and the results have been impressive. However, it is best used in combination with another antimalarial such as Fansidar – used together these will effectively kill off the parasite. For Cotexcin, you need to take six on the first day, and then three a day for the following six days. This should be followed by three Fansidar tablets on the fourth day. Both these brands are cheaply available throughout Cambodia. The standard treatment dose of mefloquine is two 250mg tablets and a further two tablets six hours later. If you were previously taking mefloquine then alternatives are Malarone (atovaquone-proguanil; four tablets once daily for three days), halofantrine (three doses of two 250mg tablets every six hours) or quinine sulphate (600mg every six hours). There is a greater risk of side effects with these dosages than in normal use if used with mefloquine, so medical advice is preferable. Be aware also that halofantrine is no longer recommended by WHO as emergency stand-by treatment because of side effects, and should only be used if no other drugs are available.

Travellers are advised to prevent mosquito bites at all times. The main messages are:

- Wear light-coloured clothing.
- Wear long trousers and long-sleeved shirts.
- Use mosquito repellents containing the compound DEET on exposed areas (prolonged overuse of DEET may be harmful, especially to children, but its use is considered preferable to being bitten by disease-transmitting mosquitoes).
- Avoid perfumes or aftershave.
- Use a mosquito net impregnated with mosquito repellent (permethrin) – it may be worth taking your own.
- Impregnate clothes with permethrin to effectively deter mosquitoes and other insects.

Dengue Fever This viral disease is transmitted by mosquitoes and occurs mainly in tropical and subtropical areas of the world. Generally, there is only a small risk to travellers except during epidemics, which are usually seasonal (during and just after the rainy season). With unstable weather patterns thought to be responsible for large outbreaks of dengue fever in South-East Asia, travellers to Cambodia may be especially at risk of infection.

The *Aedes aegypti* mosquito, which transmits the dengue virus, is most active during the day, unlike the malaria mosquito, and is found mainly in urban areas, in and around human dwellings.

Signs and symptoms of dengue fever include a sudden onset of high fever, headache, joint and muscle pains (hence its old name, 'breakbone fever') and nausea and vomiting. A rash of small red spots appears three to four days after the onset of fever. Dengue is commonly mistaken for other infectious diseases, including influenza.

You should seek medical attention if you think you may be infected. Infection can be diagnosed by a blood test. There is no specific treatment for dengue. Aspirin should be avoided, as it increases the risk of haemorrhaging. Recovery may be prolonged, with tiredness lasting for several weeks. Severe complications are rare in travellers but include dengue haemorrhagic fever (DHF), which can be fatal without prompt medical treatment. DHF is thought to be a result of second infection due to a different strain (there are four major strains) and usually affects residents of the country rather than travellers.

There is no vaccine against dengue fever. The best prevention is to avoid mosquito bites at all times – see the malaria entry earlier for more details.

Japanese B Encephalitis This viral infection of the brain is transmitted by mosquitoes. Most cases occur in rural areas as the virus exists in pigs and wading birds. Symptoms include fever, headache and alteration in consciousness. Hospitalisation is needed for correct diagnosis and treatment. There is a high mortality rate among those who have symptoms; of those who survive many are intellectually disabled.

Cuts, Bites & Stings

Cuts & Scratches Wash well and treat any cut with an antiseptic such as povidone-iodine. Where possible avoid bandages and Band-Aids, which can keep wounds wet. Coral cuts are notoriously slow to heal and if they are not adequately cleaned, small pieces of coral can remain embedded in the wound.

Bedbugs & Lice Bedbugs live in various places, but particularly in dirty mattresses and bedding, evidenced by spots of blood on bedclothes or on the wall. Bedbugs leave itchy bites in neat rows. Calamine lotion or Stingose spray may help.

All lice cause itching and discomfort. They make themselves at home in your hair (head lice), your clothing (body lice) or in your pubic hair (crabs). You catch lice through direct contact with infected people or by sharing combs, clothing and the like. Powder or shampoo treatment will kill the lice, and infected clothing should then be washed in very hot, soapy water and left to dry in the sun.

Bites & Stings Bee and wasp stings are usually painful rather than dangerous. However, in people who are allergic to them severe breathing difficulties may occur and require urgent medical care. Calamine lotion or Stingose spray will give relief and ice packs will reduce the pain and swelling.

Jellyfish Avoid contact with these sea creatures, which have stinging tentacles – seek local advice. Dousing in vinegar will deactivate any stingers that have not 'fired'. Calamine lotion, antihistamines and analgesics may reduce the reaction and relieve the pain.

Leeches & Ticks Leeches may be present in damp rainforest conditions; they attach themselves to your skin to suck your blood. Trekkers often get them on their legs or in their boots. Salt or a lighted cigarette end will make them fall off. Do not pull them off, as the bite is then more likely to become infected. Clean and apply pressure if the point of attachment is bleeding. An insect repellent may keep them away.

You should always check all over your body if you have been walking through a potentially tick-infested area as ticks can cause skin infections and other more serious diseases. If a tick is found attached, press down around the tick's head with tweezers, grab the head and gently pull upwards. Try to avoid pulling the rear of the body as this may squeeze the tick's gut contents through the attached mouth parts into the skin, increasing the risk of infection and disease. Smearing chemicals on the tick will not make it let go and this is not recommended.

Snakes To minimise your chances of being bitten always wear boots, socks and long trousers when walking through undergrowth where snakes may be present. Don't put your hands into holes and crevices, and be careful when collecting firewood.

Snake bites do not cause instantaneous death and antivenins are usually available. Immediately wrap the bitten limb tightly, as you would for a sprained ankle, and then attach a splint to immobilise it. Keep the victim still and seek medical help, if possible with the dead snake for identification. However, do not attempt to catch the snake if there is any possibility of being bitten again. The techniques of tourniquets and sucking out the poison are now comprehensively discredited.

Medical Kit Check List

Following is a list of items you should consider including in your medical kit – consult your pharmacist for brands available in your country.

☐ **Aspirin** or **paracetamol** (acetaminophen in the USA) – for pain or fever

☐ **Antihistamine** – for allergies, eg, hay fever; to ease the itch from insect bites or stings; and to prevent motion sickness

☐ **Cold** and **flu tablets, throat lozenges** and **nasal decongestant**

☐ **Multivitamins** – consider for long trips, when dietary vitamin intake may be inadequate

☐ **Antibiotics** – consider including these if you're travelling well off the beaten track; see your doctor, as they must be prescribed, and carry the prescription with you

☐ **Loperamide** or **diphenoxylate** – 'blockers' for diarrhoea

☐ **Prochlorperazine** or **metaclopramide** – for nausea and vomiting

☐ **Rehydration mixture** – to prevent dehydration, which may occur, for example, during bouts of diarrhoea; particularly important when travelling with children

☐ **Insect repellent, sunscreen, lip balm** and **eye drops**

☐ **Calamine lotion, sting relief spray** or **aloe vera** – to ease irritation from sunburn and insect bites or stings

☐ **Antifungal cream** or **powder** – for fungal skin infections and thrush

☐ **Antiseptic** (such as povidone-iodine) – for cuts and grazes

☐ **Bandages, Band-Aids (plasters)** and other wound dressings

☐ **Water purification tablets** or **iodine**

☐ **Scissors, tweezers** and a **thermometer** – note that mercury thermometers are prohibited by airlines

☐ **Syringes** and **needles** – in case you need injections in a country with medical hygiene problems; ask your doctor for a note explaining why you have them

Women's Health

Gynaecological Problems Antibiotic use, synthetic underwear, sweating and contraceptive pills can lead to fungal vaginal infections, especially when travelling in hot climates. Thrush, or vaginal candidiasis, is characterised by a rash, itching and discharge. Nystatin, miconazole or clotrimazole pessaries or vaginal cream are the usual treatment, but some people use a more traditional remedy involving the use of vinegar or lemon-juice douches, or yogurt. Maintaining good personal hygiene and wearing loose-fitting clothes and cotton underwear may help prevent these infections.

STIs are a major cause of vaginal problems. Symptoms include a smelly discharge, painful intercourse and sometimes a burning sensation when urinating. Medical attention should be sought and male sexual partners must also be treated. For more details, see Sexually Transmitted Infections earlier in this section. Besides abstinence, the best thing is to practise safe sex using condoms.

Pregnancy Most miscarriages occur during the first three months of pregnancy. Miscarriage is not uncommon and can occasionally lead to severe bleeding. The last three months should also be spent within reasonable distance of good medical care. A baby born as early as 24 weeks stands a chance of survival, but only in a good modern hospital. Pregnant women should avoid all unnecessary medication, although vaccinations and malarial prophylactics should still be taken where needed. Additional care should be taken to prevent illness and particular attention should be paid to diet and nutrition. Alcohol and nicotine, for example, should be avoided.

Less Common Diseases

The following diseases pose a small risk to travellers, and so are only mentioned in passing. Seek medical advice if you think you may have any of these diseases.

Cholera This is the worst of the watery diarrhoeas and medical help should be sought. Outbreaks of cholera are generally widely reported, so you can avoid such problem areas. *Fluid replacement is the most vital treatment* – the risk of dehydration is severe as you may lose up to 20L a day. If there is a delay in getting to hospital, then begin taking tetracycline. The adult dose is 250mg four times daily. It is not recommended for children under nine years nor for pregnant women. Tetracycline may help shorten the illness, but adequate fluids are required to save lives.

Filariasis This is a mosquito-transmitted parasitic infection found in Cambodia. Possible symptoms include fever, pain and swelling of the lymph glands, inflammation of lymph drainage areas, swelling of a limb or the scrotum, skin rashes and blindness. Treatment is available to eliminate the parasites from the body, but some of the damage already caused may not be reversible. Medical advice should be obtained promptly if the infection is suspected.

Rabies This fatal viral infection is found in Cambodia. Many animals can be infected (such as dogs, cats, bats and monkeys) and it is their saliva that is infectious. Any bite, scratch or even lick from an animal should be cleaned immediately and thoroughly. Scrub with soap and running water, and then apply alcohol or iodine solution. Medical help should be sought promptly to receive a course of injections to prevent the onset of symptoms and death.

Tetanus This disease is caused by a germ that lives in soil and in the faeces of horses and other animals. It enters the body via breaks in the skin. The first symptom may be discomfort in swallowing or stiffening of the jaw and neck; this is followed by painful convulsions of the jaw and whole body. The disease can be fatal. It can be prevented by vaccination.

Tuberculosis TB is a bacterial infection usually transmitted from person to person by coughing, but which may be transmitted through consumption of unpasteurised milk. Milk that has been boiled is safe to drink, and the souring of milk to make yogurt or cheese also kills the bacilli. Travellers are usually not at great risk as close household contact with the infected person is usually required before the disease is passed on. You may need to have a TB test before you travel as this can help diagnose the disease later if you become ill.

Typhus This disease is spread by ticks, mites or lice. It begins with fever, chills, headache and muscle pains followed a few days later by a body rash. There is often a large painful sore at the site of the bite and nearby lymph nodes are swollen and painful. Typhus can be treated under medical supervision. Seek local advice on areas where ticks pose a danger and always check your skin carefully for ticks after walking in a danger area such as tropical forest. An insect repellent can help, and walkers in tick-infested areas should consider having their boots and trousers impregnated with benzyl benzoate and dibutylphthalate.

WOMEN TRAVELLERS
Women will generally find Cambodia a hassle-free place to travel. Foreign women are unlikely to be targeted by local men, but at the same time it pays to be careful. As is the case anywhere in the world, walking or riding a bike alone late at night is risky, and if you're planning a trip off the beaten trail it would be best to find a travel companion.

Despite the prevalence of sex workers and women's employment as 'beer girls', dancing companions and the like in the entertainment industry, foreign women will probably find Khmer men to be courteous and polite. It's best to keep things this way by being restrained in your dress. Khmer women dress fairly conservatively, and it's best to follow suit, particularly when visiting wats. In general, long-sleeved shirts and long trousers or skirts are preferred. It is also worth having trousers for heading out at night on motos as short skirts aren't that functional when you sometimes have three on a bike.

Tampons and sanitary towels are widely available in the major cities and provincial capitals, but if you are heading into the wilds of Mondulkiri and Ratanakiri, it is worth having your own supply.

GAY & LESBIAN TRAVELLERS

While Cambodian culture is tolerant of homosexuality, the scene is certainly nothing like that of neighbouring Thailand. Public displays of affection, whether heterosexual or homosexual, are frowned on.

DISABLED TRAVELLERS

Depending on your disability, Cambodia is not going to be an easy country to get around in. Local labour costs though, are inexpensive, which means that you can hire a guide for around US$10 a day or less. Travellers with major disabilities would be advised to look into a tour.

SENIOR TRAVELLERS

Senior travellers are not eligible for anything in the way of discounts in Cambodia – all foreigners are rich as far as Cambodians are concerned (and they are right, comparatively). Depending on how nimble you are on your feet, it is not recommended that you take adventurous options, such as the boats that travel between Phnom Penh and Siem Reap.

TRAVEL WITH CHILDREN

Travellers considering visiting Cambodia with children should pick up a copy of Lonely Planet's *Travel with Children*. If you are planning a visit to Angkor and Phnom Penh only, there should be no problems. More adventurous travel with children in Cambodia is not recommended.

USEFUL ORGANISATIONS

Cambodia hosts a huge number of NGOs. The best way to find out who exactly is represented in Cambodia is to call in to the Co-operation Committee for Cambodia (CCC, ☎ 426009) at 35, Ph 178, Phnom Penh. This organisation has a handy list of all NGOs, both Cambodian and international, and is extremely helpful.

The following list comprises the more prominent international NGOs operating out of Phnom Penh. There are many more.

Action Internationale Contre la Faim
    (☎ 426934) 7, Bat 15
American Friends Service Committee
    (☎ 216400) 30, Ph 352
American Refugee Committee
    (☎ 426115) 18, Ph 604
Australian Catholic Relief
    (☎ 426200) 67, Ph 315
Australian People for Health Education & Development Abroad
    (☎ 216034) 10, Ph 302
Cambodian-British Centre for Teacher Education (☎ 721156) 30, Ph 29
Cambodia Canada Development Program
    (☎ 217338) 41, Ph 111
Cambodia Development Resource Institute
    (☎ 426103) 56, Ph 318
Care International
    (☎ 426233) 18A, Ph 370
Catholic Office for Emergency Relief & Refugees
    (☎ 364306) 30, Ph 232
Christian Research
    (☎ 364445) 41, Ph 476
Community Aid Abroad
    (☎ 720036) 54, Ph 352
CONCERN
    (☎ 362636) 38, Ph 388
Coopération Internationale pour le Développement et la Solidarité
    (☎ 426369) 23, Ph 294
Enfants du Cambodge
    (☎ 360040) 13 Norodom Blvd
HALO Trust
    (☎ 364063) 12, Ph 97
Handicap International
    (☎ 217300) 53 Sothearos Blvd
International Committee of the Red Cross
    (☎ 360071) 18 Samdech Sothearos Blvd
Japan International Volunteer Centre
    (☎ 366385) 35, Ph 169
Lutheran World Service
    (☎ 426350) 37, Ph 592
Marie Stopes International
    (☎ 360350) 3, Ph 75
Médecins sans Frontières, France
    (☎ 428308) 8, Ph 211
Médecins sans Frontières, Netherlands/Belgium
    (☎ 246521) 8, Ph 211
Mennonite Central Committee
    (☎ 426592) 20, Ph 475
Mines Advisory Group
    (☎ 360495) 30, Ph 294
Oxfam UK
    (☎ 720928) 54, Ph 352
Partnership for Development in Kampuchea
    (☎ 426224) 38, Ph 57
Quaker Service Australia
    (☎ 362732) 13, Ph 302

Redd Barna (Norwegian Save the Children)
(☎ 362143) 9, Ph 322
Save the Children Fund, UK
(☎ 362157) 25, Ph 71
United Nations Children's Fund (UNICEF)
(☎ 426214) 11, Ph 75
United Nations Development Programme
(UNDP)
(☎ 426217) 53, Ph 334
United Nations High Commissioner for
Refugees (UNHCR)
(☎ 362150) 2, Ph 352
United Nations Human Rights Centre
(☎ 015-913446) 45, Ph 85
Voluntary Service Overseas
(☎ 426734) 18, Ph 282
World Health Organization (WHO)
(☎ 216610) 120, Ph 51
World Food Programme
(☎ 426205) 250, Ph 63
World Vision International
(☎ 426052) 20, Ph 71

DANGERS & ANNOYANCES
Security

The security situation has long been an
Achilles heel for the tourism industry in
Cambodia, with negative publicity appearing on TV and in newspapers at regular intervals. Certainly personal security was an
issue of greater concern than in neighbouring countries during Cambodia's civil war,
and for most of the 1990s the Khmer Rouge
had a policy of targeting western tourists.
Indeed, a number were killed, and this naturally scared visitors away, while those that
came found their movements restricted. The
coup of July 1997 and the series of riots and
extra-judicial killings that followed the
elections of July 1998 further sullied Cambodia's international reputation. However,
the inconsistent situation today is better
than it used to be because the Khmer Rouge
has been eliminated from the picture.

Politically, Cambodia is an unpredictable
country and this makes it hard to judge the
relative safety of travel at any given time.
Suffice to say that you are no longer a target just because you are a tourist, although
this doesn't mean your safety is guaranteed
as with travel anywhere in the world. Many
roads that were off-limits only a few years
ago now see regular tourist traffic. These in-

clude the road between Poipet and Siem
Reap, the road from Siem Reap to Phnom
Penh and the road between the capital and
Battambang. However, there are many remote areas and some of these are not always
secure, with the problem of banditry per-
sisting. The 'bandits' are often soldiers or
former Khmer Rouge fighters who have not
received their pay cheques or promises of
better opportunities. The military is vastly
inflated for a country now officially at
peace, and serious demobilisation is required before Cambodia can move forward.
The problem remains that there are few
prospects for these soldiers once they shed
their uniforms, so many may choose to
hang on to their guns and turn to illegit-
imate means to make a living.

Cambodia is something of a lawless society in which arms are often preferred to
eloquence when settling a dispute. This
'wild east' atmosphere rarely affects tourists, but it is worth knowing about as you
can expect to hear gunshots from time to
time (usually someone firing into the air
when drunk). Phnom Penh is arguably one
of the more dangerous places in Cambodia
since peace has come to the provinces; it is
here that the most guns are concentrated
and where by far the most robberies take
place. Elsewhere in the provinces you will
be very unlucky should any incident befall
you as the vast majority of Khmers are immensely hospitable and helpful. More importantly perhaps, the majority of Khmers
are experiencing peace for the first time in
more than 30 years and don't want anything
to disturb it.

Trying to pinpoint areas of concern
around the country is always difficult as circumstances change quickly, but a few
hotspots worth researching before making a
trip include: the road between Kratie and
Stung Treng (use the boat in the wet season),
the area of National Hwy 7 between Memot
and Snuol, and any area north of Kompong
Thom and Siem Reap towards the Thai border, as much of this area was Khmer Rouge
controlled until as recently as the middle of
1998 – just because the former fighters now
wear *Titanic* t-shirts instead of Mao caps

Cambodia's Underground War

Cambodia is a country scarred by years of conflict and some of the deepest scars lie just inches beneath the surface. The legacy of land mines in Cambodia is one of the worst anywhere in the world, with an estimated four to six million dotted about the countryside awaiting their victims. These insidious inventions are not just weapons of war, but weapons against peace as they recognise no ceasefire.

In a supplement to the *Phnom Penh Post* (10-23 February, 1995) sponsored by non-governmental organisations (NGOs) and the US government, an article paints a hypothetical picture of Britain terrorised by 60 million land mines planted in more than 14,000 battlefields. With many of these land mines planted in agriculturally and industrially productive parts of the country, the job of providing for national needs becomes harder to fulfil. The scenario continues as hospitals fill with injured and dying. As tourists shun the country, industry relocates overseas and foreign investment dries up. The government declares a national emergency. The scale of the disaster is such that the military lacks the resources to find all the land mines – most will be discovered by people stepping on them. In just three years, some 245,000 Britons become amputees. Many turn to begging and crime to support themselves.

This essentially is the situation in Cambodia. As many as 40,000 Cambodians have lost limbs due to mines. Cambodia has the highest per capita rate of amputees in the world – about one in 250 people. After malaria, tuberculosis and diarrhoea, mines are Cambodia's number one killer. Land mines litter the country, buried in rice fields and on roadsides and, even after extensive mine-awareness campaigns, they still claim about 75 victims a month. This is a vast improvement on a few years ago when the figure was more like 300, but still entirely unacceptable for a country officially at peace. To make matters more complicated, areas that appear safe in the dry season become unsafe in the wet season as the earth softens. It is not uncommon for Cambodian refugees to settle on land during the dry season and begin a new life, only to have their dreams shattered when the wet season arrives as a family member has a leg blown off by a land mine.

The cost to an extensively mined country is enormous. In a developing country like Cambodia, the United Nations (UN) estimates that the lifetime rehabilitation of a land mine victim costs US$3000. With 40,000 victims, the cost is around US$120 million. Then there are indirect costs, such as the deaths of grazing livestock. Mines hamper rural development too. Much of Cambodia's agricultural land is mined, making it impossible to farm and causing shortages of food.

doesn't mean they have fundamentally changed their thinking.

For the time being, make a point of checking on the latest security situation before making a trip that you know few travellers undertake. Moreover, do not rely only on information provided by locals – they often undertake dangerous trips as a matter of necessity and have no way of assessing the risks for a foreigner. But the moral of the story is to speak with as many people as possible before undertaking any adventurous trips upcountry as conditions can change from week to week.

Checkpoints

There used to be checkpoints on roads throughout the country during the long years of civil war. These were supposedly to enhance security on provincial roads, but in reality they worsened the situation as the soldiers manning them soon learned to extort money from every vehicle passing through. However, the situation has improved vastly

Cambodia's Underground War

There are a number of groups working in Cambodia to alleviate the problem of mines. The Cambodian Mine Action Centre (CMAC) is an all-Cambodian government agency operating with technical support from overseas governments. The Hazardous Areas Life (Support) Organisation (HALO) Trust was one of the pioneers of mine clearance in Cambodia, and now has many teams working in provinces such as Pursat, Banteay Meanchey and Siem Reap. The Mines Advisory Group (MAG) is a British outfit that has been training Cambodians in mine clearance. It has launched programs to train mine victims and all-women teams in mine clearance. It has also pioneered mine awareness programs throughout the country involving puppet shows for children and posters in rural communes. The Campagna Française d'Assistance Specialisée (COFRAS) is working in Siem Reap Province to clear sites of historical importance.

Most sensible travellers will not be wandering around mined areas while they are in Cambodia. Nevertheless, there are some points worth bearing in mind while you are in the country:

- Always check with locals that paths are not mined.
- Never leave a well-trodden path in remote areas.
- Never ever touch anything that looks remotely like a mine.
- If you find yourself accidentally in a mined area, only retrace your steps if you can clearly see your footprints; if not, you should stay where you are and call for help – as advisory groups put it, 'better to spend a day standing in a minefield than a lifetime as an amputee'.
- If someone is injured in a minefield, even if they are crying out for help, do not rush in; find the help of someone who knows how to safely enter a mined area.
- Do not leave the roadside in remote areas, even for nature's calling, as your limbs are more important than your modesty.

There have been some notable breakthroughs in the campaign to ban land mines in the last few years. In 1997 more than 100 countries signed a treaty banning the production, stockpiling, sale and use of land mines under any circumstances. Some important international players in land mine production signed the treaty, including Italy, France and the UK. However, the world's major producers refused to sign, including China, Russia and the USA, so even as you read this, land mines continue to be produced.

Cambodia was a signatory to the treaty, but has yet to ratify it. While it is commendable that it has signed, the treaty does little to alleviate the everyday nightmare of life in heavily mined rural provinces. Mine clearance in Cambodia is, tragically, too often a step by step process. For the majority of Cambodians, the underground war goes on.

in recent years and many of the more commonly travelled routes have few or no checkpoints. However, if you are travelling overland throughout Cambodia, it is almost inevitable that you will run into a checkpoint at some time during your trip. If you are travelling in a taxi or pick-up truck, the driver should take care of the payment, and if you are on a motorbike you are unlikely to be stopped. However, should you find money being demanded of you, try to negotiate the sum to an acceptable level. Do not under any circumstances attempt to take photos of the individuals concerned as things could turn nasty. If the soldiers are adamant that you cannot pass, there may be a genuine security risk so turn back rather than argue.

Undetonated Mines, Mortars & Bombs

Never touch any rockets, artillery shells, mortars, mines, bombs or other war material you may come across. In Vietnam most of this sort of stuff is 20 or more years old, but in Cambodia it may have landed there or been laid in the last few years. In fact, a favourite tactic of the Khmer Rouge was to lay mines along roads and in rice fields in an effort to maim and kill civilians, thus – so the twisted logic concludes – furthering the rebel cause by demoralising the government. The only concrete results of this policy are the many limbless people you see all over Cambodia. The most heavily mined part of the country is the Battambang and Pailin area, but mines are a problem all over Cambodia. In short: do not stray from well marked paths *under any circumstances*, even around the monuments of Angkor. If you are planning any walks, even in safer areas such as the remote north-east, it is imperative you take a guide as there may be unexploded ordnance (UXO) from the American bombing campaign of the early 1970s.

Theft & Street Crime

Given the number of guns about in Cambodia, there is less armed theft than you might suppose. Still, hold-ups and motorcycle theft are regular problems in Phnom Penh. See the Dangers & Annoyances section in the Phnom Penh chapter for details. There is no need to be overly paranoid, just cautious. Riding alone late at night is not ideal, and certainly not in rural areas.

Pickpocketing and theft by stealth is more a problem in Vietnam and Thailand than in Cambodia, but it pays to be careful. Don't make it any easier for thieves by putting your passport and wads of cash in your back pocket. As a precaution, keep a 'secret' stash of cash separately from the bulk of your funds.

Begging

Begging is common throughout Cambodia, although much more evident in Phnom Penh and Siem Reap than elsewhere. There are many reasons for begging in a society as poor as Cambodia; there are, for example, amputees who may have lost their legs in frontline battles during the civil war. It is entirely up to individual visitors to give or not and how much to offer, but it should be remembered that it is common practice for

Buddhists to give to those more needy than themselves.

There are many child beggars around Phnom Penh and the temples of Angkor, and with their angelic faces it is often difficult to resist giving them some money. However, some issues to bear in mind include: giving to child beggars may create a cycle of dependency, which can continue into adulthood; the children may not benefit directly from the money as they are often made to beg by a begging 'pimp' or their family; and some child beggars, particularly around central Phnom Penh, may use the money to buy glue to feed their sniffing habit. One way to help these impoverished children is to buy them some food or drink or give them some of your time and attention – it is amazing how quickly they will forget about begging once they are being taught something simple like a whistle, a trick or a game.

The most common beggars around the country are land mine victims. Many of these victims have sustained these injuries fighting while others have had their legs blown off while working or playing innocently in the fields. You may tire of their attention after a few days in the country, but try to remember that, in a country with no social security network, begging is often all they can do to survive.

When giving to beggars, try to keep to smaller denominations to avoid making foreigners more of a special target than they already are.

Traffic Accidents

Traffic conditions in Cambodia are chaotic, though no worse than in many other underdeveloped countries. If you are riding a bike in Phnom Penh you should stay very alert and take nothing for granted. Traffic moves in all directions on both sides of the road so don't be surprised to see vehicles bearing down on you. The horn is used to alert drivers of your presence – listen out behind and get out of the way if it's a car or a truck.

None of the moto drivers in Cambodia use or provide safety helmets. Fortunately most of them drive at sensible speeds. If you encounter a reckless driver, ask them to slow down or pay them off and find another.

Having a major traffic accident in Phnom Penh would be bad enough, but if you have one in rural Cambodia you are in big trouble. Somehow you will have to get back to Phnom Penh for medical treatment.

The basic rule is drive carefully as there have been too many shattered dreams in Cambodia already: there's no need to add to them. See the Car & Motorcycle section in the Getting Around chapter for safety tips.

Snakes

Visitors to Angkor and other overgrown archaeological sites should beware of snakes, including the small but deadly light-green Hanuman snake, which often emerges after rainstorms to hunt for insects. They are very well camouflaged so keep your eyes peeled.

LEGAL MATTERS

Contrary to popular belief – and at least one guidebook – marijuana is not legal in Cambodia. Traditionally used in Khmer cooking, there would no doubt be much local opposition to a major crackdown on its availability. Still, if you are a smoker, be discreet, as the days of free bowls in guesthouses are over. It's probably only a matter of time before the Cambodian police turn the busting of foreigners into a lucrative sideline, as in neigbouring countries.

The above applies equally to other narcotic substances, which are also illegal according to the Cambodian constitution. Also think twice about visiting an opium parlour with an unfamiliar moto driver as it may end with you getting robbed after passing out.

Moral grounds alone should be enough to deter foreigners from seeking under-age sexual partners in Cambodia, but unfortunately in some cases this is not enough. Paedophiles are treated as criminals in Cambodia and several have served or are serving jail sentences as a result. There is no such thing as isolation units for sex offenders in Cambodia. Countries such as Australia and the UK have also introduced legislation that will see nationals prosecuted on their home ground for having under-age sex abroad.

Take a look at Phnom Penh's central jail on Ph 154 before you commit a crime of any sort: you really wouldn't want to end up inside.

BUSINESS HOURS

Government offices, which are open from Monday to Saturday, theoretically begin the working day at 7 or 7.30 am, breaking for a siesta from 11 or 11.30 am to 2 or 2.30 pm and ending the day at 5.30 pm. However, it is a safe bet that few people will be around early in the morning or after 4 pm.

Banking hours tend to vary according to the bank, but you can reckon on core hours of 8.30 am to 3.30 pm.

There are an incredible number of public holidays and festivals that close down offices.

PUBLIC HOLIDAYS & SPECIAL EVENTS

During public holidays and festivals, banks, ministries and embassies close down so plan ahead if visiting Cambodia during these times. These institutions also seem to take holidays on Christmas Day, New Year's Day, the Day for Remembering the Victory over the Genocidal Regime on 7 January and Chinese New Year, so all in all they spend a fair number of days on holiday each year.

The festivals of Cambodia take place according to the lunar calendar so the dates vary from year to year:

Chaul Chnam
    Held in mid-April, this is a three day celebration of Khmer New Year: Khmers make offerings at wats, clean out their homes and exchange gifts of new clothes. It is a lively time to visit as, like the Thais, Khmers go wild with water and talcum powder leaving a lot of bemused tourists looking like plastercast figures. It is not the best time to visit the temples of Angkor as half the population of the country turns up there and you will find yourself with no peace to explore the temples.
Chat Preah Nengkal
    Held in early May, this is the Royal Ploughing ceremony, a ritual agricultural festival led by the royal family. It takes place near the Royal Palace in Phnom Penh.
International Workers' Day
    1 May

P'chum Ben
  Held in late September, this is a kind of All
  Souls' Day, when respects are paid to the dead
  through offerings made at wats.
HM the King's Birthday
  30 October to 1 November
Bon Om Tuk
  Held in early November, this celebrates the re-
  versal of the current of the Tonlé Sap river
  (with the onset of the dry season, water backed
  up in the Tonlé Sap lake begins to empty into
  the Mekong; in the wet season the reverse is
  the case). This is one of the most important festivals in the Khmer calendar and a wonderful
  time to be in Phnom Penh or Siem Reap, as
  boat races are held on the Tonlé Sap river and
  the moat around Angkor Wat.
Independence Day
  9 November

The Chinese inhabitants of Cambodia celebrate their New Year in late January or early
to mid-February – for the Vietnamese, this
is Tet. As many of Phnom Penh's businesses
are run by Chinese, commerce grinds to a
halt around this time.

ACTIVITIES
Tourism in Cambodia is still in its infancy
and as yet there is little in the way of activities besides sightseeing. Phnom Penh is one
exception as the large population of foreigners has led to a boom in leisure activities. You
can try go-carting, jet-skiing, tenpin bowling
or, if that all sounds a bit dull, firing a rocket-
propelled grenade. See the Activities section
in the Phnom Penh chapter for details.

The country is slowly establishing a network of national parks with visitor facilities. Ream and Bokor, on the south coast,
are the most accessible and interesting to
visit. See the Around Cambodia chapter for
details. Hiking and elephant rides are possible to a limited extent in Ratanakiri and
Mondulkiri, but you need a guide.

Snorkelling and diving are available in
Sihanoukville, but it is not as spectacular as
in Thailand. This is also where you will find
some of Cambodia's best beaches.

LANGUAGE COURSES
The only courses available in Cambodia at
present are in Khmer and these are aimed at

expat residents of Phnom Penh rather than
at travellers. If you are going to be based in
Phnom Penh for some time, however, it
would be well worth learning basic Khmer.
Ring the CDRI (☎ 368053) for information
about classes – courses run for two months
at a time. Also check out the notice board at
the FCC, where hourly lessons are often ad-
vertised.

WORK
Jobs are available in Phnom Penh and elsewhere around Cambodia. The obvious cate-
gories are English/French teaching work
and volunteer work with one of the many
NGOs operating in the country. There is a
lot of teaching work available for English-
language speakers.

For information about work opportunities with the NGOs call into the CCC (see
the Useful Organisations section earlier in
this chapter), which has a notice board for
positions vacant and may also be able to
give advice on where to look. If you are
thinking of applying for work with NGOs,
you should bring copies of your educational
certificates and work references with you.
However, most of the jobs available are
likely to be on a voluntary basis as most re-
cruiting for specialised positions is done in
home countries.

Other places to look for work include the
classifieds sections of the *Phnom Penh Post*
and the *Cambodia Daily*, and on the notice
board at the FCC.

Do not expect to make a lot of money
working in Cambodia, but if you want to
learn more about the country and help the
locals get the place up and running again, it
may well be a very worthwhile experience.

ACCOMMODATION
The accommodation situation in Cambodia
has changed immensely over the last five to
10 years. There are options to suit all budgets in Phnom Penh, and in Siem Reap and
Sihanoukville new hotels are springing up
everywhere. Battambang is the hotel capital
of Cambodia with a surfeit of rooms at ab-
surdly reasonable prices. Elsewhere around
Cambodia, options are fairly limited.

Budget hostels exist only in Phnom Penh, Siem Reap and Sihanoukville. Costs hover around US$3 for a bed. In other parts of Cambodia, the standard rate for the cheapest hotels is US$5 – in many places this will be the standard rate for all hotels in town.

In Phnom Penh and Siem Reap, which see a steady flow of traffic, hotels improve significantly once you start spending more than US$10. For US$15 or less it is usually possible to find an air-con room with satellite TV and attached bathroom. If you spend between US$20 and US$30 you can get something quite luxurious.

Top-end accommodation is only available in Phnom Penh and Siem Reap, but represents a significant leap in price for what aren't always significantly better rooms. There are several international standard hotels in Phnom Penh and a couple in Siem Reap.

FOOD

Cambodian food is closely related to the cuisine of neighbouring Thailand and Laos and, to a lesser extent, Vietnam, but there are some distinct local dishes. The overall consensus is that Khmer cooking is similar to Thai cooking but with fewer spices.

You can try inexpensive Khmer cuisine throughout the country at local markets and cheap restaurants. For more refined Khmer dining, the best restaurants are in Phnom Penh, Siem Reap and Battambang. In Phnom Penh and Siem Reap you also have the choice of excellent Thai, Vietnamese, Chinese, French and Mediterranean cooking.

Rice is the principal staple and the Battambang region is the country's rice bowl. Most Cambodian dishes are cooked in a wok, known locally as a *chhnang khteak*.

Local Food

A Cambodian meal almost always includes a soup, or *samla*, and this is eaten at the same time as the other courses. *Samla machou banle* is a popular fish soup with a sour flavour rather like the hot and sour dishes of neighbouring Thailand. Other soups include *samla chapek* (ginger-flavoured pork soup), *samla machou bangkang* (a prawn soup

closely related to the popular Thai *tom yam*) and *samla ktis* (a fish soup with coconut and pineapple).

Much of the fish eaten in Cambodia is freshwater, from the Tonlé Sap lake or Mekong River. *Trey aing* (grilled fish) is a Cambodian speciality (*aing* means 'grilled' in Khmer and can be applied to many dishes). Traditionally, the fish is eaten in pieces that are wrapped in lettuce or spinach leaves and dipped into a fish sauce known as *tuk trey*, a close relative of Vietnam's *nam pla* or *nuoc mam* but with the addition of ground peanuts. *Trey noueng phkea* is fish stuffed with small dried prawns, *trey chorm hoy* is steamed whole fish, and *trey chean noeung spei* is fried fish served with vegetables.

Cambodian 'salad' dishes are also popular and delicious although quite different from the western idea of a cold salad. *Phlea sach ko* is a beef and vegetable salad, flavoured with coriander, mint leaves and lemon grass. These three herbs find their way into many Cambodian dishes.

Khao phoune is one of the most common Cambodian dishes and is found everywhere from street stalls to homes. Closely related to Malaysia's *laksa* dishes, the fine rice noodles are prepared in a sauce enriched with coconut milk.

At weddings and other festivities, sweet specialities like *ansam chruk* (sticky rice balls stuffed with banana) are served. *Nom bat* and *nom kom* are sticky rice cakes, or there is *phleay*, a pastry and palm sugar concoction that is fried and rolled in grated coconut. Jackfruit is used to make a pudding known as *sangkcha khnor*.

Fast Food

There are no western fast food chains represented in Phnom Penh as yet, but there are a few local rip-offs. KFC (Khmer Fried Chicken?), Pizza House and Burger Hot are some of the more illustrious.

Vegetarian

If you are not a strict vegetarian and can deal with fish sauces and the like, you should have few problems ordering meals. In Phnom Penh many of the international restaurants feature vegetarian meals, though these are not budget options. In Khmer and Chinese restaurants, stir-fried vegetable dishes are readily available, as are vegetarian fried rice dishes. If you eat fish, you can sample Khmer cooking at its best.

Self-Catering

The French influence is most clearly seen in the delicious bread, baked every day and sold in the markets. It is very cheap at around 300r to 500r, depending on size. Phnom Penh's international supermarkets have excellent supplies of goodies such as cheese, peanut butter and cold meats. By supplementing these with some vegetables from the markets, you can put together your own meals at a very reasonable cost, although this is not as cheap and fun as eating at street stalls or markets.

DRINKS
Nonalcoholic Drinks

All the well-known soft drinks are available in Cambodia. There are also a lot of lesser known drinks for sale, most of them produced in other Asian countries. Locally produced mineral water is about 500r per bottle, cheaper if you buy six-packs.

In Phnom Penh, *tuk kak* (ice) is produced with treated water, but the transportation of it in huge blocks often involves dragging it along the ground. Most people don't worry about this though and it shows up in most cold drinks. Drinking tap water is to be avoided, especially in the provinces.

Coffee is sold in most restaurants. It is either served black or *cafe au lait* – with dollops of condensed milk, which makes it very sweet. Chinese-style tea is popular and in many Khmer and Chinese restaurants a pot of it will automatically appear for no extra charge as soon as you sit down.

Tikaloks are popular throughout Cambodia. They are a little like fruit smoothies and make a great way to wash down a big meal in the provinces. Stalls come out for the evening usually near markets and the drinks cost about 1000r to 2000r. Watch out for how much sugar goes in if you don't like sweet drinks, and pass on the offer of an egg if you don't want it super frothy.

Alcoholic Drinks

The local beer is Angkor, which is produced by an Australian joint venture company based in Sihanoukville. While not quite up to the standards of Beer Lao, it is a pretty good brew and costs from US$1.50 to US$2 for a big bottle in most restaurants and bars. Most Khmer restaurants have a bevy of 'beer girls', each of whom represents a beer brand. They are always friendly and will leave you alone if you prefer not to drink beer. Brands represented include Angkor, Heineken, Tiger, San Miguel, Carlsberg, VB, Foster's and Grolsch. Cans of beer sell for around US$1 in restaurants.

In Phnom Penh, foreign wines and spirits are sold at very reasonable prices at supermarkets. Wines start at about US$4, while the famous names of the spirit world cost between US$6 and US$10.

The local spirits are best avoided, though some expats say that Sra Special, a local whiskey-like concoction, is not bad. At around 2000r a bottle it's a cheap route to oblivion. There has also been a surge in the popularity of 'muscle wines', with enticing pictures of strongmen on the labels and names like Hercules, Great Strength and King Kong. They have more unknown substances in them than an Olympic medallist and should only be drunk with care.

ENTERTAINMENT
Pubs & Bars

Phnom Penh is the place for pubs and bars. Siem Reap has a couple of quiet options, but elsewhere in Cambodia, drinking takes place in market areas, in restaurants and in nightclubs.

Discos & Clubs

Again, Phnom Penh is the place for disco nightlife: there are several nightclubs that see a good mix of locals and expats. Nightlife in Phnom Penh tends not to get going until fairly late – after midnight sessions are the popular thing to do at weekends, after a leisurely meal and some drinks at a bar.

Outside Phnom Penh, nightlife is dominated by the Khmer nightclubs. These clubs are aimed at men, though it's unlikely that a foreign woman accompanied by a foreign man would have any trouble in these places. Lighting is low to the point of pitch black and the music alternates between a live band and a disc jockey (DJ), playing an eclectic mix of Khmer, Asian and western music. The pop tunes used to be a depressing combination of Sha La La La La and Aqua, but seem to be improving as the Thai influence becomes apparent. These clubs are a good place to try to learn traditional Khmer dances as locals are keen to show you the moves. However, be aware that the hostesses charge the men to dance with them, so you might want to wait until the slow music stops.

Traditional Dance
Public performances of Khmer traditional dance are few and far between. In Phnom Penh, the best place to see regular dance displays is at the Ecole de Beaux Arts (School of Fine Arts), where pupils practice every morning from about 7.30 to 9.30 am. Performances are also held in Siem Reap. It is worthwhile checking the local English-language newspapers for news of any upcoming events.

Cinemas
See the Entertainment section in the Phnom Penh chapter for information about venues that sometimes screen foreign films. Cinemas are best avoided. Even if you can understand the proceedings, Cambodia's cinemas tend to be scruffy, hot and sometimes dangerously overcrowded.

SPECTATOR SPORTS
Sports events are held from time to time at the Olympic Stadium in Phnom Penh, including a regular Sunday football league and occasional motocross races. Check the local English-language newspapers for news of events at the stadium. Kick boxing is popular in Cambodia and is identical to Thai boxing.

SHOPPING
The checked cotton scarves everyone wears on their heads, around their necks or, if bathing, around their midriffs, are known as *krama*. Fancier coloured versions are made of silk or a silk-cotton blend. Some of the finest cotton krama come from the Kompong Cham area.

For information on where in Phnom Penh to find antiques, silver items, jewellery, gems, colourful cloth for sarongs and *hols* (variegated silk shirts), and other interesting purchases, see Shopping in the Phnom Penh chapter. However, when buying antiques be very careful of fakes as they are extremely common in this part of the world. If the prices seem too good to be true, then they usually are and you'll end up with a modern copy.

The Shopping section in the Phnom Penh chapter also has information on buying handicrafts produced by Cambodian landmine victims, handicapped people and women's groups. The proceeds go to good causes and the products are of high quality.

The Chantiers Ecoles school in Siem Reap is spearheading a revival of Khmer skills in carving and silk weaving. See Things to See & Do in the Siem Reap chapter for information on visiting its shop.

Getting There & Away

AIR
Airports & Airlines
Cambodia has two international airports: Phnom Penh's Pochentong airport and Siem Reap airport, which serves visitors to Angkor.

Flights to Cambodia are quite limited, and most of them are from neighbouring capitals. Bangkok has the most flights to Phnom Penh, and it is usually possible to get on a flight with any of the airlines at short notice. If you are heading to Cambodia for a short holiday and want a minimum of fuss, Thai Airways International (THAI) offers the best connections from major cities in Europe, the USA and Australia. Other regional centres with flights to Cambodia are Singapore, Kuala Lumpur, Hong Kong, Ho Chi Minh City (Saigon), Vientiane and Guangzhou. There are no direct flights to or from Australia, Europe or the USA, but both Air France and Aeroflot offer indirect services via Paris and Moscow respectively.

Buying Tickets
When buying airline tickets, it is always worth shopping around widely as many agents have many deals available with many airlines. Quotes for the same flight can differ significantly because one agent imposes a hefty commission while another gets a lower price from the airline. The time of year has a major impact on flight prices. If you are starting out from Europe, the USA or Australia, figure on prices rising dramatically over Christmas and during July and August, and dropping significantly during lax periods of business like February, June or October.

Thailand is the most convenient gateway from which to arrive in Cambodia. In Bangkok, the Banglamphu area, in particular Khao San Rd, is a good place to buy tickets for Cambodia.

Travellers with Special Needs
If you have any special needs, you should let the airline know as soon as possible and make a point of reminding it when you re-confirm and when you check in. Airlines can cater for victims of accidents, for passengers travelling with babies, for vegetarians and for almost any other needs, provided they are given notice.

Children under the age of two travel for 10% of the standard fare, or free with some airlines. 'Skycots', nappies (diapers) and baby food can be provided with some advance notice. Children aged between two and 12 generally travel at between half and two-thirds the full fare; they are allowed a baggage allowance.

Departure Tax
There is a hefty departure tax of US$20 on all international flights out of Pochentong airport in Phnom Penh. Well, someone has to pay for the damage inflicted during the fighting of July 1997. From Siem Reap, the international departure tax is US$10.

The USA
Competition between Asian airlines flying to and through South-East Asia has resulted in discounted tickets. Good places to start looking are the travel sections of daily newspapers such as the *New York Times*, the *Chicago Tribune*, the *LA Times*, or whatever your local newspaper is. Agents such as Council Travel and Student Travel Network are well established and have offices in most major US cities. Council on International Educational Exchange (CIEE) and STA Travel are other travel agent chains that are well represented.

From the US west coast, fares to Bangkok cost around US$700/1000 one-way/return. However, promotional fares are sometimes as cheap as US$600 return. Flights from the east coast are more expensive and it might work out cheaper to fly to London and arrange a cheap flight onward from there.

Canada
Check with the travel sections of newspapers like the *Vancouver Sun* and the *Toronto*

Air Travel Glossary

Cancellation Penalties If you have to cancel or change a discounted ticket, there are often heavy penalties involved; insurance can sometimes be taken out against these penalties. Some airlines impose penalties on regular tickets as well, particularly against 'no-show' passengers.

Courier Fares Businesses often need to send urgent documents or freight securely and quickly. Courier companies hire people to accompany the package through customs and, in return, offer a discount ticket which is sometimes a phenomenal bargain. However, you may have to surrender all your baggage allowance and take only carry-on luggage.

Full Fares Airlines traditionally offer 1st class (coded F), business class (coded J) and economy class (coded Y) tickets. These days there are so many promotional and discounted fares available that few passengers pay full economy fare.

Lost Tickets If you lose your airline ticket an airline will usually treat it like a travellers cheque and, after inquiries, issue you with another one. Legally, however, an airline is entitled to treat it like cash and if you lose it then it's gone forever. Take good care of your tickets.

Onward Tickets An entry requirement for many countries is that you have a ticket out of the country. If you're unsure of your next move, the easiest solution is to buy the cheapest onward ticket to a neighbouring country or a ticket from a reliable airline which can later be refunded if you do not use it.

Open-Jaw Tickets These are return tickets where you fly out to one place but return from another. If available, this can save you backtracking to your arrival point.

Overbooking Since every flight has some passengers who fail to show up, airlines often book more passengers than they have seats. Usually excess passengers make up for the no-shows, but occasionally somebody gets 'bumped' onto the next available flight. Guess who it is most likely to be? The passengers who check in late.

Promotional Fares These are officially discounted fares, available from travel agencies or direct from the airline.

Reconfirmation If you don't reconfirm your flight at least 72 hours prior to departure, the airline may delete your name from the passenger list. Ring to find out if your airline requires reconfirmation.

Restrictions Discounted tickets often have various restrictions on them – such as needing to be paid for in advance and incurring a penalty to be altered. Others are restrictions on the minimum and maximum period you must be away.

Round-the-World Tickets RTW tickets give you a limited period (usually a year) in which to circumnavigate the globe. You can go anywhere the carrying airlines go, as long as you don't backtrack. The number of stopovers or total number of separate flights is decided before you set off and they usually cost a bit more than a basic return flight.

Transferred Tickets Airline tickets cannot be transferred from one person to another. Travellers sometimes try to sell the return half of their ticket, but officials can ask you to prove that you are the person named on the ticket. On an international flight tickets are compared with passports.

Travel Periods Ticket prices vary with the time of year. There is a low (off-peak) season and a high (peak) season, and often a low-shoulder season and a high-shoulder season as well. Usually the fare depends on your outward flight – if you depart in the high season and return in the low season, you pay the high-season fare.

Globe & Mail for details of agents and the ticket prices they offer. Travel CUTS is probably the most well established agency chain, and it has offices throughout Canada. The frequency of flights between Hong Kong and Vancouver means it may work out cheaper to go via Hong Kong to Phnom Penh if in a rush. Travellers from the eastern side of Canada might want to consider flying to London and then arranging a cheap flight from there to Bangkok.

Australia

The best agencies to check ticket prices with in Australia are STA Travel and Flight Centre. It may be a good idea to compare the prices they give you with prices posted in the travel sections of daily newspapers such as *The Australian*, *The Age* in Melbourne and the *Sydney Morning Herald*, among others.

There are usually peak and off-peak rates for flights from Australia to South-East Asia. The peak season applies during the December to January school holiday period – flights can often be heavily booked at this time as well as more expensive.

Return fares from Sydney and Melbourne to Bangkok cost from A$700 to A$900.

New Zealand

Tickets between New Zealand and Bangkok are available with a number of major airlines. Prices start at about US$500/750 for one-way/return.

The UK

The Sunday editions of most of the major daily newspapers have travel sections with advertising for ticket prices to South-East Asia. The London listings magazine *Time Out* is also a good place to start your search.

The UK is one of the world's best places for picking up cheap tickets, and some of the best agencies for budget flights to South-East Asia are Campus Travel, Trailfinders and STA Travel. Many budget fares are with airlines that fly via Eastern Europe or the Middle East. Round-trip prices of around UK£350 are available with airlines such as Biman Bangladesh Airlines, Balkan, Kuwait Airways and Qatar Airways. A number of cheap airlines offer a free stopover in their home city – Czech Airlines is a good option as you get the opportunity to visit Prague. One-way flights start at about UK£200. Return flights to other Asian gateways are often a little more expensive, starting at about UK£400, although flight prices to Hong Kong seem to have tumbled in the wake of the handover to China. It is also worth keeping an eye out for promotional fares during the slow periods of business in February and June.

Asia

All travellers going to Cambodia will have to either pass through or fly from one of the regional air centres: Bangkok is the most likely option, but not the only one. If you are looking to arrange tickets in Cambodia for onward travel, it is cheaper to buy from a travel agent than through the airline. See Information in the Phnom Penh chapter for recommended travel agents.

Flights between Phnom Penh and Bangkok are available daily with THAI, Royal Air Cambodge (RAC) and Bangkok Airways. RAC charges US$125/240 one-way/return; THAI charges US$142/240; and Bangkok Airways flights are US$142/284. Bangkok Airways and RAC also fly daily to Siem Reap, charging US$155/310. There is talk of direct flights starting up between Phuket and Siem Reap, so keep an eye out for developments if this route suits you. All these prices were quoted in Phnom Penh. When purchasing a ticket in Bangkok, you will find prices are cheaper with fares starting at about 3000/5500B *(baht)*.

Vietnam Airlines does the short hop from Ho Chi Minh City to Phnom Penh for US$65/125; RAC charges US$65/130. Flights to Hanoi are expensive as you get charged the price of the ticket to Ho Chi Minh City plus the foreigner price of a domestic ticket from there to Hanoi, making it essentially two separate journeys.

Dragonair flies between Hong Kong and Phnom Penh, charging US$300/440. RAC has flights to Guangzhou in southern China for US$250/390.

Silk Air and RAC have flights from Singapore to Phnom Penh. RAC tickets cost about US$250/360, while Silk Air flights are about US$260/440. Flights between Kuala Lumpur and Phnom Penh are available with Malaysia Airlines for US$182/313 and RAC for US$190/300.

Flights between Vientiane and Phnom Penh cost US$125/250 with Lao Aviation and RAC.

LAND
Thailand
Poipet The land border between Cambodia and Thailand at Poipet was opened to foreigners in February 1998. An increasing number of travellers have come and gone this way since, and the roads from the crossing to either Siem Reap or Battambang are safe, but in terrible condition. International donors are upgrading the road between Poipet and Phnom Penh, but they will take a few years yet, so in the meantime prepare for a bumpy ride.

To enter at Poipet you need to obtain a Cambodian visa, which costs US$20, from Bangkok in advance. You can arrange this or you can get a travel agent to do it for a small commission.

Coming from Bangkok, there are two trains a day from Hualamphong train station to the town of Aranya Prathet, which cost 48B, but the 5.50 am is the one to go for unless you want to end up spending the night in a border town. There are also regular bus services to Aranya Prathet (144B with aircon and around 75B without). From Aranya Prathet you can take a *songthaew* (pick-up truck) the 4km to the border for about 5B. Some travel agencies around the Khao San Rd in Bangkok offer minibus services direct to the border for around 300B. Once over the border in Poipet you can jump in a pick-up to Sisophon for about 5000r in the cab or 3000r on the back, although you'll have to negotiate. Once in Sisophon, you can make for either Siem Reap or Battambang. (See the Siem Reap chapter and the Battambang section in the Around Cambodia chapter for more details.) It is worth noting that the road between Sisophon and Siem Reap can be-

come impassable at times during the wet season. If the road is impassable, you could head to Battambang and then take a fast boat from there to Siem Reap.

Leaving Cambodia, there is no departure tax by land, but guards may ask for a dollar. From Poipet, you must take a *túk-túk* (motorised three-wheeled pedicab) or songthaew to Aranya Prathet, from where there are two trains a day to Bangkok at 6.40 am and 1.45 pm, and buses every hour from 4 am until 10 pm.

Koh Kong The coastal border between Krong Koh Kong (Koh Kong Town) and Trat Province in Thailand is also open.

Coming from Bangkok you need to take a bus to Trat from platform 10 at the city's Eastern bus station (169B; five to six hours). Buses depart every half an hour from 7 am until 11.30 pm. If you take the 11.30 pm bus you can make it to Koh Kong in Cambodia in time to catch the 8 am boat to Sihanoukville and avoid spending the night in this seedy frontier town. Another convenient option for travellers staying in the Khao San Rd area is to take one of the Koh Chang minibuses as far as Trat. This might work out slightly more expensive than taking a public bus, but it saves you the hassle of getting to the Eastern bus station in Bangkok.

From Trat you can either take a minibus straight to the border at Hat Lek for 100B, charter a taxi there for about 400B, or go in stages, first to Khlong Yai and then to the border. Take either a songthaew (50B) or a seat in a share taxi (60B) to Khlong Yai and then another songthaew to Hat Lek for 30B. The border opens at 7 am so you can stay the night in Trat and still make the boat if you get up early enough. Alternatively, stay the night in Koh Kong. Once in Cambodia you can take a taxi to Neang Kok, the town just over the river from Koh Kong, for around 30B and then cross the river by boat for a further 20B a person, although make sure you are agreed on this price before you jump aboard. Fast boats from Koh Kong to Sihanoukville (500B or US$15; four hours) leave at 8 am. Make sure you don't get on a fast boat going to Sre Ambel or you'll end up in a smugglers' port some distance from Sihanoukville. From Sihanoukville there are cheap air-con buses to Phnom Penh: see the Sihanoukville section in the Around Cambodia chapter and the Getting There & Away section in the Phnom Penh chapter for details.

Leaving Cambodia, there is no real reason to stay in Koh Kong. Get off the boat at the commune of Pak Long, just before Koh Kong, and you can take a speedboat through the mangroves to the border (100B; 30 minutes). Immigration officials check your passports at Pak Long, so you will know when to abandon ship. This way you don't have to mess about with taxis in Koh Kong. If you stay on the boat right into Koh Kong town, you will have to cross the river and then take either a taxi or moto (motorcycle with driver) to the border. Once over the border you can take a songthaew/taxi combination to Trat and from Trat there are regular buses to Bangkok. However, if you want to get to Bangkok that night you will have to move fast as there are hourly buses through the day until 6 pm but then a gap until 11 pm. Alternatively, stay the night in Trat and then head to Ko Chang or the surrounding islands the following day.

Motos to and from the port in Sihanoukville cost about 1000r from the guesthouse area and nearer 2000r from the town centre.

Vietnam

The only fully functioning land crossing between Vietnam and Cambodia is at Moc Bai in Vietnam. The trip by taxi between Phnom Penh and Ho Chi Minh City should only take about six to seven hours. If you take the bus expect to be delayed at the border for a couple of hours while the locals are shaken down. You must have Moc Bai stamped on your Vietnam visa or you will not be allowed to enter the country, even if you plead. See Getting There & Away in the Phnom Penh chapter for details.

Coming from Vietnam you can easily arrange share taxis in the Pham Ngu Lao area of Ho Chi Minh City for US$5, and a number of the cafes in this area also run daily minibus services. Cheaper still, you can take a local bus to Tay Ninh from the Ben Tanh bus station for 3000d (dong) and ask to be let off at the turning for Moc Bai, the Vietnamese side of the border with Cambodia. Moto drivers can take you the rest of the way for about 10,000d.

There are daily cargo boats that run along the Lower, or Bassac, River between Phnom Penh and the Vietnamese border town of Chau Doc. It is not yet a legal entry or exit point for foreigners, but the boat operators say a few *barangs* (foreigners) have travelled this way. The boats leave at 6.30 am from a port called Psar Takhmau, near Takhmau, which is a small town about 10km south of Phnom Penh. The cost is 30,000r for the five hour trip.

Laos

At the time of writing, the land border with Laos is not officially open to westerners as the Lao authorities are paranoid about security in Cambodia. However, if security improves between Kratie and Stung Treng, and with the Lao authorities encouraging tourists in ever greater numbers, it should open during the lifetime of this book. Check the situation in Phnom Penh or Vientiane. Travellers have tried it, but have been turned back by Cambodian immigration officers as they have no exit stamp to issue. However, others have succeeded in blagging their way through.

ORGANISED TOURS

In the early days of Cambodia travel, organised tours were a near necessity. The situation has changed over the last four or five years and it is now much easier to organise your own trip. Budget and mid-range travellers in particular are best off going it alone. If you are on a tight schedule, you may like to book a return flight to Siem Reap before you leave to ensure that you get the time you want at Angkor. Once you get to Angkor, guides and drivers are plentiful.

All the same, Cambodia is not the easiest of countries to travel in and some travellers will no doubt feel more secure visiting with a tour. Some major operators are listed below.

From Australia

Orbitours (☎ 02-9221 7322, fax 02-9221 7425), GPO Box 3309, Sydney 2000, is a major tour operator for English-speaking visitors. It operates tours ex-Bangkok, and can also combine Cambodia with the other countries in Indochina.

Intrepid Travel (☎ 1300 360 667, fax 03-9419 4426), at 13 Spring St, Fitzroy 3065, has tours to South-East Asia, including a week-long trip to Cambodia.

From the UK

Regent Holidays (☎ 0117-921 1711, fax 0117-925 4866), 15 John St, Bristol BS1 1DE, is a major operator from the UK. Explore Worldwide (☎ 01252-76 0100, fax 01252-76 0001), 1 Frederick St, Aldershot, Hants, GU11 1LQ, also offers Cambodian extensions to its Vietnam trips, but the Cambodian trips are not cheap.

From Thailand

In Bangkok, Diethelm Travel is the major operator for tours to Indochina. Its office in Bangkok can be found at the Kian Gwan Building II, 140/1 Wireless Rd, Bangkok 10500 (☎ 255 9150, fax 256 0248). Diethelm also has offices in Phnom Penh (see Travel Agencies in the Phnom Penh chapter for details) and is well represented in capitals throughout the region.

WARNING

The information in this chapter is particularly vulnerable to change: prices for international travel are volatile, routes are introduced and cancelled, schedules change, special deals come and go, and rules and visa requirements are amended. Airlines and governments seem to take a perverse pleasure in making price structures and regulations as complicated as possible. You should check directly with the airline or a travel agent to make sure you understand how a fare (and ticket you may buy) works. In addition, the travel industry is highly competitive and there are many lurks and perks.

The upshot of this is that you should get opinions, quotes and advice from as many airlines and travel agents as possible before you part with your hard-earned cash. The details given in this chapter should be regarded as pointers and are not a substitute for your own careful, up-to-date research.

Getting Around

As security has improved throughout the country, the ways and means of getting around Cambodia have also increased. Domestic flights offer a quick if expensive way to travel around the country. Travel between Phnom Penh and Siem Reap is possible by fast boat and there are similar services running from the capital to both Kompong Cham and Kratie. There are also some slow boats, but they are slow, even by Cambodian standards.

Road travel is now generally safe, although after some journeys your body might well disagree. Road journeys are often long and dusty, but are certainly the cheapest way to get about. The road network that runs from Poipet via Siem Reap to Phnom Penh is in the process of being upgraded, so journey times will gradually come down. Banditry remains a problem in remote areas, so check local conditions in villages along the way, particularly if riding a motorcycle.

Train travel for tourists was long forbidden, and for good reason: three western travellers were kidnapped and subsequently killed by the Khmer Rouge in 1994 while on the way to Sihanoukville. It is once again possible; but while extremely cheap, the journey times are disturbingly slow when compared with the roads.

For sights around Phnom Penh, there is now an effective bus network operating, or it is possible to arrange share taxis or to rent motorcycles inexpensively. When visiting the temples of Angkor, it is required by law that you are accompanied by a guide, which effectively means hiring a moto driver or a taxi to get around. However, these rules are likely to be relaxed now the Khmer Rouge threat has ended.

AIR
Domestic Air Services
Royal Air Cambodge (RAC), established as a joint venture with Malaysia Helicopter Services in 1994, has flights to limited destinations around Cambodia. Siem Reap is well serviced and it is usually possible to get on a flight at short notice. Some travellers even manage to get a flight to Angkor immediately upon arrival at Phnom Penh's Pochentong airport. Demand for flights to other destinations around the country often exceeds supply; it is not always easy to get seats. However, the situation has improved somewhat with the arrival of President Airlines on the scene. President Airlines operates flights to Siem Reap, Battambang and Stung Treng, and may well add destinations if the demand is there.

RAC's fleet comprises a Boeing 737-400, which is used for international flights, and several ATR 72s.

There are seven flights a day from Phnom Penh to Siem Reap (US$55/110 one-way/return). For Battambang, there are five flights a week (US$45/90); a couple of them go via Siem Reap. Flights to Ratanakiri are scheduled five times a week (US$55/100). Other destinations are: Koh Kong, twice a week (US$50/100); Stung Treng, three times a week (US$45/90); and Mondulkiri, up to three times a week (US$50/100). Buses have replaced regular flights to Sihanoukville.

It should be noted that RAC schedules change regularly as planes go in and out of service. Check the current timetable with the RAC office in Phnom Penh.

President Airlines has fewer flights available, but you can count on at least three a week to Siem Reap and Battambang and one a week to Stung Treng and Ratanakiri.

The baggage weight limit for domestic flights is only 10kg per passenger, but unless you are way over the limit it is unlikely you will have to pay excess baggage.

The airport tax for domestic flights is US$4 from regional airports and a whopping US$10 from Pochentong Airport in Phnom Penh.

Helicopter
If you're absolutely loaded or are on an expense account, you might consider chartering

Driving up Prices

At the time of going to press, the Government had introduced both a sales tax and road tax, which amounted to 20% of income earned by pick-up, taxi and minibus operators and is likely to be passed on to travellers using transport in Cambodia. When it comes to travelling overland by pick-up trucks, the increases may be higher still, as the government has passed a law to force all right-hand drive vehicles to be converted to left-hand drive. More than three-quarters of the pick-ups have been smuggled in from Thailand and are right-hand drive. The upshot is: do not be surprised if overland journeys cost somewhat more than those quoted throughout this book.

a Soviet-built helicopter for sightseeing or aerial photography. A round-trip excursion from Phnom Penh to Angkor for up to a dozen people costs around US$6000. Helicopters can be hired by the hour for around US$2000. However, most of Cambodia's chopper fleet is grounded and the few that are still air-worthy are certainly not that safe.

BUS

Bus services have improved immeasurably in the last few years and the situation will get better as highways are upgraded. The services used most regularly by foreigners are those from Phnom Penh to Sihanoukville and Ho Chi Minh City (Saigon). Those to Sihanoukville are modern air-con buses, but to Vietnam they are often old rattletraps and it is significantly quicker to travel by share taxi.

There is now a clean and comfortable bus service to towns and villages in the vicinity of Phnom Penh. Operated by the Ho Wah Genting Bus Company, prices are very cheap and English-speaking staff can help you get on the right bus. See the Phnom Penh chapter for more details on the services to towns such as Kompong Chhnang, Udong and Takeo.

Minibuses go to Vietnam and around the south coast, but tend to be chartered by Khmer families for outings. The exceptions are those that run to Kompongs Cham, Thom and Chhnang, and Kampot.

TRAIN

Cambodia's rail system is fairly primitive, but is once again open to foreigners and is ludicrously cheap at about 15r a kilometre, or less than half a US cent! Trains travel at an average 20km/h and mechanical problems can mean unscheduled overnight stops. Bridges are not always maintained (as proven by the collapse of a bridge in Kampot in early 1998) and the ride is often as bumpy as on some of the roads. That said, the locals who use the trains regularly are very welcoming to foreigners who choose to travel this way.

The rail network consists of around 645km of single-track metre-gauge lines. The 382km north-western line, built before WWII, links Phnom Penh with Pursat (165km from the capital), Battambang (274km from the capital) and Sisophon. The line used to continue to Poipet on the Thai border, but it has fallen into disrepair. The 263km south-western line, which was completed in 1969, connects the capital with Takeo (75km from Phnom Penh), Kampot (160km from the capital), Kep (get off at Damnak Chang Aeu) and the port of Sihanoukville. The best journeys to consider undertaking are the six hours to Kampot or the section between Battambang and Pursat, which is a way of avoiding the dreadful section of National Hwy 5.

The civil war during much of the 1990s led to some unique developments in the Cambodian rail system. Each train was equipped with a tin-roofed, armoured carriage sporting a huge machine gun and numerous gun ports in its sides. In addition, the first two flat-bed carriages of the train operated as mine sweepers. Travel on the first carriage was free and on the second half-price, and, despite the risks, these options were very popular. Gladly for the Cambodian people these precautions are no longer necessary.

TRUCK, SHARE TAXI & JEEP

Long-distance pick-up trucks take on the dreadful roads to Siem Reap, Battambang and the north-west, and to Kratie, Stung Treng and the north-east. You can sit in the cab or, if you are feeling bold, on the back, and the trucks leave when seriously full. If you are on the back, try to get a seat on rice sacks as it is more comfortable, and carry a head covering and sunscreen to protect yourself from the heat. It is best to arrange pick-ups yourself as it is less expensive than getting a guesthouse to organise it. You often have to haggle patiently to ensure you pay a fair price.

Share taxis are widely available for hire in Cambodia nowadays and many travellers use them to get to Vietnam and to get around the south coast. For the major destinations you can hire them individually or pay for a seat and wait for other passengers to turn up. Guesthouses are also very helpful when it comes to arranging share taxis.

When using pick-up trucks or taxis, it is an advantage to travel in numbers as you can buy spare seats to make the journey more comfortable.

In the remote north-east of the country where the roads are so bad they look sculpted, sturdy Russian jeeps are the transport of choice. These seem to keep moving in even the most nightmarish conditions.

As a basic rule, pick-ups and jeeps are best on bad roads and taxis best on sealed roads. All these vehicles depart Phnom Penh from roads between the Psar Thmei (New Market) and Monivong Blvd for the majority of destinations around Cambodia, including those in the north and west of the country. Vehicles heading south to Kampot and Sihanoukville, however, go from Psar Dang Kor (Dang Kor Market) in the south-west of the city. Vehicles heading to Prey Veng, Svay Rieng and Vietnam go from just over the Monivong Bridge in the south of the city.

Road Distances (kms)

	Phnom Penh	Siem Reap	Battambang	Poipet	Sihanoukville	Kampot	Kompong Chhnang	Kompong Cham	Kratie	Stung Treng	Ban Lung	Moc Bai
Phnom Penh	---											
Siem Reap	311	---										
Battambang	293	183	---									
Poipet	422	152	129	---								
Sihanoukville	232	538	523	680	---							
Kampot	148	456	441	598	105	---						
Kompong Chhnang	91	399	202	331	321	239	---					
Kompong Cham	120	282	413	542	350	268	152	---				
Kratie	343	510	641	662	578	496	377	228	---			
Stung Treng	508	670	801	822	738	656	537	388	171	---		
Ban Lung	673	835	966	987	903	821	702	553	325	165	---	
Moc Bai	165	473	457	587	395	297	256	285	513	673	838	---

CAR & MOTORCYCLE

Cambodia's highways are conveniently numbered from one to seven. National Hwy 1 links Phnom Penh with Ho Chi Minh City via Svay Rieng and the Moc Bai border crossing, which is 5km east of the Cambodian town of Bavet. National Hwy 2 heads south from Phnom Penh, passing through Takhmau and Takeo on its way to Vietnam's An Giang Province and the city of Chau Doc. National Hwy 3 links the capital with the southern coastal city of Kampot. National Hwy 4 is the fastest road in the entire country and it connects Phnom Penh and the country's only port, Sihanoukville, which is on the Gulf of Thailand, southwest of the capital.

National Hwy 5 heads north from Phnom Penh, circling around to the south of the Tonlé Sap (Great Lake) and passing through Kompong Chhnang, Pursat, Battambang and Sisophon on its way northwest to the Thai frontier. National Hwy 6 crosses the Tonlé Sap river at the Japanese Bridge, heading north and then north-west on a route that goes to the north of the Tonlé Sap lake and passes through Kompong Thom, Siem Reap and Sisophon on its way to Thailand. National Hwy 7 splits from National Hwy 6 at Skuon, heading eastward to Kompong Cham and eventually to Memot, Snuol, Kratie, Stung Treng and the Lao border.

Many of these highways are in horrible shape, the one most commonly encountered by travellers being Hwy 6 between Siem Reap and Sisophon or Kompong Thom. Most of the time is spent travelling in the rice fields to avoid massive potholes! And these aren't even the worst roads in the country (see the boxed text 'Highways from Hell').

However, the international community is funding a massive project to redevelop the roads linking Thailand to Vietnam via Siem Reap and Phnom Penh, and also Hwy 7 north to Laos, including a major bridge over the Mekong River at Kompong Cham. Once this is complete, the map of overland travel in Indochina will be completely redrawn, but this work probably won't be completed for several years.

Road Rules

If there are road rules in Cambodia it is doubtful that anyone is following them. The best advice if you drive a car or ride a motorbike in Cambodia is to take nothing for granted and assume that your fellow motorists are visually challenged psychopaths. Stop before crossings and develop a habit of constant vigilance. Phnom Penh is one place where, amid all the chaos, traffic police take issue with westerners breaking even the most trivial rules. Obvious ones to look out for include no left turn signs and travelling with your headlights on during the day, although strangely, it doesn't seem to be illegal for Cambodians to travel without headlights at night. See Dangers & Annoyances in the Phnom Penh chapter for details of possible fines and how to get out of paying them.

Rental

Car hire is only available with a driver and is only really useful for sightseeing in Phnom Penh and Angkor. This is for the best, given the risks entailed in driving yourself around Cambodia. If you are working in Phnom Penh you may end up driving a 4WD or car, but you will certainly need to drive with more care than at home – in Phnom Penh traffic is a law unto itself and in the provinces roads can resemble roller coasters. If you have your own vehicle, do not attempt interprovincial travel at night.

Motorcycles are available for rent in Phnom Penh and Sihanoukville, but not in Siem Reap, as for the time being foreigners are forbidden to ride motorcycles without a driver. Costs are US$4 per day for 50cc to 100cc motorcycles and US$7 for a 250cc dirt bike. Some rental shops even have 800cc Honda Shadows available for US$12. In Siem Reap, motorbikes with driver are available to whisk you around the temples for about US$6 to US$8 a day.

Drive cautiously as medical facilities are less than adequate in Cambodia and traffic is erratic, particularly in Phnom Penh, where anarchy would be too constructive a word to

Highways from Hell

Cambodia has one of the most pathetic road systems in Asia, with many of the country's so-called national highways in a horrendous state of disrepair. Many of the roads around the country have not been maintained since the 1960s, and in some places the resultant damage from war, weather and wear and tear has been massive. There are plans, and better still funds, to upgrade some of the more important highways linking Cambodia's major cities to both Thailand and Vietnam, but even with help from the Asian Development Bank (ADB) it is unlikely anything will be completed any time soon. For now, travelling around Cambodia remains something like a steeplechase with some fast bits, some bumpy bits, and many vehicles failing far before the final hurdle.

Black cab drivers in London pride themselves on knowing every street in the city: indeed the only way they get the job is to pass a tough test of their knowledge. But that's nothing compared to the average Cambodian cabbie who has to know every pothole in the road just to keep his vehicle alive. Experienced drivers can shave an hour or two off longer journeys, while an amateur can break an axle just a few kilometres down the road. Unfortunately, there is no real trick to telling who can drive and who can't before you start the journey. However, the choice of vehicle is a start and for the most part you'll find you are better off in a pick-up truck than a taxi or minibus, as pick-ups have 4WD. That said, if the road is really shocking, it may actually be an advantage to travel by taxi as they are lighter: an overladen pick-up is more likely to come a cropper in the big holes.

Entering Cambodia at Poipet, the visitor soon gets a taste of what to expect: the section of road between Sisophon and Siem Reap is a good indicator of what is to come, though it is definitely one of the shorter stretches you have to look forward to. While bouncing and bumping their way around Cambodia, many a traveller has engaged in debate as to which is the worst of the many diabolical roads. A Lonely Planet poll came up with the following 'top five' – Cambodia's highways from hell:

- Kompong Cham to Snuol – this is 130km of pain and anguish, made worse by the possibility of bandits on the section between Memot and Snuol.
- Siem Reap to Sisophon – the most commonly travelled of Cambodia's godforsaken roads; take comfort that it doesn't get much worse than this.
- Stung Treng to Ban Lung – as on the Siem Reap to Sisophon stretch, most drivers prefer to leave the road altogether, careering through the jungle at breakneck speed.
- Kratie to Stung Treng – arguably the most insecure road in the country, it doesn't help you to relax knowing that some of the mighty holes could leave you stranded on the roadside for some time.
- Kompong Thom to Siem Reap – another commonly encountered route that was once well surfaced; the holes aren't huge but they are regular enough to leave you in pain by the end.

The good news is that there are some half-decent highways in the country, including National Hwy 4 to Sihanoukville and the road from Phnom Penh to Kompong Cham. The bad news, if you wanted more, is that once you leave these 'major' (top five) roads, it gets a lot, lot worse, particularly in the wet season. Try the road from Sen Monorom to the Bou Sraa Falls in October and you may, in time, learn to appreciate the national highways.

describe how people drive. If you have never ridden a motorbike before, the capital is not the best place to start, but once out of the city it does get easier. If jumping in at the deep end, make sure you are under the supervision of someone who knows how to ride.

The advantage of motorcycle travel is that it allows you complete freedom of movement. You can stop in small villages that westerners rarely visit (you will be assured of a lively reception) and a motorbike is great for visiting out-of-town attractions in the Phnom Penh area. It is now possible to take motorcycles upcountry for short tours, but take care if intending to ride to Siem Reap, Battambang and the north-east as road conditions are dire and security more of an issue because of military checkpoints and journey times.

For those with a reasonable amount of experience, Cambodia offers some of the best roads anywhere in the world for dirt biking, particularly in Mondulkiri and Ratanakiri. For those who don't want to ride that far, the road up to Bokor Hill Station near Kampot is exhilarating.

Security

Travelling and living in Cambodia, it is easy to lull yourself into a false sense of security and assume that down every rural road is yet another friendly village. However, even with the demise of the Khmer Rouge, banditry remains a problem in rural areas. When travelling in your own vehicle and particularly by motorcycle in rural areas, make certain you check the latest security information in communities along the way.

You may encounter military checkpoints on Cambodia's roads. For checkpoint security tips, see the Dangers & Annoyances section in the Facts for the Visitor chapter. Other general security suggestions include:

- Travel in numbers.
- When in a group, stay close together in case of any incident or accident.
- Don't be a cheapskate with petrol – to run out in a rural area could jeopardise your safety, especially if you get stranded overnight.
- Do not travel at night.
- Try to get hold of a helmet if you are going on a long journey or travelling at high speed.
- Always carry a rope for towing on longer journeys in case you break down. Things like camera straps, sarongs and *krama* (scarves) just aren't strong enough, although a couple of trusty krama are the best if you are really stuck.
- Carry a basic repair kit, including some tyre levers, a puncture repair kit and a pump.
- Do not smoke marijuana or drink alcohol and drive.
- Keep your eyes firmly fixed on the road; potholes eat people for fun in Cambodia.

BICYCLE

Cambodia doesn't see many international cyclists passing through, as you need muscles of steel to deal with some of the roads. Security concerns that apply to car and motorbike travel go double for bicycles. Mountain biking would be the only way to go and may begin to take off in parts of the north-east over the coming years.

HITCHING

Hitching is never entirely safe in any country in the world, and we don't recommend it. Travellers who decide to hitch should

MARTIN HARRIS

River travel is an important part of the transport system, with services between Phnom Penh and Siem Reap a favourite with foreigners.

understand that they are taking a small but potentially serious risk. People who do choose to hitch will be safer if they travel in pairs and let someone know where they are planning to go.

There is a severe shortage of transport in Cambodia, so most trucks – the only vehicles other than large buses able to negotiate the country's dilapidated roads – are likely to be extremely crowded. If you do hitch, expect to pay for your ride.

BOAT

Cambodia's 1900km of navigable waterways are an important element in the country's transportation system. Phnom Penh, some 320km from the mouth of the Mekong River, can be reached by ocean-going vessels with a draft of less than 3.3m. North of the capital, the Mekong is navigable as far north as Kratie, and from July to January boats can make it as far as Stung Treng.

The most popular boat services with foreigners are those that run between Phnom Penh and Siem Reap. The new express services do the trip in as little as four hours. Although often overcrowded, they remain the most popular method of travel between these destinations, and it is pretty pleasant lying dozing on the roof. There are also fast-boat services heading north up the Mekong to Kompong Cham, Kratie and, at certain times of year, Stung Treng. In the west of the country, fast boats run between Siem Reap and Battambang when the water level allows.

Slow-boat services run the same routes as fast boats, but often take many more hours, even a day or two if you are unlucky, to do the journey. They are also unstable and have been known to sink in the past. They are only worth considering between Kratie and Stung Treng.

For more information, see the Getting There & Away section of the Phnom Penh chapter.

Many travellers also use the fast boat between Sihanoukville and Koh Kong as a way of travelling between Thailand and Cambodia. See the Getting There & Away chapter for details.

LOCAL TRANSPORT

Taxi

Whereas taxi hire was once only available through government ministries, there are now many private operators working throughout Cambodia. Guesthouses, hotels and travel agents can arrange them for sightseeing. Even in Phnom Penh, however, you'll be hard pressed to find a taxi for short hops, unless leaving popular nightspots late.

Moto

Motos are small motorcycles and their drivers almost universally wear a baseball cap. They are a quick way of making short hops around towns and cities. Prices range from 500r to US$1, depending on the distance and town. Most journeys are about 1000r; expect to pay an extra 500r or so late at night. Moto drivers assume you know the cost of a trip and prices are rarely agreed before starting.

Be careful not to put your leg near the exhaust pipe after long journeys as you may get a nasty burn, which can take some time to heal in the sticky weather.

Cyclo

As in Vietnam and Laos, the *samlor* or cyclo is a quick, cheap way to get around urban areas. In Phnom Penh, cyclo drivers can either be flagged down on main roads or found hanging around markets and major hotels. In Phnom Penh and elsewhere around Cambodia, the cyclo is fast losing ground to the moto.

Remorque-Kang & Remorque-Moto

The *remorque-kang* is a trailer pulled by a bicycle; a trailer hitched to a motorbike is called a *remorque-moto*. Both are used to transport people and goods, especially in rural areas. They are not seen so much in urban Cambodia. Remorque-motos offer a cheap way to sightsee in some of the provinces, as long as you can make the driver understand where you want to get off.

Phnom Penh

Phnom Penh sits at the confluence of the Mekong, the Bassac and the Tonlé Sap rivers. Once considered the loveliest of the French-built cities of Indochina, its charm, while diminished, has managed to survive the violence of its recent history and the present invasion of property speculators and motor vehicles.

Most of Phnom Penh's attractions are low-key, which means that many travellers spend only a short time here. This is a pity. Phnom Penh is a city that is rediscovering itself and, once you have done the obligatory sightseeing circuit, it is a fascinating city to take in at leisure. The French left a legacy of now-crumbling colonial architecture, some of which has been tastefully renovated; sidewalk restaurants have sprung up all over town; crowds gather on the recently developed riverfront area at dusk; nightlife gets pretty lively at weekends; and, as the wats come back to life, monks in saffron robes can be seen wandering around town carrying alms bowls.

History

Legend has it that Phnom Penh was founded when an old woman named Penh found four Buddha images that had come to rest on the banks of the Mekong. She housed them on a nearby hill, and the town that emerged around the hill came to be known as Phnom Penh – the Hill of Penh.

The story, however, gives no clue as to why, in the 1440s, Angkor was abandoned and Phnom Penh chosen as the site of the new Cambodian capital. The move has been much lamented as evidence of cultural decline, but it nevertheless made a good deal of practical sense. Angkor was poorly situated for trade and subject to attacks from the Siamese (Thai) kingdom of Ayuthaya. Phnom Penh commanded a more central position in the Khmer territories and was perfectly located for riverine trade with Laos and China via the Mekong Delta. The Tonlé Sap river provided access to the

Highlights

- Visit the Silver Pagoda in the Royal Palace, with its 5000 silver floor tiles and an impressive collection of Buddhist treasures.

- Pray for luck at Wat Phnom, a place of legends, including the one that gave the capital its name.

- Tuol Sleng Museum is a grisly reminder of Cambodia's tragic past, but a visit is essential to understanding how far the country has progressed.

- Explore the National Museum, home to a sublime collection of sculpture from the Angkor era.

- Sample the city's vibrant nightlife with a cocktail at Hotel Le Royal, a mixer at the Foreign Correspondents' Club and a midnight journey into the Heart of Darkness.

rich fishing grounds of the Tonlé Sap (Great Lake).

By the mid-16th century trade had turned Phnom Penh into a regional power. Indonesian and Chinese traders were drawn to the city in large numbers. A century later, however, Vietnamese incursions into Khmer territory had robbed the city of access to sea lanes, and Chinese merchants driven south by the Manchu (Qing) dynasty began to monopolise trade. The landlocked and increasingly isolated kingdom became a buffer between ascendant Thais and Vietnamese. In 1772 the Thais burnt Phnom Penh to the ground. Although the city was rebuilt, in the years that followed until the French took over in 1863, Phnom Penh was buffeted by the rival hegemonic interests of the Thai and Vietnamese courts. Its population is thought never to have risen much above 25,000.

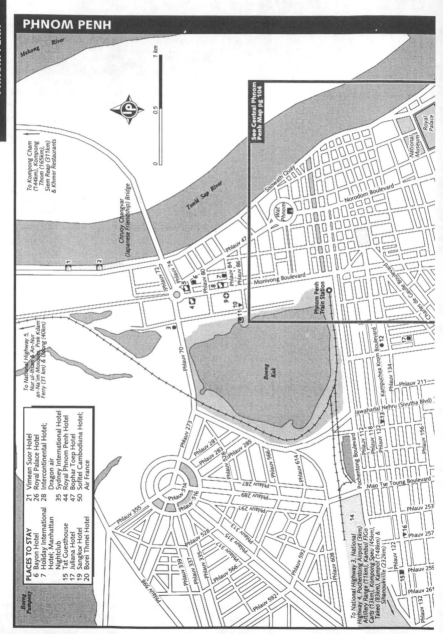

See Central Phnom
Penh Map P& 104

PLACES TO STAY
6   Bayon Hotel
7   Holiday International
    Hotel; Manhattan
    Nightclub
15 Tat Guesthouse
17 Juliana Hotel
19 Sangkor Hotel
20 Borei Thmei Hotel
21 Vimean Suor Hotel
26 Royal Palace Hotel
28 Intercontinental Hotel;
    Dragon air
35 Sydney International Hotel
44 Royal Phnom Penh Hotel
47 Bophar Toep Hotel
50 Sofitel Cambodiana Hotel;
    Air France

PHNOM PENH

PLACES TO EAT
10 Cafe Sontiepheap
13 Ly Lay Restaurant
16 La Casa Restaurant
36 Hua Nam Restaurant

OTHER
1   Slow Boats
2   Express Boats to
    Siem Reap & Kratie
3   School of Fine Arts
4   French Embassy
5   Thai Embassy
8   British Embassy
9   Calmette Hospital
11 International Mosque
12 You Nam Supermarket
14 Phnom Penh University
18 Buses to Ho Chi
    Minh City (Saigon)
22 Canadia Bank
23 Wat Moha Montrei
24 Olympic Market
25 Full Moon Bar
    & Restaurant
27 Dang Kor Market;
    Taxis to the South Coast
29 Martini Disco
30 Chinese Embassy
31 Tuol Tom Pong
    (Russian) Market
32 Wat Tuol Tom Pong
33 Tuol Sleng Museum
34 Magic Circus Cafe-
    Theatre
37 Vietnamese Embassy
38 Cham Kar Mon Palace
39 Lao Embassy
40 Former US Embassy
41 Royal Air Cambodge
42 Wat Than Handicrafts
43 European Dental
    Clinic; Ecstatic Pizza
45 Russian Embassy
46 Cambo Fun Park
48 Foreign Ministry
49 Chatomuk Theatre
51 Naga Floating Casino
52 Taxis to Ho Chi
    Minh City (Saigon)

To the Killing Fields
of Choeung Ek (13km)

To National Highway 1,
Limprevu Restaurant (8km),
Koki Beach (12km),
Svay Rieng (110km) &
Ho Chi Minh City (220km)

To National Highway 2, Takhmau,
Tonlé Bati (35km), Phnom
Tamao (42 km), Phnom
Chisor (59km) & Takeo (77km)

The population of Phnom Penh was approximately 500,000 in 1970. After the spread of the Vietnam War to Cambodian territory, the city's population swelled with refugees, reaching about two million in early 1975. The Khmer Rouge took over the city on 17 April 1975 and immediately forced the entire population into the countryside as part of its radical social program.

During the next four years, many tens of thousands of former Phnom Penhois – including the vast majority of the capital's educated people – were killed. The population of Phnom Penh during the Khmer Rouge regime was never more than about 50,000, a tiny figure when you consider the number of people living there today. Repopulation of the city began when the Vietnamese arrived in 1979. According to the population survey carried out in 1998, there are about one million residents in Phnom Penh, although exact numbers fluctuate depending on the season, with many suburban squatters returning to the countryside to harvest rice in the wet season.

Orientation

A minor hurdle to orientation in Phnom Penh is the frequency with which street names and numbers get changed. The current denominations, which date back to 1993, seem to have settled in, but there is still a chance that some of the numbered streets will change again.

The major boulevards of Phnom Penh run north-south, parallel to the banks of the Tonlé Sap and Bassac rivers. Monivong Blvd cuts north-south through the centre of town, passing just west of the Psar Thmei (New Market). Its northern sector is the main shopping strip and is also home to some of the longest-running hotels and travel agents in town. Norodom Blvd also runs north-south from Wat Phnom, and is largely administrative; the northern end contains banks, while farther south are mainly government ministries. Samdech Sothearos Blvd runs north-south near the riverfront past the Royal Palace, Silver Pagoda and National Assembly building. Sisowath Quay hugs the river and is where many of the city's most lively restaurants and bars are lo-

cated. The major east-west boulevards are Pochentong Blvd in the north of town, Preah Sihanouk Blvd, which passes the Independence Monument and ends just south of the Sofitel Cambodiana Hotel, and Mao Tse Toung Blvd (also known as Issarak Blvd). Mao Tse Toung Blvd, a ring road of sorts, also runs north-south in the west of the city.

Intersecting the main boulevards is a network of hundreds of numbered smaller streets. As a rule of thumb, streets running east-west have even numbers that increase the farther south they are in town, while north-south running streets have odd numbers that increase the farther west you go.

Most buildings around town have signs with both their building number and the *phlauv* (street) number. Finding a building purely by its address, however, is not always easy, as numbers are rarely sequential. It's not unusual to find house No 23 next door to house No 13, followed by No 11, and sometimes whole stretches of street have the same number – pity the postman. Try to get a cross-reference for an address: eg close to the intersection of Phlauv (Ph) 107 and Ph 182. The letters 'EO' after a street address stand for *étage zéro*, which means 'ground floor' in French.

Maps Local maps of Phnom Penh touted around the restaurants by children are generally of poor quality. The best city maps are the 3-D maps produced by Point Maps & Guides, which also produces a highly detailed annual listings guide to the city, useful for business travellers. The map is available in the Psar Thmei and at most book and stationery stores, while the guide is generally found only in bookshops.

The *Phnom Penh Post* and *Bayon Pearnik* include maps with regularly updated listings, though entries are sponsored by advertisers and are far from comprehensive.

The *Cambodia – Travel Map* published by Periplus is available at bookshops and includes a large fold-out map of Phnom Penh at a scale of 1:17,000. It is a colourful map, but while most streets are accurately listed many of the items included are either out of date or incorrectly placed on the map.

Information

Tourist Offices Due to lack of government funding, you can basically forget about useful tourism information in Phnom Penh. The tourist office at Pochentong international airport has information on certain hotels around town and can provide bookings, but other than this you are effectively on your own.

The head office of Phnom Penh Tourism is across from Wat Ounalom at the oblique intersection of Samdech Sothearos Blvd and Sisowath Quay. The office is officially open from 7 to 11.30 am and from 2 to 5.30 pm. It's a sleepy place with nothing in the way of useful information.

The Ministry of Tourism (☎ 426876) is in a white two-storey building on the western corner of Monivong Blvd and Ph 232. Inside chaos prevails and unless you have plans to build a large, ugly hotel you will find little assistance here. However, plans are afoot to establish a Tourism Board and this, once established, will be your best bet for dependable information.

Money The most organised bank for changing money and obtaining credit card cash advances is the Cambodian Commercial Bank (CCB), on the corner of Pochentong and Monivong Blvds. It takes most travellers cheques and can also organise cash advances for MasterCard, JCB and Visa. There is a minimum charge of US$10 for transactions of under US$500 and 2% thereafter. A limit of US$2000 is imposed on cash advances.

The Foreign Trade Bank at the northern end of Norodom Blvd is another good option, with the longest opening hours of any bank, from 7 am to 3.45 pm. If you need a cash withdrawal on credit card of less than US$250, it is cheaper here as the bank levies a flat 4%. It also boasts the lowest commission on travellers cheques at 1%, but will only deal with US dollars. This is also the best place to arrange a money transfer.

Canadia Bank is the one other bank worth singling out as it changes travellers cheques of almost any currency and has two branches, on Ph 110 near CCB, and a second, conveniently located for some of the guesthouses, near the Olympic Stadium.

Most other banks around town can change travellers cheques, but often at more than 2% commission, and credit card cash advances seem to be US$10 plus 2%!

Other banks include:

Asia Bank
    86 Norodom Blvd
Bangkok Bank
    26 Norodom Blvd
Credit Agricole Indosuez
    77 Norodom Blvd
Cambodia Asia Bank
    252 Monivong Blvd
Maybank
    2 Norodom Blvd
Thai Farmers Bank
    2, Ph 114

There are numerous small banks tucked away in the back streets, but many are rumoured to act as fronts for illegal operations.

Other options for getting money include a number of the more upmarket hotels, although this service is usually reserved for guests, and travel agents that can change travellers cheques and offer cash advances on credit card for at least a 5% fee. These places are usually open on weekends and public holidays, of which there are many in Cambodia. The Diamond Hotel near the Psar Thmei and nearby travel agents are probably the most conveniently located.

If you just want to change cash into riel, jewellery stalls around the markets of Phnom Penh are the most convenient.

Post The main post office is just east of Wat Phnom on Ph 13. It is open from 7 am to 7 pm daily and offers postal services as well as telephone and fax links. For postal rates see the Post & Communications section in the Facts for the Visitor chapter.

If you need to get your purchases or belongings home in a hurry, there are a few international courier companies represented in Phnom Penh including:

DHL
    (☎ 427726) 28 Monivong Blvd
Federal Express
    (☎ 216712) 701D Monivong Blvd
TNT
    (☎ 424022) 139 Monireth Blvd

CENTRAL PHNOM PENH

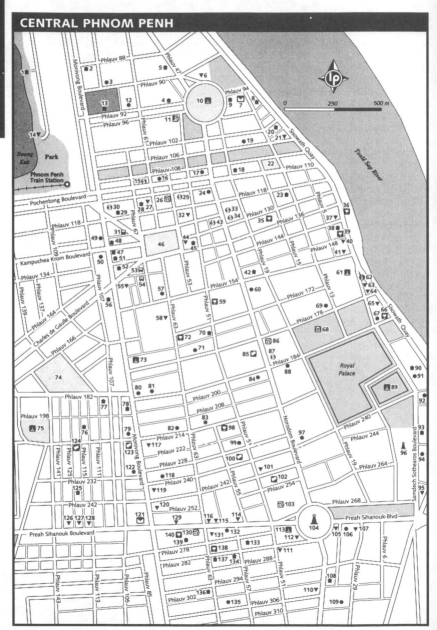

CENTRAL PHNOM PENH

PLACES TO STAY
1 No 9 Guesthouse;
  Lakeside Guesthouse
2 Tai Seng Hotel
4 Sunway Hotel
5 Sharaton Hotel;
  Casa Nightclub
8 Riverside Hotel
9 Wat Phnom Hotel
13 Hotel Le Royal
18 Cathay Hotel
20 Pyco Guesthouse
23 Dara Reang Sey Hotel
28 Fortune Hotel
29 Dusit Hotel
38 Hotel Indochine;
  Sunshine Hotel
42 Royal Guesthouse
45 Hawaii Hotel
47 Asie Hotel
48 Singapore Hotel
51 City Central Hotel
52 Diamond Hotel;
  Malaysia Airlines
56 Pailin Hotel; Silk Air
70 Walkabout Hotel
76 Lux Orisey Guesthouse
77 Capitol Guesthouse
78 Hong Kong Hotel; Lucky!
  Lucky!; New! New!
  (Motorbike Rental)
90 Renakse Hotel
93 Regent Park Hotel; Pizza House
108 One Way Guesthouse & Bar
125 Narin Guesthouse
133 Golden Gate Hotel
134 Goldiana Hotel
136 Champs Élysées Hotel
137 Amara Hotel
139 Tokyo Hotel

PLACES TO EAT
6 Il Padrino Restaurant
14 Cafe Freedom
21 Saigon House
27 Mamak's Corner
32 Cathouse Tavern
37 Rendez-Vous Restaurant
40 Riverside Restaurant
41 Banana Leaf Restaurant
44 La Paillote
55 Little India Restaurant
58 Baker's Express
63 Ponlok Restaurant;
  Istanbul Restaurant
64 Happy Herb's Pizza;
  Pink Elephant Pub;
  EID Restaurant; Wagon
  Wheel Restaurant

65 Foreign Correspondents'
  Club of Cambodia
95 Chiang Mai Restaurant
101 Baggio's Pizza
105 The Mex; Apsara Handicrafts
107 Red Restaurant
110 Baan Thai Restaurant
111 Athena Restaurant
112 L'Atmosphère
114 Nagasaki
115 California II Restaurant
116 King of King's Restaurant
117 Dararasmey Restaurant
119 Royal India Restaurant
120 Shanghai Restaurant
126 Thong Hy Restaurant
127 Chaay Heng Restaurant
128 Chez Reth Restaurant
129 Singapore Chicken Rice;
  French Bakery
131 Phnom Kiev Restaurant;
  Nike Pizza

OTHER
3 Seven Seven Supermarket
7 Main Post Office
10 Wat Phnom
11 International Youth Club
12 National Library
15 Canadia Bank
16 Tropical & Travellers Medical
  Centre
17 NCDP Handicrafts; Seeing
  Honds Massage
19 Thai Airways; Transpeed Travel
22 Psar Char
24 National Blood Transfusion
  Centre
25 Thai Farmers' Bank
26 Public Internet Centre
30 Cambodian Commercial
  Bank; Royal Air Cambodge
31 Share Taxis; Pick-ups &
  Minibuses
33 Foreign Trade Bank
34 Bangkok Bank
35 Sharky's (Disco)
36 River 3
39 Garden Bar
43 Maybank
46 Psar Thmei (New Market)
49 Bayon Market &
  City Colour Photo
50 Monument Books; Pich
  Tourist Co.
53 Ho Wah Genting Buses
54 GST Buses
57 DH Cambodia Bus Office

59 Heart of Darkness Bar
60 President Airlines
61 Wat Ounalom
62 Phnom Penh Tourism
66 The Globe Bar & Restaurant
67 UNESCO
68 National Museum; School of
  Fine Arts
69 Hanuman Tourism Voyages;
  Cafe Des Beaux Arts
71 Cooperation Committee for
  Cambodia
72 Traveller's Bar
73 Wat Koh
74 Psar O Russei
75 Wat Sampao Meas
79 International Stationery &
  Book Centre
80 Ministry of Culture & Fine Arts
81 French Cultural Centre
82 Bangkok Airways
83 Vietnam Airlines
84 Direction Des Étrangers
  (Immigration Bureau)
85 Japanese Embassy
86 Khmer Internet Development
  Services
87 Credit Agricole Indosuez
88 Language Schools
89 Silver Pagoda
91 Ministry of Justice
92 National Assembly Building
94 East West Tours
96 Cambodia-Vietnam
  Friendship Monument
97 London Bookstore
98 Monsoon
99 SOS International Medical
  Centre
100 US Embassy
102 Australian Embassy
103 NETREC Email & Internet
104 Independence Monument
106 Lao Aviation
109 Prayuvong Buddha
  Factories
113 Wat Lang Ka
118 Diethelm Travel
121 Post Office
122 Ministry of Tourism
123 German Embassy
124 Cuban Embassy
130 Khmer Web
132 Hollywood Movie Street
135 Khemara Handicrafts
138 Tom's Irish Bar
140 Lucky Supermarket;
  Ettamogah Pub

Telephone For information on making domestic and international calls, see Telephone under Post & Communications in the Facts for the Visitor chapter.

For those travelling with a mobile phone or intending to stay long term in Phnom Penh, there are several mobile telephone networks competing for your custom. The main players all offer regular promotions, so it is worth shopping around. They include:

Shinawatra
    (☎ 011-800801)
Mobitel
    (☎ 012-801801)
Samart
    (☎ 015-910220)
Camtel
    (☎ 018-810016)

Fax One of the cheaper places to send faxes is Public Internet Centre near the Psar Thmei. It charges US$3.80 per minute (depending on fax length). See also Fax under Post & Communications in the Facts for the Visitor chapter for more information.

Email & Internet Access Cambodia has finally plugged itself into the Internet, but access is expensive when compared with neighbouring countries. Charges are generally about US$5 to US$6 per hour.

You can log on at the Public Internet Centre, near the Psar Thmei; the National English Teaching Resource Centre of Cambodia (NETREC), in the school near the Independence Monument; Khmer Internet Development Services (KIDS), conveniently located near the National Museum; Khmer Web, just a couple of doors up from Lucky Supermarket; Café Asia at the Foreign Correspondents' Club (FCC); Sharky's disco; and the Ettamogah Pub. More places will undoubtedly follow suit, and provider prices may come down as demand rises.

The Public Internet Centre and NETREC are part of wider educational programs to assist Cambodia, so put your money in their direction during the day. NETREC plans to offer discounted rates for group access – US$2 an hour or less per person with four or more people. The FCC is a pleasant place

to surf the Internet, as it has drinks and snacks available and the most terminals in Phnom Penh. Khmer Web is one of the cheapest places in town.

NETREC has by far the cheapest email service in town, at US$1 to send up to five. Remember to tell folks back home to reply to your Internet address rather than just hitting reply, or all the responses will come back to NETREC's address. Most of the other email places around town charge US$1 per email sent. NETREC also offers monthly accounts for just US$10, again the cheapest in town, and a bargain if you are thinking of sticking around Phnom Penh. The Public Internet Centre charges US$13 a month, Khmer Web US$14 and the FCC charges US$15.

Travel Agencies The area near the Psar Thmei on Monivong Blvd has a few budget travel agencies, including Pich Tourist Co (☎ 246585), above Monument Books, and Khemarak Travel (☎ 367878).

One of the most reliable outfits in town is Diethelm Travel (☎ 426648, fax 219150, email dtc@gncomtext.com) at 65, Ph 240, just off Monivong Blvd. Diethelm also has offices in Siem Reap, Bangkok, Ho Chi Minh City (Saigon), and Vientiane, making it a good agency for regional flights and tours.

Hanuman Tourism Voyages (☎ 724022, fax 426194) is a very good place to arrange discounted flights and it also offers tours in and around Phnom Penh.

Another popular agency is East West Tours (☎ 427118) at 84 Samdech Sothearos Blvd, just south of the Regent Park Hotel. Like Diethelm, this office has a counterpart in Bangkok and is a reliable operator. Transpeed Travel (☎ 427366) at 19, Ph 106 is in the same building as Thai Airways and is another good option for flight bookings.

Bookshops The London Bookstore at 65 Ph 240 near Norodom Blvd is the best place in town for browsing. The shelves are stacked with second-hand stock shipped in from the UK and prices are more reasonable than in Bangkok. Reckon on paying about US$4 a book on average, and less if you have something to trade.

For new books and magazines, the bookshops at the Hotel Le Royal and the Sofitel Cambodiana Hotel are some of the best stocked in town, but prices are also five star. They have a very good selection of French newspapers, magazines and books, as well as an extensive selection of English coffee-table publications, novels and weeklies such as *Far Eastern Economic Review*, *The Economist*, *Time*, *Newsweek* and *Asiaweek*.

Monument Books is probably the best stocked new bookshop in Phnom Penh with almost every book that is currently in print about the region available here. Once again prices are high, but at least you get originals. The International Stationery & Book Centre on Monivong Blvd is mainly devoted to dictionaries, but it also stocks some locally produced maps.

Libraries The National Library (Bibliothèque Nationale), on Ph 92 near Wat Phnom, is in a delightful old building, but has only a small selection of reading material for foreign visitors. Opening hours are from 8 to 11 am and 2 to 5 pm, every day except Monday.

The Khmer Rouge turned the graceful building, constructed in 1924, into a stable and destroyed most of the books, throwing many of them out into the streets, where they were picked up by people who donated them back to the library after 1979.

Today, the National Library has about 100,000 volumes, including many crumbling books in French. Part of the English-language collection consists of books taken from the US embassy when it was sacked after the communist takeover in 1975. Cornell University is assisting the National Library to preserve its collection of palm-leaf manuscripts.

French speakers should call into the French Cultural Centre on Ph 184 (near the corner of Monivong Blvd). It has a good range of reading material.

Clubs & Associations A good opportunity to meet local expatriates is via the Hash House Harriers, usually referred to simply as 'the Hash'. A weekly run/walk takes place every Sunday. Participants meet in front of the Phnom Penh train station at 2.45

pm. The entry fee of US$5 includes refreshments (mainly beer) at the end.

The Foreign Correspondents' Club at 363 Sisowath Quay is unlike many FCCs around the world in that it is open to all comers. It is a great place to meet people, enjoy a few drinks and a meal. Membership costs US$150 per year for local residents and US$75 for overseas members. Membership provides access to the members' room (which has online news services), business facilities, a 20% discount on food and drinks and reciprocal rights to other FCCs, such as the impenetrable bastion in Hong Kong.

Look out for announcements of performances by the Phnom Penh Players in the *Cambodia Daily* and the *Phnom Penh Post* while you are in town. The players comprise residents who perform a play every few months.

Laundry Most hotels around town offer reasonably priced laundry services – in some cases for free. For dry cleaning, try Penley Dry Cleaning on the corner of Ph 13 and Ph 136.

Medical Services The SOS International Medical Centre (☎ 216911/015-912765, fax 215811) at 161, Ph 51 is one of the best medical services around town. As you might expect, costs for a consultation are on par with those overseas, so think twice about visiting if you don't have insurance. Office hours are from 8 am to 5.30 pm, Monday to Friday and 8 am to noon Saturday.

For specialist advice on tropical diseases and diligent diagnoses you can visit the Tropical & Travellers Medical Centre (☎ 015-912000) at 88, Ph 108. A good British doctor runs it in partnership with a British-trained Khmer doctor. It is open from 8.30 am to noon and 2 to 5 pm, Monday to Friday, and on Saturday morning.

The Calmette Hospital (☎ 725373), on Monivong Blvd, is French administered and the best of the local hospitals.

For dental problems, try the European Dental Clinic (☎ 015-832159) at 195A Norodom Blvd. Office hours are from 8 am to noon and 2.30 pm to 6 pm, Monday to Friday, and 8 am to 1 pm Saturday.

Emergency In the event of a medical emergency you will probably have to be flown to Bangkok. The SOS International Medical Centre (☎ 015-912765) has a 24 hour emergency service and can also organise evacuation. The European Dental Clinic also has an after hours service (☎ 018-812055). The emergency numbers for Phnom Penh's ambulance service are ☎ 724891, ☎ 426948 and ☎ 012-808915. The general emergency numbers are ☎ 117 (police), ☎ 118 (fire) and ☎ 119 (ambulance).

There is a 24 hour emergency police contact number (☎366841/015-915137) in Phnom Penh and you will be connected to an English-speaking officer. The general consensus among embassies is that the best police to deal with in the event of a crime are the nearest Flying Tigers unit (☎ 366841/720235); it's officers generally speak English.

Dangers & Annoyances Phnom Penh is not as dangerous as many people imagine, but it is still important to take care. Armed theft happens regularly, although expats tend to fall victim more than tourists as their movements are easier to predict.

Should you become the victim of a robbery, do not panic and do not under any circumstances struggle. Calmly raise your hands and let them take what they want. They will probably be as scared as you, and you will most likely get your documents back via your guesthouse or embassy later as the robbers often only want cash and valuables. For the time being, even passports and credit cards seem to be returned. Rumours abound that it may be local police doing the robberies, so this probably explains why they are so conscientious.

It is not sensible to ride a motorbike alone late at night; and if there is one area to avoid in general at night in the city, it is the area of Tuol Kauk to the north of Boeng Kak lake, which is the main brothel quarter in town and the kind of place where drunk Khmers shoot each other over a karaoke microphone after too many ales.

Those out clubbing in the evenings can expect to be stopped at checkpoints from time to time. Ostensibly police checkpoints are there to check for firearms, but occasionally foreigners will be nabbed for a cigarette or a dollar. You are under no obligation to fork out. Riding your own motorbike during the day, police will often try to fleece you for the most trivial of offences, such as turning left in violation of a no left turn sign. At their most audacious, they try to get you for riding with your headlights on during the day, although worryingly, it doesn't seem to be illegal for Cambodians to travel without headlights at night. They will most likely demand US$5 and threaten to take you to the police station and charge you US$20 if you don't pay. If you are patient and smile, you can usually get away with 1000r or a few cigarettes. The trick is not to stop in the first place.

The restaurant areas of Phnom Penh (particularly places with outdoor seating) attract many beggars, as does the Psar Thmei. Generally, however, there is little in the way of push and shove. If you give to beggars, do as the locals do and keep the denominations small – this way, hopefully, foreigners will not become special targets. See the Dangers & Annoyances section in the Facts for the Visitor chapter for more information.

Things to See & Do

The real name of the 700m Japanese Friendship Bridge, which spans the Tonlé Sap river, is the **Chruoy Changvar bridge**. It was blown up during fighting in 1975. Long a symbol of the devastation visited upon Cambodia, it was repaired in 1993 with US$23.2 million of Japanese funding. Those who have seen the film *The Killing Fields* will be interested to note that it was here on the afternoon of 17 April 1975 – the day Phnom Penh fell – that *New York Times* correspondent Sydney Schanberg and four companions were held prisoner by Khmer Rouge fighters and threatened with death.

West of the Chruoy Changvar bridge on Ph 70 is the **School of Fine Arts**. This is an active school devoted to training students in the arts of music and dance, and is not a tourist attraction. It is possible, however, to call in early in the morning and watch children rehearsing classical Khmer dance on a dais to the rear of the school. Request permission from the teachers to watch the lessons or to take photographs. There is also a circus school here where children learn acrobatics and trapeze, but the thinness of the crash mats makes it painful to observe.

The **French embassy** on the northern end of Monivong Blvd was for many years used as an orphanage and its apparently larcenous residents were blamed by local people for every theft in the neighbourhood. Today the embassy is back in place and a high wall surrounds the massive complex. The French have returned to Cambodia in a big way, promoting French language and culture in their former colony.

When Phnom Penh fell in 1975, about 800 foreigners and 600 Cambodians took refuge in the embassy. Within 48 hours, the Khmer Rouge informed the French vice-consul that the new government did not recognise diplomatic privileges and that if all the Cambodians in the compound were not handed over, the lives of the foreigners inside would also be forfeited. Cambodian women married to foreigners could stay, he was told; Cambodian men married to foreign women could not. The foreigners stood and wept as their servants, colleagues, friends, lovers and husbands were escorted out of the embassy gates. At the end of the month, the foreigners were taken out of the country by truck. Many of the Cambodians were never seen again.

There is a cluster of **private language schools** teaching English (and some French) one block west of the National Museum on Ph 184 between Norodom Blvd and the back of the Royal Palace compound. Between 5 and 7 pm, the area is filled with students who see learning English as the key to making it in post-war Cambodia. This is a good place to meet local young people.

Known collectively as the National Sports Complex, the **Olympic Stadium** is near the intersection of Preah Sihanouk Blvd and Monireth Blvd. It includes a sports arena (which doubles as the site of government-sponsored political rallies) and facilities for swimming, boxing, gymnastics, volleyball and other sports.

Just south of the Sofitel Cambodiana Hotel, the **Cambo Fun Park** is the only amusement park in Phnom Penh since the old Boeng Kak Amusement Park was demolished. It opens at around 5 pm and by 7 pm it is usually packed with school children queuing impatiently to risk their lives on what appear to be some very rickety rides – the management boasts that the whole thing

Bats in the Belfry

The elegant curves of the National Museum make for a picturesque sight framed against the pink and mauve of a sunset. It's also about this time of day that great flocks of bats stream out from the museum's roof. Most of the bats belong to a recently identified species: the Cambodian freetail.

Some bat experts claim that the National Museum has the largest bat population of any artificial structure in the world. The problem is that bat droppings are corrosive, and as they fell through the ceiling, the exhibits were gradually being destroyed. Meanwhile, museum patrons had to do their sightseeing in a miasma of bat guana.

Fortunately Australia has come to the rescue. In an agreement that saw the 'Treasures of the National Museum of Cambodia' exhibited at the Australian National Gallery, the Australian International Development Assistance Bureau (AIDAB) has undertaken to help maintain the contents of the museum and do something about the bats. It was considered ecologically unsound to remove them altogether, so a second artificial ceiling has been constructed to stop the droppings falling through. Let's just hope it holds up under the weight.

was built in just 20 days. The area between here and the Independence Monument gets pretty lively in the evening, with a whole host of *tikalok* (fruit smoothies) sellers and snack stalls. Many young Khmers hang about the fountains checking each other out.

The **Independence Monument** at the intersection of Norodom and Preah Sihanouk Blvds was built in 1958. It is now also a memorial to Cambodia's war dead and is sometimes known as the Victory Monument. Wreaths are laid here on national holidays. Nearby, beside Samdech Sothearos Blvd, is the Cambodia-Vietnam Friendship (or Liberation) Monument, built to a Vietnamese design in 1979.

In order to replace the countless Buddhas and ritual objects smashed by the Khmer Rouge, a whole little neighbourhood of private workshops producing cement Buddhas, *naga* (mythical serpents) and small stupas has grown up on the grounds of Wat Prayuvong. While the graceless cement figures painted in gaudy colours are hardly works of art, they are part of an effort by the Cambodian people to restore Buddhism to a place of honour in their reconstituted society. The **Prayuvong Buddha factories**, as they are known, are on the eastern side of Norodom Blvd about 300m south of the Independence Monument (between Ph 308 and Ph 310).

The **former US embassy** is on the northeastern corner of the intersection of Norodom and Mao Tse Toung Blvds. Much of the US air war in Cambodia (1969-73) was run from here. The building now houses the Department of Fisheries of the Ministry of Agriculture.

On the morning of 12 April 1975, 360 heavily armed US Marines brought in by helicopter secured a landing zone several hundred metres from the embassy. Within hours, 276 people – Americans, Cambodians and others – were evacuated by helicopter relay to US ships in the Gulf of Thailand. Among the last to leave was US Ambassador John Gunther Dean, carrying the embassy's US flag under his arm.

Cham Kar Mon Palace, on the west side of Norodom Blvd between Ph 436 and Ph 462, was once the residence of Prince Sihanouk.

The palace, whose name means 'silkworm fields', is now used by visiting heads of state.

Very few individual travellers bother with **Mekong Island**, which lies north of Phnom Penh and is reached via an organised boat trip that leaves from the Sofitel Cambodiana Hotel. The trip includes entertainment on the island including elephant rides, classical dancing and handicraft production. Boats leave at 9.30 am and return at 3 pm. The trip costs US$32, including lunch. Bookings can be made at the Sofitel Cambodiana Hotel or at Mekong Island Tours (☎ 427225), 13, Ph 240.

It's possible to visit the island without taking the tour boat, but bribes will be required if you want to get in to see the tourist operations. If you want to visit the island this way (it involves an inexpensive ferry ride), ask one of the English-speaking moto drivers about how to do it.

The **Seeing Hands Massage** is intended to raise funds to empower disabled Cambodians in the capital. It is administered by well-trained blind masseurs and costs US$3 per hour. It is well worth it, particularly if you have arrived in Phnom Penh by pick-up truck from Siem Reap. There are two centres in the capital, one at the National Centre for Disabled Persons (NCDP) at 3 Norodom Blvd, and the other on the northwest corner of Ph 19 and Ph 178.

National Museum

The National Museum of Cambodia is housed in a graceful terracotta structure of traditional design (built 1917-20) just north of the Royal Palace. It is open from 8 to 11.30 am and 2 to 5.30 pm, Tuesday to Sunday; entry is $2. Photography is prohibited inside. The School of Fine Arts (École des Beaux-Arts) has its headquarters in a structure behind the main building.

French- and English-speaking guides are available, and there is also a useful exhibition booklet, *Khmer Art in Stone*, available at the front desk. The museum comprises four courtyards, which face a garden. The most significant displays of sculpture are in the courtyards to the left and straight ahead of the entrance.

Some highlights include the eight-armed statue of Vishnu from the 6th or 7th century, the statue of Shiva (circa 866-877) and the sublime statue of Jayavarman VII seated (circa 1181-1218), his head bowed slightly in a meditative pose. Elsewhere around the museum are displays of pottery and bronzes dating from the pre-Angkor periods of Funan and Chenla (4th to 9th centuries), the Indravarman period (9th and 10th centuries), the classical Angkor period (10th to 14th centuries), as well as more recent works.

See the Sculpture section in the Facts about Cambodia chapter for more information about some of the exhibits in the National Museum.

Tuol Sleng Museum

In 1975 Tuol Svay Prey High School was taken over by Pol Pot's security forces and turned into a prison known as Security Prison 21 (S-21). It soon became the largest such centre of detention and torture in the country. More than 17,000 people held at S-21 were taken to the extermination camp at Choeung Ek to be executed; detainees who died during torture were buried in mass graves in the prison grounds. S-21 has been turned into the Tuol Sleng Museum, which serves as a testament to the crimes of the Khmer Rouge. The museum's entrance is on the western side of Ph 113, just north of Ph 350, and it is officially open from 7 to 11.30 am and from 2 to 5.30 pm daily except Mondays, although you can usually visit any time of day; entry is US$2.

Like the Nazis, the Khmer Rouge was meticulous in keeping records of its barbarism. Each prisoner who passed through S-21 was photographed, sometimes before and after being tortured. The museum displays include room after room of these photographs of men, women and children covering the walls from floor to ceiling; virtually all the people pictured were later killed. You can tell in what year a picture was taken by the style of number-board that appears on the prisoner's chest. Several foreigners from Australia, France and the USA were held here before being murdered. Their documents are on display. It is worth paying US$2 to have a guide show you

around, as they can tell you the story behind some of the people in the photographs.

As the Khmer Rouge 'revolution' reached ever greater heights of insanity, it began devouring its own children. Generations of torturers and executioners who worked here killed their predecessors and were in turn killed by those who took their places. During the first part of 1977 when the party purges of eastern-zone cadres were getting underway, S-21 claimed an average of 100 victims a day.

When the Vietnamese army liberated Phnom Penh in early 1979, it found only seven prisoners alive at S-21. Fourteen others had been tortured to death as Vietnamese forces were closing in on the city. Photographs of their gruesome deaths are on display in the rooms where their decomposing corpses were found. Their graves are nearby in the courtyard.

Altogether, a visit to Tuol Sleng is a profoundly depressing experience. The sheer ordinariness of the place makes it even more horrific: the suburban setting, the plain school buildings, the grassy playing area where today children kick around balls, rusted beds, instruments of torture and wall after wall of harrowing black and white portraits conjure up images of humanity at its worst. Tuol Sleng is not for the squeamish.

Killing Fields of Choeung Ek

Between 1975 and 1978 about 17,000 men, women, children and infants (including nine westerners) detained and tortured at S-21 prison were transported to the extermination camp of Choeung Ek. They were often bludgeoned to death to avoid wasting precious bullets.

The remains of 8985 people, many of whom were bound and blindfolded, were exhumed in 1980 from mass graves in this one-time longan orchard; 43 of the 129 communal graves here have been left untouched. Fragments of human bone and bits of cloth are scattered around the disinterred pits. Over 8000 skulls, arranged by sex and age, are visible behind the clear glass panels of the Memorial Stupa, which was erected in 1988.

[Continued on page 114]

THE ROYAL PALACE & THE SILVER PAGODA

Phnom Penh's Royal Palace, which stands on the site of the former citadel, Banteay Kev (built in 1813), fronts Samdech Sothearos Blvd between Phlauv (Ph) 184 and Ph 240. Since Sihanouk's return to Cambodia, visitors are only allowed to visit the palace's Silver Pagoda and its surrounding compound. Entry is not, at present, permitted to the rest of the palace complex. The Silver Pagoda is open to the public from 8 to 11 am and from 2 to 5 pm daily. The entry fee is US$2. There is an additional US$2 charge to bring a still camera into the complex; movie or video cameras cost US$5. Photography is not permitted inside the pagoda.

Chan Chaya Pavilion Performances of classical Cambodian dance were once staged in the Chan Chaya Pavilion, through which guests enter the grounds of the Royal Palace.

Throne Hall The Throne Hall, topped by a 59m-high tower inspired by the Bayon Temple at Angkor, was inaugurated in 1919 by King Sisowath; the present cement building replaced a vast wooden structure built on this site in 1869. The Throne Hall was used for coronations and ceremonies such as the presentation of credentials by diplomats. Most of the items once displayed here were destroyed by the Khmer Rouge.

Silver Pagoda The Silver Pagoda, so named because the floor is covered with over 5000 silver tiles weighing 1kg each, is also known as Wat Preah Keo (Pagoda of the Emerald Buddha). It was constructed of wood in 1892 during the rule of King Norodom, who was apparently inspired by Bangkok's Wat Phra Keo; it was then rebuilt in 1962. The Silver Pagoda was preserved by the Khmer Rouge in order to demonstrate to the outside world its concern for the conservation of Cambodia's cultural riches. Although some 60% of the pagoda's contents were destroyed under Pol Pot, what remains is spectacular. This is one of the few places in all of Cambodia where objects embodying some of the brilliance and richness of Khmer civilisation can still be viewed.

The staircase leading to the Silver Pagoda is made of Italian marble. Inside, the Emerald Buddha, said to be made of Baccarat crystal, sits on a gilt pedestal high atop the dais. In front of the dais stands a life-size gold Buddha decorated with 9584 diamonds, the largest of which weighs 25 carats. Created in the palace workshops during 1906 and 1907, the gold Buddha weighs some 90kg. Directly in front of it, in a Formica case, is a miniature silver-and-gold stupa containing a relic of Buddha brought from Sri Lanka. To the left is an 80kg bronze Buddha, and to the right a silver Buddha. On the far right, figurines of solid gold tell the story of the Buddha.

Behind the dais is a standing marble Buddha from Myanmar (Burma) and a litter (portable bed), used by the king on coronation day and designed to be carried by 12 men; its gold parts weigh 23kg. To either side are silver models of King Norodom's stupa and Wat Preah Keo's library. At the back of the hall is a case containing two gold Buddhas, each decorated with diamonds weighing up to 16 carats; the lower figure weighs 4.5kg, the upper 1.5kg.

RICHARD I'ANSON

RICHARD I'ANSON

Top: Part of the Royal Palace complex in Phnom Penh.

Bottom: A royal procession makes its way to the Chat Preah Nengkal (Royal Ploughing Ceremony).

The Royal Palace & The Silver Pagoda

BERNARD NAPTHINE

RICHARD I'ANSON

RICHARD I'ANSON

Top, Middle & Bottom:
Incredible and intricate,
these murals are a
feature of the Silver
Pagoda.

Along the walls of the pagoda are examples of extraordinary Khmer artisanship, including bejewelled masks used in classical dance and dozens of solid and hollow gold Buddhas. The many precious gifts given to Cambodia's monarchs by foreign heads of state appear rather spiritless when displayed next to such diverse and exuberant Khmer art.

The epic of the *Ramayana* (Sanskrit poem) is depicted on a colossal mural, created around 1900, painted on the wall enclosing the pagoda compound; the story begins just south of the east gate.

Other structures in the complex (listed clockwise from the north gate) include the Mondap (library), which used to house richly illuminated sacred texts written on palm leaves; the shrine of King Norodom (ruled 1860-1904); an equestrian statue of King Norodom; the shrine of King Ang Duong (ruled 1845-59); a pavilion housing a huge footprint of the Buddha; Phnom Mondap, an artificial hill at the top of which is a structure containing a bronze footprint of the Buddha from Sri Lanka; a shrine dedicated to one of Prince Sihanouk's daughters; a pavilion for celebrations held by the royal family; the shrine of Prince Sihanouk's father, King Norodom Suramarit (ruled 1955-60); and a bell tower, whose bell is rung to order the gates to be opened or closed.

1 Entrance to Royal Palace
2 Chan Chaya Pavilion
3 Building with Elephant Dock
4 Throne Hall
5 Royal Treasury
6 Royal Offices
7 Gift of Napolean III
8 Banquet Hall
9 Route from Royal Palace to Silver Pagoda
10 Street Entrance to Royal Palace
11 North Gate (Entrance to Silver Pagoda
12 Galleries around Silver Pagoda
13 Mondap (Library)
14 Bell Tower
15 Stupa of King Norodom
16 Equestrian Statue of King Norodom
17 Silver Pagoda
18 East Gate (closed)
19 Stupa of King Ang Duong
20 Beginning of Ramayana Mural
21 Pavilion containing Buddha Footprint
22 Phnom Mondap
23 South Gate (closed)
24 Stupa of Sihanouk's Daughter
25 Pavilion of Royal Celebrations
26 Stupa of King Norodom Suramarit
27 West Gate (closed)

THE ROYAL PALACE & THE SILVER PAGODA

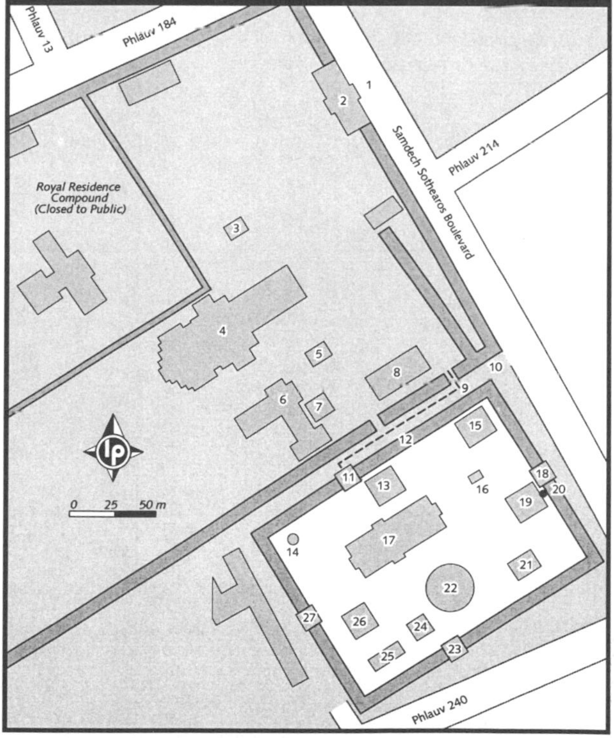

[Continued from page 111]

The Killing Fields of Choeung Ek are 15km from central Phnom Penh. To get there, take Monireth Blvd south-westward out of the city from the Psar Dang Kor (Dang Kor Market) bus depot. The site is 8.5km from the bridge near Ph 271. Take the left fork when the road splits and pretty soon you will find yourself in rural surroundings. Look out for an archway on the right and it's another kilometre or so down this track. A memorial ceremony is held annually at Choeung Ek on 9 May. Entry costs US$2.

Wats & Mosques

Wat Phnom Set on top of a 27m-high tree-covered knoll, Wat Phnom is the only hill in town. According to legend, the first pagoda on this site was erected in 1373 to house four statues of Buddha deposited here by the waters of the Mekong River and discovered by a woman named Penh. The main entrance to Wat Phnom is via the grand eastern staircase, which is guarded by lions and naga balustrades.

Today, many people come here to pray for good luck and success in school exams or business affairs. When a petitioner's wish is granted, he or she returns to make the offering (such as a garland of jasmine flowers or bananas, of which the spirits are said to be especially fond) promised when the request was made.

The *vihara* (temple sanctuary) was rebuilt in 1434, 1806, 1894 and, most recently, in 1926. West of the vihara is an enormous stupa containing the ashes of King Ponhea Yat (reigned 1405-67). In a small pavilion on the south side of the passage between the vihara and the stupa is a statue of a smiling and rather plump Madame Penh.

A bit to the north of the vihara and below it is an eclectic shrine dedicated to the genie Preah Chau, who is especially revered by the Vietnamese. On either side of the entrance to the chamber in which a statue of Preah Chau sits are guardian spirits bearing iron bats. On the tile table in front of the two guardian spirits are drawings of Confucius, as well as two Chinese-style figures of the sages Thang Cheng (on the right) and Thang Thay (on the left). To the left of the central altar is an eight-armed statue of Vishnu.

Down the hill from the shrine is a royal stupa sprouting full-size trees from its roof. For now, the roots are holding the bricks together in their net-like grip, but when the trees die the tower will slowly crumble. If you can't make it out to Angkor, this stupa gives a pretty good idea of what the jungle can do (and is doing) to Cambodia's monuments.

Curiously, Wat Phnom is the only attraction in Phnom Penh that is in danger of turning into a circus. Beggars, street urchins, women selling drinks and children selling birds in cages (you pay to set the bird free – locals claim the birds are trained to return to their cage afterwards) pester everyone who turns up to slog the 27m to the summit. Fortunately it's all high-spirited stuff, and it's difficult to be annoyed by the vendors, who, after all, are only trying to eke out a living. You can also have a short elephant ride around the base of the hill, perfect for those elephant trekking photos without the accompanying sore butt.

It is hardly the most stunning location you are likely to visit in Cambodia, but as a symbol of the city it is worthwhile visiting. It costs US$1.

Wat Ounalom Wat Ounalom, the headquarters of the Cambodian Buddhist patriarchate, is across the road from Phnom Penh Tourism. It was founded in 1443 and comprises 44 structures. As you might expect, it received a battering during the Pol Pot era, but today the wat is coming back to life. The head of the country's Buddhist hierarchy lives here along with an increasing number of monks.

On the 2nd floor of the main building, to the left of the dais, is a statue of Samdech Huot Tat, Fourth Patriarch of Cambodian Buddhism, who was killed by Pol Pot. The statue, made in 1971 when the patriarch was 80, was thrown in the Mekong but retrieved after 1979.

Nearby, a bookcase holds a few remnants of the once-extensive library of the Buddhist Institute, which was based here until

1975 and is being re-established. To the right of the dais is a statue of a former patriarch of the Thummayuth sect, to which the royal family belongs.

On the 3rd floor of the building is a marble Buddha of Burmese origin broken into pieces by the Khmer Rouge and later reassembled. On the right front corner of the dais on the 3rd floor are the cement remains of a Buddha from which the Khmer Rouge stripped the silver covering. In front of the dais to either side are two glass cases containing flags – each 20m long – used during Buddhist celebrations. The walls are decorated with scenes from the life of the Buddha: they were painted when the building was constructed in 1952.

Behind the main building is a stupa containing an eyebrow hair of the Buddha. There is an inscription in Pali (an ancient Indian language) over the entrance.

Wat Lang Ka Wat Lang Ka on Preah Sihanouk Blvd by the Victory Monument is another wat that is enjoying a new lease on life. It is a colourful place with plenty of new paint and young monks in saffron robes strolling around. It was the second of Phnom Penh's wats repaired by the post-1979 government (the first was Wat Ounalom). Around the main building are reconstructed stupas. Both the ground level and 2nd floor chambers of the vihara have been newly painted with scenes from the life of Buddha.

Wat Koh Wat Koh on Monivong Blvd between Ph 174 and Ph 178 is one of Phnom Penh's oldest pagodas. It was established centuries ago (around the time when Wat Phnom was founded), but only became popular with the masses after the lake surrounding its very small vihara was filled in during the 1950s.

Wat Moha Montrei Wat Moha Montrei, which is one block east of the Psar Olympic (Olympic Market), is on the southern side of Preah Sihanouk Blvd between Ph 163 and Ph 173 (across from the Olympic Stadium). It was named in honour of one of King Monivong's ministers, Chakrue Ponn,

who initiated the founding of the pagoda (*moha montrei* means 'the great minister'). The cement vihara, topped with a 35m-high tower, was completed in 1970. Between 1975 and 1979, the building was used to store rice and corn.

Note the assorted Cambodian touches incorporated in the wall murals of the vihara, which tell the story of Buddha. The angels accompanying Buddha to heaven are dressed as classical Khmer dancers and the assembled officials wear white military uniforms of the Sihanouk period. Along the wall to the left of the dais is a painted and carved wooden lion from which religious lessons are preached four times a month. The golden wooden throne nearby is used for the same purpose. All the statues of Buddha here were made after 1979.

International Mosque This completely rebuilt mosque is beside the Boeng Kak. It was built with US$350,000 in donations from Saudi Arabia. Prayers are held five times daily.

Nur ul-Ihsan Mosque The Nur ul-Ihsan Mosque in Khet Chraing Chamres, founded in 1813, is 7km north of central Phnom Penh on National Hwy 5. According to local people, it was used by the Khmer Rouge as a pigsty and reconsecrated in 1979. It now serves a small community of Cham and ethnic Malay Muslims. Next to the mosque is a *madrasa* (religious school). Visitors must remove their shoes before entering the mosque.

Not many of the moto drivers know Nur ul-Ihsan Mosque, so you may need to ask around a bit to get out there. Buses leave from Psar O Russei (O Russei Market) towards Khet Prek Phnou, passing the mosque en route.

An-Nur an-Na'im Mosque The original An-Nur an-Na'im Mosque was built in 1901 and razed by the Khmer Rouge. A new, more modest brick structure – topped with a white dome holding a star and crescent aloft – has been constructed by the local Muslim community. The mosque is in Chraing Chamres II, about 1km north of Nur ul-Ihsan Mosque.

Markets

All Phnom Penh's markets have food stalls where you can buy cheap and tasty food. These make perfect places for a lively breakfast or lunch.

Psar Thmei The dark-yellow Art Deco Psar Thmei (New Market) is also referred to as the Central Market, a reference to its location and size. The central domed hall resembles a Babylonian ziggurat, and has four wings filled with shops selling gold and silver jewellery, antique coins, fake name-brand watches and other such items. Around the main building are stalls offering *krama* (checked scarves), stationery, household items, cloth for sarongs, flowers and second-hand clothes, usually from Europe and the US. For photographers, the fresh food section affords a lot of opportunities. There are a host of good value food stalls on the structure's western side, which faces Monivong Blvd.

Psar Thmei is undoubtedly the best of Phnom Penh's markets for browsing. It is the cleanest and has the widest range of products for sale. Opening hours are from early morning until early evening.

Psar Tuol Tom Pong More commonly referred to by foreigners as the Russian Market, this is located at the corner of Ph 440 and Ph 163, south of Mao Tse Toung Blvd. It's the best place in town for souvenir shopping, having a large range of real and fake antiquities. Items for sale include miniature Buddhas, silk, silver jewellery, gems, videos, ganja (both ready-rolled and roll-your-own!) and a host of other goodies. It's well worth popping in for a browse.

Psar O Russei Not to be confused with the aforementioned Psar Tuol Tom Pong, the Psar O Russei sells luxury foodstuffs, costume jewellery, imported toiletries and second-hand clothes from hundreds of stalls. The market is normally on Ph 182 between Ph 111 and Ph 141; this is a real labyrinth of a place. A new indoor market is under construction on the site, and at the time of writing, the market is temporarily located a couple of blocks west, where Ph 182 hits Charles de Gaulle Blvd.

Psar Olympic A great deal of wholesaling is done at the Psar Olympic, which is near the Olympic Stadium and Wat Moha Montrei. Items for sale include bicycle parts, clothes, electronics and assorted edibles. This is the most modern market set in a covered location.

Psar Dang Kor Psar Dang Kor is just north of the intersection of Mao Tse Toung Blvd and Monireth Blvd, where the modern Municipal Theatre building stands. Taxis for the south coast leave from this market.

Psar Char The Psar Char (Old Market) on Ph 110 lives up to its name. It's a scruffy place that deals in household goods, clothes and jewellery. Small restaurants, food vendors and jewellery stalls are scattered throughout the area.

Activities

Swimming There is a large swimming pool at the Olympic Stadium, olympic-sized in fact, and it is only US$2 entry to escape the heat of the city. There is also a diving pool at the complex with some high boards. Women should note that one-piece swimsuits are required, and should this be a problem, there are some flamboyant, frilly numbers available. There is also a pool at the International Youth Club, but this is expensive as the club boasts other facilities such as tennis courts and gym.

Shooting Many travellers decide Cambodia is the place to do the Rambo thing and fire off a few rounds on an AK-47 or aim a rocket launcher at a cardboard cut-out of a tank. It costs about US$12 for an AK-47 clip, US$30 for 100 bullets on an M-60 mounted machine gun and US$40 for a go on a B-40 rocket propelled grenade launcher. For US$100 the soldiers say they will chuck in a cow: were you sick enough to want to do it, they would inevitably adjust the sights anyway so you would miss.

The artillery range is out beyond Pochentong airport, so don't forget to aim low. Motos can be arranged outside guesthouses for about US$4. It is best to go in a group as you can get some excellent photographs and negotiate a discount on arms.

Go-Carting There are a couple of go-cart tracks in the Phnom Penh area. Tompuon is located about 10km or so across the Monivong Bridge and charges US$3 for 10 minutes. The track is pretty small and the carts have seen better days. Much more professional is Kambol F1, located abut 10km beyond Pochentong airport, just off the road to Sihanoukville. It costs US$7 for 10 minutes, including helmets and racing suits. It organises races on Sundays, so if you fancy yourself as a new Niki Lauda, turn up then.

Mini Golf There is a nine hole mini golf course at L'Imprevu Restaurant, about 8km down National Hwy 1 to Vietnam. It costs just US$2 a round, and some of the holes are quite difficult, with myriad obstacles blocking the route to your goal. This is a pretty cheap way to get in a round of golf when compared with the price of US$80 a round at the Cambodia Country Club.

Places to Stay

Where once there were just a few ineptly run government 'institutions', there is now a wide selection of guesthouses, mid-range *pensions* and hotels, and a growing number of top-end choices for travellers.

The best hotel deals in Phnom Penh fall into the mid-range category. For the most part, it is still slim pickings for budget travellers, though there are signs that the situation is gradually improving. Similarly, top-end travellers will often find that Phnom Penh's top hotels are expensive; there is often far better value for money at the mid-range hotels.

For the time being, traffic conditions, while slightly chaotic, are not as bad as they are in many Asian cities. Provided you are happy to jump on a moto or take a *cyclo* (bicycle rickshaw), it makes little difference where in town you are based. Some of the best mid-range deals, for example, are in the south of town near the Independence Monument, but even from there it is only a 10 minute moto drive to the centre of town.

Places to Stay – Budget

The most popular guesthouses are scattered around town, which makes checking them out for comfort difficult. There aren't that many budget places in Phnom Penh when compared with Siem Reap, but this will undoubtedly change as visitor numbers take off in the next few years, so if you hear of a great new place that isn't mentioned here it is probably worth a try.

The longest running, though by no means the best, is the *Capitol Guesthouse* (☎ 364104) on Ph 182 not far from Psar O Russei. The owners have expanded operations into two adjacent buildings under the names Happy Guesthouse and Capitol II. Basic singles/doubles (no bathroom, often no window) cost US$3/5, while rooms with bathroom cost US$4/6.

There is a slightly seedy atmosphere pervading the place, but the restaurant downstairs is always a lively, cheap place to eat. The Capitol is the best budget centre to arrange transport for sightseeing in the Phnom Penh area, as the friendly management is the most experienced in the business. It can also change most foreign currencies and assist with visa arrangements.

Narin Guesthouse (☎ 213657, 50, Ph 125) is probably the most popular budget place in town. It's a clean and friendly, family-run place that provides excellent meals. Clean rooms with windows and shared bathroom cost US$3/5, or US$6 for a double with bathroom in the corner annex. Bookings are advised. If the rooms are full, the guesthouse will let you sleep on the terraces for US$1. The family has guesthouses throughout Cambodia so can also help with transport and visa arrangements.

Not far from the Capitol and Narin on Ph 115 is the *Lux Orisey Guesthouse* (☎ 721761), which has some decently priced rooms for US$5 for a double bed and bathroom and US$8 for two beds, a bathroom and a TV. It is a quiet place, and makes for a handy retreat if Narin is full.

Elsewhere around town, the two most popular spots are *No 9 Guesthouse* (☎ 018-815569) and *Lakeside Guesthouse*. Both have a great setting by Boeng Kak, and

PHNOM PENH

there's a wooden pavilion area with hammocks. The food served at these guesthouses is reasonable, and it is definitely the place to be for dramatic sunsets over the lake. It's advisable that you check in any valuables with management if you stay – the rooms are not particularly secure. Very basic rooms start at US$2, but are prone to attacks from squadrons of mosquitoes living on the lake. The biggest drawback of staying here is access, as both guesthouses are at the end of a long dirt road that becomes a bog in the wet season.

If you are in Phnom Penh for the first time and want to experience the sights and nightlife, Narin is better than the guesthouses by the lake; but if you've done all you want to do and are just waiting for a visa or a plane, you might want to chill out by the water.

A relative newcomer that is rapidly acquiring a great reputation among backpackers is the *Walkabout Hotel* (☎ 012-851787) on the corner of Ph 51 and Ph 174, not far south of the Heart of Darkness bar. Rooms start at US$6, but are slowly being upgraded so prices may rise a little. Air-con rooms are available for US$10. It has a 24 hour bar with a pool table. If you are into your nightlife you may end up saving a considerable sum on moto rides to the Heart of Darkness.

The *Pyco Guesthouse* (☎ 012-862824, 79 Sisowath Quay), formerly Bert's Books, has little atmosphere for such a good location – it's a joint venture in waiting really. Rooms with fan and bathroom cost US$5 or US$10 with air-con.

If you don't mind staying a little way out from the city centre, then the *Tat Guesthouse* (☎ 012-858709), just off Kampuchea Krom Blvd on Ph 259, is a good place. It offers clean, modern rooms for US$3/5, or US$6 with a bathroom. It also has a rooftop restaurant. It is a convenient location if you have to catch an early flight from Pochentong airport.

If you want to spend a little more for a lot more comfort, the friendly *Royal Guesthouse* (☎ 360298, 91, Ph 154), just off Norodom Blvd, has a good selection of rooms with bathroom, TV, fridge and air-con. It has a couple of basic rooms for

US$4/5, while rooms with all the trimmings cost US$7/10. It has a good cafe downstairs.

A similar deal is available at the *Dara Reang Sey Hotel* (☎ 428141), on the corner of Ph 118 and Ph 13. It has well-appointed air-con rooms for US$12/15 and some cheaper fan rooms with bathroom for US$6. The restaurant downstairs has Khmer-priced food and drinks.

Places to Stay – Mid-Range

If you are happy spending US$10 to US$20 for a room in Phnom Penh there are some excellent deals to be had around town. The average price for a double with air-con, attached bathroom, TV (sometimes with satellite) and laundry service is US$15, and occasionally prices dip to US$10 or lower for a single.

As with the budget guesthouses, there is no single mid-range hotel area. The stretch of Monivong Blvd between Pochentong and Preah Sihanouk Blvds is the old hotel district, but many of the hotels in this area have been renovated and refurbished into the top-end category: those that haven't are generally poor value. Some of the best deals in town are south of Preah Sihanouk Blvd, but there are also some good deals elsewhere.

Central Phnom Penh On the waterfront, on the corner of Ph 144, is *Hotel Indochine* (☎ 427292), a very friendly place with spacious air-con rooms with bathroom and TV for US$10/12 for singles/doubles and those with a river view for US$12/15. There are also some rooms with hot water for US$20. It can help with travel arrangements and sells cheaper return boat tickets to Siem Reap than most other places.

Next door is the slightly more sophisticated *Sunshine Hotel* (☎ 725684, fax 218256), which has slightly higher prices to match the image. Well-equipped rooms with air-con, TV, fridge and telephone are US$15/20, or US$25 a double with a dubious city view and US$30 with a commanding river view.

In the south of town is the *Amara Hotel* (☎ 362824), on the corner of Ph 63 and Ph 282. The Amara looks slightly the worse for wear, but it has a business centre, and rooms with air-con and bathroom are just US$10/13. There are also functional triples available for US$15.

The *Singapore Hotel* (☎ 725552), on the corner of Kampuchea Krom and Monivong Blvds, is an average kind of place with rooms for US$15.

The *Cathay Hotel* (☎ 427178), just north of the corner of Ph 19 and Ph 110, has been around for a while, and is a popular place with resident journalists and photographers, who swear by the hotel's answering service and business facilities. The rooms are a good deal too. Air-con rooms on the 1st and 2nd floors cost US$20, while those on the 3rd and 4th floors cost US$15. One of the high points of this hotel (besides its location) are the encircling verandas on every floor.

Not far from the Cathay is the *Fortune Hotel* (☎ 428216, 2, Ph 67). It does a steady business with regular visitors to Phnom Penh and seems to have cleaned up its once slightly seedy image. Rooms cost US$15. The *Wat Phnom Hotel* (☎ 725320) is also US$15 for a room and is not far away on the Wat Phnom circle road. The Wat Phnom is a little tired these days – the rooms are musty and look the worse for wear.

A favourite with long-termers is the *Golden Gate Hotel* (☎ 721161, fax 427618). It is close to the corner of Ph 57 and Ph 278. Unfortunately it is not unusual for this extremely friendly Chinese-run hotel to be full – it's a good idea to ring ahead and book. The Golden Gate has a downstairs restaurant and verandas. The rooms are spotless, have air-con and are fitted with satellite TV and minibars. There is also a free laundry service. Costs are US$30/40 for rooms in the main building, or US$15/20 in the less impressive annex.

If the Golden Gate is full, the *Tokyo Hotel* (☎ 721050, fax 721051, 13, Ph 278) is not far away. It is good value with rooms for US$10/15. Another nearby option is the *Champs Élysées Hotel* (☎ 721080, fax 724153, 185, Ph 63). This place deserves to be more popular than it is. The staff are helpful and the doubles at US$20 are among the best value in town. Two-room apartments

are available for US$30, and there are also some triples for US$22 and a couple of singles without bathrooms for US$15.

Also close to the Golden Gate, but a definite notch up in price and comfort is the *Goldiana Hotel* (☎ 218490, fax 217558/9). The only fault of this excellently run place is the gaudy pink decor in the rooms. Standard doubles cost US$25, spacious deluxe rooms US$35 to US$45 and suites US$55. The standard doubles here would cost US$50 or upwards at any of the self-proclaimed three- or four-star hotels around town. It also boasts a fitness centre. The restaurant downstairs is Chinese, but the food is very average.

Nearby, the small *One Way Guesthouse* (☎ 215621) on Norodom Blvd to the south of Independence Monument has four rooms with air-con, TV and hot bath for US$20. It's popular with the French crowd in Phnom Penh. You need to book ahead if you hope to stay here.

There are very few good mid-range deals to be had on the Monivong Blvd commercial stretch nowadays. The *Asie Hotel* (☎ 427825) on the corner of Monivong and Kampuchea Krom Blvds has some singles for US$18, but they are grim, windowless coffins; better rooms cost from US$22.

The *Tai Seng Hotel* (☎ 427220, 56 Monivong Blvd) has a good location west of Wat Phnom and is heavily promoted by the tourist office at Pochentong airport. Rooms here cost US$25, or US$20 on the higher floors – some of these have good views of Boeng Kak. The hotel also has a reasonably good restaurant.

The *Hong Kong Hotel* (☎ 211891, fax 211890, 419 Monivong Blvd) has standard fare at its attached Cantonese restaurant. It is popular with the Chinese business set. Rooms cost US$20/25.

The *Pailin Hotel* (☎ 426697, fax 426376, 219 Monivong Blvd) has rooms for US$20/28, or deluxe rooms for US$45 and suites for US$55. Add 20% tax to the price. The *Dusit Hotel* (☎ 427483, 2, Ph 118) is a sprawling place not far from the Psar Thmei; rooms cost US$20/30.

La Paillote (☎ 722151), opposite the Psar Thmei on Ph 130, is a clean, well-run place in a good location; rooms cost from US$20 to US$30.

For more upmarket accommodation, one of the best choices around is the *Hawaii Hotel (☎ 426652)* on the corner of Ph 51 and Ph 136 near the Psar Thmei. The Hawaii has Chinese and Thai restaurants, and the rooms cost US$22/33, or US$44 for junior suites. Discounts of 10% are available for a stay of a week or more.

The *Renakse Hotel (☎ 722457, fax 428785, email renakse_htl@camnet.com.kh)*, superbly located opposite the Royal Palace, is an old colonial building set amidst an attractive leafy garden. The rooms have recently been tastefully renovated and start at US$25/30, or US$45 for a deluxe double with more space. These rates include breakfast, making it one of the best places to stay in Phnom Penh for this sort of money, especially for those that are unable to afford a similar ambience at Hotel Le Royal.

Due to the proliferation of hotels in Phnom Penh, prices of some of the town's nicer hotels have dropped dramatically in the last few years. Places to look out for include the *Diamond Hotel (☎ 427325, fax 426635)* on Monivong Blvd, which has halved its prices lately and offers rooms for US$40/50.

The *Foreign Correspondents' Club (☎ 724014, fax 427758)* offers a similarly stylish location to rest your head at night, with two rooms for US$35, including breakfast. The rooms have breezy balconies overlooking the Tonlé Sap river and include a minibar clearly aimed at the journalists who pass through town – the spirits come in litre bottles rather than miniatures. It is advisable that you book ahead.

Beyond the City Centre On Charles de Gaulle Blvd opposite the Psar Olympic there are a few more mid-range places. The best of these is the Borei Thmei Hotel (☎ 880239), where spacious, clean, air-con singles/doubles cost US$15/20. The nearby Sangkor Hotel (☎ 427144) and the Vimean Suor Hotel (☎ 364070) offer the same rates, but are not quite as welcoming or comfortable.

The *Bophar Toep Hotel (☎ 724251)*, opposite Sofitel Cambodiana Hotel, is a noisy place with attached karaoke/dancing club; seedy rooms cost US$15.

The *Paradise Hotel (☎ 722951, fax 427280, 213 Monivong Blvd)* has double rooms from US$20.

A popular place with long-term residents is the *Sydney International Hotel (☎ 428312, fax 427907)*, inconveniently located just west of the intersection of Monivong Blvd and Ph 360. This place is recognisable by the oversize Foster's can outside and a miniature Sydney Opera House inside the foyer. As you might expect, it's popular with the Aussie contingent. Rooms range from US$25 to US$35, though discounts are sometimes available.

The *Bayon Hotel (☎ 427281, 2, Ph 75)* is a new French-run hotel with a bar and excellent restaurant plus video room with over 1500 titles. Singles/doubles/triples cost US$25/35/45; deluxe rooms cost from US$55.

The highly recommended *Royal Palace Hotel (☎ 720875, fax 720874)*, located near Psar Dang Kor on Monireth Blvd, has faultless rooms with all the trimmings for US$40 – excellent value given it boasts a swimming pool.

Places to Stay – Top End

Historic *Hotel Le Royal (☎ 981888, fax 981168, email raffles.hlr.ghda@bigpond .com.kh)*, next to the National Library on the corner of Monivong Blvd and Ph 92, opened its doors once more for business at the end of 1997. It is Phnom Penh's finest hotel, with a heritage to match its comfort and class. Rooms are not as expensive as you would at first imagine given the opulence. Singles/doubles start at US$120/135 if booked through travel agents in Phnom Penh, although walk-in rates are generally higher. Its personality suites are rather expensive at US$360; if you are really flush, there is a Royal Suite for US$2000, but surely people can find a better way to spend this much money.

The hotel has a swimming pool, gym, spa, business centre, and bars and restaurants with lavish food and drink. It is worth visiting the Elephant Bar for a tipple, even if you are not staying here. See the Bars entry in the Entertainment section later in this chapter for more details.

Between 1970 and 1975 most journalists working in Phnom Penh stayed here, and part of the film *The Killing Fields* was set in the hotel (though filmed in Hua Hin, Thailand). When foreign-aid workers set up shop in the country after the Vietnamese takeover, this is where they stayed.

The city's first five-star hotel, the *Intercontinental Hotel* (☎ 424888, fax 424885, email phnompenh@interconti.com), is the city's tallest building and is located on the corner of Mao Tse Toung and Monireth Blvds. It has a fitness centre, a swimming pool, business centre and conference facilities. Rooms start at US$170/200.

The *Sofitel Cambodiana Hotel* (☎ 426288, fax 426392, email sofitel.cambodiana@ worldmail. com.kh) took almost a quarter of a century to complete. Begun around 1967, when Prince Sihanouk was chief of state, the unfinished structure and its spacious grounds were used as a military base by the Lon Nol government. Refugees from the fighting in the countryside sheltered under its concrete roof between 1970 and 1975. Work was resumed in 1987 after a Cambodian expatriate living in Hong Kong and two Singaporeans decided to invest at least US$20 million in the project.

It has restaurants, bars, a swimming pool, health centre, business centre and shops. Room prices start at US$120/150, and executive suites cost US$400.

Just south of the Russian embassy on Samdech Sothearos Blvd is the highly rated *Royal Phnom Penh Hotel* (☎ 360026, fax 360036). This Thai-managed hotel has a pleasant garden setting, offers Thai and Chinese dining, a nightclub, bar and coffee shop. Room rates are a flat US$180. Bookings can be made in Bangkok (☎ 589 2021).

The *Juliana Hotel* (☎/fax 366070) on Ph 152 north-west of Psar O Russei is one of the best options in its price range. Again it features a garden setting with a large swimming pool. Other amenities include a fitness centre and sauna, barber, bar and restaurants. Singles cost US$60, twins US$70 and

deluxe rooms US$80, which is excellent value for the standard provided and half the price of a few years ago.

One of the newest hotels on the Phnom Penh scene is the *Sunway Hotel* (☎ 430333, fax 430339, email asunway@bigpond .com.kh), which has an excellent location overlooking Wat Phnom. The comfort is of a high standard and facilities include restaurants, a business centre and conference rooms. It also has an art gallery on the 1st floor, which includes some innovative paintings produced by local artists. Room prices are US$72/94.

There are several cheaper upmarket hotels around the city, which charge a standard US$60/70: the *Regent Park Hotel* (☎ 427131, fax 361999, email regentpark@bigpond .com.kh) is housed in a rather incongruous looking building near the Cambodia-Vietnam Friendship Monument; the *City Central Hotel* (☎ 722022, fax 722021, email citycentralhotel@camnet.com.kh) has a lively location on Monivong Blvd, near the Psar Thmei; the recently refurbished *Riverside Hotel* (☎ 725050, fax 725551), overlooking the Tonlé Sap river and just around the corner from Wat Phnom, is the best of these places.

Popular with the Chinese business set is the *Holiday International Hotel* (☎ 427402, fax 427401), on Ph 84, just off Monivong Blvd, and the *Sharaton Cambodia Hotel* (no, not *Sheraton*; ☎/fax 361199), on Ph 47, just north of Wat Phnom. Both these places have Chinese restaurants and karaoke entertainment. Rates start at US$60 at the Holiday and US$50 at the Sharaton.

Places to Eat

The increasing affluence of at least some urban Phnom Penhois and the large foreign non-governmental organisation (NGO) population of the city has led to an explosion of restaurants. Visitors to Phnom Penh are quite literally spoilt for choice.

Most of the foreign restaurants around town (and there are a lot of them) are expensive by local standards, but it's worth splashing out at least once on a good French or Italian meal, or at least a pizza.

Many of the guesthouses around town have reasonably priced restaurants and some tasty food, but with so much decent food available in Phnom Penh it seems a shame to get into the habit of chowing down on the nearest terrace. Guesthouse restaurants are a good place for trading tales about the latest situation upcountry, but you won't meet many locals dining in these places.

If you want to eat up at Boeng Kak, several of the guesthouses offer reasonable food. *Cafe Freedom* has tasty Thai food, but prices are higher than in the guesthouses. *Cafe Sontiepheap*, between Monivong Blvd and the International Mosque, has some pretty good pub-style grub during the day, including huge sandwiches, and at night the menu even includes Cumberland sausages.

Other pub-style places include the *Cathouse Tavern*, on the corner of Ph 118 and Ph 51, which is a Filipino style bar with mock tropical decor and good counter lunches. It opens only in the late afternoons and evenings, however, and the meals are not cheap. *Tom's Irish Bar*, not far from Phnom Kiev, has a basic selection of typical pub food including bacon sandwiches.

The good news at the time of writing is that none of the big fast-food chains grace Phnom Penh, just a host of copies including *KFC* (Khmer Fried Chicken?) on Monivong Blvd, *Pizza House*, under the Regent Park Hotel, and *Lucky Burger*, next to Lucky Supermarket.

If you are on a tight budget, Phnom Penh's many markets all have small food courts where you can eat very cheaply. Baguettes are widely available around town, and usually cost from 200r to 500r. For something to eat with them, Phnom Penh's supermarkets are remarkably well stocked. Naturally, imported items tend to be expensive. For around US$3 to US$4 you can pick up treats such as salami, Camembert and Brie. The markets are well stocked with fruit and vegetables, fish and meat, all at reasonable prices if you are prepared to bargain a little.

The best of the Phnom Penh supermarkets is the *Lucky Supermarket*, at 160 Preah Sihanouk Blvd, but prices tend to be high. Other good stores are the *Seven Seven Supermarket* at 13, Ph 90, the *You Nam Supermarket* on Kampuchea Krom Blvd and the *Psar Bayon* (Bayon Market) at 133 Monivong Blvd.

For fresh bread and cakes, the best place in town is *Baker's Express*, on Ph 63. It was established by an overseas Khmer family returning to Cambodia after years of running a bakery in New Zealand. It has everything from jam tarts and gingerbread men to cheesecake and eclairs. Another good option is the *French Bakery* opposite the Lucky Supermarket on Preah Sihanouk Blvd. Most of the city's best hotels also operate bakery outlets, but prices are higher than elsewhere.

Cambodian Scattered around town are numerous Khmer restaurants, which set up outdoor tables and chairs in the evenings. These places rarely have English signs and are as much about drinking beer as about eating, but they're lively places for an inexpensive meal and the food is usually very good.

Cook-your-own soup restaurants are very popular with Khmers and are great fun if you go in a group. Other diners will often help you with protocol as it is important to cook things in the right order so you don't massively overcook half the ingredients and eat the rest raw. On the corner of Ph 214 and Monivong Blvd is a popular *restaurant* with a US$2.50 all-you-can-eat deal, and nearby on Ph 214 is another place, the *Dararasmey Restaurant*, which always seems to be packed in the evenings.

Some of the best places for the Khmer experience are along Preah Sihanouk Blvd, just to the west of Monivong Blvd. On the corner of Ph 125 near Narin Guesthouse is the *Chaay Heng Restaurant*, which is heaving every night and seems to have almost as many beer girls as dishes on the menu. Meals are about 6000r with rice, and beer is about US$1 a can. Down a block on the corner of Ph 141 is the *Thong Hy Restaurant*, which has better food than its rivals and extremely helpful staff, but is quieter at nights because it does a lot of its trade at lunch time. On the corner of Ph 115 is yet another place, *Chez Reth*, which offers the option of customising your food, as the hand-written English menu lists all the ingredients available.

There are many more places around town that are worth trying. Some of the more popular areas include: south of the Psar Thmei on Ph 63, north-east of the National Museum on Ph 178 and the area of Ph 51 south of Baggio's Pizza.

It's a bit of a trek out of town, but on Norodom Blvd, south of the Monivong (Vietnam) Bridge are a string of restaurants dealing in 'crusty rice' dishes served with meat and vegetable stews. The food in these places is inexpensive and very tasty.

The reconstruction of the Chruoy Changvar bridge over the Tonlé Sap river has blessed Phnom Penh with a multitude of new Khmer restaurants by opening up access to the Mekong riverfront. These are the places to eat for well-to-do Khmers, and at the weekend are packed with literally thousands of people on a big night out. Most charge US$3 and up for a dish and about US$2 for a big bottle of beer. Heading north, the restaurants start to appear about a kilometre or so over the bridge, and they range from small, family-run places to enormous complexes with fountains, neon and festooned fairy lights. The *Hang Neak* is probably the most popular with resident foreigners, but it is also one of the more opulent places on this stretch of road. Another good one with more than 250 dishes on the menu is the *Boeng Kak Restaurant*. Other popular places worth trying out include: *Kompong Cham*, *Continental Restaurant* (big, all mod cons, complete with a small zoo), *Som Tam Restaurant*, *Neak Samot* (favoured by affluent Phnom Penhois) and the *Ta Ta Restaurant* (Chinese-style Khmer cuisine). There are dozens more.

For upmarket Khmer cuisine, one of the best places around is the *Ponlok Restaurant*, on Sisowath Quay just a few doors up from the FCC. This place has good views of the river from its upstairs dining area, and the English menu takes you on a guided tour of the local cuisine. The house speciality is hotpot. This restaurant is popular with the Khmer mobile-phone set – prices are not cheap, but are reasonable when compared with the European competition on the riverfront (figure on a minimum of US$5 per head).

For inexpensive Khmer food with a Gallic touch, head down to the *Phnom Kiev Restaurant*, on Preah Sihanouk Blvd. The restaurant has a popular garden area out front, and it does good salads and some excellent beef dishes, all between US$2 and US$4.

American There are a few places around town that do steaks, French fries and so on. *California I* is on Sisowath Quay, just north of the FCC. *California II* is at 55 Sihanouk Blvd. Both are popular with the local expat community. *Wagon Wheel* is close to California I and is celebrated for its inexpensive breakfasts of fried eggs and hash browns; its lunch time and evening meals are good too.

Australian No-frills Aussie pub grub is available at the *Ettamogah Pub* on Preah Sihanouk Blvd, next to the Lucky Supermarket. The fish and chips and hamburgers are among the best in town. It also offers Internet and email services at reasonable prices.

Chinese While there are numerous Chinese restaurants around Phnom Penh, few of them are particularly authentic. The *King of Kings Restaurant* on Preah Sihanouk Blvd opposite the Phnom Kiev Restaurant is a shabby place with outside seating, but it has cheap dim sum from morning until mid-afternoon.

Probably the best affordable Chinese cuisine in town is at the *Ly Lay Restaurant* on Kampuchea Krom Blvd near the intersection of Sivutha Blvd. Another good, cheap place to try is the *Shanghai Restaurant* on Monivong Blvd just north of the intersection with Preah Sihanouk Blvd. The *Hua Nam Restaurant* at 753 Monivong Blvd (near the intersection of Mao Tse Toung Blvd) is another contender, but meals here are very expensive by local standards.

Continental The Foreign Correspondents' Club on Sisowath Quay has a restaurant and bar on its 3rd floor with fabulous views of the Tonlé Sap river on one side and the National Museum on the other. The food here is pretty good, although portions are sometimes a little *nouvelle cuisine*. With great views, good music and a friendly crowd of regulars, the club is an essential stop on the Phnom Penh restaurant circuit.

North of the club, the riverfront is now crowded with European restaurants, all pleasant locations for a meal, but the best of them is the *Rendez-Vous*, on the corner of Ph 144. The menu looks small at first, but there are plenty of dishes on the daily specials board. Both the *filet mignon* in mustard sauce and the Moroccan chicken stuffed with pistachio sauce are excellent. Draught Angkor is US$1 and wine is available by the glass. One block south is *Garden Bar*, which serves mid-priced European cuisine on its pavement tables, and is worth mentioning for its friendly and attentive service.

There are a number of pizzerias around town and opinion is divided as to which is the best. Odds-on favourite, however, is *Baggio's Pizza* on Ph 51 not far from the intersection of Preah Sihanouk Blvd. Small pizzas (a meal for one) start at around US$5.

Happy Herb's on Sisowath Quay is as close as you get to a Phnom Penh institution. Apparently Herb taught the local chefs to do the pizzas, and he was always happy – hence the name for pizzas with marijuana as a topping. If you want your pizza to leave you with a grin for the rest of the day (or evening), tell the waiter you want it 'happy' – those with nothing to do for a couple of days might request 'very happy'. Pizzas are about US$4 and up depending on size.

Other decent pizza places around town include *Ecstatic Pizza* (don't get the wrong idea just because of Happy Herb's), south of the Independence Monument on Norodom Blvd, and *Nike Pizza*, just south off Preah Sihanouk Blvd on Ph 63.

For a splash-out meal, *Red*, on Preah Sihanouk Blvd not far from the Independence Monument is a restaurant with real ambience. It's upstairs, over Perfumerie Jolie Madame, in a converted French villa. The menu is eclectic and changes periodically, but the friendly staff are happy to make recommendations. Most main courses are around US$7.

Out of town, over the Monivong (Vietnam) Bridge on National Hwy 1 to Vietnam are a couple of continental restaurants that are popular with residents of Phnom Penh, particularly on the weekends, but are unfortunately a little overpriced. Around 4.5km from Phnom Penh is the *River View Restaurant*. It overlooks the Mekong River and has Khmer/French meals starting at around US$5 for a main course. *L'Imprevu* is 2.5km farther on, on the other side of the road. It offers French cuisine, steaks and so on in a delightful garden setting with a swimming pool, but is a little pricey. There are also *bungalows* for rent here.

French A bit of a distance out of town, *La Casa* is just off Kampuchea Krom Blvd on Ph 257, but the journey there is for a very worthy cause. Established by the French NGO Krousar Thmey (New Family), all income generated goes to funding this organisation's programs to help impoverished and unprotected children both in the capital and the countryside. Along with traditional French cuisine, La Casa also does very good pizzas all served in the cultured atmosphere of an old French villa. If you are going to have just one splash, this is the place to do it.

La Paillote, on Ph 130 near the Psar Thmei, is an excellent French restaurant that serves a wide selection of dishes and has an atmosphere of the Paris suburbs that is not unlike the Santisouk Restaurant in Vientiane, Laos. The menu includes some well-dressed salads accompanied by fresh bread, a wide range of steaks and fish and a mouth watering selection of desserts, such as creme brulee, creme caramel and chocolate mousse.

L'Atmosphère is on the corner of Preah Sihanouk Blvd and Norodom Blvd, and is a French-style wine bar with a reasonably priced menu. *Riverside*, opposite the Garden Bar, is a French restaurant with lunch time and Sunday discounts.

Greek The *Athena*, on the corner of Ph 51 and Ph 282, can safely claim to be the first and only Greek restaurant in town. The atmosphere is surprisingly authentic with scenes from Mykonos adorning the walls and tunes from Zorba gracing the stereo. It offers set lunches from US$4 to US$8, and sells wine by the glass to wash down your *dolmades*.

Indian The *Little India Restaurant*, near the Psar Thmei, has huge vegetarian *thali* (mixed plate) for US$3, including a drink, while those wanting meat will have to pay US$4. Down on the riverfront is the *Banana Leaf Restaurant*, offering a slice of the subcontinent's cuisine from US$3 and up.

The *Indian Restaurant* on Monivong Blvd near the Phnom Penh train station is another very popular option. *Royal India Restaurant* on the corner of Ph 240 and Monivong Blvd has perhaps the best tandoori in town, but service can be haphazard – check your order before it goes in and check the bill afterwards. *King's Bar* is a popular Indian restaurant down the road from the Capitol Guesthouse.

Italian On the Wat Phnom circle road, north of the wat, *Il Padrino* is a spacious bar and restaurant with good pastas, sandwiches and wines. It's an inexpensive place for a light lunch or for evening drinks.

Japanese As is the case almost everywhere, Japanese food in Phnom Penh is expensive. *Nagasaki* on the corner of Preah Sihanouk Blvd and Ph 55 is reasonably authentic and has pleasant rooms with tatami (woven matting) if there is a group of you. There's something galling about paying Tokyo prices for a meal in Phnom Penh, however. Another good Japanese restaurant is *Heisei* on Sisowath Quay. *Midori*, just south of the Independence Monument on Norodom Blvd, is probably the most authentic Japanese restaurant in town – naturally you pay for the privilege.

Malaysian It's possible to eat well for about US$3 at *Mamak's Corner* on Ph 61. It's a good place for an early-morning *roti chanai* (flat bread with dhal or curry) and a coffee. The decor is minimal, but the food is authentic. Another good Malaysian place is *Singapore Chicken Rice* on Preah Sihanouk Blvd.

Mexican Yes, it's possible to get Mexican fast food in Phnom Penh. *The Mex*, on the corner of Preah Sihanouk and Norodom Blvds, has takeaways and inexpensive sit-down meals. You can fill yourself up with a massive burrito for US$2.50.

Thai The nicest Thai restaurant in town, but one with the least marks for originality of name, is the *Baan Thai* (meaning Thai house), located just off Norodom Blvd on Ph 302. It is set in a multilevel wooden house, is beautifully laid out with tropical plants, and offers a choice of traditional floor seating or tables and chairs. Most dishes cost from US$3 to US$5 and the presentation of some is quite flamboyant.

There are some good Thai restaurants on Sisowath Quay. Here you will find *Chiang Mai* and *EID* (generally pronounced 'eed'). EID has a very loyal following. It's a small place and very basic, but it has some of the best Thai food in town for the prices, including a healthy *pad thai* (noodle dish) for just US$1.50. Most dishes range from US$2 to US$4. Chiang Mai is a few doors up. Prices are slightly higher but the restaurant is more of a dining experience, and there is more seating – the sit-down area with cushions at the back is good if there is a group of you. There is another branch of Chang Mai located near the Cambodia-Vietnam Friendship Monument.

Turkish The ubiquitous kebab shop has finally made it to the shores of Cambodia, although unfortunately the Istanbul Restaurant closes at 10 pm so you are not able to stumble out of a bar after midnight and pick up a chilli-sauce special. More seriously, it has a good location with a nice balcony overlooking the Tonlé Sap river and pretty reasonable prices when compared to other places popular with expats nearby.

Vietnamese Just south of Pyco Guesthouse on Sisowath Quay is *Saigon House*. It's a small friendly place with prices that won't break the budget. There are also numerous Vietnamese soup places selling *pho* (noodle soup) on Monivong Blvd.

Entertainment

All kinds of events take place in Phnom Penh that are impossible to predict. For news of what's going on where while you are in town, check with the latest issue of the *Phnom Penh Post* or the *Bayon Pearnik*, or with the Friday edition of the *Cambodia Daily*.

Bars If you want to save yourself a bit of money, it is worth hitting the early evening happy hours in some of the bars around town, as many drinks are often half price. One of the best happy hours in Phnom Penh is at the *Elephant Bar* at Hotel Le Royal: an elegant bar in the city's finest hotel. All drinks are buy-one-get-one-free, which means two cocktails for US$5 by the time you factor in tax and service. Wednesday is ladies' night with cocktails for US$3 all night, and Thursday is gentlemen's night, when 'half yards' of ale cost US$3.50 all night. Happy hour is from 5 to 7 pm.

Other worthwhile happy hours to look out for down by the river include the *Globe Bar & Restaurant* from 6 to 8 pm, a place that also serves good food and occupies one of the finest colonial buildings in the city; and the *Garden Bar*, which is open from 5.30 to 7.30 pm.

One of the most popular evening drinking spots is the *Foreign Correspondents' Club*, on Sisowath Quay. Drinks are a little expensive, but you pay for the ambience as much as anything and it is the best place from which to watch a storm come in over the Tonlé Sap river. Happy hour, when Angkor draught is US$1 a mug, is from 5 to 7 pm. This is one bar you should check out.

The riverfront is one of the most pleasant areas in Phnom Penh and quite a lot has been invested in redeveloping it in recent years. There are now a string of pavilions on the edge of the river that serve very cheap beer and good food. *River 3* and *River 2* (such original and daring names) will no doubt be followed by River 1 and River 4! However, you can't fault them when they serve jugs of Angkor draught beer for just 10,000r and a wide range of Cambodian food for 6000r a plate. The only thing that would improve these fine places is a toilet!

There are a few more decent bars near the river including *The Pink Elephant*, which has a free pool table and serves cheap drinks.

Naga, the floating casino behind the Cambodiana, has surprisingly cheap drinks – the Vegas technique – but you need to take a crowd as it lacks atmosphere. Upstairs in the world of the high rollers beer is free, so look important and you will have a cheap night. The *Cathouse Tavern*, at the top end of Ph 51, has an intimate feel and sees its fair share of customers, mostly men. However, it charges for pool, which is pretty uncommon in Phnom Penh. *Tom's Irish Bar* on Ph 63 just south of Preah Sihanouk Blvd is an Irish bar with a loyal following and cheap drinks for an expat haunt. The *Travellers' Bar*, a few blocks south of the Psar Thmei on Ph 63, has very affordable drinks including a host of shots for just US$1.

Two new places are *Teukei Bar (23, Ph 111)* not far from the Capitol Guesthouse, and *Gecko Tales*, near the Foreign Correspondents Club on Ph 178.

The most popular late night haunt in town is *Heart of Darkness*. It's on Ph 51, south of the Psar Thmei. The Heart, as locals call it, is generally deserted before 10 pm but often packed after midnight. Most drinks cost US$1 to US$2 or not much more, and the music is some of the best in town. There is also a pool table out back, but get your name up early as it is a popular institution. It usually stays open until the last person leaves.

Discos Phnom Penh is not exactly the club capital of Asia, but its nightlife is certainly renowned. The few discos that there are around town are largely the domain of the expat community, as Khmers stick to karaoke bars or hostess clubs of the sort you see in the provinces. Ask around at some of the bars for the latest hot spots, as places come in and out of fashion quickly.

The *Manhattan Club*, near the Holiday International Hotel, is the closest thing Cambodia has to a decent club with banging tunes. Don't get too excited, as the music is mainly mainstream techno, but it is usually heaving most nights and stays open until daylight. Entry is free, but drinks are overpriced, so if you are feeling thirsty, pop across the road to the drink stalls where beer is available for just US$1 a can.

Monsoon has the most chilled out atmosphere in town come the weekend. It is set in a delightful colonial building above Papparazzi Italian Restaurant on Ph 214. There is a pool table, a cool veranda and a dance floor. Beers start at about US$1.50 and it generally stays open until the last people leave.

Casa was pretty popular for a while, but seems to have gone out of favour again. It is part of the Sharaton Hotel and may pick up again, so ask around.

Sharky's on Ph 130 near the corner of Ph 15 has free entry. Most drinks are US$2. It's essentially a disco with a chill-out veranda area and a lot of pool tables. However, there are a lot of young sex workers hanging around attracting older western men, which gives it something of a sleazy atmosphere.

Last but not least, *Martini*, just off Mao Tse Toung Blvd, has been around since the United Nations Transitional Authority in Cambodia (UNTAC) days, and is one of the only places in town that can be counted on to be packed at 1 am on a Thursday, Friday or Saturday night. Martini has both a beer garden (with movies) and a dark dance space. Many of the local women who populate the place are sex workers, but they do not work for the bar – they are freelance. They are more numerous than ever with the clampdown on brothels in the last few years. The atmosphere is pretty hard-sell these days, but if you go with a crowd, it remains a place to have a good night out.

Live Music There's little in the way of live music in Phnom Penh. The *Ettamogah Pub*, on Preah Sihanouk Blvd, has a live band every Friday night. The *Duck Tub*, just down the street from the Heart of Darkness, has live music on Saturdays. On Sundays *The Globe Bar & Restaurant* hosts an informal jam session – anyone is welcome to join in as long as they can play.

Traditional Dance Check the latest information on performances at the *Chatomuk Theatre*, just north of the Sofitel Cambo-

diana Hotel. It is occasionally the venue for displays of traditional dance.

The *Sofitel Cambodiana Hotel* has a Khmer buffet dinner and traditional dance from 7.30 pm every Friday night. During the dry season the performances are held outside. The US$17 per head for the performance and for the meal is steep, but worth it if you have the money. Bookings can be made in the foyer of the hotel.

The *Magic Circus Cafe-Theatre (111, Ph 360)* has traditional song and dance at 8 pm on Saturday night. Performances are more folk-oriented than at the Sofitel Cambodiana or the Chatomuk Theatre. Circus performances are held at 5 pm on Sunday. Tickets are US$2 and drinks and food are available. This place closes periodically, so check it out in advance to avoid disappointment.

Private performances by the National Royal Dance Group can be organised through the Ministry of Tourism or the Ministry of Culture and Fine Arts (both on Monivong Blvd). The going rate for a show (normally held at the Institute of Science) is US$350, so you'll need a big group of you to make it affordable.

Cinemas Even if you understand Khmer, Phnom Penh's cinemas are probably best avoided. The patrons are crowded into poorly ventilated halls with no fire escapes.

The *Foreign Correspondents' Club* has movie screenings on Tuesday and Sunday evening. Entry is free for members, US$2 for nonmembers. The movies shown are advertised at the FCC from around a week in advance. At the video store *Hollywood Movie Street*, on Preah Sihanouk Blvd near the Independence Monument, you can hire films to watch in the store's private rooms. It pretty much has all the latest titles from Hollywood and the UK and charges about US$8 per screening.

The *International Youth Club*, not far from Wat Phnom, screens two films a night, at 8 and 10 pm. The French Cultural Centre has frequent movie screenings – generally at 6 pm several times a week. Check at the centre, where a monthly programme is available.

PHNOM PENH

Casinos The few casinos in Phnom Penh that used to exist were big-buck establishments popular with Asian business travellers, but these were all shut down during 1999 after a spate of kidnappings of prominent gamblers. Only the *Naga* floating casino survived the cull, but others may well open up again.

Spectator Sports

It's worth checking the Friday edition of the *Cambodia Daily* or asking locals about events at the Olympic Stadium, which is occasionally the venue for kick boxing or international football. There are regular football matches on Sunday afternoons and once every few months a supercross (moto-cross) race is held here.

Shopping

Souvenirs The best place for an overview of antiques, silver items, jewellery, silks and clothes is the Psar Tuol Tom Pong. Most of the 'antiques' here are fake and bargaining is required, but it's still a worthwhile place for a browse. The Psar Thmei is also worth checking out.

For really tasteful souvenirs, consider calling into one of the workshops set up by NGOs, local disabled people and mine victims. The National Centre of Disabled Persons (NCDP) has a shop called NCDP Handicrafts at 3 Norodom Blvd. Articles on sale include silk and leather bags, slippers, krama, shirts, wallets and purses, and notebooks. The standard of craft work is very high. Prices for some of the items tend to be high too. Part of the building is an inexpensive cafe, where staff serve a variety of food and cheap Tiger draught – a good place to relax after a Seeing Hands Massage.

Along similar lines is the handicraft shop at Wat Than. The emphasis here is on products made from Khmer silk. Khemara is run by a local NGO and women's self-help groups. It is at 18, Ph 302 and has a great garden setting. Downstairs is a cafe, while the shop upstairs is a relaxing place for some hassle-free browsing. Near the Independence Monument on Norodom Blvd is Apsara, another good gift shop helping disabled people in Cambodia.

Postcards Postcards are widely available in Phnom Penh. The easiest places to find them are the Psar Thmei or the Psar Tuol Tom Pong, where books of 10 cost from US$1 to US$1.50 depending on your negotiating skills. Better quality, but more expensive postcards are available at bookstores in upmarket hotels and at the FCC.

Daily Needs Most supermarkets stock essentials such as shampoo, UV sunscreen lotion, toothbrushes and the like.

Getting There & Away

Air For information on air services to/from Phnom Penh, see the Getting There & Away and Getting Around chapters.

The Royal Air Cambodge head office (☎ 428055) is at 206 Norodom Blvd. Opening hours are from 7 to 11 am and 2 to 5 pm, Monday to Saturday. You can get flights at short notice to Siem Reap, but for other destinations like Ratanakiri and Battambang it's wise to book well in advance. There is another, more convenient booking office located next to Cambodian Commercial Bank on Ph 110. Other airlines include:

Air France
  (☎ 426426) Office 11, Sofitel Cambodiana Hotel
Bangkok Airways
  (☎ 426707) 61, Ph 214. It offers flights to Bangkok and can book onward connections to Ko Samui and Phuket. It can also book Siem Reap to Bangkok tickets.
Dragonair
  (☎ 217665) 104 Regency Square, Intercontinental Hotel
Lao Aviation
  (☎ 426563) 58 Preah Sihanouk Blvd. Lao Aviation offers flights to Vientiane and can also organise Lao visas for US$25. The office open from 8 to 11.30 am and 2 to 5 pm, Monday to Saturday.
Malaysia Airlines
  (☎ 426588) Diamond Hotel, 182 Monivong Blvd
President Airlines
  (☎ 212887) 50 Norodom Blvd (Head Office). It has regular flights to Siem Reap, Battambang and Stung Treng.
Silk Air
  (☎ 364747) Pailin Hotel, Monivong Blvd

Lively and loud, local markets are a marvellous insight into Cambodian cuisine.

JULIA WILKINSON

English lessons are on hold as lunch is served on a Phnom Penh street.

BERNARD NAPTHINE

Education, once banned, is back on the agenda and school children are again a common sight.

Thai Airways International
  (☎ 722335) 19, Ph 106
Vietnam Airlines
  (☎ 363396). The office is on Ph 214, almost
  opposite Monsoon. It has daily flights to Ho
  Chi Minh City, and can also issue Vietnam
  visas (US$50 for a five day service). Opening
  hours are from 8 to 11.30 am and 2 to 5 pm,
  Monday to Saturday.

Bus New bus services are opening as security improves. For Sihanoukville (12,000r;
three to four hours), GST and Ho Wah
Genting both have large, comfortable air-con
buses offering kung fu videos and complimentary water. GST departs at 8 am and 1
pm and Ho Wah Genting at 7.30 and 8.45 am
and 12.15 (9000r in a smaller bus) and 1.30
pm. Ho Wah Genting has the most comfortable buses. Buses depart from the ticket offices, located south-west of the Psar Thmei.

Buses back to Phnom Penh leave from
company offices in Sihanoukville (see the
Sihanoukville section in the Around Cambodia chapter for details). GST departs at the
same times as from Phnom Penh, but Ho
Wah Genting departs at 7 (9000r in a smaller
bus) and 8 am and noon and 2 pm.

Ho Wah Genting has started services to
Kompong Cham (6000r; two hours). Buses
leave Phnom Penh at 6.45, 7.45, 9.30 and
11.30 am and 1.45 and 3.45pm. Buses leave
Kompong Cham at 6.45, 7.45 and 9.30 am
and 12.30, 1.30 and 3.30 pm.

Ho Wah Genting also runs air-con provincial services to towns around Phnom Penh,
including Kompong Chhnang via Udong, and
Takeo via Tonlé Bati and Phnom Chisor,
which makes sightseeing around the capital
much cheaper than it used to be. The buses
are clean, comfortable and cheap. Buses to
Kompong Chhnang (5000r) via Udong start
from 6.30 am and run regularly through the
day until the last bus at 4.30 pm. There are
also smaller buses to Udong (2000r) every 45
minutes. Buses to Takeo (4500r) via Tonlé
Bati (3000r) and Phnom Chisor (4000r) start
running at 6.50 am and run regularly until the
last at 4.30 pm. Buses to Kompong Speu
(3000r) start at 6 am and run every 45 minutes until 6 pm; to Takhmau (1200r) they go
every 15 minutes and to Neak Luong (4000r)

via Kien Svay (1200r) every hour, which offers travellers a cheaper, if less convenient
way of getting to Vietnam than a share taxi.
See the Getting There & Away chapter for
more details on getting to the border.

Ho Chi Minh City There is a daily (except
Sundays) bus service to Ho Chi Minh City
that leaves at 4.30 am from the Ho Chi
Minh bus station, on a little dirt road off Ph
182, just past the Shell garage. Monday to
Wednesday is the rattletrap bus (US$5) and
Thursday to Saturday is the modern air-con
bus (US$12). The office is open from 5 to
10 am. It is better to use share taxis as the
bus gets stuck at the border for ages, making journey times as long as 10 hours.

Minibuses depart Capitol Guesthouse at
6.45 am daily. Tickets cost $8 and should be
bought a day in advance. This is probably the
most convenient way to travel to Vietnam.

Train Train travel is now once again possible for foreigners with the nationwide improvement in security. It may be ludicrously
cheap, but it is generally not the most time-
effective way to travel, as trains are extremely slow. Trains to Kampot (2500r; six
hours; 166km) and Sihanoukville (4000r;
11 hours; 270km) leave at 6.20am every
Tuesday, Thursday and Saturday and return
the following day.

Trains to Battambang (4000r; 14 to 16
hours; 274km) via Pursat (about 2000r; six
hours) depart from the Phnom Penh train
station at 6.30 am everyday.

Taxi, Pick-up & Minibus Taxis, pick-ups
and minibuses leave Phnom Penh for destinations all over the country. Different vehicles run different routes depending on the
quality of the road. The following prices
are those quoted for the most commonly
used vehicle on that particular route. For
more information, see the individual town
entries in later chapters and the Getting
Around chapter.

Six share-taxis to Sihanoukville (10,000r;
three hours) and the south coast leave from
the Psar Dang Kor in the south-west of the
city. It's not a pleasant way to travel when

compared to the bus services. Minibuses cost 7000r. Taxis go to Kampot (8000r; three hours), but the minibuses are cheaper (6000r). To travel as far as Takeo costs just 6000r in a taxi and only 3000r in a minibus.

Taxis go to the Vietnam border (US$25 to charter or US$5 per person; four hours). Minibuses also make the journey and are cheaper; they cost 10,000r. From Moc Bai it costs about US$5 per person to downtown Ho Chi Minh City (two hours). Taxis and minibuses leave from the east side of the Monivong Bridge in the south of town. The Capitol Guesthouse has a US$6 per person service with no more than four to a car, while other guesthouses can usually arrange a car to come to you.

It is also possible to hire taxis on a per-day basis. Rates start at US$25 for around Phnom Penh and for nearby destinations, and then go up according to distance and the language skills of the driver.

Pick-up trucks are the best bet for tackling most of the country's harsher roads, including the journey to Siem Reap (15,000r seated inside and 7000r on the back; eight to 10 hours) and Battambang (20,000r in and 7000r out; about seven hours).

Minibuses run to Skuon (4000r), Kompong Cham (5000r) and Kompong Thom (6000r). From Kompong Cham you can continue on to the north-east of the country, while from Kompong Thom you can continue to Siem Reap.

Boat There are numerous ferry operators north of the Chruoy Changvar. Boats go to Kompong Cham, Kratie, Stung Treng, Kompong Chhnang and Siem Reap.

Siem Reap The most popular boat services are those to Siem Reap. It is certainly the most pleasant way to get to Angkor, with attractive views of life along the Tonlé Sap river and a couple of hours rest on the lake to sleep off the 6 am start. Express services to reach Siem Reap (US$25; four to five hours) are overcrowded, and often appear to have nothing in the way of safety gear. It's best to sit on the roof of the express boats, but don't forget a head covering and sun-

screen. Try not to sit inside the boats, which are mostly Malaysian vessels superannuated from the Rejang River in Sarawak, as you would have little chance of survival if the boat overturned.

Guesthouses can save you anything from US$2 to US$5 on the price. The Hotel Indochine on the riverfront offers return tickets for US$40. The US$25 is an unofficial foreigner price (locals pay 40,000r to 50,000r), which will hopefully come down as more people opt to take the road. The boat operators and accommodation owners probably split the difference between them, but there is little you can do about it apart from travelling by another means: the boat companies will not sell you a ticket for under US$25 under any circumstances. Several companies have daily services at 7 am, arriving at about 11.30am and usually take it in turns to make the run. You can save some money and see an extra town by taking a cheap bus to Kompong Chhnang and picking up the fast boat there. See the Kompong Chhnang section in the Around Cambodia chapter for details.

Slow boats to Siem Reap (25,000r; 36 hours) leave on an irregular basis, so you will need to ask ahead for the next departure. They are not the most stable of boats if the winds pick up across the Tonlé Sap lake. If you really want to travel this way, buy a hammock at the Psar Thmei and stock up on food and drinks for the trip.

Up the Mekong Possible stops on the Mekong River are Kompong Cham, Kratie and Stung Treng.

There are daily express boats from Phnom Penh to Kompong Cham (10,000r; 2½ hours) and Kratie (30,000r; five hours). Boats leave at 7 am and also stop at Chhlong (25,000r; 4½ hours), the start of the new logging road to Mondulkiri. Express services from Phnom Penh to Stung Treng are irregular because of security problems and the river level, but fast boats have been known to do a 10 hour run for 60,000r.

From July until January, extremely slow boats do the run, but think carefully about how much you like being on a cargo boat for several days before taking this trip as it takes three days and two nights to get there. From Phnom Penh to Kompong Cham takes one day and to Kratie two days and one night. It is much more sensible to take the fast boat to Kratie and arrange a slow boat north from there.

For more details on boat services up the Mekong, see the Kompong Cham and Kratie entries in the Around Cambodia chapter.

Getting Around

To/From the Airport Pochentong international airport is 7km west of central Phnom Penh via Pochentong Blvd. Official taxis from the airport to the city centre cost US$7, but you can negotiate a taxi for about US$4 to US$5 outside the terminal. A moto costs about US$1 per passenger.

Bus Local buses don't really exist in Phnom Penh. Most Cambodians use motos or cyclos to get around the city.

Motorcycle There are numerous motorbike hire places around town. Bear in mind that motorbike theft is a problem in Phnom Penh, and if yours gets stolen you will be liable. The best places for motorbike hire are Lucky! Lucky! and New! New! on Monivong Blvd next to the Hong Kong Hotel. A 100cc Honda costs US$4 per day or US$25 per week and 250cc dirt bikes cost US$7 per day or US$40 a week.

Taxi There are no metered taxis of the sort you see in Vietnam these days. Vantha Taxi (☎ 018-810267) is available 24 hours a day and has a few old air-con cars (including a groovy 1970s Mercedes) that work out at about US$1 every couple of kilometres, and this includes a security guard at night.

Unmetered taxis tend to wait outside popular nightspots, but you must agree on a price in advance.

Bicycle It is possible to hire bicycles at the Capitol Guesthouse for 4000r a day, but take a look at the chaotic traffic conditions before venturing forth.

Moto Motos are easily recognisable by the baseball caps favoured by the drivers. In areas frequented by foreigners, moto drivers generally speak English and sometimes a little French. Elsewhere around town it can be difficult to find anyone who understands where you want to go, which can be a real problem if you don't know the location of your destination either. It is not uncommon for a moto driver who doesn't speak English just to keep driving along the same road until you tell them to turn, so unless you want to end up in Thailand or Vietnam, it is best to carry a map and plan your route. Most trips are about 1000r and an extra 500r at night, although if you want to get from one end of the city to the other you have to pay more. Prices are rarely negotiated in advance.

Many of the moto drivers that wait outside the Capitol Guesthouse, Narin Guesthouse and Hotel Indochine have good English and are able to act as guides for a daily rate of about US$6.

Cyclo Cyclos are still common on the streets of Phnom Penh, but have lost a lot of business to the moto drivers. It is a more relaxing way to see the sights in the centre of town, but they are just too slow for going from one end of the city to another. Costs are generally 500r for a short trip, 1000r for longer ones.

Boat The Lotus D'Or cruise boat can take up to 30 passengers and can be chartered from Phnom Penh Tourism or at the landing place just across from the tourism office. For one to six people the boat costs US$18 per hour, for seven to 10 people US$3 each and for 11 to 30 people it's US$2 each.

Around Phnom Penh

There are several attractions around Phnom Penh that make good day trips out of the capital, although they are quite low key when compared with other parts of the country. The Angkorian temple of Tonlé Bati and the hilltop pagoda of Phnom Chisor are best visited in one trip, and can be incorporated into a southward journey to either Takeo or Kampot. Phnom Udong, once the capital of Cambodia, is also a pleasant day trip and can be combined with a visit to Kompong Chhnang, a 'genuine' Cambodian town.

There is now a clean, comfortable and cheap bus network operated by the Ho Wah Genting Bus Company covering most of the places in this chapter. Motorcycles are another interesting way to visit these attractions, as you can stop in small villages along the way. See the Phnom Penh chapter for details on motorbike rentals. If you value time above money, you can rent a taxi to whisk you around for between US$20 and US$30 a day.

PHNOM UDONG

Udong ('the Victorious') served as the capital of Cambodia under several sovereigns between 1618 and 1866. A number of kings, including King Norodom, were crowned there. The main attractions these days are the two humps of Phnom Udong, which have several stupas on them. Both ends of the ridge have good views of the Cambodian countryside dotted with innumerable sugar palm trees. From Phnom Penh's taller buildings, weather permitting, the bluffs of Udong appear as two symmetrical hills – one of which is topped with spires – in the middle of the plains stretching northward from the city.

Udong is not a major attraction, but for those with the time it's worth seeing. It's generally very quiet, though picnickers tend to arrive from Phnom Penh on the weekends.

The smaller ridge has two structures – both heavily damaged – and several stupas on top. **Ta San Mosque** faces westward towards Mecca. Only the bullet and shrapnel-pocked walls survived the years of Khmer Rouge

> ## Highlights
>
> • Tonlé Bati is an Angkor-era temple without the Angkor tourists.
>
> • Udong was once Cambodia's royal capital and is the final resting place of many kings.
>
> • Phnom Da is an ancient hill temple set among lush paddy fields.
>
> • Phnom Chisor offers fantastic views across the Cambodian countryside.

rule, though there are said to be plans to rebuild it. From the mosque you can see, across the plains to the south, Phnom Vihear Leu, a small hill on which a *vihara* (sanctuary) stands between two white poles. To the right of the vihara is a building used as a prison under Pol Pot. To the left of the vihara and below it is a pagoda known as **Arey Ka Sap**.

The larger ridge, Phnom Preah Reach Throap (Hill of the Royal Fortune), is so named because a 16th century Khmer king is said to have hidden the national treasury here during a war with the Thais. The most impressive structure on Phnom Preah Reach Throap is **Vihear Preah Ath Roes** (Vihara of the 18 Cubit Buddha). The vihara and the Buddha, dedicated in 1911 by King Sisowath, were blown up by the Khmer Rouge in 1977; only sections of the walls, the bases of eight enormous columns and the right arm and part of the right side of the Buddha remain.

About 120m north-west of Vihear Preah Ath Roes is a line of small viharas. The first is **Vihear Preah Ko**, a brick-roofed structure that contains a statue of Preah Ko, the sacred bull; the original of this statue was carried away by the Thais long ago. The second structure, which has a seated Buddha inside, is **Vihear Preah Keo**. The third is **Vihear Prak Neak**, its cracked walls topped with a temporary thatch roof. Inside is a seated Buddha guarded by a *naga*, or mythical serpent (*prak neak* means 'protected by a naga').

At the north-west extremity of the ridge stand three large stupas. The first is the cement **Chet Dey Mak Proum**, the final resting place of King Monivong (ruled 1927 to 1941). Decorated with *garudas* (half bird, half human), floral designs and elephants, it has four Bayon-style faces on top. The middle stupa, **Tray Troeng**, is decorated with coloured tiles; it was built in 1891 by King Norodom for the ashes of his father, King Ang Duong (ruled 1845 to 1859). But some say King Ang Duong was buried next to the Silver Pagoda in Phnom Penh. The third stupa, **Damrei Sam Poan**, was built by King Chey Chethar II (ruled 1618 to 1626) for the ashes of his predecessor, King Soriyopor.

An eastward-oriented staircase leads down the hillside from the stupa of King Monivong. Just north of its base is a pavilion decorated with graphic murals depicting Khmer Rouge atrocities.

At the base of the ridge, close to the path, is a **memorial** to the victims of Pol Pot containing the bones of some of the people who were buried in approximately 100 mass graves, each containing about a dozen bodies. Instruments of torture were unearthed along with the bones when a number of the 2m by 2.5m pits were disinterred in 1981 and 1982.

Getting There & Away

Udong is 40km from the capital. To get there, head north out of Phnom Penh on National Hwy 5. Continue past Prek Kdam ferry for 4.5km and turn left (south) at the archway. Udong is 3.5km south of the turnoff; the access road goes through the village of Psar Dek Krom, and passes by a memorial to Pol Pot's victims and a structure known as the Blue Stupa, before arriving at a short staircase.

The cheapest and best way to get to Udong is by air-con local bus from Phnom Penh. Buses from near the Psar Thmei (New Market) run every 45 minutes throughout the day and cost 2000r. They drop you at the access road to Udong from where you can arrange a moto to the base of the hill for about 1500r. Buses also run the other way every 45 minutes. Buses to/from Kompong Chhnang also stop here, so you can combine your visit to the temples with a visit to a Cambodian town that sees few tourists.

A taxi to Phnom Udong and back will cost around US$20. It might be a good idea to hire the car for the day and include another destination such as Kompong Chhnang. The Capitol Guesthouse in Phnom Penh can arrange share taxis for US$5 per head for the return trip to Udong.

Moto drivers also run people to Udong for about US$6 for the day, but when compared with the bus this isn't the most pleasant way to go.

TONLÉ BATI
Ta Prohm

The laterite temple of Ta Prohm was built by King Jayavarman VII (ruled 1181 to 1201) on the site of a 6th century Khmer shrine. A stele found here dates from 1574. The site is open all day every day.

The main sanctuary consists of five chambers; in each is a totem, or *lingam* (all of which show signs of the destruction wrought by the Khmer Rouge).

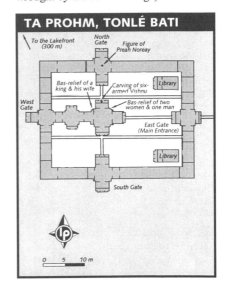

TA PROHM, TONLÉ BATI

To the Lakefront (300 m)

North Gate

Figure of Preah Noreay

Bas-relief of a king & his wife

Carving of six-armed Vishnu

Library

West Gate

Bas-relief of two women & one man

East Gate (Main Entrance)

Library

South Gate

0   5   10 m

Entering the sanctuary from the east gate, 15m ahead on the right is a bas-relief depicting a woman and a man who is bowing to another, larger woman. The smaller woman has just given birth and failed to show proper respect for the midwife (the larger woman). The new mother has been condemned to carry the afterbirth on her head in a box for the rest of her life. The husband is asking that his wife be forgiven.

Around the corner to the right from the north gate of the sanctuary building is a bas-relief in which a king sits to the right of his wife. Because she has been unfaithful, a servant is shown in the scene below putting her to death by trampling her with a horse.

Inside the north gate is a damaged statue of the Hindu god Preah Noreay. Women come here to pray for children.

Yeay Peau

Yeay Peau temple, named after King Ta Prohm's mother, is 150m north of Ta Prohm. Legend has it that Peau gave birth to a son, Prohm. When Prohm discovered his father was King Preah Ket Mealea, he set off to live with the king. After a few years, he returned to his mother but did not recognise her and, taken by her beauty, asked her to become his wife. He refused to believe Peau's protests that she was his mother.

To settle the matter, Peau suggested that she and Prohm build a temple; whoever finished first would get their way. The contest was held at night, with the women helping Peau and the men helping Prohm. After many hours, Peau sent aloft an artifical morning star. The men, thinking it was dawn, went to sleep. Meanwhile Peau's temple was completed, and Prohm, defeated, recognised Peau as his mother.

Nearby is Wat Tonlé Bati, a modern cement structure heavily damaged by the Khmer Rouge. The only remnant of the pagoda's pre-1975 complement of statues is an 80cm-high Buddha's head made of metal.

The Lakefront

About 300m north-west of Ta Prohm, a long, narrow peninsula juts into the Bati River. It used to be packed on Sunday with vendors selling food, drink and fruit, but their high prices have led most Phnom Penh residents to give the place a miss or bring picnics. You are best doing likewise.

Getting There & Away

The access road to Ta Prohm intersects National Hwy 2 at a point 33km south of Phnom Penh, 21km north of the access road to Phnom Chisor and 44km north of Takeo town. The temple is 2.5km from the highway.

Buses leave for Takeo at fairly regular intervals throughout the day and can let you off at the access road. The fare is 3000r. The first bus from Phnom Penh leaves at 6.50 am and then there are hourly services between 8 and 10 am. Buses returning from Takeo in the afternoon leave at 2, 3.30 and 4.30 pm and take about one hour to get to Tonlé Bati. If you are heading to the zoo at Phnom Tamao (see the following entry), these services also apply.

Taxis from the Capitol Guesthouse in Phnom Penh charge US$5 per head.

PHNOM TAMAO

Phnom Tamao is the site of Cambodia's leading zoo. It occupies a vast site south of the capital and its animals are kept in varying conditions. Spread out as it is, it feels like a zoo crossed with a safari park; hopefully some of this space will be used to provide a better habitat for the larger animals. The flagship enclosure is that of the sun bears, funded by an Australian non-governmental organisation (NGO). Other animals include tigers, gibbons and a lion, but these all live in tiny cages. If you don't like zoos you won't like this one, but it is certainly better than many of the animal prisons you see elsewhere in the developing world. It costs 1000r to visit.

Getting There & Away

Phnom Tamao is about 44km from Phnom Penh down National Hwy 2. Take a left turn after the sign for the zoo, and it is a few kilometres down a sandy track. At weekends, you can combine an air-con bus ride with a *remorque-moto* (trailer hitched to a motorbike), but on weekdays it may be easier to rent a motorbike. See the previous Tonlé Bati section for details on bus times and prices.

PHNOM CHISOR

Try to get to the hill-top pagoda of Phnom Chisor early in the day or in the late afternoon, as it is a very uncomfortable climb in the heat of the midday sun.

The main temple stands at the eastern side of the hill top. Constructed of laterite and brick with carved lintels of sandstone, the complex is surrounded by the partially ruined walls of a 2.5m-wide gallery with windows.

Inscriptions found here date from the 11th century, when this site was known as Suryagiri. The wooden doors to the sanctuary in the centre of the complex, which open to the east, are decorated with carvings of figures standing on pigs. Inside the sanctuary are statues of the Buddha.

On the plain to the east of Phnom Chisor are the sanctuaries of **Sen Thmol** (at the bottom of Phnom Chisor) and **Sen Ravang** (farther east), and the former sacred pond of **Tonlé Om**. All three of these features form a straight line from Phnom Chisor in the direction of Angkor. During rituals held here 900 years ago, the Brahmans and their entourage would climb up to Suryagiri from this direction on a monumental stairway of 400 steps.

There is a spectacular view of the temples and plains from the roofless gallery opposite the wooden doors to the central shrine. Near the main temple is a modern Buddhist vihara used by resident monks.

There are two paths up the 100m-high ridge, which takes about 15 minutes to climb. The northern path, which has a mild gradient, begins at a cement pavilion with windows shaped like the squared-off silhouette of a bell. The building is topped with a miniature replica of an Angkor-style tower. The steeper southern route, which begins 600m south of the northern path, consists of a long stairway. A good way to see the view in all directions is to go up the northern path and come down the southern stairway.

Getting There & Away

The intersection of National Hwy 2 and the east-bound access road to Phnom Chisor is marked by the two brick towers of Prasat Neang Khmau (Temple of the Black Virgin), which may have once served as a sanctuary to Kali, the dark goddess of destruction.

Prasat Neang Khmau is on National Hwy 2 at a point 55km south of central Phnom Penh, 21km south of the turn-off to Tonlé Bati and 23km north of Takeo town. It's a bit over 4km from the highway to the base of the hill.

The cheapest way to get to Phnom Chisor is to take a Takeo bus from Phnom Penh and ask to be let off at Prasat Neang Khmau. This costs 4000r and from here you can take a moto to the bottom of the hill for about 1500r. See the Getting There & Away section of the Tonlé Bati entry earlier in this chapter for details on times. Alternatively you can charter a taxi for about US$25 to visit both Phnom Chisor and Tonlé Bati, or there is the option of hiring a motorcycle in Phnom Penh.

TAKEO

Takeo, capital of the province of the same name, is best used as a base to visit the old temples in the area of Angkor Borei. It lacks the charm of some of the other provincial capitals because it has fewer examples of colonial architecture than seen elsewhere. However, in the wet season, it becomes a lakeside town as much of the surrounding countryside floods.

Places to Stay & Eat

The *Phnom Sonlong Guesthouse* is around the corner from the Restaurant Stung Takeo, near the river. It's a basic outfit with fan-cooled doubles for US$5. Another good option near the lake is the *Boeung Takeo Guesthouse*. Rooms with fan are US$6 or US$10 with air-con. This is a nicer part of town to stay than down by the market. Near the market is the *Chhouk Meas Hotel*, which has rooms with fan and bathroom for US$7 and air-con rooms for US$12.

Restaurant Stung Takeo, overlooking the Takeo River, is on the road that demarcates the eastern extremity of town. It's one of the most popular restaurants in town and a good place for lunch during a journey along National Hwy 2.

Getting There & Away

National Hwy 2, which links Phnom Penh with Takeo town (77km), is in a good state as far as Takeo. Air-con buses (4500r; two hours) leave Phnom Penh from the Psar Thmei at 6.50, 8, 9, 10 and 11.30 am and 1, 2, 3.30 and 4.30 pm. From Takeo back to the capital they depart at 6.30, 7.30, 9.30, 10.30 and 11.30 am and 12.45, 2, 3.30 and 4.30 pm. These buses also go past Tonlé Bati and Phnom Chisor, so you can build these attractions into your trip.

The price from Phnom Penh by share taxi is 6000r, while minibuses are cheaper at 3000r. If you are going by road to Kampot, take a remorque-moto or moto for the 13km journey to Angk Tasaom and then arrange a seat in a minibus or share taxi to Kampot.

There are also train services linking Takeo to Phnom Penh in the north and, to the south, Kampot and Sihanoukville. Trains from Phnom Penh leave at 6.20 am every Monday, Wednesday and Friday for Takeo (1500r; three hours). Coming from Kampot, they depart for Takeo (1500r; three hours) at around 10 am on Tuesday, Thursday and Saturday, depending on what time the train arrives from Sihanoukville.

ANGKOR BOREI & PHNOM DA

Angkor Borei was known as Vyadhapura when it served as the capital of 'water Chenla' in the 8th century. Angkor Borei is actually a small town, but in this instance it is used to refer to a group of temples in the vicinity. Four artificial caves, built as shrines, are carved into the north-east wall of Phnom Da, a hill south of Angkor Borei. On top of Phnom Da is a square laterite tower open to the north. In the wet season, it is worth approaching Phnom Da by water as the island is spectacularly isolated. During the dry season, it is possible to make it there by road.

The town has a small **museum** housing a decent collection of Chenla-era artefacts. Entry is US$1.

Getting There & Away

Angkor Borei and Phnom Da are about 20km east of Takeo town along Canal No 15 (visible only in the dry season). A boat to Angkor Borei or Phnom Da is about 4000r a person, but you may have to charter a speedboat for more like US$20 for the day if no-one else is making the journey. In the dry season it is also possible to visit by road. Expect to pay 2000r in a share taxi or about 5000r each way by moto.

The best option is to take the road to Angkor Borei and arrange a boat to Phnom Da from there.

KOKI

Koki (pronounced kaw-**kee**) refers to the beach on the Mekong River in Kien Svay district; beach being a rather misleading name, unless your idea of a beach is a mud-flat on the Mekong covered in 'picnic restaurants' on stilts.

Koki, east of Phnom Penh, is a peculiarly Cambodian institution, a mixture of the universal love of picnicking by the water with the unique Khmer fondness for lounging about on mats. It works like this: for 1500r or so an hour, picnickers rent an area about 2.5m square on a raised pier covered with reed mats. Be sure to agree on the price *before* you rent a space. On Sunday, these piers are packed.

Places to Eat

All sorts of food is sold at Koki beach on Sunday, though at prices higher than in Phnom Penh. The beach is deserted during the week, but food is available at *restaurants* along National Hwy 1 between the Koki turn-off and the capital.

Getting There & Away

Koki Beach is in Kandal Province in the Koki sub-district of Kien Svay district. To get there from Phnom Penh, turn left off National Hwy 1, which links Phnom Penh with Ho Chi Minh City (Saigon) at a point 12km east of the Monivong (Vietnam) Bridge. Buses depart from the Psar Thmei regularly for Kien Svay and cost just 1500r. There are taxis to Koki from the Chba Ampou share-taxi station, which is just east of the Monivong (Vietnam) Bridge. A moto will take you out there and back for a few US dollars.

TEMPLES OF ANGKOR

JULIA WILKINSON

The temples of Angkor were built between the 9th and 14th centuries, when Khmer civilisation was at the height of its extraordinary creativity. Unparalleled in South-East Asia – though the temples of Bagan in Myanmar (Burma) are a close runner-up – Angkor rates among the foremost architectural wonders of the world.

From Angkor, the kings of the mighty Khmer empire ruled over a vast territory that extended from the tip of what is now southern Vietnam north to Yunnan in China and from Vietnam west to the Bay of Bengal. Angkor's 100 or so temples constitute the sacred skeleton of a spectacular administrative and religious centre. Its houses, public buildings and palaces were constructed of wood – now long decayed – because the right to dwell in structures of brick or stone was reserved for the gods.

It is easy to spend a week or more at Angkor, seeing the temples at a leisurely pace, perhaps returning to the main attractions several times to see them in different light conditions. Many travellers feel that about four or five days is the optimum length of time to spend before saturation starts to set in. Even with only two days at your disposal, however, you can get a lot of sightseeing done providing you get an early start in the mornings. If your time is limited and you only have one day to tour the Angkor complex, it would probably be best to organise a tour to get the most out of the day.

HISTORY
Early Years

The Angkor period, in which the temples of Angkor were built and the Khmer empire consolidated its position as one of the great powers of South-East Asia, covers more than 600 years from 802 to 1432. This is quite a sweep of history, encompassing periods of decline and revival, and wars with rival powers in Vietnam, Thailand and Myanmar (Burma). This brief history deals only with the periods that produced the temples of Angkor.

The Angkor period begins with the rule of Jayavarman II (ruled 802-50). Little is known of this king. It is thought that he spent his early years in Java, where he was resident at the Shailendras' court. He returned to Cambodia in the late 8th century and established himself as the head of an independent Khmer kingdom. His court was variously sited in four different locations, notably at Roluos and at Phnom Kulen, 40km north-east of Angkor.

Jayavarman II set a precedent that became a feature of the Angkor period and accounts for the staggering architectural productivity of the Khmers at this time. He established himself as a 'god king' or 'universal king' whose all-reaching power expressed the god-like qualities of Shiva. Shiva's dwelling place is the mythical Mt Meru, and consequently Jayavarman built a 'temple mountain' at Phnom Kulen, which

Title page:
The amazing sight of a silhouetted Angkor Wat (photograph by Mick Elmore).

Facing page: An apsara or 'heavenly nymph', Angkor Wat. Apsara are often depicted in the decorative sculptures that are such a feature of Angkor.

TEMPLES OF ANGKOR

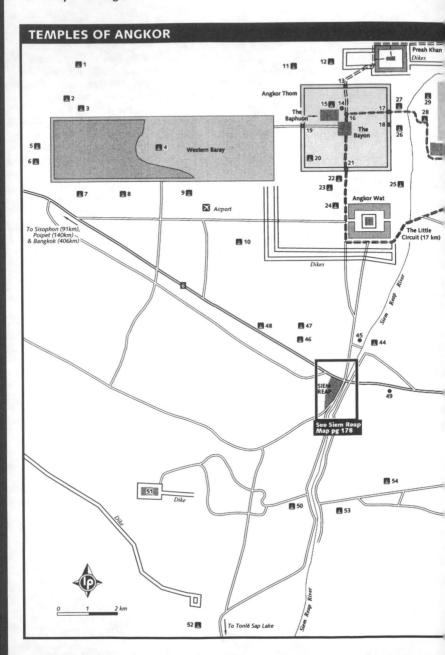

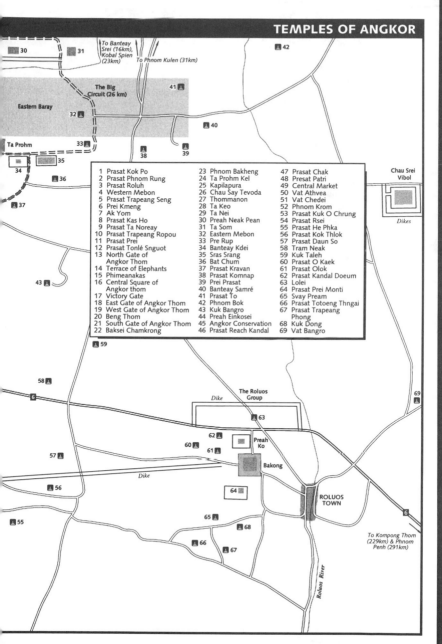

TEMPLES OF ANGKOR

30 · 31 · To Banteay Srei (16km), Kobal Spien (23km) · To Phnom Kulen (31km) · 42

The Big Circuit (26 km) · 41

Eastern Baray · 32

Ta Prohm · 33 · 35 · 38 · 39 · 40

34 · 36

37

43

1 Prasat Kok Po
2 Prasat Phnom Rung
3 Prasat Roluh
4 Western Mebon
5 Prasat Trapeang Seng
6 Prei Kmeng
7 Ak Yom
8 Prasat Kas Ho
9 Prasat Ta Noreay
10 Prasat Trapeang Ropou
11 Prasat Prei
12 Prasat Tonlé Snguot
13 North Gate of Angkor Thom
14 Terrace of Elephants
15 Phimeanakas
16 Central Square of Angkor thom
17 Victory Gate
18 East Gate of Angkor Thom
19 West Gate of Angkor Thom
20 Beng Thom
21 South Gate of Angkor Thom
22 Baksei Chamkrong
23 Phnom Bakheng
24 Ta Prohm Kel
25 Kapilapura
26 Chau Say Tevoda
27 Thommanon
28 Ta Keo
29 Ta Nei
30 Preah Neak Pean
31 Ta Som
32 Eastern Mebon
33 Pre Rup
34 Banteay Kdei
35 Sras Srang
36 Bat Chum
37 Prasat Kravan
38 Prasat Komnap
39 Prei Prasat
40 Banteay Samré
41 Prasat To
42 Phnom Bok
43 Kuk Bangro
44 Preah Einkosei
45 Angkor Conservation
46 Prasat Reach Kandal
47 Prasat Chak
48 Presat Patri
49 Central Market
50 Vat Athvea
51 Vat Chedei
52 Phnom Krom
53 Prasat Kuk O Chrung
54 Prasat Rsei
55 Prasat He Phka
56 Prasat Kok Thlok
57 Prasat Daun So
58 Tram Neak
59 Kuk Taleh
60 Prasat O Kaek
61 Prasat Olok
62 Prasat Kandal Doeum
63 Lolei
64 Prasat Prei Monti
65 Svay Pream
66 Prasat Totoeng Thngai
67 Prasat Trapeang Phong
68 Kuk Dong
69 Vat Bangro

Chau Srei Vibol

Dikes

59

58

6

69

57

The Roluos Group · Dike · 63

56 · 62 · Preah Ko · 60 · 61

Bakong

Dike

64 · ROLUOS TOWN

55

65 · 68

66 · 67

To Kompong Thom (229km) & Phnom Penh (291km)

Roluos River

symbolised the holy mountain at the centre of the universe. This cult of the god king is known as *devaraja*.

Indravarman I (ruled 877-89) is believed to have been an usurper, and probably inherited the mantle of god king through conquest. He built a 650 hectare reservoir, or *baray*, at Roluos and established the temple Preah Ko. The baray marked the first stage of a massive irrigation system that, eventually, was to extensively water the lands around Angkor. But it also had religious significance in that Mt Meru, according to legend, is flanked by lakes. As is often the case, necessity and symbolism dovetail nicely. Indravarman's final work was the Bakong, a pyramidal representation of Mt Meru.

For some reason, the son of Indravarman I, Yasovarman I (ruled 889-910), looked further afield when it came time to celebrate his divinity and glory in a temple mountain of his own. After building Lolei on an artificial island in the baray established by his father, he began work on the Bakheng, siting it on the hill known today as Phnom Bakheng (a favoured spot for sunset photographs of Angkor Wat). A raised highway was constructed to connect Bakheng with Roluos, 16km to the south-east, and a large baray was formed to the east of Phnom Bakheng – it is now known as the Eastern Baray.

Following the death of Yasovarman I, power briefly shifted away from the Angkor region to Koh Ker, around 80km to the north. In 944 power returned again to Angkor under the leadership of Rajendravarman II (944-68), who built the Eastern Mebon and Pre Rup. The rule of his son, Jayavarman V (ruled 968-1001), produced the temples Ta Keo and Banteay Srei.

Classical Age

The so-called classical age refers to the period that produced the temples that are now the highlights of any tour of Angkor: Angkor Wat and the city of Angkor Thom. The classical appellation conjures up images of a golden age of abundance and leisured temple construction; but while this period is marked by fits of remarkable productivity, it was also a time of much turmoil, of conquests and setbacks. The city of Angkor Thom, for example, owes its existence to the fact that the old city of Angkor that stood on the same spot was destroyed in an invasion.

There is much debate as to the origins of Suryavarman I (ruled 1002-49) – he may have been of Malay origin, but is more likely to have hailed from a noble family in the north-east of Cambodia. He was an usurper to the throne who won the day through strategic alliances and military conquests. Although he adopted the Hindu cult of the god king, he is thought to have come from a Mahayana Buddhist background and may even have sponsored the growth of Buddhism in Cambodia. Certainly, Buddhist sculpture became more commonplace in the Angkor region during his time.

Little physical evidence of Suryavarman I's reign remains at Angkor, but his military exploits brought much of southern Thailand and southern Laos into the ambit of Angkorian control. His son, Udayadityavarman II (ruled 1049-65), embarked on further military expeditions, extending the empire still further. He built the Baphuon and the Western Mebon.

From 1065 until the end of the century, Angkor was again divided by various contenders for the throne. The first important monarch of the new regime, when it came to be founded, was Suryavarman II (ruled 1112-52). Suryavarman II unified Cambodia and led campaigns against Vietnam, extending Khmer influence to Malaya, Myanmar (Burma) and Thailand. He also set himself apart religiously from earlier kings through his devotion to the Hindu deity Vishnu, to whom he devoted the largest and arguably the most magnificent of all the Angkor temples, Angkor Wat.

The reign of Suryavarman II and the construction of Angkor Wat marks one of the high-water marks of Khmer civilisation. But if decline was not inevitable, there were signs that it was waiting in the wings. It is thought that the hydraulic system of reservoirs and canals that supported the agriculture of Angkor had by this time probably been pushed beyond capacity. The construction of Angkor was a major strain on resources, and on top of this Suryavarman II led a disastrous campaign against Vietnam late in his reign.

In 1177 the Chams of southern Vietnam, long annexed by the Khmer empire, rose up and sacked Angkor. They burned the wooden city and carried off its accumulated wealth. Four years later Jayavarman VII (ruled 1181-1201) struck back, driving the Chams out of Cambodia and reclaiming Angkor.

Jayavarman VII's reign has given scholars much to debate. It represents a radical departure from those of his predecessors. For centuries the fount of royal divinity had reposed in the Hindu deity Shiva and, occasionally, Vishnu. Jayavarman VII, however, adopted Mahayana Buddhism and looked to Avalokiteshvara, the Buddha of Compassion, for sponsorship of his reign. In doing so he may very likely have been converting to a religion that already enjoyed wide popular support among his subjects. It may also be that the destruction of Angkor was such a blow to royal divinity that a new religious foundation was thought to be needed.

In his reign Jayavarman VII embarked on a dizzying catalogue of temple projects centred on the Baphuon, which was the site of the city destroyed by the Chams. Angkor Thom, Jayavarman VII's new city, was surrounded by walls and a moat (which became another component of Angkor's complex irrigation system). The centrepiece of Angkor Thom was the Bayon, the temple mountain studded with faces that, along with Angkor Wat, is the most famous of the temples of Angkor. Other temples built during the reign of Jayavarman VII include Ta Prohm, Banteay Kdei and Preah Khan.

After the death of Jayavarman VII around 1220, the Khmer empire went into decline. The Thais sacked Angkor in 1351 and in 1431 they sacked it again. The Khmer court moved to Phnom Penh.

Angkor Rediscovered

The French 'discovery' of Angkor in the 1860s made an international splash and created a great deal of interest in Cambodia. But 'discovery',

TEMPLES OF ANGKOR

Angkor Conservation

The organisation Angkor Conservation is responsible for the study, preservation and upkeep of the Angkor monuments. It has its headquarters in a large compound between Siem Reap and Angkor Wat. More than 5000 statues, linga and inscribed steles are stored here because of the danger of theft from the hundreds of nearby sites where these artefacts were found. As a result, Angkor's finest statuary is inside Angkor Conservation's warehouses, meticulously numbered and catalogued. Unfortunately, without the right contacts, getting a peek at the statues is a lost cause. Hopefully, some of the statuary will eventually go on public display.

with all the romance it implied, was something of a misnomer. For a start, as historian David Chandler points out, when French explorer Henri Mouhot first stumbled across Angkor Wat it was found to contain a 'prosperous monastery ... tended by more than 1000 hereditary slaves'. What is more, Portuguese travellers in the 16th century seem to have come across Angkor, referring to it as the Walled City. A 17th century Japanese pilgrim even drew a detailed plan of Angkor Wat, though he mistakenly concluded he had seen it in India and not in Cambodia.

Still, it was the publication of *Voyage à Siam et dans le Cambodge* by Mouhot in 1868 that first brought Angkor to the public eye. Although the explorer himself made no such claims, by the 1870s he was being posthumously celebrated as the discoverer of the lost temple city of Cambodia. The fact is, a French missionary known as Charles-Emile Bouillevaux had visited Angkor 10 years before Mouhot and had published his own account of his findings. It was roundly ignored. It was Mouhot's account, with its rich descriptions and tantalising pen and ink colour sketches of the temples, that turned the ruins into an international craze.

From the time of Mouhot, Angkor became the target of financed French expeditions. A few individuals, such as John Thomson (a Scottish photographer who took the first photographs of the temples and was the first to posit the idea that the temples were symbolic representations of the mythical Mt Meru), managed to make their way to the region, but for the most part it was to be the preserve of French archeological teams.

The first of these expeditions was led by Ernest Doudart de Lagrée, and its principal mission was to determine whether the Mekong River was navigable into China. Doudart de Lagrée died upstream in Yunnan, but not before taking his team on a detour to the Temples of Angkor. The team assembled its findings at Angkor into *Voyage d'exploration en Indo-Chine*, which contained valuable archeological details concerning Angkor.

Angkorian Monarchs

A mind-numbing array of kings ruled the Khmer empire from the 9th century to the 14th century. The following list includes the dates they reigned and the more significant monuments built during their reign.

king	dates of reign	temples built
Jayavarman II	802-50	
Jayavarman III	850-77	
Indravarman I	877-89	Preah Ko, Bakong (Roluos)
Yasovarman I	889-910	Lolei (Roluos), Bakheng
Harshavarman I	910-28	
Jayavarman IV	928-42	
Harshavarman II	942-44	
Rajendravarman II	944-68	Eastern Mebon, Pre Rup, Phimeanakas
Jayavarman V	968-1001	Ta Keo, Banteay Srei
Udayadityavarman I	1001-02	
Suryavarman I	1002-49	
Udayadityavarman II	1049-65	Baphuon, Western Mebon
Harshavarman III	1065-90	
Jayavarman VI	1090-1108	
Dharanindravarman I	1108-12	
Suryavarman II	1112-52	Angkor Wat, Banteay Samré
Harshavarman IV	1152	
Dharanindravarman II	1152-81	
Jayavarman VII	1181-1201	Angkor Thom, Ta Nei, Preah Khan, Preah Palilay, Ta Prohm, Banteay Kdei
Indravarman II	1201-43	
Jayavarman VIII	1243-95	
Sri-Indravarman	1295-1307	
Sri-Indrajayavarman	1307	
Jayavarman Paramesvara	mid-1300s	

Louis Delaporte, who had joined Doudart de Lagrée on the first mission, led the second assault on Angkor. The aim was to produce plans of the monuments and return to France with examples of Angkorian art. Delaporte brought some 70 pieces back, and his sketches aroused the interest of some Parisian architects, who saw in the monuments of Angkor a bold clash of form and function. Lucien Fournereau, an architect, travelled to Angkor in 1887 and produced plans and meticulously executed cross-sections that were to stand as the best available until the 1960s.

In 1901 the École Française d'Extrême Orient began a long association with Angkor by funding an expedition to the Bayon. In 1907 Angkor, which had been under Thai control, was returned to Cambodia and the École took responsibility for clearing and restoring the whole site. In the same year, the first tourists arrived in Angkor – an unprecedented 200 of them in three months. Angkor had been 'rescued' from the jungle and was assuming its place in the modern world.

ARCHAEOLOGY OF ANGKOR
Angkor Restored

With the exception of Angkor Wat, which was restored for use as a Buddhist shrine in the 16th century by the Khmer royalty, the monuments of Angkor were left to the jungle for many centuries. A large number of the monuments are made of sandstone, which tends to dissolve when in prolonged contact with dampness. Bat droppings took their toll, as did sporadic pilfering of sculptures and cut stones. In the cases of some monuments, such as Ta Prohm, the jungle had stealthily waged an all-out invasion, and plant-life could only be removed at great risk to the structures it now supported in its web of roots.

Initial attempts to clear Angkor under the aegis of the École Française d'Extrême Orient were fraught with technical difficulties and theoretical disputes. On the technical front, the jungle tended to grow back as soon as it was cleared, and on a theoretical front scholars debated the extent to which temples should be restored and whether later additions (such as Buddha images in Hindu temples) should be removed.

It was not until the late 1920s that a solution came along. It was the method the Dutch had used to restore Borobudur in Java and it was called anastylosis. Put simply, it was a method of reconstructing monuments with the original materials used and in keeping with the original form of the structure. New materials were only permitted where the originals could not be found and were to be used discreetly. An example of this method can be seen on the right side of the causeway leading to the entrance of Angkor Wat – it is largely the result of French restoration work.

The first major restoration job was carried out on Banteay Srei in the 1930s. It was deemed such a success that more extensive restoration work was undertaken elsewhere around Angkor, a project that culminated in a massive restoration job on Angkor Wat in the 1960s. Cranes and earth-moving machines were brought to bear, and the operation was backed by an armoury of surveying equipment.

The Khmer Rouge victory and Cambodia's subsequent slide into civil war resulted in far less damage to Angkor than many had assumed.

Nevertheless, turmoil in Cambodia resulted in a long interruption of restoration work, allowing the jungle to grow back and once again resume its assault on the monuments. The illegal trade of *objets d'art* on the world art market has also been a major threat to Angkor, although it is the more remote sites that are now being targeted. Angkor has been under the jurisdiction of the United Nations Educational Scientific and Cultural Organisation (UNESCO) since 1992 as a World Heritage Site, and international and local efforts continue to preserve and reconstruct the monuments.

ARCHITECTURAL STYLES

From the time of the earliest Angkorian monuments at Roluos, Khmer architecture was continually evolving, often from the rule of one king to the next. Archaeologists therefore divide the monuments of Angkor into nine separate periods, each named after the foremost example of the art style in question.

To a certain extent, however, the evolution of Khmer architecture was the elaboration of a central theme: the idea of the temple mountain. The earlier a temple was constructed the closer it adheres to this fundamental idea. Essentially the mountain was represented by a blunt-topped tower mounted on a tiered base. At the summit was the central sanctuary, usually with an open door to the east, and three false doors at the remaining cardinal points of the compass.

By the time of the Bakheng period, this layout was being embellished. The summit of the central tower, for example, was crowned with five 'peaks', in a quincunx arrangement – four cells at the points of the compass and one in the centre. Even Angkor Wat features this layout, though on a grand scale. Other features that came to be favoured included an entry tower and a causeway lined with *naga* (mythical serpent) balustrades or sculpture leading up to the temple.

As the temples grew in ambition, the central tower became a less prominent feature, although it was the focus of the temple. Courtyards enclosed by colonnaded galleries, with the galleries themselves richly decorated, came to surround the central tower. Smaller towers were

Periods of Angkorian Architecture

style	date	
Preah Ko style	875-93	
Bakheng style	893-925	
Koh Ker style	921-45	
Pre Rup style	947-65	
Banteay Srei style	967-1000	
Kleang style	965-1010	
Baphuon style	1010-80	
Angkor Wat style	1100-75	
Bayon style	1177-1230	

Right: An etching of the Bayon, Angkor Thom, by the French explorer Louis Delaporte, published in 1880 in Paris.

placed on gates and on the corners of walls, their overall number generally having a religious or astrological significance.

These refinements and additions culminate in Angkor Wat, which effectively showcases the evolution of Angkorian architecture. The architecture of the Bayon period breaks with tradition to a certain extent in temples such as Ta Prohm and Preah Khan, in which the horizontal layout of galleries, corridors and courtyards seems to completely eclipse the central tower.

The curious narrowness of the corridors and doorways in these structures can be explained by the fact that Angkorian architects only engineered arches by laying blocks on top of each other, until they met at a central point. These are known as false arches; they can only support very short spans.

ORIENTATION

Angkor's monuments are spread throughout the forest. Heading north from Siem Reap, you first come to Angkor Wat, then the walled city of Angkor Thom. To the east and west of this city are two vast reservoirs, which helped to feed the Angkor Thom population. Further east are temples including Ta Prohm. North of Angkor Thom is Preah Kahn and way beyond in the north-east, Banteay Srei and Phnom Kulen. To the east of Siem Reap is the Roluos group of early Angkor temples.

Maps

There are quite a number of excellent maps of the Angkor area that have been published over the years. Angkor Tourism sells a good one reproduced from the Henri Parmentier guidebook. The May 1982 issue of *National Geographic* also has an excellent map that shows Angkor in its prime.

INFORMATION
Visitor Fees

Entrance fees to Angkor have finally settled to affordable levels. Visitors have a choice of a one day pass (US$20), a three day pass (US$40) or a one week pass (US$60). This gives you access to all the monuments of Angkor, but does not currently include the recently opened attractions of Phnom Kulen and Kobal Spien, which due to their distance from Siem Reap aren't really firmly under the control of the provincial tourism office.

It is best to buy your entry pass from the official entrance booth on the road to Angkor Wat, as then you can be certain that the pass is genuine and that the money is going to the right place. Hang on to your ticket once your visit is over or it may be resold, the money going straight into the pockets of guesthouse operators, moto drivers or checkpoint guards.

Suggested Itineraries

The chief attractions of Angkor can be summed up in Angkor Wat, the 'city' of Angkor Thom (principally the Bayon) and Ta Prohm, which famously has been left to the jungle. On a short visit to Angkor, you might restrict your sightseeing to these three attractions – attempting too much is likely to reduce the whole experience to a whirl of impressions.

A curious lore of itineraries and times for visiting the monuments has coalesced around Angkor since tourism first started in the 1920s. It is received wisdom that as Angkor Wat faces west, one should be there for the sunset, and in the case of the Bayon, which faces east, at sunrise. Ta Prohm, most people seem to agree, can be visited in the middle of the day because of its umbrella of foliage. This is all well and good: Angkor Wat is indeed stunning at sunset and the Bayon is a good place to be for sunrise if you can get out of bed on time. If you reverse the order, however, the temples will still look good – and you'll miss the crowds.

Back in the early days of tourism, the problem of what to see and in what order was left to two basic temple courses: the Little (petit) Circuit and the Big (grand) Circuit. It's difficult to imagine that anyone follows these to the letter any more, but in their time they were an essential component of the Angkor experience and were often undertaken on the back of an elephant.

Little Circuit

The 17km Little Circuit began at Angkor Wat, headed north to Phnom Bakheng, Baksei Chamkrong and Angkor Thom (in which one visited the city wall and gates, the Bayon, the Baphuon, the Royal Enclosure, Phimeanakas, Preah Palilay, Tep Pranam, the Preah Pithu group, the Terrace of the Leper King, the Terrace of Elephants, the Central Square, the North Kleang, the South Kleang and the 12 Prasat Suor Prat), exited from Angkor Thom via Victory Gate (in the eastern wall), continued to Chau Say Tevoda, Thommanon, Spean Thma and Ta Keo, went north-east of the road to Ta Nei, turned south to Ta Prohm, continued east to Banteay Kdei and the Sras Srang, and finally returned to Angkor Wat via Prasat Kravan.

Big Circuit

The 26km Big Circuit was an extension of the Little Circuit: where the latter exited at the east gate of the walled city of Angkor Thom, the Big Circuit exited at the north gate and continued to Preah Khan and Preah Neak Pean, east to Ta Som then south via the Eastern Mebon to Pre Rup. From there it headed west and then south-west on its return to Angkor Wat.

One Day

If you only have one day to visit Angkor a good itinerary would be the Bayon for sunrise (or early morning) and a tour of the other attractions of Angkor Thom, before heading over to Ta Prohm late in the morning or early in the afternoon. From here you might visit Ta Keo and then the Victory Gate of Angkor Thom en route to Angkor Wat for the last two or three hours before sunset.

Two Days

A two day itinerary might be very similar to the one above, but with more time to explore the temples. Possible additions would be a late afternoon at Phnom Bakheng, which provides a hilly overview of the sunset at Angkor Wat, and Preah Khan, which is in a good state of repair but sees less visitors than many of the other main temples. The exquisite carvings at Banteay Srei are certainly worth the long journey, but you have to weigh up whether or not you can afford a whole morning or afternoon required for the visit.

Three Days or More

If you have three days or more to explore Angkor, you should be able to see most of the important sites described in this chapter. One way to approach a three day tour of Angkor is to see as much as possible on the first day (as in the One Day entry above) and then spend the next two days combining visits to other sites such as Roluos and re-visiting the places you liked best on the first day.

If you have more than three days in and around Siem Reap, it is certainly worth trying to make the trip to the River of a Thousand Lingas at Kobal Spien and the holy mountain of Phnom Kulen, which can just about be done in a day trip, but check that the security situation is stable before making such a trip.

Organised Tours

One day tours to Angkor do not give you very long to explore the ruins. They can be booked by tour agencies in Phnom Penh for around US$250; this includes the return flight, entry fees, guide, transport and lunch. Two-day, one-night tours cost US$350 to US$400; three days and two nights cost US$400 to US$450. The increasing flight frequency between Phnom Penh and Siem Reap makes tours easier to schedule, but they are heavily booked.

For something a little more adventurous and personal, Terre Cambodge (email tc@worldmail.com.kh) offers tours including picnics at Beng Mealea and expeditions to Phnom Kulen.

Getting Around

For information on transport to and around the temples see Getting Around in the Siem Reap chapter.

ANGKOR WAT

Angkor Wat is the largest and undoubtedly the most breathtaking of the monuments of Angkor. It is also the best preserved and never fails to reward repeat visitors with previously unnoticed details. Most probably it was constructed as a funerary temple for Suryavarman II (ruled 1112-52) to honour Vishnu, the Hindu deity who the king identified with.

There is much about Angkor Wat that is unique among the temples of Angkor. The most significant point is its westward orientation. West is symbolically the direction of death, which once led many scholars to conclude that Angkor Wat was primarily a tomb. This was supported by the fact that the magnificent bas-reliefs of Angkor Wat were designed to be viewed in an anticlockwise direction, a practice which has antecedents in Hindu funerary rites. Vishnu, however, is often associated with the west, and it is commonly accepted nowadays that Angkor Wat was probably both a temple and a mausoleum for Suryavarman II.

Symbolism

The casual visitor to Angkor Wat is struck by its imposing grandeur and, at close quarters, its fascinating decorative flourishes and extensive bas-reliefs; but a scholar at the time of its construction would have revelled in its multilayered levels of meaning in much the same way as a contemporary literary scholar might delight in James Joyce's *Ulysses*.

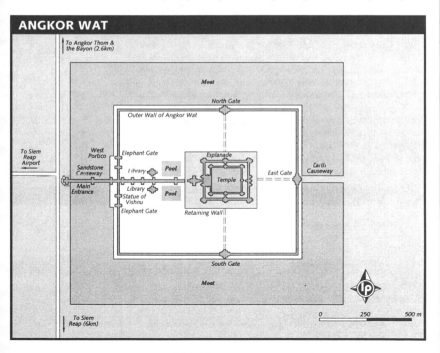

ANGKOR WAT

To Angkor Thom & the Bayon (2.6km)

Moat

North Gate

Outer Wall of Angkor Wat

To Siem Reap Airport

West Portico

Elephant Gate

Esplanade

Library

Pool

Earth Causeway

East Gate

Sandstone Causeway

Temple

Main Entrance

Library

Pool

Statue of Vishnu

Elephant Gate

Retaining Wall

South Gate

Moat

To Siem Reap (6km)

0   250   500 m

David Chandler, drawing on the research of Eleanor Moron, points out in his book *History of Cambodia* that the spatial dimensions of Angkor Wat parallel the lengths of the four ages, or Yuga, of classical Hindu thought. Thus the visitor to Angkor Wat who walks the causeway to the main entrance and through into the courtyards to the final main tower, which once contained a statue of Vishnu, is metaphorically travelling back in time to the first age of the creation of the universe.

Of course, like the other temple mountains of Angkor, Angkor Wat also replicates the spatial universe in miniature. The central tower is Mt Meru, with its surrounding smaller peaks, surrounded in turn by continents (the lower courtyards) and the oceans (the moat). In the central tower, the king prefigures the heaven that awaits him after death, the lofty peak where *apsara* (heavenly nymphs) frolic with boundless amorous desire.

Architectural Layout

Angkor Wat is surrounded by a moat, 190m wide, that forms a giant rectangle measuring 1.5km by 1.3km. From the west, a sandstone causeway crosses the moat; the holes in the paving stones held wooden pegs that were used to lift and position the stones during construction, after which the pegs were sawn off. The sandstone blocks from which Angkor Wat was built were apparently quarried many kilometres away (perhaps at Phnom Kulen and Kobal Spien) and floated down the Siem Reap River on rafts.

The rectangular outer wall, which measures 1025m by 800m, has a gate on each side, but the main entrance, a 235m-wide porch richly decorated with carvings and sculptures, is on the western side. In the gate tower to the right as you approach is a statue of Vishnu, 3.25m in height and hewn from a single block of sandstone. Vishnu's eight arms hold a mace, a spear, a disk, a conch and other items. You may even see locks of hair lying about. These are cut off as an offering by both young women and men preparing to get married or by people who seek to give thanks for their good fortune (such as successful recovery from an illness).

An avenue, 475m long and 9.5m wide and lined with naga balustrades, leads from the main entrance to the central temple, passing between two graceful libraries and then two pools.

The central temple complex consists of three storeys, each made of laterite, which enclose a square surrounded by intricately interlinked galleries.

The corners of the second and third storeys are marked by towers, each of them topped with pointed cupolas. Rising 31m above the third level and 55m above the ground is the central tower, which gives the whole ensemble its sublime unity. At one time, the central sanctuary of Angkor Wat held a gold statue of Vishnu mounted on a *garuda* (half eagle, half human) that represented the deified god-king Suryavarman II.

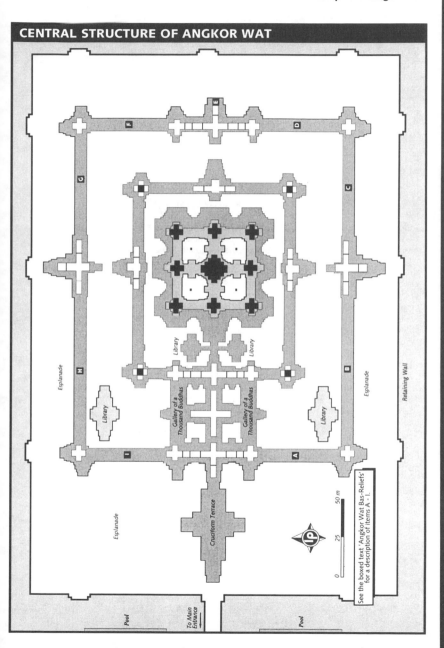

CENTRAL STRUCTURE OF ANGKOR WAT

Pool

To Main Entrance

Pool

Esplanade

Cruciform Terrace

Library

Library

Esplanade

Esplanade

Gallery of a Thousand Buddhas

Gallery of a Thousand Buddhas

Library

Library

I

A

H

B

G

C

F

D

E

Retaining Wall

0   25   50 m

See the boxed text 'Angkor Wat Bas-Reliefs' for a description of items A - I.

Angkor Wat Bas-Reliefs

Stretching around the outside of the central temple complex, which is enclosed by an esplanade framed by a *naga* (mythical serpent) balustrade, is an 800m-long series of extraordinary bas-reliefs. The carvings were once sheltered by the cloister's wooden roof, which long ago rotted away (except for one original beam in the western half of the northern gallery; the other roofed sections are reconstructions). The following is a brief description of the epic events depicted on the panels in the Gallery of Bas Reliefs. They are described in the order in which you'll come to them if you begin on the west side and keep the bas-reliefs to your left.

(A) Battle of Kurukshetra The southern portion of the west gallery depicts a battle scene from the Hindu *Mahabarata* epic, in which the Kauravas (coming from the north) and the Pandavas (coming from the south) advance in serried ranks towards each other, meeting in furious battle. Infantry are shown on the lowest tier, officers on elephant-back and chiefs on the second and third tiers. Among the more interesting details (from left to right): a dead chief lying on a pile of arrows and surrounded by his grieving parents and troops; a warrior on an elephant who, by putting down his weapon, has accepted defeat; and a mortally wounded officer, falling from the conveyance in which he is riding into the arms of his soldiers. Over the centuries, some sections have been polished by the millions of hands that fall upon them to look like black marble. The portico at the south-west corner is decorated with sculptures representing subjects taken from the *Ramayana* (Sanskrit epic poem).

(B) Army of Suryavarman II The remarkable western section of the south gallery depicts a triumphal battle-march of Suryavarman II's army. In the south-west corner about 2m from the floor is Suryavarman II on an elephant, wearing the royal tiara and armed with a battle-axe; he is shaded by 15 umbrellas and fanned by legions of servants. Farther on is a procession of well-armed soldiers and officers on horseback; among them are elephants carrying their chiefs, who appear bold and warlike. Just west of the vestibule is the rather disorderly Thai mercenary army, at that time allied with the Khmers in their conflict with the Chams. The Khmer troops have square breastplates and are armed with spears, the Thais wear headdresses and skirts and carry tridents.

The rectangular holes were created when, long ago, pieces of the scene – reputed to possess magical powers – were removed. Part of this panel was damaged by an artillery shell in 1971.

(C) Heaven & Hell The eastern half of the south gallery, the ceiling of which was restored in the 1930s, depicts the punishments and rewards of the 37 heavens and 32 hells. On the left, the upper and middle tiers show fine gentlemen and ladies proceeding towards 18 armed Yama, judge of the dead, seated on a bull; below him are his assistants, Dharma and Sitragupta. On the lower tier is the road to hell, along

Angkor Wat Bas-Reliefs

which the wicked are dragged by devils. To Yama's right, the tableau is divided into two parts separated by a horizontal line of garudas: above, the elect dwell in beautiful mansions, served by women, children and attendants; below, the condemned suffer horrible tortures.

(D) Churning of the Ocean of Milk The south section of the east gallery is decorated by the most famous of the bas-relief scenes at Angkor Wat, the Churning of the Ocean of Milk. This brilliantly executed carving depicts 88 *asura* (devils; on the left) and 92 *deva* (gods) with crested helmets, churning up the sea to extract the elixir of immortality, which both groups covet. The demons hold the head of the serpent and the gods hold its tail. At the centre of the sea, the serpent is coiled around Mt Mandala, which in the tug of war between the demons and the gods turns and churns up the water. Vishnu, incarnated as a huge turtle, lends his shell to serve as the base and pivot of Mt Mandala. Brahma, Shiva, Hanuman (the monkey god) and Lakshmi (the goddess of beauty), all make appearances, while overhead a host of heavenly female spirits sing and dance in encouragement.

(E) Elephant Gate This gate, which has no stairs leading to it, was used by the king and others for mounting and dismounting elephants directly from the gallery. North of the gate is a Khmer inscription recording the erection of a nearby stupa in the 18th century.

(F) Vishnu Conquers the Demons The northern section of the east gallery shows a furious and desperate encounter between Vishnu, riding on a garuda, and innumerable *danava* (demons). Needless to say, he slays all comers. Scholars conjecture that this gallery was executed at a later date, perhaps in the 15th or 16th century.

(G) Krishna & the Demon King The eastern section of the north gallery shows Vishnu incarnated as Krishna riding a garuda. He confronts a burning walled city, the residence of Bana, the demon king. The Garuda puts out the fire and Bana is captured. In the final scene Krishna kneels before Shiva and asks that Bana's life be spared.

(H) Battle of the Gods & the Demons The western section of the north gallery depicts the battle between the 21 gods of the Brahmanic pantheon with various demons. The gods are featured with their traditional attributes and mounts. Vishnu, for example has four arms and is seated on a garuda, while Shiva rides a sacred goose.

(I) Battle of Lanka The northern half of the west gallery shows scenes from the *Ramayana*. In the Battle of Lanka, Rama (on the shoulders of Hanuman), along with his army of monkeys, battles 10-headed Ravana, seducer of Rama's beautiful wife Sita. Ravana rides on a chariot drawn by monsters and commands an army of giants.

ANGKOR THOM

The fortified city of Angkor Thom, some 10 sq km in extent, was built by Angkor's greatest king, Jayavarman VII (ruled 1181-1201), who came to power just after the disastrous sacking by the Chams of the previous Khmer capital. Centred on the Baphuon, Angkor Thom is enclosed by a square wall 8m high and 12km in length and encircled by a moat 100m wide, said to have been inhabited by fierce crocodiles.

The city has five monumental gates, one each in the north, west and south walls and two in the east wall. The gates, which are 20m in height, are decorated to either side of the passageway with stone elephant trunks and crowned by four gargantuan faces of the bodhisattva Avalokiteshvara facing the cardinal directions. In front of each gate stand giant statues of 54 gods (to the left of the causeway)

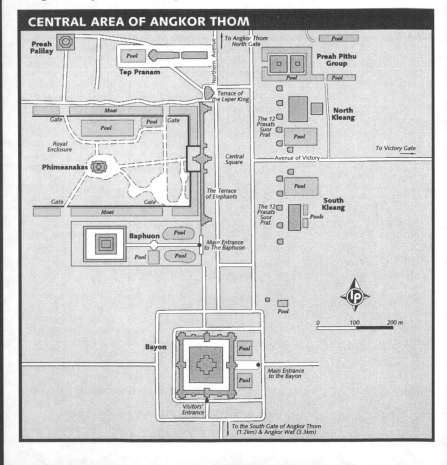

CENTRAL AREA OF ANGKOR THOM

and 54 demons (to the right of the causeway), a motif taken from the story of the Churning of the Ocean of Milk illustrated in the famous bas-relief at Angkor Wat. In the centre of the walled enclosure are the city's most important monuments, including the Bayon, the Baphuon, the Royal Enclosure, Phimeanakas and the Terrace of Elephants.

Bayon

The Bayon takes an easy second place after Angkor Wat as the most popular of Angkor's many monuments. It's a place of stooped corridors, precipitous flights of stairs and, most of all, a collection of 54 gothic towers decorated with over 200 coldly smiling, gargantuan faces of Avalokiteshvara. As you walk around, a dozen or more of the visages are visible at any one time – full-face or in profile, almost level with your eyes or peering down from on high.

The Bayon is now known to have been built by Jayavarman VII, though for many years its origins were obscure. Shrouded in dense jungle, it also took researchers some time to realise that it stands in the exact centre of the city of Angkor Thom. There is still much mystery associated with the Bayon – its exact function and symbolism – and this seems only appropriate for a monument whose signature is an enigmatically smiling face.

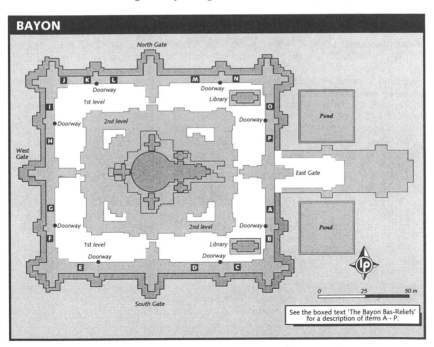

BAYON

North Gate

J K L M N

Doorway · 1st level

Doorway · Library

I

· Doorway · 2nd level · Doorway ·

O

Pond

H

P

West Gate · East Gate

G

A

· Doorway · 2nd level · Doorway ·

B

Pond

F

1st level · Library

· Doorway · Doorway ·

E D C

South Gate

0   25   50 m

See the boxed text 'The Bayon Bas-Reliefs' for a description of items A - P.

The Bayon Bas-Reliefs

The Bayon is decorated with 1200m of extraordinary bas-reliefs incorporating over 11,000 figures. The famous carvings on the outer wall of the 1st level depict vivid scenes of everyday life in 12th century Cambodia. The bas-reliefs on the 2nd level do not have the epic proportions of those on the 1st level or the ones at Angkor, and tend to be fragmented. The reliefs described in this section are those on the 1st level. The sequence assumes that you will enter the Bayon by the east entrance and view the reliefs in a clockwise direction.

(A) Just south of the east gate is a **three level panorama**. On the first tier, Khmer soldiers march off to battle; notice the elephants and the ox carts, which are almost exactly like those still in use. The second tier depicts the coffins being carried from the battlefield. In the centre of the third tier, Jayavarman VII, shaded by parasols, is shown on horseback followed by legions of concubines (to the left).

(B) The first panel north of the south-east corner shows **Hindus praying** to a linga. This image was probably originally a Buddha, later modified by a Hindu king.

(C) The next panel has some of the best carved reliefs. The scenes are combinations of **naval battles** between the Khmers and the Chams (with head coverings) and pictures of everyday life by the shores of the Tonlé Sap lake, where the battle was fought. Look out for images of people picking lice from each other's hair, of hunters hunting and, towards the western end of the panel, a woman giving birth.

(D) In the next panel the **scenes from daily life** continue and the naval battle shifts to the shore; the Chams are given a thorough thrashing by the Khmers. Scenes include two people playing chess (or a similar board game), a cockfight and women selling fish in the market. The later scenes of meals being prepared and served are in celebration of the Khmer victory over the Chams.

(E, F) The last section of the south gallery, depicting a **military procession**, is unfinished, as is the next panel, in which elephants are being brought in from the mountains. Brahmans have been chased up two trees by tigers.

(G) This panel depicts scenes that some scholars maintain is a **civil war**. Groups of people, some armed, confront each other, and the violence escalates until elephants and warriors join the melee.

The Bayon Bas-Reliefs

(H) The fighting continues on a smaller scale in the next panel. At the bottom, an **antelope** is being swallowed by a gargantuan fish. Among the smaller fish is a prawn, under which an inscription says that the king will seek out those in hiding.

(I) This panel depicts a **procession** that includes the king (carrying a bow). Presumably it is a celebration of his victory.

(J) At the western corner of the north wall is a **Khmer circus**. You can see a strong man holding three dwarfs and a man on his back spinning a wheel with his feet; above, there is a group of tightrope walkers. To the right of the circus, the royal court watches from a terrace, below which a procession of animals is marching. Some of the reliefs in this section remain unfinished.

(K) The **two rivers**, one next to the doorpost and the other 3m to the right, are teeming with fish.

(L, M, N) West of the North Gate on the lowest level of this unfinished three tiered scene, the **Cham armies** are being defeated and expelled from the Khmer kingdom. The next panel depicts the Cham armies advancing, and the next, badly deteriorated panel shows the Chams (on the left) chasing the Khmers.

(O) This panel shows the **war of 1177**, when the Khmers were defeated by the Chams and Angkor was pillaged. The wounded Khmer king is being lowered from the back of an elephant and a wounded Khmer general is being carried on a hammock suspended from a pole. Directly above, despairing Khmers are getting drunk. The Chams (on the right) are in hot pursuit of their vanquished enemy.

(P) This panel depicts another **meeting of the two armies**. Notice the flag bearers among the Cham troops (on the right). The Chams were defeated in the war, which ended in 1181, as depicted on panel A.

Right: With the sacking of the former capital fresh in his mind, King Jayavarman VII left nothing to chance during construction of Angkor Thom, which incorporates the Bayon. A 100m-wide moat and massive stone walls surround the royal city, a section of which is depicted here in an 1868 engraving by Louis Delaporte.

A number of locals point out that the Khmer empire was divided into 54 provinces at the time of the Bayon's construction, hence the all-seeing eyes of Avalokiteshvara were keeping watch on the kingdom's far-flung subjects. You would certainly think twice about a rebellion knowing these faces were watching you.

The eastward orientation of the Bayon leads most people to visit it early in the morning, preferably at sunrise, when the sun inches upwards, lighting face after face with warmth. The Bayon, however, looks equally good in the late afternoon, and if you stay for the sunset you get the same effect as at sunrise, in reverse. A Japanese team is restoring the north gate.

Architectural Layout

Unlike Angkor Wat, which looks impressive both close up and from a distance, the Bayon looks like a muddle of rock from a distance. It's only when you enter the temple and make your way up to the third level that its magic appears.

The basic structure of the Bayon is a simple one of three levels, which correspond more or less to three distinct phases of building. The first two levels are square and adorned with bas-reliefs. They lead up to a third circular level, which is whee you will find the towers and the faces. The central sanctuary of the third level is a cave-like cell in a massive, round mass of intricately embellished rock.

Baphuon

The Baphuon, a pyramidal representation of mythical Mt Meru, is 200m north-west of the Bayon. It was constructed by Udayadityavarman II

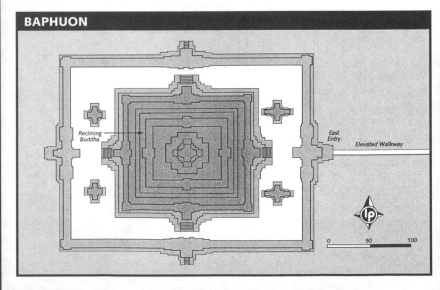

BAPHUON

Reclining Buddha

East Entry

Elevated Walkway

0   50   100

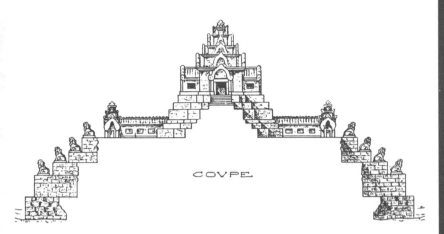

COVPE.

(reigned 1049-65) and marked the centre of the city that existed before the construction of Angkor Thom. The Baphuon is in pretty poor shape and at the time of writing it was being restored by a French team, with much of the temple off-limits. It is approached by a 200m elevated walkway made of sandstone. The central structure is 43m high, but unfortunately its summit has collapsed (it may be restored).

On the west side of the temple, the retaining wall of the second level was fashioned – apparently in the 15th century – into a reclining Buddha 40m in length. The unfinished figure is difficult to make out, but the head is on the northern side of the wall and the gate is where the hips should be; to the left of the gate protrudes an arm. When it comes to the legs and feet – the latter are entirely gone – imagination must suffice.

Royal Enclosure & Phimeanakas

Phimeanakas stands close to the centre of a walled area that once housed the royal palace, not that there's anything left of it today except two sandstone pools near the northern wall. Once the site of royal ablutions, these are now used as swimming holes by local children. It is fronted to the east by the Terrace of Elephants. The palace was used by Jayavarman V and Udayadityavarman I.

Phimeanakas means 'Celestial Palace', and some scholars contend that it was once topped by a golden spire. Today it only hints at its former splendour and looks a little the worse for wear.

The temple is another pyramidal representation of Mt Meru with three levels. Most of the decorative features of the temple are broken or have disappeared. Still, it is worth trudging up to the second and third levels (the stairs to the third level are steep) for good views of the Baphuon.

Preah Palilay

Preah Palilay, a rather deteriorated temple 200m north of the Royal Enclosure's northern wall, was erected during the rule of Jayavarman VII

Above right: This cross-section of Phimeanakas, published in the 1911 *Inventaire Descriptif des Monuments du Cambodge*, reveals a common Angkorian theme: the temple is a representation of the mythical Mt Meru.

(ruled 1181-1201). The temple originally housed a Buddha, which has long since disappeared.

Tep Pranam

Tep Pranam, an 82m by 34m cruciform Buddhist terrace 150m east of Preah Palilay, was once the base of a pagoda of lightweight construction. Nearby is a Buddha 4.5m high – it is a reconstruction of the original. A group of Buddhist nuns live in a wooden structure close by.

Preah Pithu Group

Preah Pithu, which is located across Northern Ave from Tep Pranam, is a group of five 12th century Hindu and Buddhist temples enclosed by a wall.

Terrace of the Leper King

The Terrace of the Leper King, just north of the Terrace of Elephants, is a platform 7m high. On top of the platform stands a nude, though sexless, statue. It is another of Angkor's mysteries. The original of the statue is in Phnom Penh's National Museum, and various theories have been advanced to explain its meaning. Legend has it that at least two of the Angkor kings had leprosy, and the statue may represent one of them. A more likely explanation is that the statue is of Yama, the god of death, and that the Terrace of the Leper King housed the royal crematorium.

The front retaining walls of the terrace are decorated with five or more tiers of meticulously executed carvings of seated apsara; other figures include kings wearing pointed diadems, armed with short double-edged swords and accompanied by the court and princesses, who are adorned with rows of pearls. The terrace, built at the end of the 12th century, between the construction of Angkor Wat and the Bayon, once supported a pavilion made of lightweight materials.

On the south side of the Terrace of the Leper King (facing the Terrace of Elephants) there is an entry to a long, narrow trench, excavated by archaeologists. This passageway follows the front wall of an earlier terrace that was covered up when the present structure was built. The four tiers of apsara and other figures, including naga, look as fresh as if they had been carved just yesterday.

Terrace of Elephants

The 350m-long Terrace of Elephants was used as a giant reviewing stand for public ceremonies and served as a base for the king's grand audience hall. As you stand here, try to imagine the pomp and grandeur of the Khmer empire at its height, with infantry, cavalry, horse-drawn chariots and elephants parading across the Central Square in a colourful procession, pennants and standards aloft. Looking on is the god-king, crowned with a gold diadem, shaded by multitiered parasols and attended by mandarins and handmaidens bearing gold and silver utensils.

The Terrace of Elephants has five outworks extending towards the Central Square, three in the centre and one at each end. The middle section of the retaining wall is decorated with life-size garudas and lions; towards either end are the two parts of the famous parade of elephants.

Kleangs & Prasat Suor Prat

Along the east side of Central Square are two groups of buildings, the North Kleang and the South Kleang, that may at one time have been palaces. The North Kleang dates from the period of Jayavarman V (reigned 968-1001).

Along the Central Square in front of the two Kleangs are 12 laterite towers – 10 in a row and two more at right angles facing the Avenue of Victory – known as the Prasat Suor Prat. Archaeologists believe the towers, which form an honour guard of sorts along Central Square, were constructed by Jayavarman VII (reigned 1181-1201). It is likely that each one originally contained either a linga or a statue.

Above right: Baksei Chamkrong is an example of the temple mountain structure. Built of laterite and brick, it features a tower supported by a four-tiered pyramid with four staircases, as shown in this cross-section, published in the 1911 *Inventaire Descriptif des Monuments du Cambodge*.

AROUND ANGKOR THOM
Baksei Chamkrong

Located south-west of the south gate of Angkor Thom, Baksei Chamkrong is one of the few brick edifices in the immediate vicinity of Angkor. It was once decorated with a covering of mortar of lime. Like virtually all the structures of Angkor, it opens to the east. In the early 10th century, Harshavarman I erected five statues in this temple: two of Shiva, one of Vishnu and two of Devi.

Phnom Bakheng

Around 400m south of Angkor Thom, the main attraction of Phnom Bakheng is the sunset view of Angkor Wat. Unfortunately and inevitably the whole affair has turned into something of a circus, with crowds of tourists gasping up the steep slope of the hill, pestered all the way by nimble-footed soft-drink vendors. To get a decent picture of Angkor Wat in the warm glow of the late afternoon sun you will need a 300mm lens and a tripod, as the temple is 1.3km away. Still, the sunset over the Tonlé Sap lake is very impressive from the hill. It is also now possible to arrange an elephant ride up the hill and the location certainly makes for one of the more memorable journeys you will make.

Phnom Bakheng is also home to the first of the temple mountains built in the near vicinity of Angkor. Yasovarman I (ruled 889-910) chose Phnom Bakheng over the Roluos area, where previous temples had been built.

Phnom Bakheng is a five-tiered temple mountain with seven levels, including the base and the summit. At the base are (or were) 44 towers. Each of the five tiers had 12 towers. The summit of the temple has four towers at the cardinal points of the compass as well as a Central Sanctuary. All of these numbers are of symbolic significance. The seven levels, for example, represent the seven Hindu heavens, while the total number of towers, excluding the Central Sanctuary, is 108, a particularly auspicious number and one which correlates to the lunar calendar.

Prasat Kravan

The five brick towers of Prasat Kravan, which are arranged in a north-south line and oriented to the east, were built for Hindu worship in 921. The structure is unusual in that it was not constructed by royalty and this

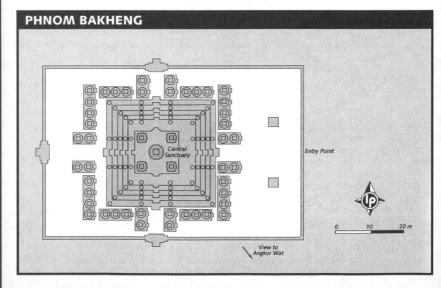

PHNOM BAKHENG

Central Sanctuary

Entry Point

View to Angkor Wat

0　10　20 m

accounts for its slightly remote location, away from the centre of the capital. Prasat Kravan is just south of the road between Angkor Wat and Banteay Kdei.

The group was partially restored in 1968 and is notable for the bas-reliefs cut into the bricks on the interior walls. The images of Vishnu in the largest central tower show eight-armed Vishnu on the back wall; taking the three gigantic steps with which he reclaimed the world on the left wall; and riding a garuda on the right wall. The northernmost of the towers has reliefs of Vishnu's consort, Lakshmi.

One of Vishnu's best-loved incarnations was as the dwarf Vamana who reclaimed the world from the demon-king Bali. The dwarf polite-ly asked the demon for a patch of ground upon which to meditate, saying that the patch need only be big enough so that he could walk across it in three paces. The demon agreed, only to see the dwarf swell into a giant who strode across the universe in three mighty steps. From this legend Vishnu is sometimes known as the 'long strider'.

Banteay Kdei & Sras Srang

Banteay Kdei, a massive Buddhist temple of the second half of the 12th century, is surrounded by four concentric walls. The outer wall meas-ures 500m by 700m. Each of its four entrances is decorated with garuda, which hold aloft one of Jayavarman VII's favourite themes, the four visages of Avalokiteshvara. The inside of the central tower was never finished.

Just east of Banteay Kdei is a basin of earlier construction, Sras Srang (Pool of Ablutions), measuring 800m by 400m. A tiny island in the middle once bore a wooden temple, of which only the stone base remains.

There is a mass grave of hundreds of victims of the Khmer Rouge a bit north of Sras Srang on the other side of the road. It is marked by a wooden memorial.

Ta Prohm

The temple of Ta Prohm rates with Angkor Wat and the Bayon as one of the most popular attractions of Angkor. Its appeal lies in the fact that, unlike the other monuments of Angkor, it has been left to be swallowed by the jungle, and looks very much the way most of the monuments of Angkor appeared when European explorers first stum-bled upon them.

This deliberate neglect has not been without controversy. As long ago as 1942 the French restorer Maurice Glaize lashed out at the sent-iments that justify the neglect of Ta Prohm, arguing:

> The tourist ... who travels in style and comfort to visit ruins where he expects to experience the exhilaration of Mouhot discovering Angkor Wat in 1860 ... is driven by an outdated individualism, and all that counts for him is a ro-manticism fuelled by spectacular effects, as symbolised by a section of wall crumbling in the passionate tentacled embrace of voracious trees.

Ideological qualms aside, Ta Prohm is a unique other-world experience. The temple is cloaked in dappled shadow, its crumbling towers and walls locked in the slow muscular embrace of vast root systems. If Angkor Wat, the Bayon and other temples are testimony to the genius of the Angkor-period Khmers, Ta Prohm reminds us equally of the awesome fecundity and power of the jungle.

Built in approximately 1186, Ta Prohm was a Buddhist temple dedicated to the mother of Jayavarman VII. It is one of the few temples in the Angkor region where an inscription provides information about the temple's dependents and inhabitants. The numbers quoted really are staggering: close to 80,000 people were required to maintain or attend at the temple, among them more than 2700 officials and 615 dancers.

Ta Prohm is a temple of towers, close courtyards and narrow corridors. Many of the corridors impassable, clogged with jumbled piles of delicately carved stone blocks dislodged by the roots of long-decayed trees. Bas-reliefs on bulging walls are carpeted by lichen, moss and creeping plants, and shrubs sprout from the roofs of monumental porches. Trees, hundreds of years old – some supported by flying buttresses – tower overhead, their leaves filtering the sunlight and casting a greenish pall over the whole scene.

There are generally some children at Ta Prohm who, for a small tip, will show you around. This is one temple where it is well worth having a local guide. Most of the children know the best spots for photographs, and will lead you into courtyards you might otherwise spend all day trying to find.

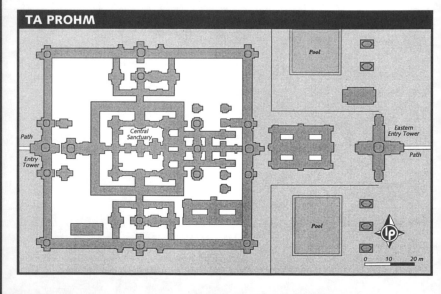

TA PROHM

COVPE

SVIVANT A B

Ta Keo

Above: The temple of Ta Keo was the first Angkorian monument built entirely of sandstone. This cross-section was published in the 1911 *Inventaire Descriptif des Monuments du Cambodge.*

Ta Keo, built by Jayavarman V (ruled 968-1001), was dedicated to Shiva and was the first Angkorian monument built entirely of sandstone. The summit of the central tower, which is surrounded by four lower towers, is more than 50m high. This quincunx arrangement with four towers at the corners of a square and a fifth tower in the centre is typical of many Angkor temple mountains.

The process of decorating Ta Keo's particularly hard sandstone was never completed and the temple has a spartan feel compared to the lavish decoration of other Angkor monuments.

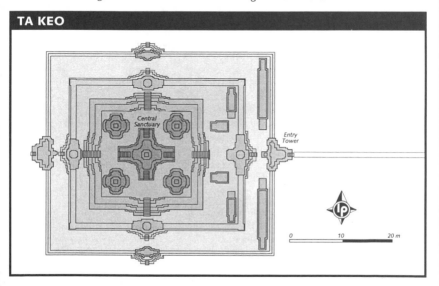

Ta Nei

Ta Nei, 800m north of Ta Keo near the north-west corner of the Eastern Baray, was built by Jayavarman VII (ruled 1181-1201).

Spean Thma

Spean Thma (Stone Bridge), of which an arch and several piers remain, is 200m east of the Thommanon temple. It was one of the final projects for the last great builder of Angkor, Jayavarman VII, and is the only large bridge in the vicinity of Angkor of which anything remains. Just north of the bridge is a large and surprisingly elegant water wheel.

Chau Say Tevoda

Just east of Angkor Thom's East Gate is Chau Say Tevoda. It was probably built during the second quarter of the 12th century and dedicated to Shiva and Vishnu.

Thommanon

The Thommanon temple is just north of Chau Say Tevoda and over the road. Although unique, it complements its neighbour as it was built around the same time and has a similar plan. The Thommanon is in much better condition than the rather ruinous Chau Say Tevoda. It was also dedicated to Shiva and Vishnu.

Preah Khan

The temple of Preah Khan (Sacred Sword) is a good counterpoint to Ta Prohm, though it gets far fewer visitors. Preah Khan was built by Jayavarman VII (it may have served as his temporary residence while Angkor Thom was being built), and like Ta Prohm it is a place of towered enclosures and shoulder-hugging corridors. Unlike Ta Prohm, however, the temple of Preah Khan is in a reasonable state of preservation and ongoing restoration efforts should maintain and even improve this situation.

The central sanctuary of the temple was dedicated in 1191 and a large stone stelae originally located within the first eastern enclosure, but now housed safely at Angkor Conservation (see the boxed text 'Angkor Conservation' in this chapter), says much about Preah Khan's role as a centre for worship and learning. The temple was supposed to have been dedicated to 515 divinities and during the course of a year, 18 major festivals took place here, requiring a team of thousands just to maintain the place.

Preah Khan covers a very large area, but the temple itself is within a rectangular enclosing wall of around 700m by 800m. Four processional walkways approach the gates of the temple, and these are bordered by gods carrying a serpent, as in the approach to Angkor Thom. From the central sanctuary, four long vaulted galleries extend in the cardinal directions. Many of the interior walls of Preah Khan were once coated with plaster held in place by holes in the stone.

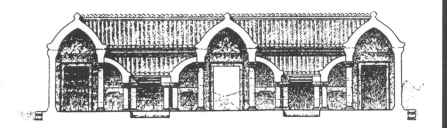

The main entrance to Preah Khan is, as with most of the other Angkor temples, in the east, but the standard practice is to enter at the west gate and walk from here to the north gate (your driver will automatically go to the north gate to wait for you). Make sure that you walk the length of the temple to the east entrance before doubling back to the central sanctuary and making your way to the north entrance. The function of the two storey structure inside the east entrance is unknown, but its columns give it an unexpected Mediterranean aspect.

Above: In better condition than many of its neighbours, Preah Khan is one of Angkor's largest monuments. This sketch was published in the 1911 *Inventaire Descriptif des Monuments du Cambodge.*

Just north of Preah Khan is Banteay Prei, which dates from the same period.

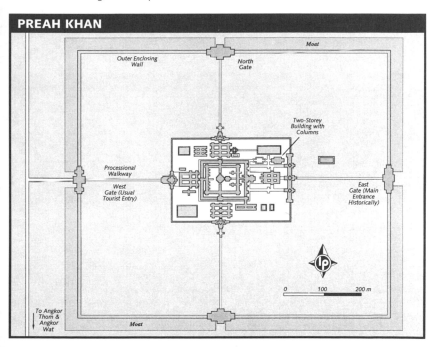

PREAH KHAN

Preah Neak Pean

The late 12th century Buddhist temple of Preah Neak Pean (Inter-twined Naga), which was built by Jayavarman VII, consists of a square pool with four smaller square pools arranged on each axis. In the centre of the large central pool is a circular 'island' encircled by the two naga whose intertwined tails give the temple its name. Although it has been many centuries since the pools were last filled with water, it's easy for a modern visitor to envisage the complex as a huge swim-up bar at some fancy hotel.

In the pool around the central island there were once four statues, but only one remains, reconstructed from the debris by the French ar-chaeologists who cleared the site. The curious figure has the body of a horse supported by a tangle of human legs. It relates to a legend that Avalokiteshvara once saved a group of shipwrecked followers from an island of ghouls by transforming himself into a flying horse.

Water once flowed from the central pool into the four peripheral pools via ornamental spouts, which can still be seen in the pavilions at each axis of the pool. The spouts are in the form of an elephant's head, a horse's head, a lion's head and a human's head. The pool was used for ritual purification rites and the complex was originally in the centre of a huge 3km by 900m lake, now dried up and overgrown.

Ta Som

Ta Som, which stands to the east of Preah Neak Pean, is yet another of the late 12th century Buddhist temples of Jayavarman VII. Much of Ta Som is in a ruined state.

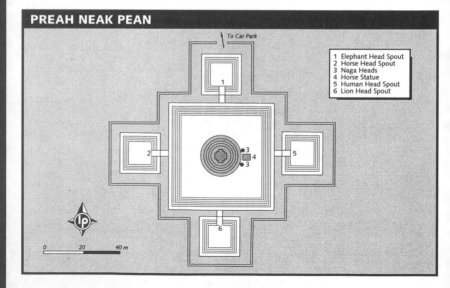

PREAH NEAK PEAN

To Car Park

1 Elephant Head Spout
2 Horse Head Spout
3 Naga Heads
4 Horse Statue
5 Human Head Spout
6 Lion Head Spout

0   20   40 m

ANDERS BLOMQVIST

ANDERS BLOMQVIST

Top: The Bayon, Angkor Thom, is best viewed at dawn or dusk.

Bottom: One of the 200 smiling faces of the Bayon, Angkor Thom.

Temples of Angkor

ANDERS BLOMQVIST

ANDERS BLOMQVIST

ANDERS BLOMQVIST

Top: Giant tree roots are locked in an embrace with the crumbling Ta Prohm.

Middle: A false wall and door at Banteay Srei.

Bottom: The Bayon bas-relief depicts a battle on the Tonlé Sap lake.

Eastern Baray & Eastern Mebon

The enormous one-time reservoir known as the Eastern Baray was excavated by Yasovarman I (ruled 889-910), who marked its four corners with steles. This basin, the most important of the public works of Yasodharapura, Yasovarman I's capital, is 7km by 1.8km. It was fed by the Siem Reap River.

The temple known as the Eastern Mebon, erected by Rajendravarman II (ruled 944-68), is on an islet in the centre of the Eastern Baray. This Hindu temple is very similar in design though smaller in size to the Pre Rup temple, which was built 15 to 20 years later and lies immediately to the south. The temple mountain form is surmounted by the usual quincunx of towers. The elaborate brick shrines are dotted with neatly arranged holes, which have given some observers the idea that they were once covered in metal plates. In fact, the towers were covered in plaster. The base of the temple is guarded at its corner by stone figures of harnessed elephants, some of which are still in a reasonable state of preservation.

Pre Rup

Pre Rup, built by Rajendravarman II, is about 1.5km south of the Eastern Mebon. Like its nearby predecessor, the temple consists of a pyramid-shaped temple mountain with the uppermost of the three tiers carrying five square shrines arranged as a quincunx. Also like the Eastern Mebon, the brick sanctuaries were once decorated with a plaster coating, fragments of which remain on the south-west tower. There are some fine lintel carvings here.

PRE RUP

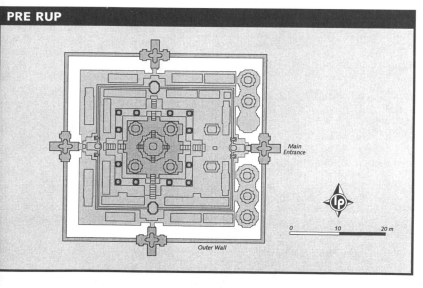

Main
Entrance

0   10   20 m

Outer Wall

Pre rup means 'turning the body' and refers to a traditional method of cremation in which the corpse's outline is traced in the cinders, first in one direction and then in the other.

Banteay Samré

Banteay Samré, 400m east of the south-east corner of the Eastern Baray, was built in the third quarter of the 12th century. It consists of a central temple with four wings preceded by a hall and accompanied by two libraries, the southern example remarkably well preserved. The ensemble is enclosed by two concentric walls.

The road to Banteay Samré should only be attempted in vehicles with high ground clearance.

The Western Baray

The Western Baray (Baray Occidental), measuring 8km by 2.3km, was excavated to provide water for the intensive cultivation of lands around Angkor. In the centre of the basin is the Western Mebon, where the giant bronze statue of Vishnu, now in the National Museum in Phnom Penh, was found. It is accessible by boat.

Above left: Legend suggests that Pre Rup was the site of an important cremation. This cross-section, published in the 1911 *Inventaire Descriptif des Monuments du Cambodge*, shows the temple's pyramidal structure.

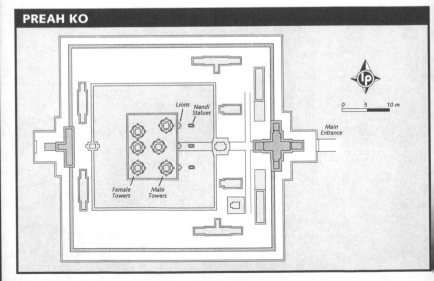

PREAH KO

ROLUOS GROUP

The monuments of Roluos, which served as the capital of Indravarman I (reigned 877-89), are among the earliest large, permanent temples built by the Khmers and mark the beginning of Khmer classical art. Before the construction of Roluos, only lighter (and nondurable) construction materials had been employed, even for religious structures.

The temples can be found 13km east of Siem Reap along National Hwy 6: Preah Ko is 600m south of National Hwy 6 and the Bakong is 1.5km south of the highway.

To get to Lolei from the turn-off to Preah Ko and Bakong, head east for 400m, turn left (north-west) and continue for 500m. There are modern-day Buddhist monasteries at Bakong and Lolei.

Preah Ko

Preah Ko was erected by Indravarman I in the late 9th century. The six *prasat* (brick towers), aligned in two rows and decorated with carved sandstone and plaster reliefs, face east; the central tower of the front row is larger than the others. There are inscriptions in Sanskrit on the doorposts of each temple.

The temples of Preah Ko (Sacred Ox) feature three Nandi (sacred oxen) in front of the first row of temples. It was dedicated by Indravarman I to

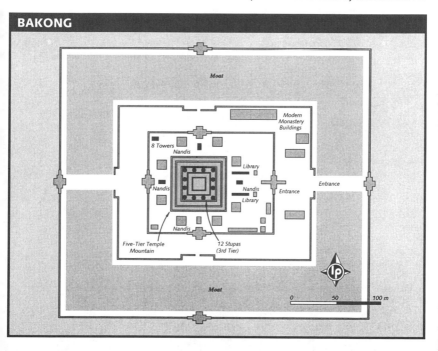

BAKONG

his deified ancestors in 880. The front towers relate to male ancestors or gods, the rear towers to female ancestors or goddesses. Lions guard the steps up to the temple platform.

Bakong

Bakong is the largest and most interesting of the Roluos group temples, and has an active Buddhist monastery just to the north of the east entrance. It was built and dedicated to Shiva by Indravarman I. Built as a representation of Mt Meru, it served as the city's central temple. The east-facing complex consists of a five-tier central pyramid of sandstone, 60m square at the base, flanked by eight towers (or what's left of them) of brick and sandstone and by other minor sanctuaries. Several of the eight towers down below are still partly covered by their original plasterwork.

The complex is enclosed by three concentric walls and a broad moat. Note the stone elephants on each corner of the first three levels of the central temple. There are 12 stupas – four to a side – on the third tier. The sanctuary on the 5th level was a later addition. There is a modern Buddhist monastery at the north-east corner.

Lolei

The four brick towers of Lolei, an almost exact replica of the towers of Preah Ko although in much worse shape, were built on an islet in the centre of a large reservoir – now rice fields – by Yasovarman I (ruled 889-910), the founder of the first city at Angkor. The sandstone carvings in the niches of the temples are worth a look and there are Sanskrit inscriptions on the doorposts. According to one of the inscriptions, the four towers were dedicated by Yasovarman I to his mother, his father and his maternal grandparents on 12 July 893.

AROUND ANGKOR
Phnom Krom

The temple of Phnom Krom, 12km south of Siem Reap on a hill overlooking the Tonlé Sap lake, dates from the 11th century. The three towers, dedicated (from north to south) to Vishnu, Shiva and Brahma, are in a ruined state. The fast boats from Phnom Penh dock near here.

Banteay Srei

Banteay Srei was for many years kept off the visitor map by Khmer Rouge activity. With the area now under government control, it is possible to visit this artistic jewel for no extra fee, although moto drivers may want more money to take you there. It is not a particularly extensive temple site, but it is wonderfully well preserved and its bas-reliefs are among the most accomplished Angkor has to offer.

Banteay Srei was built in the late 10th century and is a Hindu temple dedicated to Shiva. The temple is square with entrances at the east and west. The east entrance is approached by a causeway. Of chief interest are the three central towers, which are decorated with male and female divinities and beautiful filigree relief work.

Banteay Srei is 21km north-east of the Bayon and 8km west of Phnom Kulen. You can combine a visit here with a trip to the River of a Thousand Lingas at Kobal Spien and the sacred mountain of Phnom Kulen. Check that the security situation is still okay before planning a trip out here.

Kobal Spien

More commonly referred to in English as the River of a Thousand Lingas, this is an area of riverbed carvings not unlike Phnom Kulen, but far less popular with Khmers, so a mite more peaceful. For the most part it also lacks intimidating goons demanding money like at Phnom Kulen so a visit is altogether more easy going. The path up the hill begins amid what appears to be a slick military logging operation. It is about a half hour walk to where the carvings begin along a pleasant path that winds its way up into the jungle. It is sensible although not entirely necessary to get someone to guide you up there who can also tell you a bit about what you are actually seeing.

The river eventually appears on your left and the first carvings include a large image of Vishnu. As you continue, you come to an area with several good images of Rama, Lakshmi and Hanuman, and further up some lingas. On the way back down there is a path that follows the river for a time and along this stretch are hundreds of lingas giving rise to the name the River of a Thousand Lingas. These eventually give way to a waterfall and a scenic pool below. Although this area is of less significance to Khmers than Phnom Kulen, in some ways it is actually nicer as it lacks the crowds and the quality of the riverbed carvings is better.

Getting There & Away

Kobal Spien is about 30km north-east of the Bayon and about 9km beyond the temple of Banteay Srei on a good dirt road. Keep an eye out for a barrier on the left, behind which is the military logging camp. It is only a 15 minute drive on from Banteay Srei. Moto drivers will no doubt want extra money to take you here, but if you are a canny bargainer you should be able to get it included in a package with both

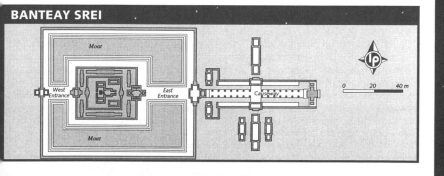

BANTEAY SREI

Banteay Srei and Phnom Kulen. The road from Kobal Spien to Phnom Kulen forks to the left about 1km back towards Banteay Srei, and the total distance is about 13km.

Phnom Kulen

Phnom Kulen is considered by Khmer people to be the most sacred mountain in Cambodia and is a popular place of pilgrimage during weekends and festivals. It played a significant role in the history of the Khmer empire, as it was from here in 802 that Jayavarman II proclaimed independence from Java, giving birth to modern-day Cambodia. There is a small wat at the summit of the mountain, which houses a large reclining Buddha carved into the sandstone boulder upon which it is built. Nearby is an attractive waterfall in which you can swim and there are a number of carvings in the riverbed, including numerous lingas. Be careful of land mines though: in 1998 two young boys were killed and one seriously injured when they darted off the path to take a leak.

Phnom Kulen has only recently opened to tourism and getting here can be fraught with the inconvenience of checkpoints and corruption, making the trip an expensive proposition. The situation will no doubt improve once the tourism authorities get a better grip on the place, but for now tread warily with the military. It is not that long since many of them were Khmer Rouge and they seem to owe little allegiance to the government in Phnom Penh.

Once you arrive at the base of the mountain, be prepared for a long march to the top, no less than 1½ hours even if you are walking briskly. Bring a steady supply of drinking water unless you are prepared to pay the outrageous 1500r demanded by drink sellers along the way. At the time of writing, some unfriendly military personnel at the bottom were demanding US$10 per person for security, but this is simply extortion as, according to most Khmers, security is not a problem. Try not to pay this and if you have to, then make them earn their money like everyone else by walking up and down with you.

The sandy trail winds its way to a small pagoda called Wat Chuop, set into the cliff face from which a tuk chuop (spring) emerges. Being a holy mountain, this is considered holy water and Khmers like to bottle it up to take home with them. This water source eventually flows into the Tonlé Sap lake and is considered to bring good fortune to the waterways of Cambodia.

From this point the climb is steep until you emerge on the plateau, where, incredibly, there are a host of motos waiting to whisk you along the path if you are too tired to walk. They want a hefty 30,000r for the round trip, perhaps a form of compensation for carting the bikes up there, but 10,000r seems a more sensible price and more like the amount Khmers pay. The walk is easy enough though: it is mostly shaded and flat and takes no more than 30 to 45 minutes. You have to cross a small river, into the bed of which are carved numerous linga. There is an official ticket booth just before this where Khmers pay 10,000r and tourists are asked for US$10. This is an absurd price. When

WARNING

! ● At no point during your visit to Kobal Spien or Phnom Kulen should you leave well-trodden paths as there are land mines.

you add it to the security charge, you are paying the same as you pay to visit the temples for a day. However, this should soon change.

The waterfall here would be an attractive spot were it not for all the litter left here by Khmer families picnicking at the weekend. You can bathe here if you like and, if you have a bit of time to kill, it is a worthwhile exercise clearing up some of the mess and burning it. In some ways it's a little like pissing in the ocean, but if locals can be shown how much more beautiful it is without their leftovers then they might start disposing of things properly themselves. Near the waterfall is a jungle-clad temple dating from the 9th century, but think twice before clambering around it as there may be land mines inside.

The image of the reclining Buddha, set inside a small pagoda, is memorable as it is carved into the top of a massive sandstone boulder. This is the focal point of a pilgrimage here for Khmer people, so make sure you take off your shoes and any head covering before climbing the stairs to the sanctuary. The views from the top are tremendous as you can see right across the forested plateau. The highest point on Phnom Kulen is 487m.

Getting There & Away

Phnom Kulen is more than 40km from Siem Reap and about 15km from Banteay Srei. The easiest way to go is to visit the River of a Thousand Lingas at Kobal Spien first, then head back towards Banteay Srei, taking the left fork in the road after about 1km. That road goes direct to Phnom Kulen on a good surface. It is about 13km from Kobal Spien to Phnom Kulen. There are several other routes as there are a multitude of logging trails in the area. Moto drivers that take you up this way will no doubt have their own idea of which way they want to go, but if you are coming with your own vehicle, take the Kobal Spien route. Moto drivers are likely to want about US$10 to bring you out here due to additional petrol costs and the perceived lack of security in the area.

Beng Mealea

Beng Mealea is one of the most interesting of Angkor's many temples, but also one of the hardest to reach. The 12th century temple is about 40km east of the Bayon (as the crow flies) and 6.5km south-east of Phnom Kulen. Beng Mealea is enclosed by a moat measuring 1200m by 900m. It is nearly the size of Angkor Wat, but utterly subsumed by jungle. Many of the carvings have recently been plundered due to the temple's isolation, but that doesn't detract from the atmosphere. Check security conditions before heading out this way.

It is best to combine a trip to Beng Mealea with a visit to Phnom Kulen or Kobal Spien. Make sure you find a moto driver who knows the route as many Khmers in Siem Reap know very little about the temple.

Getting There & Away

The best way to get to Beng Mealea is to get a group together and charter a pick-up from Siem Reap's central market; expect to pay about US$50, with driver. In the wet season, no vehicle will make the last 10km.

Siem Reap

Siem Reap (pronounced see-*em* ree-*ep*) is a fast-developing town just north of the western extent of the Tonlé Sap (Great Lake). The name Siem Reap means 'Siamese Defeated' (Siem means Siamese or Thais).

Even if Siem Reap was not the nearest town to Angkor, it would probably still be worth a short visit. There's a sleepy, rural quality to the place, and this coupled with a good range of accommodation and some fine restaurants makes it a great place to unwind for a few days. If there was a more developed arts and crafts industry it would be easy to draw parallels with Ubud in Bali before the advent of mass tourism (for the moment at least). Siem Reap is obviously destined for big things, and major changes can be expected over the next few years.

Several upmarket hotels are under construction, so sleepy Siem Reap is slowly waking up. Fortuitously, the Asian economic crisis halted a number of the more ambitious plans for the area being touted around by Malaysian investors. These included golf courses and sound and light shows at Angkor Wat, but their lack of funds has, for the time being at least, spared Siem Reap for a few more years.

Orientation

It is possible to walk around Siem Reap in an hour or so; there is no risk of getting lost. National Hwy 6 cuts through the north of town past the Grand Hotel d'Angkor and the central market. The Siem Reap River flows north to south through the centre of town, and has enough bridges that you don't have to worry too much about being on the wrong side.

There is no central accommodation area in Siem Reap. The most popular budget guesthouses are scattered across town, as are the town's mid-range hotels.

Angkor Wat and Angkor Thom are around 6km north of town, while the Roluos group of temples is 12km east of town along National Hwy 6.

Highlights

- Angkor Massage has the right medicine for weary bodies.
- A bird lovers' paradise, Prek Toal is home to rare storks and pelicans.
- The Vietnamese floating village promises outstanding sunset scenery.
- The town's dark and noisy nightclubs are great for learning groovy moves.

Information

Tourist Offices The Angkor office of Cambodia Tourism is in a new white structure opposite the Grand Hotel d'Angkor. There's a sign saying 'Tourist Information', but you will be very lucky to find the staff here awake.

For the most part, budget and mid-range travellers in Angkor get their travel information from other travellers or from their guesthouses.

Money There are several banks where you can change money in Siem Reap. The Cambodian Commercial Bank is open from 8 am to 3.30 pm, Monday to Friday, and changes travellers cheques at 2% commission. Cash advances (with a limit of US$2000) are available on credit card for a flat fee of US$10.

The National Bank of Cambodia has slightly longer opening hours, from 7.30 am to 4 pm weekdays. This bank also charges a 2% commission for changing travellers cheques, but it does not provide credit card cash advances.

The other banks in town offer similar deals on travellers cheques.

Post & Communications The post office is along the river, 400m south of the Grand Hotel d'Angkor. It would probably be best to save your post for Phnom Penh or Bangkok, where services are more reliable.

Making international calls from Siem Reap is as simple as from Phnom Penh. There are several Ministry of Post and Telecommunications (MPTC) and Camintel public phone booths around town, including one outside the Cambodia Tourism office. You can buy phone cards at hotels around town.

Domestic calls within Cambodia are still expensive and should be avoided if possible.

If you need to send or receive faxes and you are not based in a hotel that offers this service, try either the Angkor Swiss Centre at the top of Sivatha St or Lotus Temple Communications, a business centre near the old market.

There are a few email places around town that have deals that work out at US$1 per email. Most convenient are probably the Chao Saya Guesthouse and Lotus Temple Communications, and they also offer unlimited monthly accounts for US$15. If you want to access the Internet for your email it is going to hurt as it requires a long distance call to Phnom Penh. It is at least US$1 a minute and the connection is slow. Until Siem Reap gets its own service provider, you will do better to wait until you're in Phnom Penh or Thailand to get connected.

Emergency If you fall seriously ill in Siem Reap, do not check yourself into the hospital as standards are appalling and you'll need to pay cash for what may turn out to be wrong treatment. There are two clinics considered to offer western standards of hygiene and training. One is French speaking Dr Kong Rithy (☎ 012-853937), just across the road from the Angkor Saphir Hotel, while the other is a bigger operation further down the highway towards the central market. There are plenty of pharmacies in the centre of town if you need basic medication.

Dangers & Annoyances Siem Reap is perfectly safe to stroll around, even at night. Out at the temples, however, stick to clearly marked trails. There are still mines out there. It is also not recommended that you visit remote sites such as Phnom Kulen or Beng Mealea alone as there is the possibility of bandit activity.

Things to See & Do

Most people are in Siem Reap to see Angkor. The sights in and around Siem Reap rather pale in comparison, but they make interesting options for those who find themselves all templed out after a few days.

Wat Bo is one of the town's oldest wats and has a collection of well-preserved wall paintings depicting the life of Buddha. Another wat to consider visiting while in town is **Wat Inkosei**, built on the site of an early Angkorian temple, which still stands today. Nearby is a workshop called the **House of Peace Association**, where leather shadow puppets are made along with other exquisite leather artistry, including characters from Hindu mythology. Small puppets cost about US$10 while larger pieces can be as much as US$150. **Wat Thmei**, on the left-hand side of the road to Angkor Wat, has a small memorial stupa containing the skulls and bones of victims of the Khmer Rouge.

Shadow puppetry displays are often held near the town at the protection centre for children run by Krousar Thmey. Money raised from the shows helps fund its program in Cambodia. Contact La Noria guesthouse for further details or phone ☎ 380166.

Siem Reap has become something of a centre in the drive to revitalise Khmer cultural skills, which were dealt such a harsh blow by the Khmer Rouge and the years of instability that followed its rule. **Les Chantiers Ecoles** (☎ 380187, email artcefp@rep.forum.org.kh) is a school in town that specialises in teaching wood and stone carving techniques to young people from impoverished backgrounds. It was opened to the public during 1998, but the project directors found that having large groups tramping through the buildings was disrupting pupils. It is still willing to show genuinely interested individuals or small groups around, but you have to make an appointment. It has a craft shop on the premises where you can buy anything from simple carvings to household furniture. Tucked down a side road the school can be quite hard to find. Look out for a large sign on the left side of the road heading west from Villa Bakong. The sign reads 'Direction Provinciale: Education, jeunesse et sports',

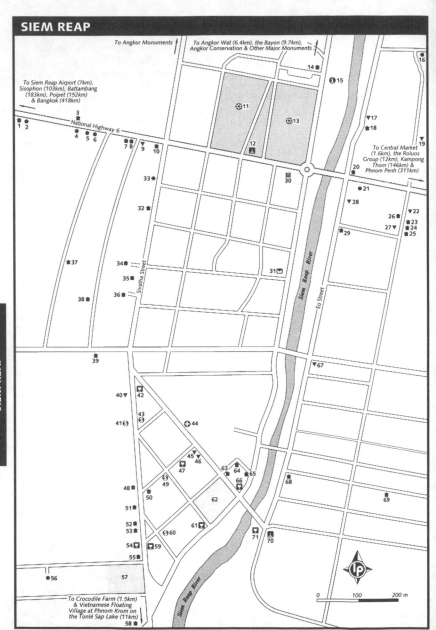

SIEM REAP

SIEM REAP

To Angkor Monuments

To Angkor Wat (6.4km), the Bayon (9.7km),
Angkor Conservation & Other Major Monuments

To Siem Reap Airport (7km),
Sisophon (103km), Battambang
(183km), Poipet (152km)
& Bangkok (418km)

National Highway 6

To Central Market
(1.6km), the Roluos
Group (12km), Kampong
Thom (146km) &
Phnom Penh (311km)

Sivatha Street

Siem Reap River

Eo Street

To Crocodile Farm (1.5km)
& Vietnamese Floating
Village at Phnom Krom on
the Tonlé Sap Lake (11km)

SIEM REAP

PLACES TO STAY
1 Banteay Srei Hotel
3 Angkor Hotel
7 Apsara Angkor Guesthouse
8 Takeo & Chenla
   Guesthouses
10 Golden Angkor Hotel
14 Grand Hotel d'Angkor
18 La Noria Guesthouse
20 Angkor Saphir Hotel
23 Mom's Guesthous
24 Sunrise Guesthouse
25 Mahogany Guesthouse;
   Pailin Guesthouse
26 Garden House
29 Diamond Hotel
32 Neak Pean Hotel
34 Green Garden Guesthouse
35 Eclipse Guesthouse
36 Smiley Guesthouse
37 Salina Hotel
38 Auberge Mont Royal
39 Naga Guesthouse
48 Royal Hotel
50 Golden Apsara
   International House
51 Vimean Thmei Hotel
52 Reaksmey Chanreas Hotel

53 Villa Phkay Proeuk
55 Villa Bakong
58 Popular Guesthouse
63 Chao Saya Guesthouse
   & Restaurant
64 Stung Siem Reap Hotel
65 Rasmei Angkor Guesthouse;
   Continental Cafe
68 Bayon Hotel
69 Angkor Village

PLACES TO EAT
9 Greenhouse Restaurant
17 Arun Restaurant
19 Sawasdee Restaurant
22 Bayon Restaurant
27 Chavlit Thai Restaurant
28 Samapheap Restaurant
40 Angkor Green Restaurant
45 New Delhi Restaurant;
   Roof Rack Shack
46 Little India Restaurant
67 Angkor Borey Restaurant

OTHER
2 Bangkok Airways
4 Angkor Massage
5 Royal Air Cambodge

6 Apex Cambodia Travel
11 Lotus Gardens
12 Wat
13 Royal Gardens
15 Cambodia Tourism
16 Angkor Wat &
   Banteay Srei Replicas
21 Medical Clinic
30 Sihanouk's Villa
31 Post Office
33 Angkor Swiss Centre
41 Cambodian Commercial
   Bank
42 Vimean Akas Nightclub
43 Pacific Commercial Bank
44 Hospital
47 The Angkor What?
49 First Overseas Bank
54 Zanzybar
56 Les Chantiers Ecoles
57 Night Market
59 Bakheng Nightclub
60 National Bank of Cambodia
61 Ivy Bar & Guesthouse
62 Old Market
66 Bar Only One
70 Wat Dam Nak
71 Martini Nightclub

SIEM REAP

and underneath it is a smaller sign 'Chantiers Ecoles de Formation Professionelle', and you've made it.

The school also maintains a **Silk Farm** about 18km outside Siem Reap. All stages of the production process can be seen here, from the cultivation of mulberry trees to the dyeing and weaving of the silk. The work produced here is the best in the country as many of the patterns on the clothing are ancient royal designs rediscovered with assistance from experts from neighbouring Thailand. Items can be purchased at the farm or in the shop at the school. If you want to arrange a visit, telephone or email Les Chantiers Ecoles.

Another worthy place deserving your patronage is **Angkor Massage**. It is similar to the Seeing Hands Massage in Phnom Penh in that it trains blind people in the art of massage and uses the money raised to assist blind people in Siem Reap Province. It is very reasonable costing just US$3 an hour, and you will certainly need a massage if

you have arrived by road from Phnom Penh or Poipet. If you are only going to have one massage while in the country, this is the place to do it, as Angkor Massage needs the custom more than Seeing Hands Massage in Phnom Penh, which is already very popular.

About 2km outside town is a **crocodile farm**, which costs US$2 to visit, but is worth it for photos of the feeding frenzy.

One of the more quirky sights in town are the **miniature replicas** of Angkor Wat and Banteay Srei that the town's master sculptor has constructed in his garden. It is a bluffer's way to get that aerial shot of Angkor without chartering a helicopter, although cynics might question the presence of gigantic insects in the shot. Work is currently underway on a miniature Bayon. There is no charge to have a look and even King Sihanouk has praised the sculptor's work in the past.

The covered **central market**, 1.6 km east of the Siem Reap River (towards Roluos), is a sprawling affair.

Places to Stay

The hotel scene in Siem Reap has changed immensely from the early days of Angkor tourism, when travellers were essentially restricted to the venerable Grand Hotel d'Angkor and its Villa Apsara annex. A large number of family run guesthouses have sprung up for budget travellers, while those on mid-range budgets can choose from *pension*-style villas at around US$10 to US$15 or hotels, which cost from around US$15. In fact, it wouldn't be an exaggeration to say there are now more places to stay than there are temples out at Angkor. There are even a few mid-range to top-end hotels around town, including the fully restored Grand Hotel d'Angkor, and these will soon be supplemented by further arrivals.

Places to Stay – Budget

Touts for the budget guesthouses wait at the airport and at the port. They will usually give you a free ride into town. You are not obligated to stay at their guesthouse if you don't like the look of the place. Many guesthouses in Phnom Penh have partnerships with places in Siem Reap, so you may be greeted with a sign when you disembark from your plane or boat. Apart from the guesthouses listed here, there are many other places around town with rooms ranging from US$3 to US$5. Most of the less popular places are known simply by numbers – Guesthouse 258, and so on.

One of the cheapest guesthouses in town is the *Naga Guesthouse* (☎ 963439), where singles/doubles start at US$2/3. It's a surprisingly big place, and between the early morning sunrise seekers and the late-night drinking crowd it tends to be lively at all times of day.

Smiley Guesthouse (☎ 012-852955), just off Sivatha St, is run by the same family that operates Narin Guesthouse in Phnom Penh, and offers a similar deal with rooms for US$3/5, or a dollar more with bathroom. It has expanded into adjacent buildings and also offers rooms with air-con for around US$12. This is one of the friendliest places to enjoy your stay and the menu at the guesthouse restaurant is reasonably good, with a few local specialties. Nearby, the *Eclipse Guesthouse*

(☎ 380195) has big, clean doubles with bathroom for US$6, similar singles for US$5 and rooms with shared facilities for just US$3.

The *Popular Guesthouse* (☎ 015-917377, email chom@camnet.com.kh), in the south of town near the river is, as its name suggests, pretty popular with backpackers. Basic singles cost US$2 to US$3, doubles are US$4; rooms with bathroom rise to US$5/7. There is a pleasant roof-top restaurant, with a menu that bears an uncanny resemblance to that of Smiley Guesthouse.

East of the Siem Reap River, just off National Hwy 6, is a cluster of long-running guesthouses. *Mom's Guesthouse* (☎ 964037), next door to the Bayon Restaurant, has been around for quite a while and is overseen by the ever-fussing 'Mom' herself. Singles are US$4 to US$5 and doubles are US$6 or US$8 with bathroom. There are also air-con rooms available for the rather ambitious price of US$20. Mom's has a pleasant balcony and does a good coffee, baguette and egg breakfast.

Mahogany Guesthouse (☎ 963417), just a couple of doors from Mom's, is the most popular place in this part of town. It's a large two storey building with a veranda area for hanging out. Rooms with one or two beds cost US$5, while doubles with bathroom are US$8. Across the road is the *Garden House* (☎ 963523), which also has rooms for US$5/7. There are a couple of rooms with bathrooms for US$8. The other two options here are *Sunrise Guesthouse* (☎ 015-635883) and *Pailin Guesthouse* (☎ 015-850973), which offer pretty much the same deal as the rest.

The other budget section of town is the area just west of the Greenhouse Restaurant on National Hwy 6. Pick of the pack is probably the *Apsara Angkor Guesthouse* (☎ 963476), a big operation. The rooms are spacious and there's a leafy restaurant area in the garden. Singles/doubles/triples cost US$3/5/6, and food is cheap as the menu is priced in riel.

Takeo Guesthouse is the best value in this part of town at US$2 a person, or US$3 with bathroom. Dinner with the family is US$1. Next door is the family-run *Chenla Guest-*

house (☎ 015-630046), a clean and friendly place with kitchen facilities. Nice doubles with bathrooms are US$6 in the newer buildings at the back, where there are also some air-con rooms for US$15. In the old house it is US$3 for a simple double.

The *Rasmei Angkor (☎ 015-834264)* is the one guesthouse with a riverside location. It is in a pleasant, breezy building above the Continental Cafe, but the rooms are a bit plain. Rooms cost US$5/10. It has a lot of potential for renovation.

If you want to spend just a little more to attain guesthouse intimacy with greater comfort, the *Green Garden Guesthouse (☎ 015-631364)* has a wide variety of rooms starting at US$8 for a double with fan and bathroom, rising to US$17 for a modern room with air-con and fridge. There is, as you might imagine, an attractive communal area set in a lush garden.

Places to Stay – Mid-Range

As is the case in Phnom Penh, there has been a mid-range hotel boom in Siem Reap, and there are some very good deals around.

Undoubtedly the best choice of accommodation in this range is *La Noria Guesthouse (☎ 964242, fax 964243, email lanoria@rep.forum.org.kh)*, a tasteful and charming small operation on the east bank of the river. The rooms are thoughtfully decorated with traditional crafts and the bathrooms have some nice touches, as well as hot water. All have their own veranda area and such comfort is remarkably well priced at US$20 or US$30 with air-con. You should really try to book ahead if you want to be sure of a room. There is also a good restaurant here serving European and Khmer food in elevated surroundings.

Hanuman Alaya (☎ 023-724022, fax 023-426194, email hanuman@bigpond.com.kh) overlooks the river just south of Angkor Conservation. Traditionally decorated rooms cost US$30, including breakfast. Book with Hanuman Tourism-Voyages in Phnom Penh.

The *Golden Apsara International House (☎ 963533)* is highly recommended. It's a wonderfully hospitable villa with verandas and a pleasant family atmosphere. Fan rooms with bathroom start at US$10, while air-con singles/doubles cost US$15/20. Doubles with hot showers cost US$25.

Across the road from the Golden Apsara are several more villa-style hotels. The *Villa Phkay Proeuk (☎ 380175)* has rooms with fan for US$5/10 and air-con doubles for US$15. There are a couple of air-con triples, and these are a good deal at US$20. Rooms are large and well-equipped making it the best value place of its kind. The *Vimean Thmei Hotel (☎ 015-636993)* and *Reaksmey Chanreas (☎ 380068)* are similar kinds of outfits, with fan rooms for US$10 and air-con rooms for US$15. *Royal Hotel (☎ 015-639114)* is overpriced at US$20 a room. South of these hotels is *Villa Bakong (☎ 380126)*, offering spotless modern rooms in an attractive house for US$15 a double with air-con and bathroom with hot water.

On the old market housed in an attractive colonial building, is the *Chao Saya Guesthouse (☎ 380055, fax 380065, email lotus@worldmail.com.kh)*, which has clean rooms with bathroom costing US$10/15 with fan/air-con. These rates drop to US$8/12 if you book by email or through the Hotel Indochine in Phnom Penh. The Belgian-Khmer owners sell a full range of Walls ice cream, which is flown in regularly. Another good-value option is the *Golden Angkor Hotel (☎ 964039)*, which is on the corner of Sivatha St and National Hwy 6. Large rooms with TV, fridge, air-con and bathroom cost US$15 and with fan only US$10.

Tucked away on a dirt road on the west side of town is the *Auberge Mont Royal (☎ 964044, email mont-royal@worldmail .com.kh)*, a modern villa with air-con rooms with minibar and bathroom for US$25/30, plus US$5 for an extra bed. While these prices are quite high, they include a continental breakfast. The management plans to add a roof-top bar and swimming pool sometime soon.

On the eastern bank of the Siem Reap River is a string of mid-range hotels. None of them stand out, but they can be relied on for basic comforts and decent service. They all sport air-con rooms, satellite TV and hot and cold water. The **Diamond Hotel** (☎ 015-633130, fax 380038) has a popular Thai restaurant and slightly musty rooms for US$35/45. The **Hotel Bopha** (☎ 015-917176) is better value with spacious rooms for US$30/35. The **Bayon Hotel** (☎ 963507, fax 963993) has some pleasant rooms overlooking the river and costs US$35/40 plus US$10 for an extra bed.

The **Stung Siem Reap Hotel** (☎ 015-913074) is a good alternative to the riverside places. The extremely friendly management of this place offers rooms with air-con, satellite TV and fridges, costing from US$30 to US$40. One factor to bear in mind is that several of the town's brothels are located just around the corner.

The **Freedom Hotel** is near the central market. Fan rooms with attached bathroom are US$10, basic air-con rooms US$15, air-con rooms with hot water US$20, and rooms with satellite TV US$25. The friendly Khmer manager speaks excellent English and is a good source of information about Siem Reap and Angkor.

Out on the airport road is the **Banteay Srei Hotel** (☎ 015-913839), which was once one of the better places in town and now offers rooms at very competitive rates. Singles with all the amenities cost US$30 and similarly smart and spacious doubles are US$35. This is a very good deal.

Two more places just in the mid-range category are the **Neak Pean Hotel** (☎/fax 380073), on Sivatha St, and the **Angkor Saphir Hotel** (☎ 963566, fax 380233), just over the bridge on the road to the central market. Both lack any atmosphere but have well-appointed rooms with all the trimmings for about US$40 to US$50.

Places to Stay – Top End

Most of the hotels in this range levy an additional 10% charge for service and 10% government tax, so don't forget to factor it in as an extra cost, but breakfast is included, so there is no need to head off to a market for your baguettes. Competition in this sector has driven down prices at some of the town's older top-end hotels so some quite good deals are available.

One of the classiest acts in town is **Angkor Village** (☎ 963561/2/3, fax 380104, email angkor.village@worldmail.com.kh). Designed by its owner, a French architect, this all-timber collection of bungalow units set around a recessed restaurant area is quite indulgent at US$50/75 for rooms with fan/air-con, US$100 for a deluxe air-con and US$125 for a suite. This doesn't prevent it being regularly full due to its sophisticated ambience, so it is advisable to book ahead. Breakfast, lunch and dinner are offered at US$5, US$8 and US$10 respectively. It also arranges culture shows with a set meal for US$20.

The cheapest hotel in this range is the Thai-managed **Salina Hotel** (☎ 380221/4, fax 380035), signposted from the airport road. Its rates are low considering the quality of rooms and service. Singles/doubles cost US$40/50, and the two suites are US$70.

The **Ta Prohm Hotel** (☎ 380117, fax 380116) has a good location in the south of town next to the Siem Reap River. It's popular with European tour groups, and has room rates of US$60/70, or suites for US$100/110.

Some of the best hotels in town are on National Hwy 6 on the way out to the airport. The **Hotel Nokor Kok Thlok** (☎ 015-920487, fax 380022) used to be rated as the best hotel in Siem Reap. Apart from the fact that virtually none of its foreign guests are able to pronounce its name, this hotel lacks character and it's hard to justify the room rates of US$85/95. Suites are also available for US$110.

A better option towards the airport is the new **Angkor Hotel** (☎ 964301, fax 964302, email angkor_hotel@worldmail.com.kh), which opened at the start of 1999. It is modern in appearance, but its interior has been tastefully decorated using local materials. Its 62 international standard rooms start at US$100/125, and rise to US$210 for the Angkor Suite, with a number of options in between. The hotel also has business facilities, a swimming pool and a health club, and an international management team to keep staff on their toes.

If money is no object then the hotel of choice in town is the historic **Grand Hotel** d'Angkor (☎ 963888, fax 963168, email raffles.grand@bigpond.com.kh), which was recently fully renovated and extended by the Raffles Group of Singapore. It is in these sort of opulent surroundings that you can imagine what it was like to be a tourist in colonial days. All the rooms are extremely well appointed and options include personality suites named in honour of earlier visitors to Angkor. The four of these cost US$460, while standard rooms are US$310/360. It has all the facilities you would expect of one of the region's finest hotels, including a library and map room with old works on Angkor. If, like most, this is a little beyond your budget, it is worth visiting the *Elephant Bar* for happy hour between 4 and 8pm, when two drinks can be had for the price of one and staff welcome you heartily.

Places to Eat

The restaurant scene in Siem Reap is not developing as fast as the hotel scene, but there are still some very good restaurants around. There are good restaurants at several of the guesthouses and hotels, including *Smiley Guesthouse* and, for something in more sophisticated surroundings, *La Noria*, but if you are staying at these places, it is still nice to venture out into the town to see some new faces.

One of the most popular places in town is the *Bayon Restaurant*, next door to Mom's Guesthouse, just off National Hwy 6. It has a pleasant garden setting and the food is consistently excellent, including the popular curry chicken in baby coconut.

The *Angkor Borey Restaurant* on the east side of the river is a lively place for an evening meal. There is a huge choice of Khmer dishes and other Asian classics. The place is not short on beer girls and always draws a healthy local crowd. Prices are in the US$2 to US$4 range. Further up the river, the *Arun Restaurant* is an inexpensive Khmer place, with some of the best prices in town and it is always busy at night.

For Thai food the best restaurant in town is the *Chavlit Thai* opposite Mahogany Guesthouse. The setting is delightfully traditional with raised eating platforms and the

large menu offers all the favourites for US$2 to US$4. Unless you are a fire eater don't ask for anything extra spicy. On the same road over the other side of National Hwy 6 is the *Sawasdee Restaurant*, which offers a similar selection of dishes at slightly lower prices, but in a less appealing environment.

The *Samapheap Restaurant*, next to the river, has a Thai atmosphere – complete with twinkling fairy lights at night – and the food is Khmer, Thai and generic western.

The *Greenhouse* is near the corner of Sivatha St and National Hwy 6. It has a good atmosphere and is the one of the few restaurants in town that sells red and white wine by the glass, although the friendly staff aren't really sure of the difference. It has a large range of Thai, Khmer and western standards on the menu. Success has led to expansion into a second location called the *Angkor Green Restaurant*; the building used to be the excellent Rasmey Meanchey Restaurant.

There are two Indian restaurants in town, but if they are busy service can be hit and miss. Prices are average at US$2 to US$4 a main course. *Little India* has better food, but *New Delhi* has a roof-top bar where you can eat your meal.

Chao Saya Restaurant has an experienced European chef who can put together exquisite Khmer and European food for about US$4 to US$6, accompanied by some of France's finest wines. The steaks are some of the best in the country as the owner operates a farm near Angkor. For the indulgent, the desserts warrant a tasting, particularly the chocolate mousse or lemon sorbet with half a bottle of vodka on top.

The *Continental Cafe* is a very popular place with local expats and has a happy hour from 6 to 8 pm when draught beer is US$1 a mug. Owned by the Foreign Correspondents' Club, it also has good food, but is quite expensive with pizzas pushing US$8 and most meals at least US$5.

Another place with a wide selection of continental food is the *Angkor Swiss Centre* on Sivatha St. Run by a Swiss guy with years of experience in the hotel business, the outdoor location makes it a pleasant place for an evening meal.

The *old market* has some cheap stalls with signs in English and these are becoming increasingly lively places for an atmospheric local meal at very reasonable prices.

When packing in a heavy day of sightseeing out at the temples, the *Khmer restaurants* opposite the main entrance to Angkor Wat are good places for lunch.

Entertainment

Several hotels offer cultural performances during the evening which are open to outsiders. The *Ta Prohm Hotel* offers the cheapest in a small garden over the road. The *Grand Hotel d'Angkor* and *Angkor Village* also have shows, but as these include dinner they are quite expensive at US$15 and US$20.

Nightlife in Siem Reap has a provincial feel to it despite the number of tourists starting to come through the town. A lot of people congregate early in the evening on guesthouse verandas to drink cheap beer and then venture out later. There are a few expat bars in town including *Bar Only One* and *Zanzybar*, but rather inflated prices seem to keep backpackers away. The *Roof Rack Shack* above the New Delhi restaurant is an atmospheric place for more reasonably priced drinks, but bring a crowd in case it is quiet. It claims to stay open until the last person leaves.

Fortunately, things are starting to move on the bar scene. The *Ivy Bar*, overlooking the old market, the *Angkor What?*, and the *Continental Cafe* are decent places for a drink.

There are several nightclubs in town. *Vimean Akas* is the most expensive, but possibly the worst. *Martini* has nothing to do with its namesake in Phnom Penh and is worth a visit as there is no dodgy cover band banging out songs you have loved to hate from the last 30 years. *Bakheng* is the cheapest with almost guesthouse-priced drinks and the occasional bizarre floorshow that includes a ballroom routine and scantily clad dancers with lit candles.

Shopping

There is no shortage of gift shops around town, though the items on sale are rarely of much interest. Look out for Bayon temple coffee mugs. For information on high quality souvenirs where the money spent is going to a good cause, see Les Chantiers Ecole in the Things To See & Do section earlier in this chapter.

At Angkor, you will end up spending a lot of your time fighting off hordes of souvenir sellers. Items being touted include temple bas-relief rubbings, curious musical instruments, ornamental knives, T-shirts, and crossbows that might raise a few eyebrows with customs should you try to take them home!

You can get your Angkor photos printed in Siem Reap quickly and cheaply. Most of the photo shops are on National Hwy 6, just east of the river, and charge about US$4 to process 36 prints.

Getting There & Away

There are now direct flights between Bangkok and Siem Reap and the frequency of flights to Phnom Penh has increased dramatically over the last few years. For those on a smaller budget it is possible to take a fast boat between Siem Reap and Phnom Penh and, more recently, overland travel has opened up with improved security in Cambodia. You can now come overland from Bangkok (see the Land entry in the Getting There & Away chapter for more details), Battambang and Phnom Penh.

Air Flights to Siem Reap are available from Phnom Penh with Royal Air Cambodge (RAC) and President Airlines, and from Bangkok with RAC and Bangkok Airways.

Flights between Phnom Penh and Siem Reap cost US$55 one-way, US$105 return with President Airlines, and US$110 return with RAC. RAC has several daily flights in both directions, and several more that go once or twice a week. They are well spread throughout the day so you can travel in the early morning or late afternoon. There is no need to book your return flight in Phnom Penh as this can be done in Siem Reap.

RAC and Bangkok Airways (☎ 380191/2) operate daily flights to Bangkok for US$155/310 one-way/return. Coming from Bangkok, visas are available on arrival at Siem Reap airport.

The RAC office (☎ 963422, 015-635994) in Siem Reap is on National Hwy 6 out towards the airport and is open from 7.30 to 11.30am and 1.30 to 5.30pm daily. The Bangkok Airways office (☎/fax 380191) is on the same road and open from 8am to 5pm daily. The President Airlines office is way out past the Nokor Kok Thlok Hotel.

Flying out of Siem Reap, international departure tax is US$10, while domestic departure tax is US$4.

Pick-up As the security situation has improved, travel by road between Phnom Penh and Siem Reap is becoming increasingly popular among backpackers. Sections of the road are far from pretty, but pick-up trucks complete the journey in about eight to 10 hours. Basically, the road is in total disrepair as far as Kompong Thom and then pretty good from there to Phnom Penh. When travelling between Siem Reap and Phnom Penh by road, consider making a stop in Kompong Thom for the night in order to visit the pre-Angkorian temples at Sambor Prei Kuk. See the Around Kompong Thom section in the Around Cambodia chapter for details. It costs about 15,000r in the cab or 7000r on the back between Siem Reap and Phnom Penh. Guesthouses can help you arrange this, but you will likely have to pay a bit more for the privilege.

The 152km road to Thailand is also open and something of a joke, as about half the time is spent driving in the paddy fields to avoid potholes and downed bridges. Pick-ups to Poipet take four to five hours and cost about 20,000r in the cab or 10,000r behind, although be prepared for some negotiating. To Sisophon, where you can change for Battambang, pay about 15,000r in the cab and about 7000r on the back for the three to four hour ride.

Boat See the Getting There & Away section in the Phnom Penh chapter for information about the boats running between Siem Reap and Phnom Penh and their costs.

Boats from Siem Reap to Phnom Penh leave from Phnom Krom, 11km south of Siem Reap. A moto out there costs US$1.

Most of the guesthouses in town sell boat tickets, and the companies tend to take it in turns to make the run so you could well end up on a different boat in each direction.

There are also boats travelling between Siem Reap and Battambang, which can be a good way of avoiding the misery of National Hwy 6 between Siem Reap and Sisophon. Express boats make the run when the water is high enough between the months of August and January (US$15; four hours). During this period, slower boats also make the journey (US$10; seven hours). From roughly February to June, when the water level is too low for bigger boats, tiny speedboats travel this route for about US$15 a person. This boat journey is probably the most spectacular in Cambodia as you pass through protected wetlands and narrow channels.

Getting Around
To/From The Airport Many of the hotels and guesthouses in Siem Reap have a free airport pick-up service. The 7km ride from the airport on the back of a moto costs US$1. Taxis are also usually available at US$3 to US$5.

Car & Motorcycle Most of the hotels and guesthouses can organise taxi hire to see Angkor. The going rate is US$20 to US$25. Minibuses are available from Diethelm Travel (☎ 963524, fax 963694) and Apex Cambodia Travel (☎ 963994, fax 380047). A 12 seat minibus costs US$40 per day, a 25 or 30 seat minibus US$80 to US$100 per day, depending on the time of year.

Bicycle Some of the guesthouses around town hire out bicycles. Motorcycles are no longer available for hire. The government now demands that tourists visiting Angkor use a 'qualified guide', which means you are compelled to hire a motorbike or car with a driver. However, if you decide to rent a bicycle you could quite easily cycle out to the temples if you have the stamina.

Moto Motos are available at daily rates of US$6 to US$8. Some of the drivers have excellent English and can tell you much about the temples as you zip between them. Many people end up going around the temples with the moto driver they take from the ferry to town, particularly if it is a free lift arranged by a guesthouse, but there are many to choose from so don't be afraid to shop around.

Currently, it is illegal for locals to rent motorbikes to foreigners, unless journalists or non-governmental organisation (NGO) representatives, illegal for them to show visitors back routes into the temple complex and illegal for moto drivers to carry more than one passenger. Don't go trying to persuade residents into bending these rules as they will likely get into a lot more trouble than you, possibly even having their moto confiscated. Also, it is worth remembering that this situation exists in the interests of visitor safety. A few wrong turns could have foreigners in places they shouldn't be either because of land mines or isolated cases of robbery. However, the rules are being revised at the time of writing and some guesthouses are starting to rent motorbikes to tourists for speeding about town. No doubt it will soon become possible to use rented motorbikes to visit the temples themselves.

The average cost for a short trip within town is 500r and 1000r across the river or at night.

Cyclo You can get around Siem Reap in the town's unique and rather uncomfortable cyclos, which are essentially standard bicycles with a two seat trailer in hitch. You can reach anywhere in town for about 1000r.

AROUND SIEM REAP
Bird Sanctuary & Biosphere of Prek Toal
This is one of three biospheres on the Tonlé Sap lake and the establishment of the bird

sanctuary makes it the most worthwhile and straightforward to visit. It is an ornithologist's fantasy with a significant number of rare breeds gathered in one small area, including the huge lesser and greater adjutant storks, the milky stork and the spot-billed pelican. If you are able to visit in the dry season (December to May), the concentration of birds is like something out of a Hitchcock film as water starts to dry up elsewhere.

To arrange a visit you can contact the project director on ☎ 023-360991 or arrange a boat trip in Siem Reap. A nonprofit agency called Osmose (email osmose@worldmail.com.kh) runs day trips there including breakfast and lunch and a lengthy boat trip through the flooded forest for US$40. It aims to promote the benefits of responsible tourism to the Cambodian people and financially contribute to the conservation of the area. The *Heart of Gold* boat makes regular journeys out here. For details contact La Noria Guesthouse or call ☎ 015-630893. The Chao Saya Guesthouse can also arrange boats and no doubt more guesthouses will move into this business as word of the sanctuary spreads.

Vietnamese Floating Village
This has become a popular excursion for visitors wanting a break from the temples and is easy enough to arrange yourself. Visitors arriving by fast boat get a preview, as the floating village is near Phnom Krom where the boat docks. The village moves location depending on the season and you will need to rent a boat to get around properly. This costs around US$8 to US$10 an hour, regardless of the number of people, and regardless of safety too, so make sure you don't overfill it. It is very scenic in the warm light of early morning or late afternoon. To get out here from Siem Reap costs US$1 by moto each way.

Around Cambodia

South Coast

The south coast of Cambodia is becoming increasingly popular with visitors and offers a number of diverse attractions that, with a little planning, can be seen in less than a week. For travellers arriving in Sihanoukville from Thailand by boat, there is the option of heading along the coast to Kampot, a sleepy riverside town that makes a good base from which to explore the abandoned seaside resort of Kep and the beautiful Bokor National Park. From Kampot there is a direct road back to Phnom Penh; or you can make your way back slowly via Takeo and the nearby ruined temples around Angkor Borei, and include some of the attractions along National Hwy 2, such as the hill-top temple of Phnom Chisor, the zoo at Phnom Tamao or the Angkorian temple at Tonlé Bati. See the Around Phnom Penh chapter for details on these places.

For those starting in Phnom Penh it may be better to run the route in reverse, wearing yourself out sightseeing before relaxing on the beach at Sihanoukville at the end of it all. All the places mentioned can be visited by public transport or moto, although highlights such as Bokor are not always cheap. For those with rental motorbikes the circuit is pretty straightforward.

SIHANOUKVILLE

Sihanoukville (also known as Kompong Som) is Cambodia's only maritime port. Its chief attractions are the four beaches that ring the headland. None of them rival Thailand's finest, but during weekdays you quite often have the beach to yourself. It isn't the world's most sophisticated resort, but if you feel the need to escape the searing heat of Cambodia's dry season, this makes a pleasant retreat all the same. It is popular during festivals and remains dry and hot from December to July.

Malaysian investors had big plans for the place a few years ago, with talk of a casino

Highlights

- Set atop a commanding plateau, the abandoned buildings of Bokor hill station offer breathtaking views across the Gulf of Thailand.
- Kampot has some of the best-preserved colonial architecture in the country and a low-key, laid-back feel.
- Kep, a beachside ghost town slowly coming back to life, features abandoned villas and unexplored islands.
- Pods of endangered freshwater dolphins can be seen in the Mekong River at Kratie.
- Home to many of Cambodia's ethnic minorities, the rolling hills of Mondulkiri are unlike any other region of Cambodia.

resort on one of the nearby islands and direct flights from Kuala Lumpur to Sihanoukville, but it turned out to be all talk and no action. A lot of hotels were constructed in anticipation of a boom in visitor numbers, but with the political climate of 1997 and 1998, tourists never materialised to fill the rooms. Plans to promote Sihanoukville's beaches were dealt a further blow at the end of 1998 by a toxic waste scandal involving a Taiwanese firm. Many Khmers are now opting to visit Kep at weekends, but the beaches are definitely better at Sihanoukville. It is also a good base from which to visit Ream National Park and a convenient way to travel between Cambodia and Thailand.

Orientation

Sihanoukville is not a small place, so the best way to get around is to hail a moto driver or hire a motorbike. Sihanoukville is east of Victory Beach, the main backpackers' beach, and closer to the mid-range Ochheuteal Beach and popular Sokha Beach. West of

SIHANOUKVILLE

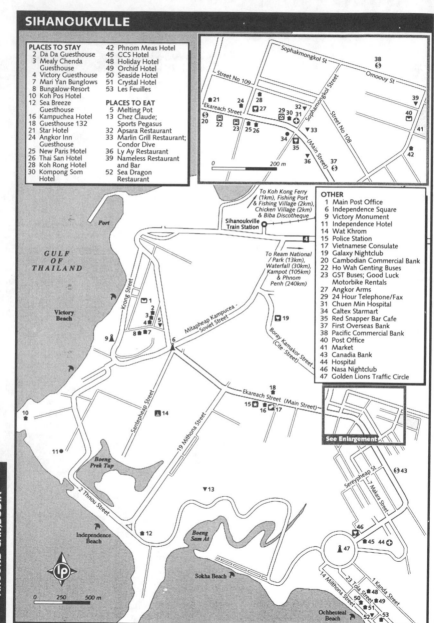

PLACES TO STAY
2 Da Da Guesthouse
3 Mealy Chenda
   Guesthouse
4 Victory Guesthouse
7 Mari Yan Bunglows
8 Bungalow Resort
10 Koh Pos Hotel
12 Sea Breeze
   Guesthouse
16 Kampuchea Hotel
18 Guesthouse 132
21 Star Hotel
24 Angkor Inn
   Guesthouse
25 New Paris Hotel
26 Thai San Hotel
28 Koh Rong Hotel
30 Kompong Som
   Hotel

42 Phnom Meas Hotel
45 CCS Hotel
48 Holiday Hotel
49 Orchid Hotel
50 Seaside Hotel
51 Crystal Hotel
53 Les Feuilles

PLACES TO EAT
5 Melting Pot
13 Chez Claude;
   Sports Pegasus
32 Apsara Restaurant
33 Marlin Grill Restaurant;
   Condor Dive
36 Ly Ay Restaurant
39 Nameless Restaurant
   and Bar
52 Sea Dragon
   Restaurant

OTHER
1 Main Post Office
6 Independence Square
9 Victory Monument
11 Independence Hotel
14 Wat Khrom
15 Police Station
17 Vietnamese Consulate
19 Galaxy Nightclub
20 Cambodian Commercial Bank
22 Ho Wah Genting Buses
23 GST Buses; Good Luck
   Motorbike Rentals
27 Angkor Arms
29 24 Hour Telephone/Fax
31 Chuen Min Hospital
34 Caltex Starmart
35 Red Snapper Bar Cafe
37 First Overseas Bank
38 Pacific Commercial Bank
40 Post Office
41 Market
43 Canadia Bank
44 Hospital
46 Nasa Nightclub
47 Golden Lions Traffic Circle

AROUND CAMBODIA

town is tiny Koh Pos Beach and the larger Independence Beach, which is home to the decaying and empty Independence Hotel.

Information

The ultimate source of information on Sihanoukville is the Sihanoukville Visitor's Guide. It is a pocket-sized directory put together every year and you can pick up a copy at local hotels and guesthouses. There are several banks in town, the best being Cambodian Commercial Bank (CCB), which has its usual services and charges, including credit card cash advances with a US$10 minimum charge. Canadia Bank is another useful option if you are carrying non-US dollar travellers cheques. The main post office is near the port, and there is a small branch office near the market.

There is also a Vietnamese consulate in Sihanoukville, which offers the same visa services as the embassy in Phnom Penh. Travellers who don't want to hang around Phnom Penh waiting for a visa might prefer to relax on the beach while the Vietnamese do their bureaucratic thing.

Things to See & Do

The best of the **beaches** are Sokha and Ochheuteal, although the beach near the guesthouses is easier to reach. It's worth visiting **Independence Beach** and checking out the old Independence Hotel. Some locals claim the hotel is haunted, and it does indeed have an eerie look about it. At night it seems to function as some sort of brothel, so if you hear some groaning and moaning, don't worry, it's probably not the ghosts that locals talk about.

Just 2km north of the main port is a **fishing port**, which offers some good photo opportunities at sunrise or sunset. Otherwise the town, although not an unpleasant place, lacks major attractions. There is no colonial architecture in town as it was founded in 1959.

There are several dive operations in town, all offering comparable deals. Condor Dive (☎ 015-831373) operates out of the Marlin Grill restaurant and offers single tank dives for US$35. Chez Claude (☎ 012-824870) offers similar prices. Both outfits can arrange picnics on board. Naga Dive (☎ 023-365102) operates classes at the Olympic Stadium in Phnom Penh and has a qualified PADI instructor. At weekends the operation heads south to Sihanoukville, and a single tank is US$25, but you have to chip in for a boat on top of that. It occasionally does three-day trips out to small islands beyond Koh Rong and Koh Tang, and at least you'll be in safe hands in pretty uncharted waters. Contact Marc at Phnom Penh's Olympic Stadium. Unless you are a dedicated diver, it is better to save diving for cheaper, more bountiful waters in Thailand and Indonesia.

About an hour's drive out of town is a **waterfall**, which is becoming a popular excursion with travellers. It is a pleasant place for a swim and all the moto drivers will want to take you there at some stage during your visit. Pay about US$3 for a morning or afternoon visit.

Sihanoukville is also the base from which to organise a visit to **Ream National Park**, a protected area that is home to dolphins, myriad bird species and a number of isolated beaches. See the Ream National Park entry under Around Sihanoukville later in this chapter.

Places to Stay

Sihanoukville has witnessed a boom in hotel construction during the last few years, but visitors have not materialised in quite the numbers anticipated. The upshot of this is that you should not be afraid to ask for rate reductions in the mid-range hotels. Most budget accommodation is a couple of kilometres west of town, near the port area.

Mealy Chenda Guesthouse is on the hill above Victory Beach. It's a friendly place run by the family that owns Narin Guesthouse in Phnom Penh and is very popular with backpackers. Rooms in the old house cost US$2 a dorm bed, US$3 a single and US$5 a double with shared bathroom. In the newer building behind, doubles cost US$5 to US$7 and a triple with shared facilities costs US$8. The neighbours have obviously decided they can make some money in this business as well, and both *Victory Guesthouse* and *Da Da Guesthouse* have clean, spacious doubles with bathroom for US$8, or US$5 without.

On the same hill, *Bungalow Resort* has basic huts for US$5. Slightly more upmarket is the *Mari Yan*. Huts with bathrooms are US$8 for one person and US$10 for two, or there are rooms in a longhouse for US$6. The setting is pleasant, but restaurant prices seem more geared to expats than backpackers. Both sets of bungalows get pretty hot during the day as they have tin roofs.

Ekareach St, the road that leads to town from Victory Beach, has recently seen the opening of several family-run guesthouses. The location is pretty poor, but the prices are some of the lowest in town. The best of the bunch is the nameless *guesthouse* at No 132, which is opposite the Kampuchea Hotel and has spotless rooms with fan and bathroom for US$6.

There are also cheap rooms for rent at *Les Feuilles* restaurant, one block from Ochheuteal Beach. You can expect to pay US$5 a bed, which is a good deal for this part of town.

If you're looking for some peace and quiet, the isolated *Koh Pos Hotel* is an option. It has its own small stretch of beach and a beachfront restaurant, and is signposted from town. Rates are US$15 for a big air-con double with attached bathroom and US$20 a triple, but the rooms are showing their wrinkles. Given the alternatives on other beaches it is a little overpriced. The *Sea Breeze Guesthouse* (☎ 320217), on Independence Beach, has clean, air-con singles/doubles with TV and fridge for US$15/25.

The centre of town has a host of midrange hotels offering air-con rooms with fridge, TV and attached bathroom with hot water: there is nothing much to choose between them. Bear in mind that it is quite a long way to the beaches. One of the cheapest is the *Angkor Inn Guest House*, with air-con rooms for US$8 and those with fan for US$6. Some of the best value establishments are those that charge just US$10 for all the trimmings. These include the *Star Hotel*, the *Thai San Hotel*, the *Koh Thas Hotel* and the *Phnom Meas Hotel*. Moving up the price range, the *Kompong Som*

Hotel has rooms for US$10/13, the *Koh Rong Hotel* for US$10/15 and the *New Paris Hotel* for US$15; these three hotels are all on or just off Ekareach St.

The other major concentration of hotels is on Ochheuteal Beach, but they cost a few more dollars than at Victory Beach. The beachfront *Crystal Hotel* (☎ 933523) has rooms for US$25/35, but is rather overshadowed by the most expensive place in town, the *Seaside Hotel* (☎ 933662), looking rather like a junior version of the Cambodiana in Phnom Penh. It offers a variety of well-appointed rooms from US$25, to US$50 for the politician Hun Sen's regular room, suite 214. A block back from the beach are the well-appointed *Orchid Hotel*, with rooms for US$15/20, and the *Holiday Hotel*, with rooms for US$15/20/25. One other place worth considering, particularly for families, is the *CCS Hotel* near the Golden Lions Traffic Circle, which has standard rooms for US$20 and large bungalows with two bedrooms for US$40.

Places to Eat

There are a lot of restaurants in the town centre and each of the beaches has one or two, although you are expected to pay higher prices for the pleasures of a sea view. *Mealy Chenda Guesthouse* has an extensive, reasonably priced restaurant with a wider choice of seafood than at the family's other guesthouses. It is a good place to watch the sunset, but service can be slow if there is a crowd. The *Melting Pot*, on the hill above Victory Beach, also has a good selection of Western food and is fast getting a reputation as the bar in which to hang out. It is all too easy to hang around these places if you're staying at this end of town, but it is worth venturing into the centre of town or to Ochheuteal Beach for an evening out.

Apsara Restaurant, right in the centre of town, has a mixture of Asian cuisine and some western dishes for US$2 to US$4. *Ly Ay Restaurant*, on Ekareach St, is a cheap noodle shop that stays open late into the night, so it's a good option if you get a munchies attack after the nightclubs close. Opposite the market is a nameless draught

Angkor Beer *emporium,* which has a couple of menus in English encouraging diners to sample such exotic delights as lizard and deer. 'Fried crap with peper' is one for the brave. *Marlin Grill Restaurant,* on Ekareach St, is the place in town to get western food, but it is also the place to pay western prices. It is a good place to indulge.

Down on Ochheuteal Beach there are a few more restaurants offering the advantage of a sea breeze. *Les Feuilles* serves steaks in blue cheese sauce for US$6 and a selection of pastas for about US$4. It also has a pool table. On the seafront, the *Sea Dragon Restaurant* has one of the most extensive menus around. It offers just about every combination of food and flavours you can imagine.

Chez Claude has reopened after Franco-Vietnamese owner Claude's extensive land dispute with local authorities was settled. Perched on a hill overlooking Sokha and Independence beaches, the views are breathtaking. The predominantly seafood menu is expensive by Sihanoukville standards, but the food is among the best in Cambodia, with a wine cellar to match.

Entertainment

Nightlife in Sihanoukville is pretty limited compared with Phnom Penh.

The nameless beer *emporium* is a great place for cheap draught at 2000r a mug, and worth stopping at before venturing out to dance as beers are much more expensive at nightclubs – and you'll likely dance better with a bit of fuel in the tank! The *Angkor Arms* is on the main drag and aims to offer the atmosphere of a British pub with darts and draught, with slightly higher prices to match. The *Red Snapper Bar Cafe,* just off the main drag, has a good roof-top location and stays open into the early hours if customers have the legs.

There are several nightclubs around town, but they are quite expensive for those on a budget and wind down by midnight. Most are the dark, Sha La La La La variety frequented by Khmers and Chinese and teeming with girls who charge for their company. *Galaxy* on Boray Kamakor St and

Nasa, near the Golden Lions Traffic Circle, are probably the best of this genre. For something later into the night you have to brave a drive through Chicken Village, the brothel strip, beyond which you will find *Biba Discotheque,* little unlike a formal brothel itself. It is worth a visit just for the surreal service: your drink is topped up almost constantly by the bar staff, even after the tiniest sip. Most of the girls seem to have numbers on them as in Bangkok and there is very little atmosphere.

Getting There & Away

Bus Both Ho Wah Genting and GST have services running to the capital and in Sihanoukville, and their offices are located on Ekareach St near the centre of town. Going to Phnom Penh, GST departs at 8 am and 1 pm and Ho Wah Genting at 7.30 and 9.30 am and 12.30 and 2 pm. See the Getting There & Away section of the Phnom Penh chapter for more details.

Train The train service to Sihanoukville is extraordinarily slow when compared with the bus service, but is remarkably cheap. Trains leave Phnom Penh and go via Kampot at 6.20 am on Monday, Wednesday and Friday and return at the same time on Tuesday, Thursday and Saturday. The cost is around 4000r, but 10 hours is a long time to sit on the train. If you really want to try the trains, you are better off just going from Phnom Penh to Sihanoukville by road and then taking a train for the shorter journey to Kampot.

Motorcycle You can use motorbikes rented in Phnom Penh to get to Sihanoukville. They are useful for exploring areas along the south coast and it is becoming increasingly popular to do a circuit that takes in Kampot, Kep and Bokor hill station. You can either ride the motorbikes to Sihanoukville or put them on the train and relax. See the Getting Around section in the Phnom Penh chapter for rental details. There are also motorcycles available for rent in Sihanoukville.

Taxi Taxis between Phnom Penh and Sihanoukville leave from the south-west of the

AROUND CAMBODIA

capital near Psar Dang Kor (Dang Kor Market), and from Sihanoukville opposite the market. Prices have dropped in the last few years, as the checkpoints on the road (numbering more than 100 some days), have been dismantled. Prices are negotiable, but you can expect to pay about US$25 a vehicle, 10,000r a head in cramped conditions or US$4 each with just three in the back. Most drivers seem to think they are Michael Schumacher, so if you don't like blind overtaking you may want to sit in the back with some Valium. Travelling by pick-up truck is cheaper; it costs about 7000r. From Sihanoukville to Kampot (8000r; two hours) is 105km and the road is excellent while you stay on National Hwy 4, but pretty poor for the next 30km.However it does improve for the final stretch. Taxis can be arranged from near the market.

Boat For details on the boat service operating between Sihanoukville and Koh Kong, see the Getting There & Away chapter earlier in the book.

Getting Around

Motorcycle In Sihanoukville, motorbike rentals can be arranged at Good Luck (you'll need it with some of their bikes) on Ekareach St, or through some of the guesthouses. It costs US$7 a day for 250cc dirt bikes and about US$5 for a standard moped, sometimes cheaper if you take them for several days. There are dirt bikes available here but they are not as good as those for rent in Phnom Penh.

Moto Apart from hiring your own bike, the only way to get around Sihanoukville is by moto. There are plenty about and in the evenings they tend to wait in droves outside popular nightspots. From the guesthouse area to the market is about 1000r, to Sokha and Ochheuteal beaches more like 2000r and late at night an extra 500r might be requested. From the centre of town to any of the beaches should only be about 1000r. From the guesthouse area to the fast boat dock is about 1000r, and nearer 2000r from the centre of town.

AROUND SIHANOUKVILLE
Ream National Park

Also known as Preah Sihanouk National Park, it was established as a protected area in 1993 and its 21,000 hectare area is home to a variety of animal and bird species, an expanse of mangrove swamp and forests and, beneath the surface of the Gulf of Thailand, some dolphins and coral.

The park now accepts visitors and has boats to transport them along the river to untouched beaches. Along the estuary, you may see monkeys, eagles and even dolphins, and from the empty sands on the coast it is possible to explore some nearby creeks that disappear into the forest.

The program is very much in its infancy, but deserves support as the boat trip can be both adventurous and educational and the income generated will ensure that the rangers protect the park instead of using its resources to make a living. The boat trip costs about US$5 a person, although this depends on numbers, and you will need to bring lunch unless you can arrange something with the rangers. There is also some beachfront accommodation available in the Keng Kong Recreation Area near Ream Naval Base, from where rangers may be able to take you on walks into the park.

Getting There & Away Ream National Park is located about 18km east of Sihanoukville. The park's headquarters is a short distance down a turn-off from the Naga statue in Ream. Lookout for the Preah Sihanouk National Park sign carved in stone. The building, white with a green roof, is right next to the little used airport that serves Sihanoukville. Contact the rangers to organise a trip or try organising one through a guesthouse in town. To get to the headquarters, take a moto from Sihanoukville for about US$1, or squeeze in a share taxi and get off at Ream.

KAMPOT

The somnolent riverside town of Kampot is beginning to attract more visitors. It is a charming place with some lovely examples of French architecture and a relaxed atmosphere.

Security concerns that have kept travellers away from Kampot Province in the past are no longer a problem and the town is a good base from which to explore the nearby crumbling beach resort of Kep and the abandoned hill station of Bokor, part of Bokor National Park.

Information

The main post office is on the river to the south of the Kampot Bridge. There are several telephone and fax offices around town from where you can make international calls. There are no banks in town so come armed with a fistful of dollars.

Tek Chhouu Falls

The falls are 8km out of town. Waterfall enthusiasts should prepare themselves for a disappointment as it is really just a series of small rapids, which don't even move very rapidly in the dry season. It is, however, a pleasant bathing spot should you want to cool off and is very popular with locals.

There is a proper waterfall 18km further up a dirt track from Tek Chhouu, but access is not straightforward as the road is bad and there are one or two checkpoints manned by Khmer Rouge defectors. They don't seem to have a problem with foreigners, but their

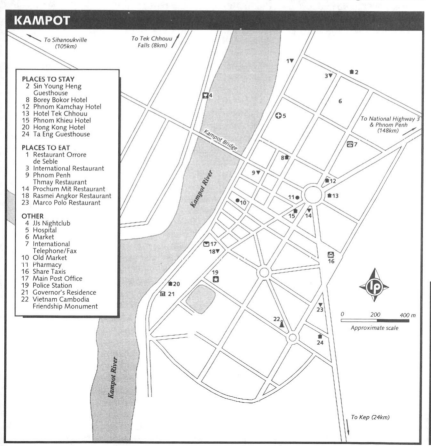

KAMPOT

To Sihanoukville (105km)

To Tek Chhouu Falls (8km)

To National Highway 3 & Phnom Penh (148km)

Kampot Bridge

Kampot River

Kampot River

PLACES TO STAY
2 Sin Young Heng Guesthouse
8 Borey Bokor Hotel
12 Phnom Kamchay Hotel
13 Hotel Tek Chhouu
15 Phnom Khieu Hotel
20 Hong Kong Hotel
24 Ta Eng Guesthouse

PLACES TO EAT
1 Restaurant Orrore de Seble
3 International Restaurant
9 Phnom Penh Thmay Restaurant
14 Prochum Mit Restaurant
18 Rasmei Angkor Restaurant
23 Marco Polo Restaurant

OTHER
4 JJs Nightclub
5 Hospital
6 Market
7 International Telephone/Fax
10 Old Market
11 Pharmacy
16 Share Taxis
17 Main Post Office
19 Police Station
21 Governor's Residence
22 Vietnam Cambodia Friendship Monument

0   200   400 m
Approximate scale

To Kep (24km)

relations with the army are somewhat strained so you may be told in Kampot that it is not possible to visit. Ask around before you head up there and take a guide.

Boat Trips

Kampot's riverside location makes it a good place to organise a short boat trip upstream. Ask around among local boat owners and you should be able to arrange something for about US$5 an hour. For something a little more organised, the Marco Polo Restaurant rents out a boat for US$30 a day. It has capacity for up to 12 people and can take you into the jungle at the foot of Bokor National Park. This works out pretty good value if you can get enough people together.

Places to Stay

There isn't a tremendous variety of hotels in Kampot, but beyond domestic tourists there have been very few people to fill them until recently. One thing worth bearing in mind is that if you are making a day trip up to Bokor hill station on a wet or cloudy day you will kill for a hot shower by the time you make it back to town.

The *Ta Eng Guesthouse* is the closest thing to backpacker accommodation in town. The friendly owner speaks decent English and French and has three-double rooms available with mosquito net, ceiling fan and shared bathroom for US$5. Nearby, the *Marco Polo Restaurant* has a couple of similar rooms, also for US$5. On the riverfront in the south of town is the *Hong Kong Hotel*, which is a little rundown, but has cheap rooms for US$7 a double with bathroom; most rooms can sleep three. In a lively location near the market is the *Sin Young Heng Guesthouse*, which has plain rooms with fan and bathroom for US$6, or US$10 should you opt to use the air-con.

The other hotels in town are a little more upmarket and are clustered around the central roundabout, but given the competition don't be afraid to bargain if there are few tourists around. *Hotel Tek Chhouu* has an atmosphere of decay, but offers doubles with bathroom as cheap as US$6 and something similar with air-con for US$10. It has a dark

nightclub below and a number of the punters seem to head upstairs after a few dances. The *Phnom Khieu* has some very good value rooms starting at US$5 for a large room with double bed, bathroom and fridge and US$10 for a room with air-con. The *Phnom Kamchay* offers basically the same deal, but singles/doubles are better equipped and a little more expensive with air-con, fridge and hot water for US$12/15, and US$15 for a cavernous triple without air-con. The town's newest hotel is the *Borey Bokor*, just off the central roundabout, and its presence has helped push prices down. It has the best rooms in town, which include TV, fridge, hot water and air-con, all in spotless surroundings, for US$10/15.

Places to Eat

There is a good range of dining opportunities in town, although you may have trouble making yourself understood at the hole in the wall establishments. Several restaurants have English menus and offer a fairly standard selection of dishes. One of the best places in town is the *Phnom Penh Thmay Restaurant*, one block up from the bridge. It has an extensive menu and most dishes cost US$1 to US$$3. Come the evening, the same street plays host to a large number of *tikalok* (fruit smoothies) sellers. The *Prochum Mit Restaurant* is right in the centre of town, has good food and often attracts a Khmer crowd come the evening. The *International Restaurant* has long been popular with the small expat community in Kampot. Near the market, it serves breakfast, lunch and dinner, and has a mixed menu of Khmer, Chinese and western dishes from about US$1.50 to US$4. If you are staying in the Hong Kong Hotel, it is worth checking out the nearby *Rasmei Angkor Restaurant*, which is one block back from the river. The food is good and service is relatively quick as its location means it is never too busy.

Restaurant Orrore de Seble has the best location for an evening meal; its series of simple bamboo huts are built over the river's edge. The food is good, with most dishes costing about US$2, and the service attentive to the point of over-eager. The *loklak* (diced beef, French fries and an egg) is excellent as the French fries are some of the best in Cambodia, but 'fork soup' sounds a bit painful! There are quite a number of girls purveying anything from Labatts to Angkor and it is a great place to sip a beer watching sunsets over Phnom Bokor. Both the Borey Bokor and Phnom Kamchay hotels also have *restaurants* that have the usual suspects on the menu and are convenient for breakfast if you are staying there, but are more expensive than the cheap *diners* around the market.

The *Marco Polo Restaurant*, just south of the share taxi stand on the road to Kep, is a new establishment that has brought a taste of Europe to Kampot. Prices are high, at US$4 to US$6, because it caters primarily to expats weekending from Phnom Penh and well-heeled tourists, but you might expect to pay for the privilege of pizzas and pastas in a town that didn't have telephone links with the capital until recently. Cornflakes with fresh milk are available for breakfast and decent wine is available with meals. The owner has been in Cambodia many years and organises boat and 4WD excursions in the area.

Entertainment

Expats tend to drink at the *Phnom Kamchay Hotel*. There are a couple of nightclubs in town, but they are even more provincial than those in Siem Reap and Battambang. The one under the *Hotel Tek Chhouu* appears to be little more than a disco brothel, and *JJs* across the river isn't much better. Diplomatically put, Kampot is a good place to recharge the batteries before hitting the town in Phnom Penh or Sihanoukville.

Getting There & Away

Kampot is 148km from Phnom Penh and due to the deteriorating condition of National Hwy 3, the journey takes about three hours. Share taxis cost about 8000r per person and leave Kampot from near the Total station in the south of town; minibuses cost 5000r; pick-ups cost 4000r. There is also a selection of vehicles making the journey to Sihanoukville. The prices are about the same as for Phnom Penh. For road conditions see the Sihanoukville section earlier in

this chapter. Some travellers make their way on 250cc motorbikes from the capital; see the Getting Around section in the Phnom Penh chapter for rental details. From Kampot to Takeo is not so straightforward as there are rarely any direct services. Jump in a vehicle going to Phnom Penh and ask to get off at the Takeo turn-off, which should cost about 5000r in a share taxi, less in a minibus or a pick-up. From here you can arrange a moto or a cheaper *remorque-moto* (motorcycle towing a trailer) for the 13km trip to Takeo.

Then there is the train, which in terms of time is the least sensible option, but time is something many travellers have to spare. It takes about six hours and is very cheap at about 2500r from Phnom Penh or Sihanoukville. It is quite a beautiful journey for the last hour or so and you can ride on the roof if you like. The train runs between Phnom Penh and Sihanoukville, so if you want to take it from Phnom Penh to Kampot it departs at 6.20 am Monday, Wednesday and Friday, arriving around midday before continuing to Sihanoukville. The train returns to Phnom Penh from Sihanoukville at 6.20 am every Tuesday, Thursday and Saturday, arriving in Kampot some time after 10 am before continuing on to the capital.

KEP

The seaside resort of Kep-sur-Mer was founded as a colonial retreat for the French elite in 1908. Cambodian high rollers continued the tradition, flocking here to enjoy gambling and water sports, and like most privileged revolutionaries it is likely the Khmer Rouge had its dachas down here in case things got too hot in the capital. Little remains except skeletons of buildings, as locals were forced to loot the villas for materials to sell to the Vietnamese to survive the famine of 1979 and 1980. Kep is on a small headland and has a 6km palm-fringed road extending along the coastline.

There are regular rumours of redevelopment plans, although there are only a few new villas appearing in town. Kep has certainly benefited from the toxic waste scandal

AROUND CAMBODIA

that brought so much bad publicity to Sihanoukville at the end of 1998, and Khmers are once again flocking here at the weekends. The beach is rather scruffy and often overcrowded at weekends, but there is a certain atmosphere about the place that brings expats back again and again.

On top of the hill near the beach is one of King Sihanouk's many palaces constructed in the early 1990s. Before his overthrow in 1970, Kep had been one of Sihanouk's favourite spots in Cambodia. He perhaps harboured thoughts of retirement here, but his ill-health and political instability in the country has meant he has never actually stayed at the palace.

Places to Stay & Eat

There are several places to stay in town. The first place you come to following the one-way coastal road through Kep is the *Seaside Guesthouse*, which has clean singles/doubles with attached washroom for US$6/8. This is the best of the budget deals in town. The *Phuong Bon Guesthouse*, about 3km on from the statue of the mermaid, has fan rooms for US$5 or US$7 with two beds and a bathroom. The decrepit *Krong Kep Hotel* has doubles for US$10 to US$15. The Marco Polo Restaurant in Kampot offers a tastefully furnished beautiful *wooden villa* above the beach at Kep. It can sleep six people in relative luxury. It is available for US$110 per night weekdays, US$140 a night at weekends or US$500 per week. It is beyond the range of most budget travellers, but is worth the money if you are in Cambodia for only a short time.

Eating in Kep is easy as there are numerous *bamboo shacks* all along the road offering fresh seafood, although be prepared to agree on a price in advance. It is one of the cheapest places in the country to gorge on fresh crab at about 5000r a kilogram. There are also a few nameless *restaurants* springing up in small wooden properties along the coast road. If you are staying in Kep for the night and don't want to go hungry, put in an order before dark for something later as most of the *food stalls* pack up by late afternoon.

Getting There & Away

Kep is 24km from Kampot, 172km from Phnom Penh and 49km from the Vietnamese town of Ha Tien. From Kampot you can arrange a moto for the day for about US$6 to US$8 day or you can get a moto driver to take you out there for about US$2 and come and collect you at a pre-arranged time for the same price. Cheaper by a long way is to go by remorque-moto if you can find one going all the way. However, not having your own transport makes exploration of the surrounding area more difficult. You could also charter a share taxi from the centre of town, but they are likely to want US$20 for the day as they won't be able to do the run to Phnom Penh.

There is a border crossing 8km to the north of Ha Tien, but it is not presently open to foreigners. The direct road from Kep to Phnom Penh offers some interesting limestone peaks before rejoining National Hwy 3, but is in atrocious condition and only really passable in a 4WD or on a motorbike. The journey to the capital takes about four hours, but is easier via Kampot.

AROUND KEP
Koh Tonsay

Koh Tonsay (Rabbit Island) is just a short boat ride off the coast of Kep. It has several beaches, all much nicer than those at Kep, and it is possible to stay with families on the island as long as you can sort out a price for food and lodging. Malaria is prevalent on most islands off Cambodia's coast so come prepared with an arsenal of chemical weapons. Boats can be arranged at the first cluster of food stalls on the coast road. Expect to pay about US$20 a day for the boat, although the price may depend on numbers. You can negotiate your way to the island for less if you are planning to stay overnight.

It is possible to get to islands further afield on day trips organised through the Marco Polo Restaurant in Kampot. The boat costs US$30 for the day and carries up to 12 people.

Caves of Phnom Sia

There are quite a lot of caves in and around the limestone hills near Kep. There are a number of unexplored cave systems on the road that winds along the Vietnamese border. However, these are only accessible with the help of locals and may be hazardous. The most convenient caves to visit are those at Phnom Sia, just a couple of kilometres on from the junction with the statue of the white horse on the road from Kep to Kampot. It is considered a holy place and there is a small wat at the bottom of the hill. Concrete steps wind their way past altars and statues on a circuit that takes you to several major caves.

The biggest cave is called **Rung Damrey Saa (White Elephant Cave)** because of a stalactite formation said by locals to resemble a white elephant head, although whatever they had been taking when they came up with this, it must have been strong. Further on the right is a sign pointing to **100 Fields Cave**, and by following a precarious path to a small hole in the cave wall, you are rewarded with a peep show of terraced paddy fields. The final cave is home to many bats and you can hear them squeaking before you descend. It must be quite spectacular to see them streaming out come sunset. The circuit ends near a small **stupa** from where there are impressive views.

The caves at Phnom Sia are certainly worth a stop on the way back to Kampot. They may not be as spectacular as some of those in Vietnam, but they boast almost no visitors, which gives them a peace and serenity unmatched by major tourist attractions.

BOKOR NATIONAL PARK

Officially known as Preah Monivong National Park, but more commonly referred to as Bokor, it is one of the country's largest national parks. It is now open to visitors, having long been kept off the map due to Khmer Rouge activity and more recently the presence of illegal loggers. Within its boundaries are the nascent tourist attractions of the abandoned French hill station of Bokor and the Popokvil Falls, a two tiered waterfall where you are able to swim on a warm day. It is home to significant numbers of birds and mammals, including elephants whose dung litters the road to the hill station. However, most of the animals are nocturnal, so you are

only likely to see them should you stay overnight. The park has a ranger post at the foot of the hill and a ranger station with accommodation at the old hill station. There is a US$2 entry fee to the park, which will hopefully provide the rangers with much needed revenue to combat illegal logging.

There are possibly a few land mines dotted about the park, so if you really want to do some serious exploring it is imperative that you take a ranger as a guide. They have trail bikes and will be able to take you to both the hill station and the falls. A fee of about US$10 to US$15 for the day on the trail bikes should cover their services, petrol and maintenance for the machines, but if the rangers are using their bikes for park duties they may not be able to take you up. Although these prices may sound high, you are helping to preserve Cambodia's forests by ensuring the rangers have a sustainable income. Their government wage is negligible and is not guaranteed to arrive every month, so they need money from tourism to resist the temptation of elephant poaching or logging.

The park is best visited as a day trip from Kampot, but should you want to visit coming to or from Sihanoukville it is possible, but arduous.

Bokor Hill Station

The old French hill station of Bokor (1080m) is known for its cool climate, secluded waterfalls and jungle vistas. Founded by the French in 1922, the town was abandoned twice in its history, once when the Vietnamese overran the place in the late 1940s while fighting for independence against the French, and then again in 1972 when it was overrun by the Khmer Rouge in its guerrilla war against the Lon Nol regime. It has since remained uninhabited, save for the presence of either Vietnamese troops or Khmer Rouge guerrillas during much of the past two decades. Its altitude and commanding views made it a place of strategic importance to all sides during the long years of conflict in Cambodia, and it was one location the Vietnamese really had to fight for during their invasion in 1979. The Khmer Rouge held out for three months; one unit was ironically holed up in the Catholic church while the Vietnamese shot at it from the Bokor Palace Hotel only half a kilometre away.

The place really has a ghost town feel, and the old **Catholic church** looks like it was locked up only yesterday. Inside, the altar remains intact and drawings of what look like Khmer Rouge fighters adorn the wall.

The old hotel, the **Bokor Palace**, is straight out of the film *The Shining* and if you walk to the edge of what was once an outdoor terrace you will be rewarded with a magnificent view over lush jungle stretching almost to the sea. However, do not stray from the narrow path as there is still at least one land mine in an isolated corner of the hotel grounds, according to Khmer Rouge defectors. Inside the hotel, you can wander up and down the corridors from the kitchens below through the ballroom to the suites above, imagining what it was like before it was gutted. On a cold and gusty day it can get pretty creepy up there as visibility drops to nothing and the wind howls through the building.

There is also the ruin of an old wat up at the hill station known locally as **Five Boats Wat** due to the five large rocks, which some say resemble boats. It was built in 1924 and, like the Bokor Palace Hotel, affords tremendous views over the jungle to the coastline below. Other buildings dotted around include an old **casino** just opposite the ranger station, a post office, which looks like it has taken a mortar at some stage in its history, and an old water tower that looks like a spacecraft.

It is possible to stay the night up at Bokor hill station in the *ranger station*. There are three rooms with six bunks available for US$5 a person, and one room with a double and single bed available for US$20. Bathroom facilities are shared and there is a basic communal kitchen for the use of guests and rangers. Don't forget to bring some food from Kampot as nothing much is available here. Running water and electricity keep going until about 9 pm. It can get very cold at night so take some extra layers for after dark. If the wind is blowing, you might want to prop a mattress up against the windows as they are not very well sealed.

Popokvil Falls

This two-tiered waterfall is a fine place to bathe on a sunny day. The upper falls are 14m high and are the best place to take a swim. The lower falls are 18m high, but getting to the bottom is a bit of a headache. The name translates into 'Swirling Clouds' in English and there do appear to be swirling clouds just above the falls most of the time. The falls are located about 15 minutes by road and another hour or so walking from the Bokor hill station. It is best to take a guide as the falls are not easy to find and there may be land mines in the area. If you really are set on doing it yourself, keep going straight at the concrete sign pointing towards an abandoned building and when you get to the river with some sort of small dam or bridge foundations across it, follow it to the left and try to stick near it until you eventually hit the falls. If you are visiting the falls before the hill station, take the right fork in the road when up on the plateau; the left fork continues to the hill station.

Getting There & Away

Bokor National Park is 41km from Kampot, 132km from Sihanoukville and 190km from Phnom Penh. The access road is 7km outside Kampot marked by an elaborate interchange system. There is a ranger post and a ticket booth at the bottom of the hill. If they will not let you pass it is usually for a good reason, such as the unwanted presence of armed loggers.

The road up to Bokor is one of Cambodia's most exciting, but in terrible condition for the first 25km and only passable on a motorbike or in a sturdy 4WD vehicle. It winds its way up through thick jungle and in places the foliage is trying to reclaim the road. Trees do get blown across the road from time to time, and if this is the case you will have to go up with the rangers, so they can clear the road. The poor surface ends when you emerge on top of the plateau, and this is where the first buildings appear with a wonderful view over the coast.

The building nearest the road was part of Sihanouk's villa complex at Bokor, known as the **Black Palace**. From this point the road is

AROUND CAMBODIA

pretty good for the final 10km to the hill station, and the scenery is decidedly different with scrub everywhere. It is about 6km to the right fork to Popokvil, and it is up on this desolate plateau that you start encountering elephant dung. If you are riding your own bike use the brakes carefully as it is seriously big stuff.

As well as the ranger service to get you up the hill, moto drivers in Kampot will offer to take you up there for about US$10, but it is less comfortable and of less benefit to the park this way. Otherwise you can arrange your own motorbike in Phnom Penh. Finally, the Marco Polo Restaurant in Kampot offers a 4WD trip for US$50 with space for six people, so it's a fair price if you can fill it, but overpriced otherwise.

KIRIROM NATIONAL PARK

The hill station of Kirirom, set amid pine forests 675m above sea level, has been established as a national park. It is 112km south-west of Phnom Penh in the **Chuor Phnom Damrei (Elephant Mountains)** to the west of National Hwy 4. It is popular with Khmers at weekends, although this has led to something of a litter problem, which blights parts of the park. It is not the most interesting of Cambodia's national parks, but it is the most accessible from the capital and the scenery is notably different from the flat agricultural land that surrounds Phnom Penh. There is a small *guesthouse* in the park should you want to stay the night with rooms for US$5.

Unless you have your own transport it is not that easy to get to because it is about 25km east of National Hwy 4. You could get one of the buses going down to Sihanoukville and ask to be let off at Kirirom or Preah Suramarit Kossomak National Park (the full name in Khmer). However, you would still have to get a moto to drive you around the park itself. The best way to visit would be to hire a motorcycle in Phnom Penh or get a group of people together and charter a taxi from somewhere like the Capitol Guesthouse. Coming in your own vehicle, the turn-off for the park is about 85km from the centre of Phnom Penh, and is marked by a sign.

KOH KONG

Koh Kong is a pretty dull town, but increasing numbers of travellers are staying here when journeying from Thailand to Cambodia by sea. It has been something of a boom town for trade, both legal and illegal, and this has begun to attract migrants from other parts of the country seeking opportunities in this fast growing frontier area. It is also popular with Thais as casinos are a legal and thriving business in Cambodia. In a few years time, it may become some sort of base from which to explore Cambodia's nearby islands, but for now it remains primarily a transit stop and not somewhere people really want to hang around.

Information

There is a branch of Pacific Commercial Bank in town where you can change cash or travellers cheques in most major currencies. However, if you come with a solid supply of US dollars and a few hundred Thai baht (B), you will have no need to visit the bank as you can use either currency or change a little into riel at the market. There is a post office in town, but you are better off sending mail from Thailand before you get here or waiting until you arrive in Phnom Penh. There are several phone and fax offices around town and, like other towns in western Cambodia, prices are reasonable as the system is connected to Thailand.

Places to Stay & Eat

Being Cambodia's original 'wild west', long before Pailin started to muscle in on the gambling and prostitution business, quite a lot of the town's hotels double as brothels, so you may not get as much sleep as you hope for.

Out beyond the market are a few cheap guesthouses, but these are mainly the domain of one hour customers, with very spartan rooms, paper-thin walls and little in the way of security. The *Preas Chann Penh Vong Hotel* is the friendliest of these cell-like places and has rooms for 150B. Others include the *Koh Kong Guesthouse*, the *Punleathe Nay Hotel* and the *Rasmay Bunthan Hotel;* they all charge about 200B a night.

A much better choice is the **Koh Kong Hotel** on the riverfront, which offers fan-cooled rooms with shared bathroom for 100B, with bathroom inside for 150B and with a TV for 200B.

Moving a little more upmarket, the **Phkaousaphea Hotel** has air-con rooms with bathroom and TV for 300B; the Phkaousaphea seems to get the bulk of its custom from Thai businessmen.

The biggest hotel in town is the **Koh Pick Hotel**, which has some spacious doubles with air-con, bathroom and TV for 300B, and some surprisingly affordable basic rooms with fan behind the main building for 100B. This hotel employs security guards so you would have to consider it the safest place in town.

There are a string of small **riverfront restaurants** from where you can enjoy a sunset meal and almost forget the dirt and dust of the town.

During the day you can get a cheap meal or snack from the **market**, but most of the food places there are closed by dark. Some of the larger hotels also have reasonably priced **restaurants** with fresh seafood on the menu.

Entertainment

There is arguably more to do by night in Koh Kong than during daylight hours. Thais have been crossing the border for years to gamble or for a bit of womanising, and bars and nightclubs have sprung up to cater for them. The town's best nightclub is in the **Koh Pick Hotel** and it has an 11 member house band that, early on at least, outnumbers the clients. Just near the Rasmay Bunthan Hotel is a pretty seedy **bar** that has several bears in cages and some pretty unfriendly regulars so you might want to avoid it.

Getting There & Away

Royal Air Cambodge (RAC) operates three flights a week between Phnom Penh and Koh Kong. The price is US$50/100 one-way /return. For details on land and sea travel to Thailand or Sihanoukville see the Getting There & Away chapter.

Western Cambodia

BATTAMBANG

Cambodia's second largest city is an elegant riverside town, home of the best-preserved colonial architecture in the country and some of the most hospitable Khmers you can hope to meet. Until recently, security concerns kept Battambang off the map for all but those willing to fly in and out. However, improved conditions have opened the city to overland traffic and it makes a great base from which to explore nearby temples and scenic villages. For now it remains a secondary hub on the overland trade route between Thailand and Vietnam, but there are fears that with the upgrading of National Hwy 6 from Poipet to Siem Reap and on, eventually, via Kompong Cham to Vietnam, that it could find itself wiped off the map of commerce. However, for visitors, this will probably only add to the charm of the city.

Orientation

Although it is a major city, Battambang is fairly compact and easily negotiable on foot. The centre of town is the market square and all commercial activity and most of the city's hotels are located within a few blocks of here. The central area is bordered to the west by the railway line and to the east by the Sangker River. Across the river are a number of old colonial buildings serving as administrative centres for the large numbers of non-governmental organisations (NGOs) represented in the province.

Information

There are several banks in town. CCB, near the train station, will do the usual credit card cash advances for US$10, and travellers cheques for 2%. Canadia Bank is north of the market and changes travellers cheques in most major currencies for 2% commission. The main post office is on the riverfront, but for international telephone calls use the Interphone offices located all over town. Calls are routed via Thailand so it is only 10B a minute to Bangkok and

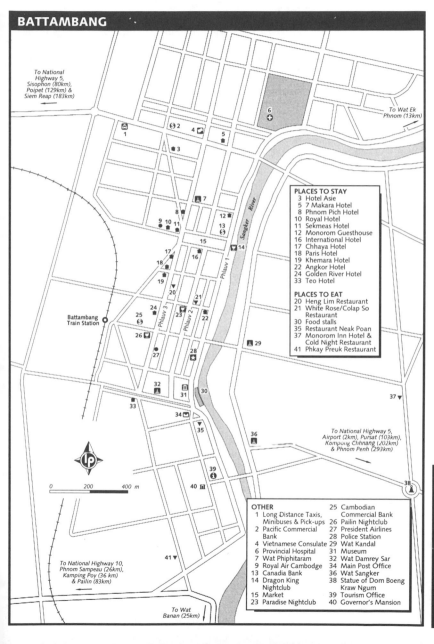

BATTAMBANG

To National
Highway 5,
Sisophon (80km),
Poipet (129km) &
Siem Reap (183km)

To Wat Ek
Phnom (13km)

Sangker River

Phlauv 1

Phlauv 3

Phlauv 2

Battambang
Train Station

To National Highway 5,
Airport (2km), Pursat (103km),
Kompong Chhnang (202km)
& Phnom Penh (293km)

To National Highway 10,
Phnom Sampeau (26km),
Kamping Poy (36km)
& Pailin (83km)

To Wat
Banan (25km)

0   200   400 m

PLACES TO STAY
3 Hotel Asie
5 7 Makara Hotel
8 Phnom Pich Hotel
10 Royal Hotel
11 Sekmeas Hotel
12 Monorom Guesthouse
16 International Hotel
17 Chhaya Hotel
18 Paris Hotel
19 Khemara Hotel
22 Angkor Hotel
24 Golden River Hotel
33 Teo Hotel

PLACES TO EAT
20 Heng Lim Restaurant
21 White Rose/Colap So
   Restaurant
30 Food stalls
35 Restaurant Neak Poan
37 Monorom Inn Hotel &
   Cold Night Restaurant
41 Phkay Preuk Restaurant

OTHER
1 Long Distance Taxis,
   Minibuses & Pick-ups
2 Pacific Commercial
   Bank
4 Vietnamese Consulate
6 Provincial Hospital
7 Wat Phiphitaram
9 Royal Air Cambodge
13 Canadia Bank
14 Dragon King
   Nightclub
15 Market
23 Paradise Nightclub
25 Cambodian
   Commercial Bank
26 Pailin Nightclub
27 President Airlines
28 Police Station
29 Wat Kandal
31 Museum
32 Wat Damrey Sar
34 Main Post Office
36 Wat Sangker
38 Statue of Dom Boeng
   Kraw Ngum
39 Tourism Office
40 Governor's Mansion

AROUND CAMBODIA

US$2 a minute for Europe, Australia and the US.

There is a small provincial tourist office near the Governor's Mansion, which has little to offer in the way of handouts, but staff can tell you quite a lot of information about places of interest near Battambang if you stick around and chew the cud.

Things to See & Do

Much of Battambang's charm lies in the network of old **French shop houses** nestled on the riverbank. There are a number of wats around town, including **Wat Phiphitaram**, north of the market, where a number of the monks speak English and are glad for the chance to practise their conversation. The city has a small **museum** on the riverfront with a collection of Angkorian-era artefacts assembled from temples in the province. Beyond the town are a number of attractions including hill-top temples, Angkorian-era wats and a large lake.

Places to Stay

Battambang's hotels are the best value in the country as many were built to house United Nations Transitional Authority in Cambodia (UNTAC) personnel and are now suffering a long hangover, with no guests to patronise them. Prices are fairly uniform so you can expect to pay US$5 for a spacious double with bathroom, TV and fridge, and US$10 for the added luxuries of air-con and hot water. Most hotels have their own adult movie channel, which kicks in at night and is beyond explicit.

There isn't the vast selection of cheap guesthouse karaoke brothels you find in cities like Kompong Cham and Kratie, so really cheap accommodation is limited to the *7 Makara Hotel*, which is north of Wat Phiphitaram and pretty run down compared with the competition, but offers basic rooms for just 10,000r.

The best choice is the *Chhaya Hotel*, in the centre of town, which has helpful and friendly staff and attentive service, all for US$5. The cheapest hotel rooms, at US$4, are in the nearby *Sekmeas Hotel*, also known as the Golden Parrot Guesthouse, but they are a little musty. Other hotels with cheap rooms include the nearby *Phnom Pich Hotel* and a little further north *Hotel Asie*. 23 Tola Hotel, near Sekmeas Hotel, is being renovated and will reopen as *Royal Hotel*. This should prove to be serious competition to the Chhaya.

Moving up to the US$10 establishments, the friendliest staff are at the *Golden River Hotel,* and the desk manager has excellent English. There is a pool table upstairs. Head south to the top joint in town, the *Teo Hotel*, where doubles go for US$12. The exterior is pretty extravagant, but the rooms are similar to those elsewhere. It has a restaurant downstairs, which is a popular place for local expats to sink a beer or two at night.

If you want a room overlooking the river, the only choices are the *Angkor Hotel*, a modern affair incongruously clinging to the end of some fine old buildings, which has rooms for US$10, and the *Monorom Guesthouse*; which has fan rooms for US$5/6/7 for one, two or three people, making it good value. Other central, worthwhile options include *Paris Hotel*, *Khemara Hotel* and *International Hotel*, the latter overlooks the bustling market area.

Places to Eat

Like the city's hotels, restaurants in Battambang offer good value for money. Undoubtedly the best food in town, and a contender for all Cambodia, is the *Phkay Pruek Restaurant* on the road to Pailin. The menu is full of Thai and Khmer delights and it has, believe it or not, Wall's ice-cream sundaes for only US$1. Try 'four comrades to play fire with shrimp', the 'comrades' being carrots, peas, baby corn and mushrooms, or if you prefer something super spicy try something 'drunken'.

There are popular restaurants near Paradise Nightclub, which offer cheap local food and divine tikaloks. The best of the bunch is *White Rose*, or *Colap So* in Khmer, as it tends not to put too much sugar in the drinks. There is no English sign so look for the white rose on the rear wall. It also sells inexpensive sandwiches throughout the day, which are basically a piece of baguette and a large assortment of goodies to cram inside. ***Heng Lim Restaurant*** has a healthy menu of mixed Asian cuisine and some of the staff speak English. It is good value for money and centrally located.

If you are willing to venture a bit further afield or are staying in the Monorom Inn Hotel, then the ***Cold Night Restaurant***, east of the river, has a massive menu with about 300 dishes. There is a wide selection of Asian food and a surprising amount of western food including burgers and pastas for about US$2 and pizzas from US$3.

If you want to eat by the river, ***Restaurant Neak Poan*** has a beer garden and is popular with locals in the evening. Nearby are a host of ***food stalls*** that set up for business in the late afternoon and make a good place to observe life in this pleasant city. Cheap dining is also available in and around the ***market***, although the places inside the main building seem to specialise in what can only be described as 'unusable bits' soup.

Entertainment

For such a large city, Battambang's nightlife is somewhat limited. For evening drinking, the ***Teo Hotel*** is popular with expats, while the cheap ***riverside food stalls*** near the museum attract a good Khmer crowd, with their cheap prices. Khmer nightclubs are about the only option after 9 pm and none of these are exactly spectacular. The ***Pailin Nightclub***, east of the train station, is marginally cheaper than the alternatives, but ***Dragon King***, on the river, goes on until later. Be prepared to be attacked by the myriad beer girls using their charms to encourage you to drink their particular brand – it is like something out of a wrestling ring.

Getting There & Away

Air Flights to Phnom Penh leave daily except Tuesday, and on Monday, Wednesday and Thursday go via Siem Reap. Direct flights take 45 minutes and indirect a little under 1¾ hours. It is US$45/90 one-way/return.

Train It is a harsh 274km journey to Phnom Penh of at least 15 hours if the train encounters no problems on the way. The train leaves at 6 am every day. It is cheap at just

over 4000r, but locals advise against using the service for reasons of comfort and personal security. You could take the train as far as Pursat, avoiding the worst stretch of road, and then continue to Phnom Penh by taxi. There is also a train to Sisophon (1500r; four hours), which departs at 8 am and returns to Battambang at 2 pm every day. The journey is tediously slow when compared with the road.

Taxi, Pick-up & Minibus The 293km road to Phnom Penh is a case of the good, the bad and the ugly. It is plain ugly between the town of Muong Russei and Pursat, bad from Pursat to Kompong Chhnang and good into Phnom Penh, although the annual wet season can leave it pretty potholed. Security is not a problem, but check this is still the case before departing. Share taxis and pick-ups leave Battambang from near the Sisophon roundabout north-west of the town centre. Pick-ups to Phnom Penh cost 20,000r inside or 7000r outside, but you really don't want to ride on the back given both weather and road conditions. Taxis cost about 20,000r a person, although they may start much higher. Minibuses sometimes pass by and will take you for US$5.

Sisophon is 80km north-west of Battambang on a reasonable road. Aim to pay 5000r in the cab of a pick-up, 3000r on the back and about 6000r in a taxi. From Sisophon you can arrange transport to Poipet or Siem Reap.

Getting Around

To/From the Airport The airport is east of the river about 2km from the centre of town. Pay about 2000r by moto.

Moto Battambang is compact enough to explore on foot. Motos are cheap and plentiful. Most rides are 500r, although you may pay more if you go out across the river or use them at night.

AROUND BATTAMBANG

Before setting out on trips around Battambang province, try to link up with an English-speaking moto driver as it will help you to get more out of the experience. As the area sees few tourists, prices are a little sketchy and different drivers may want different amounts. The following prices are meant to be indicative rather than definitive. Remorque-moto is the cheapest way to get to these places, but it takes longer and may require more than one ride to get to some of the more distant places.

Wat Ek Phnom

Wat Ek Phnom is a rather dilapidated 10th century temple. It is something of a disappointment after Angkor, but the attractive ride out there on a winding road following the banks of the Sangker River makes the trip worth the time. Take a US$2 moto for the 25km round trip. Some drivers will take you on a loop through the countryside on the way back.

Phnom Sampeau

The hill-top temple of Sampeau was formerly the front line in the government's defence of Battambang, but with the late 1996 defection of Ieng Sary and his Khmer Rouge units, the area is safe to visit. There is a long, hot climb to reach the summit, which is topped by both a small **wat** and a **stupa**. Nearby are a couple of large **field guns**, which local children claim are defended with mines. This may not be true, but in the meantime take your photos from the path and do not approach them. For this information alone it is worth letting a child tag along with you and give them something like 1000r at the end. There is another mountain nearby, which locals call **crocodile mountain**, long occupied by the Khmer Rouge during the civil war and used to lob shells at government troops guarding Phnom Sampeau.

The children will also guide you to a rather horrific **killing field** located in a cave on another part of the hill. A small staircase leads down to a platform covered in the skulls and bones of victims. Look up to the right and you will see a skylight hole where victims were bludgeoned before being thrown into the pit beneath.

Phnom Sampeau is 26km south-west of Battambang and a moto costs about US$2 to US$3, depending on wait time.

Wat Banan

Wat Banan is like a smaller version of the rather more illustrious Angkor Wat. Built in the 10th century, it is in a better state of repair than Wat Ek Phnom and its hillside location makes it more striking. It is very popular at weekends with Khmer families out on picnics.

Wat Banan is 25km south of Battambang and the round trip costs US$2 to US$3.

Kamping Poy

Kamping Poy is the site of both a **recreational lake** and one of the Khmer Rouge's grander schemes, a massive **hand-built dam** stretching for about 8km between two hillsides. Some locals claim the dam was intended as a sort of final solution for enemies of the revolution, who were to be invited to witness its inauguration and instead drown as dynamite charges were set to detonate. It was more likely another step on the road to recreating the complex irrigation network that Cambodia enjoyed under the kings of Angkor. Whatever the truth, as many as 10,000 Cambodians are thought to have perished in its construction. Near the dam is the lake, which is a popular swimming spot for locals at the weekend.

Kamping Poy is 36km west of Battambang down a small turn-off just after Phnom Sampeau. It is best combined with a visit to this hillside wat. A moto for a full day is about US$6.

PAILIN

This small town near the border with Thailand, with its gem and timber resources, was long the economic crutch that kept the Khmer Rouge hobbling along. It was used as a base from which to launch regular dry-season offensives against government positions in and around the city of Battambang, which was actually taken by the Khmer Rouge for a very short time in 1994. However, in August 1996, Ieng Sary, former brother No 3 during the Khmer Rouge regime and Khmer Rouge supremo in these parts, defected to the government side bringing with him up to 3000 fighters and their dependents. This was critical in bringing about the eventual demise of the Khmer Rouge, as it cut off much needed sources of revenue for fighters in the north and allowed the Royal Cambodian Armed Forces (RCAF) to concentrate its resources on one front.

Today Pailin occupies a curious position as a semiautonomous zone in which leaders of the former Khmer Rouge can seek haven, avoiding the long arm of international law. There is little of interest to the tourist here, unless you know a bit about gemstones or like hanging out with geriatrics responsible for mass murder. It is indeed ironic that this one time Khmer Rouge model town is these days a centre of vice and gambling.

Places to Stay

Quite a few of the guesthouse brothels that you see in frontier towns like Koh Kong have sprung up in Pailin so you can get rooms for as little as 10,000r. There are also a few more upmarket places in town, which were built to cater for all the gem speculators that flocked here from other parts of Asia during the mid-1990s. The *Pailin Guesthouse* has rooms from US$5 with fan, TV and bathroom.

Getting There & Away

Pailin lies 80km south-west of Battambang and only about 30km from Thailand. This border is not presently open to foreigners, but may be soon, so if you hear it is open, check for confirmation in Phnom Penh or Bangkok. Share taxis make the journey between Battambang and Pailin (30,000r; two to three hours). Pick-ups want 30,000r in the cab and 15,000r in the back. These prices are very high for Cambodia, but then Cambodian cabbies probably consider the trip to Pailin as the equivalent of driving to Hades itself!

SISOPHON

Sisophon is not one of Cambodia's more inspiring towns, and for tourists it is more often than not no more than a quick transit stop between Thailand and the temples of Angkor near Siem Reap. However, a number of travellers do find themselves having to spend the night here, particularly in the wet season. Thai baht is the currency of choice here, but as in the rest of Cambodia, US dollars will never be ignored.

Shadow Puppet Theatre

In the centre of Sisophon near the hospital is a workshop run by the NGO Krousar Thmey (New Family), which teaches disadvantaged children the art of shadow puppetry and leatherwork techniques for making the puppets. Shows take place on an irregular basis, but if you can muster a group together Krousar Thmey may be able to arrange a one-off performance in return for a donation.

Places to Stay

There are quite a lot of guesthouses and hotels in Sisophon. The cheapest places to stay are the guesthouses on the road to Siem Reap, which offer simple fan rooms at reasonable rates. These include the *Thmor Da Guesthouse*, with rooms for 10,000r; the *Pat Paining Guesthouse*, which charges 100B/150 for singles/doubles; and the *Reaksmey Santephiep Guesthouse*, with rooms for US$4. Whatever currency you are carrying you are sure to get a bed somewhere!

Moving up the price range, the *Sourkear Hotel*, also on the road to Siem Reap, has 11 rooms with bathroom for US$10 with aircon, and US$5 with a double bed and fan. Next door is the *Roeung Rong Hotel*, which has fan rooms with bathroom for 200B and a few with air-con for US$10. On the same road is the town's fanciest place, the *Phnom Sway Hotel*, which has a wide variety of rooms starting at US$6 for a single with fan, bathroom and TV and rising to US$10 for an air-con double with hot water. This is the hotel of choice with visiting UN or NGO workers and is affectionately known as the birthday cake because it looks a little like one. The *Proum Meanchey Hotel*, near the market, is another modern, clean hotel with good value rates. Rooms with air-con, TV, fridge and bathroom with hot water are US$10. It also runs a restaurant next door.

Places to Eat

The choice of restaurants is not as good as the choice of hotels, but there are a few places where you can get a good meal. Many places offer food as an afterthought to their steady diet of karaoke. There are a lot of inexpensive *food stalls* all over town, particularly near the taxi stand. Apart from the *Morning Sky Restaurant* (the town's best eatery), which is next to the Phnom Sway Hotel, there are only a couple of proper restaurants in Sisophon: the *Sereisophon Restaurant* and the *Penh Cheth Restaurant*. The Penh Cheth is more lively.

Getting There & Away

Pick-ups travel from Sisophon to Poipet (5000r in the cab, 3000r on the back), to Siem Reap (20,000r inside, 7000r outside), and to Battambang (5000r inside, 3000r outside; 1½ hours). Coming from Thailand to Siem Reap, you should consider spending the night in Sisophon if you arrive much after 3 pm.

There are also trains to Battambang (1500r; four hours) leaving at 2 pm each day.

BANTEAY CHHMAR

Banteay Chhmar (Narrow Fortress), 71km north of Sisophon, was one of the capitals of Jayavarman II (ruled 802-50). The city, enclosed by a 9km-long wall, had in its centre one of the largest and most impressive Buddhist monasteries of the Angkor period. The sandstone structure, built in the 11th century and dedicated to the deity Avalokiteshvara, suffered significant damage during repeated Thai invasions, although many of its huge bas-reliefs, which are said to be comparable to those of the Bayon and Angkor Wat, are extant. Many of the remaining works of art

were plundered during 1998, and at least one full truckload was confiscated by the Thai authorities on the road to Bangkok, so there may be very little left by now. The road is in bad shape and there is the possibility of robbery because of its remoteness.

POIPET

If Cambodia can be said to have an armpit, then Poipet is it. If this is your first port of call in Cambodia, then take heart as this really is an aberration. Until as recently as 1996, it was under regular mortar fire from the Khmer Rouge and so has always been a transient place with a transient look. It feels like a shanty town without a city to justify its existence, but it has Thailand instead. Conditions worsen significantly during the wet season, when the roads become rivers of mud and detritus. There is absolutely no reason to spend any time here. If you enter Cambodia with US dollars or baht then you don't really need to change this into riel until later in your trip, but should you want to get your hands on some local currency the market is the best place to do so.

Places to Stay & Eat

Should you for some masochistic reason want to stay in Poipet, there are a few guesthouses around town with basic rooms: the *Khemarak Hotel* has fan rooms for 200B; the *Santephiep Guesthouse* has similar rooms for US$5; the *O Chrow Hotel* has rooms with air-con for

A Bitter Pill

Several travellers have warned of bogus doctors at the Poipet immigration point demanding cash for cholera or typhoid 'vaccine' – and threatening to refuse entry into Cambodia if the money failed to materialise.

Border guards insisted the travellers go through quarantine, where, if they could not produce an International Health Card proving vaccination for cholera or typhoid, they were charged about US$5 for two pills. The pills were antimalarials (doxycycline).

One traveller even showed quarantine their own 60 pill pack. However, it took a lot more to convince immigration that its health care help was unnecessary. But immigration obviously knows this already: there is no insistence that travellers swallow the pills, just that they pay for them.

Once inside Cambodia, things might just get worse. Fake antimalarials are on sale in pharmacies around the country. The best bet is to buy the more expensive, packaged brands that come with instruction leaflets. If in doubt, get a doctor to check them out.

US$8; and the *Neak Meas Hotel* has air-con rooms for US$10. There are a couple of *restaurants* and plenty of *street stalls* here so it is a good place to pick up water or snacks for the journey into Cambodia.

Getting There & Away
Poipet is connected by road to Thailand to the west and Sisophon to the east. For details of travelling between Thailand and Cambodia via Poipet, see the Land section in the Getting There & Away chapter. Pickups are available to Sisophon (5000r in the cab, 3000r on the back) and direct to Siem Reap (25,000r inside, 10,000r outside).

Central & Eastern Cambodia

KOMPONG CHAM
Cambodia's third largest city is a peaceful provincial capital spread along the banks of the Mekong River where you can get away from it all. It was an important trading post during the French period and the colonial legacy is evident as you wander through the streets. It is a crucial travel hub and acts as gateway to eastern and north-eastern Cambodia. This role will only be enhanced with the construction of a Japanese-financed bridge across the Mekong, which was started in late 1998 and will eventually form a crucial link in the direct road from Bangkok to Ho Chi Minh City (Saigon).

Orientation
Kompong Cham may be Cambodia's third largest city, but it is not that difficult to find your way around. Arriving from Phnom Penh, all roads east end up at the Mekong River, near many of the guesthouses and hotels. The market is a few blocks back from the river.

Information
There are banks in town that can change travellers cheques and cash, but no credit card cash advances. Canadia Bank, north of the market, is the most efficient. Phone calls and faxes can be arranged at offices around

town and there are also a few Camintel phone booths, but it is not that easy to find cards for sale. Vannat is a good local guide, and if you sip an evening drink by the Mekong, he'll likely find you before long. He speaks English and French.

Wat Nokor
Just outside town is an 11th century Mahayana Buddhist shrine of sandstone and laterite, which today houses an active **Hinayana wat**. It is a kitsch place as it is really a temple within a temple and many of the older building's archways have been incorporated into the new building as shrines for worship. On weekdays, you will find just a few monks in the complex and you can wander slowly among the many alcoves and their hidden shrines. There is also a large **reclining Buddha**.

Heading out of town on the road back to Phnom Penh, you need to take the left fork at the large roundabout and the shrine is about half a kilometre down a dirt road.

Phnom Pros & Phnom Srei
The name of the two hills translate as 'man hill' and 'woman hill' respectively. Local legend has it that two teams, one of men and the other of women, toiled by night to be the first to construct a stupa on their summit by daybreak. The women built a big fire, which the men took to be the rising sun and gave up work. The women, having won, no longer had to ask for the man's hand in marriage. Phnom Srei has good views of the countryside during the wet season. Phnom Pros is an interesting place for a cold drink as the trees are populated by some rather cheeky monkeys.

The hills are about 7km out of town and can be reached by moto for about US$2 (round trip) depending on wait time.

Places to Stay
There are an incredible number of cheap rooms to rent in this city as they were originally let to Cambodian soldiers when Kompong Cham was near the frontline in the war against the Khmer Rouge. In most hotels rates are negotiable, as few customers come their way.

One street off the market has a whole row of *cheap guesthouses* advertising rooms for 5000r, although most 'guests' seem to pay by the hour, so it could get noisy. There is another 5000r establishment on Rue Pasteur, just off the river, sporting a Foster's sign. This place has a cleaner image than its immediate competitors.

If a riverside view is required, the *Chumnor Tonlé* has big doubles with bathroom for US$5 or US$10 with air-con, but the staff speak little English. Nearby are two more places, the *Ponleur Rasmei 2 Guesthouse* and the *Kim Srun Guesthouse*,

Laundry and Karaoke, but you might not get a lot of sleep at the latter between the washing and the wailing. Rooms at both cost the usual US$5/10 with fan/air-con.

Further along the riverfront is the vast *Mekong Hotel*, with corridors in which you can play Frisbee and football. It has large, well-equipped rooms for US$7/15 with fan/air-con. It gets little business so push for US$5/10. The Japanese team overseeing the construction of the bridge across the Mekong has taken over half the building and there seems to have been a coincidental rise in the number of attractive Viet-

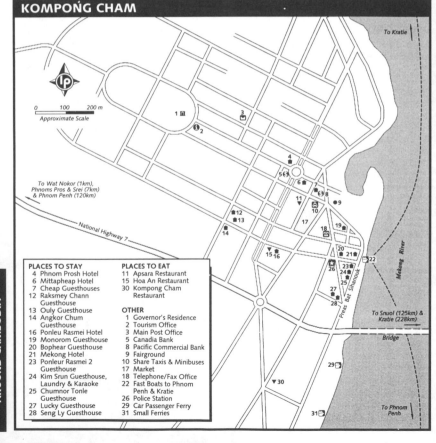

KOMPONG CHAM

To Kratie

0   100   200 m
Approximate Scale

To Wat Nokor (1km),
Phnoms Pros & Srei (7km)
& Phnom Penh (120km)

National Highway 7

Mekong River

To Snuol (125km) &
Kratie (228km)

Bridge

Preas Bat Sihanouk

To Phnom
Penh

PLACES TO STAY		PLACES TO EAT
4	Phnom Prosh Hotel	11 Apsara Restaurant
6	Mittapheap Hotel	15 Hoa An Restaurant
7	Cheap Guesthouses	30 Kompong Cham
12	Raksmey Chann	Restaurant
	Guesthouse	
13	Ouly Guesthouse	**OTHER**
14	Angkor Chum	1 Governor's Residence
	Guesthouse	2 Tourism Office
16	Ponleu Rasmei Hotel	3 Main Post Office
19	Monorom Guesthouse	5 Canadia Bank
20	Bophear Guesthouse	8 Pacific Commercial Bank
21	Mekong Hotel	9 Fairground
23	Ponleur Rasmei 2	10 Share Taxis & Minibuses
	Guesthouse	17 Market
24	Kim Srun Guesthouse,	18 Telephone/Fax Office
	Laundry & Karaoke	22 Fast Boats to Phnom
25	Chumnor Tonle	Penh & Kratie
	Guesthouse	26 Police Station
27	Lucky Guesthouse	29 Car Passenger Ferry
28	Seng Ly Guesthouse	31 Small Ferries

AROUND CAMBODIA

namese girls offering clients a massage in the 'karaoke' rooms downstairs.

The *Bophear Guesthouse* is a friendly, clean place one block off the river on Rue Pasteur. Doubles with bathroom, fan and complimentary water cost US$5, making this the best of the budget places in town. Other guesthouses between the river and market include *Monorom Guesthouse*, *Lucky Guesthouse* and *Seng Ly Guesthouse*. Monorom is tucked away behind the Mekong Hotel and has large rooms with bathroom for US$5 and smaller rooms with one bed for US$4. Lucky has US$5 doubles with fan and bath, while Seng Ly is a touch more luxurious, including air-con and TV for US$10 a double. West of the market are the *Ouly Guesthouse*, the *Angkor Chum Guesthouse* and the *Raksmey Chann Guesthouse*, but their location isn't as good as the riverside places and they still want the same sort of money.

The *Ponleu Rasmei Hotel*, south of the market, is popular with local NGOs and the staff there speak reasonable English and French. Rooms with fan and bathroom cost US$5, while those with air-con are US$10.

The *Mittapheap Hotel* and the *Phnom Prosh Hotel*, near the roundabout in the centre of town, are the newest hotels in town. The Mittapheap Hotel has well-appointed rooms with bathroom, TV, fridge and air-con for US$12. The Phnom Prosh Hotel has similar rooms for the same price, but also has a few rooms with fan instead of air-con and these go for just US$5, making them about the best deal in town when you add in the TV and bathroom. It is owned by the nephew of Samdech Hun Sen, Cambodia's first prime minister, so as long as the political winds continue to blow the same way, you should be safe here. It also has the town's only nightclub downstairs.

Places to Eat

There are several good restaurants in town and a lot of cheaper places with no signs dotted around the market square. Probably the best restaurant in town is the *Hoa An Restaurant*, near the Ponleu Rasmei Hotel. The Hoa An was resurrected in late 1998 after

being bulldozed to make way for the construction of a bridge. It is an impressive looking place and prices are pretty reasonable at about 6000r to 10,000r a dish. The service is good and there is always a regiment of beer girls to ensure you don't go thirsty.

The *Kompong Cham Restaurant*, on Rue Pasteur about 1km up from the Mekong River, is another fine establishment. There are more than 100 dishes on the menu, including Khmer, Thai and Chinese influences. Prices are reasonable and the Kompong Cham attracts a number of local expats. The curries are particularly good here. The last of the restaurants sporting English-language menus is the *Apsara Restaurant*, opposite the market. It is Chinese run and has pretty good food, but watch out for the beer girls opening a surfeit of lagers and expecting you to pay for them.

There are a lot of unnamed *restaurants* around town selling inexpensive Khmer classics, some stop and dip *food stalls* in the market and a number of *tikalok stalls* near the police station.

Entertainment

Leave your platform heels in the capital as the only nightclub in town is the extremely provincial *Phnom Prosh Nightclub*. Somehow it manages to be even darker than normal, but is a good place to shape up on your Khmer dancing if your moves are getting a little rusty. Locals gather on the waterfront outside the Mekong Hotel where a number of stalls sell cheap drinks and cold beers in the evening.

Getting There & Away

Kompong Cham is 120km north-east of Phnom Penh. The road has been upgraded by the Japanese so is excellent. The Ho Wah Genting Bus Company has regular air-con bus services to Kompong Cham (6000r; two hours). Minibuses also do the run (5000r). National Hwy 7 on to Kratie is in horrific condition and swings way out east to Snuol before cutting west again. Pick-ups do the run for about 25,000r, or 15,000r on the back. For more details of road routes, see Kratie later in the chapter.

AROUND CAMBODIA

The Eight-Legged Food Routine

There is a small town in Cambodia, Skuon, which is otherwise known affectionately as Spider-ville, where the locals eat eight-legged furry friends for breakfast, lunch and dinner. Most tourists travelling between Siem Reap and Phnom Penh pass through Skuon without ever re-alising they have been there. This is hardly surprising, as it has nothing much to attract visit-ors, but it is the centre of one of Cambodia's more exotic culinary delights, the fried spider.

Pick-up trucks usually pause in Spiderville, so take a careful look at the goodies the food sellers are offering. The creatures, decidedly dead, are piled high on platters, but don't get too cocky: there are normally live samples lurking nearby.

The spiders are bred in holes in the ground in villages around Skuon and are quite an inter-esting dining experience. They are best treated like a crab and eaten by cracking the body open and pulling the legs off one by one, bringing the juiciest flesh out with them – a cathartic ex-perience indeed. They taste a bit like ... mmm chicken – well doesn't everything new and ex-otic? Alternatively, for a memorable photo, just bite the thing in half and hope for the best. Watch out for the abdomen, which seems to be filled with some pretty nasty tasting brown sludge, which could be anything from eggs to excrement.

No-one seems to know exactly how this micro-industry developed around Skuon, although some have suggested that the population may have developed a taste for these creatures dur-ing the years of Khmer Rouge rule, when food was in short supply.

Skuon is located about 90km from Phnom Penh where National Hwy 6 splits, the western branch continuing to Siem Reap and Thailand, and the eastern branch, National Hwy 7, head-ing to Kompong Cham and then north to the Lao border.

Fast boats for Phnom Penh (10,000r to 15,000r; 2½ hours) and Kratie (20,000r; three hours) leave from near the Mekong Hotel at 7 and 9.30 am respectively. There are also slower boats up to Kratie (10,000r; four hours), one of which leaves at 9 am. Then there are a host of different slow boats and ferries making sporadic runs with no particular timetable. Travel is slow (it takes pretty much all day), departures infrequent and security not always good, but it's cheap: to Phnom Penh or Kratie the fare is only 5000r.

Between July and January, boats con-tinue up to Stung Treng (fast boats cost 50,000r, seven to eight hours; slow boats cost 25,000r, two days and a night). If you are intent on getting a slow boat, you are better off getting to Kratie first then picking one up there to save some time.

Getting Around

Motos are available in Kompong Cham and most journeys around town are only 500r.

KOMPONG THOM

Kompong Thom, north-west of Kompong Cham on National Hwy 6, is another one of those towns that overland travellers stop at when speeding between destinations, but never really hang around long enough to get a feel for the place. If you are travelling on the arduous road between Phnom Penh and Siem Reap, it is a pleasant place to break the journey for a night and is a good base from which to explore the pre-Angkorian Chenla capital of **Sambor Prei Kuk** and the hill-top temple of **Phnom Suntonk**. It is another sleepy provincial capital, but the proximity of Sambor Prei Kuk makes it a more re-warding stop than many of the others.

Information

There are no banks in town, but there are phone and fax offices near the market. There is a tourism office down the road op-posite the Neak Meas Hotel. It is upstairs in an old wooden building and the staff there speak a little English and better French.

Places to Stay

There is quite a range of accommodation available in Kompong Thom to suit every budget.

At the budget end there are several guest-houses, some of which make more money as brothels, down a side road off National Hwy 6 opposite the market. Furthest from the highway is the *Penh Chet Guesthouse*, where some French is spoken and basic rooms with double bed, fan and shared bathroom cost 7000r. Heading towards the main road, the *Sok San Guesthouse* has similarly rudimentary rooms, but for US$4 it is not good value. Next door is the *Visal-sok Guesthouse*, which doesn't seem to want to rent rooms to tourists as it cuts into its lucrative one hour trade. The last place on this strip, just off the main road, is the *Mohaleap Guesthouse*, which offers the best deal. It is a new place with clean doubles with fan and basic bathroom for US$3.

The *Neak Meas Hotel*, on National Hwy 6, has air-con doubles with TV, fridge and bathroom for US$15, and only US$10 if you are prepared to walk to the top floor. This is a good deal for those with strong legs. Nearby is the *Vimean Suor Guesthouse*, which has clean double rooms with ceiling fan and well-appointed bathrooms for just US$6. It is one of the better budget deals in town if you can no longer stand the brothel hotels.

The most expensive hotel in town is the *Stoeng Sen Hotel*, which has fully furnished air-con rooms for US$20 or US$25 if you want something slightly bigger. It seems a little incongruous in such a small town, and expensive compared with the Neak Meas Hotel, but it may draw some package tourists if they start to visit Sambor Prei Kuk in numbers.

Places to Eat

There aren't a whole lot of restaurants in town and some of those that claim to be are more like nightclubs: little food gets served, just lots of beer. The best establishment in town, the *Monorom Restaurant*, is just over the river on the right side next door to the *7 Makara Nightclub*. The location and atmosphere is not unlike the Khmer restaurants out beyond the Japanese bridge in Phnom Penh, set up on stilts and with a healthy Khmer crowd at night. The *Arunas Restaurant* is another good option in the centre of town.

Getting There & Away

Strategically located on National Hwy 6, Kompong Thom is about 165km north of Phnom Penh and about 146km south-east of Siem Reap. Share taxis, pick-ups and minibuses make the run from Phnom Penh. Pick-ups are cheapest (6000r in the cab; 3000r on the back), then minibuses (6000r) and share taxis (8000r). The journey from the capital takes about three hours as the road is in pretty good shape by Cambodian standards. Between Kompong Thom and Siem Reap the road degenerates into some sort of pothole horror show. Pick-ups (10,000r inside, 4000r outside) are the most sturdy for dealing with the terrible conditions, and cost about 10,000r in the cab and 4000r on the rear. Minibuses charge 8000r, but your spine will feel every bump, and share taxis are faster but more expensive (10,000r).

AROUND KOMPONG THOM
Sambor Prei Kuk

Sambor Prei Kuk is home to the most impressive group of pre-Angkorian monuments anywhere in Cambodia and there are more than 100 small temples scattered through the forest. They are some of the oldest structures in the country. It was the capital of Chenla during the reign of the early 7th century king Isanavarman, and continued to be an important centre of scholarship during the Angkorian period.

The complex of Ishanapura consists of four groups of edifices, most of which are made of brick, whose design prefigures a number of later developments in Khmer art. The northernmost group is dedicated to Gambhireshvara, one of Shiva's many forms, while the other groups are all dedicated to Shiva himself. Future generations of brochure writers will no doubt attempt to draw comparison with Bagan in Myanmar (Burma), but this is a fanciful description to say the least.

It is best visited on the way to Siem Reap as it gives the visitor a chronological insight into the development of temple architecture in Cambodia. Coming from Siem Reap, you might have seen enough temples to last a lifetime and those at Sambor Prei Kuk are certainly not in the same league as Angkor.

Getting There & Away The roads between Kompong Thom and Sambor Prei Kuk are in pretty poor shape so the 35km takes about 1½ hours. There are two routes, neither of which is straightforward, so it is best to take a guide from Kompong Thom even if you have your own transport. Arrange a moto driver for the day and expect to pay US$6 to US$8. The cheapest way to get here is by remorque-moto, but it will take nearer three hours this way.

Locals often refer to the temples themselves as Prasat Prei Kuk as distinct from the nearby village of Sambor Prei Kuk.

Phnom Suntonk

Not far out of Kompong Thom on the road to Phnom Penh is the hill-top pagoda of Phnom Suntonk. It is an attractive location, set high above the surrounding countryside, but this means there are a lot of stairs to climb – 980 in fact. They wind their way up through a forest and emerge at a colourful pagoda with many small shrines, quite unlike others you see around Cambodia. There are a number of interesting sandstone boulders balanced around the wat, into which have been carved **images of the Buddha**.

It is a good place from which to watch the sunset if you are staying the night in Kompong Thom. A round trip by moto costs about US$2 to US$3, depending on how long the drivers have to wait.

Preah Khan

The vast laterite and sandstone temple of Preah Khan, originally dedicated to Hindu deities, was reconsecrated to Buddhist worship in the early 11th century. Nearby monuments include **Preah Damrei**, guarded by massive elephants; **Preah Thkol**, a cruciform shrine 2km east of the central group; and **Preah Stung**, 2km south-east of the main group, which includes a tower with four faces.

Koh Ker

Koh Ker (also known as Chok Gargyar) served as the capital of Jayavarman IV (ruled 928-42) who, having seized the throne, left Angkor and transferred his capital here, where it remained throughout his reign. The principal monument of this large group of interesting ruins is **Prasat Thom** (also known as Prasat Kompeng), which includes a 40m-high sandstone-faced pyramid of seven levels. Some 40 inscriptions, dating from 932 to 1010, have been found at Prasat Thom.

PREAH VIHEAR

The important temple complex of Preah Vihear, built on a crest of the Chuor Phnom Dangkrek (Dangkrek Mountains) at an altitude of 730m, dates from the reign of Suryavarman I (ruled 1002-49). This is probably the most dramatic location of any temple in Cambodia. The main drawback is that it is almost inaccessible from Cambodia unless you have the funds to charter a helicopter or are willing to spend a few tough days getting there.

It is now open to visitors from Thailand and many people are going this way and leaving their passports at the border. Should you really want to make the journey from the Cambodian side, go to Kompong Thom, and from there to Tbeng Meanchey, the capital of Preah Vihear province, before making a final assault on Preah Vihear.

Remember that the site was the scene of heaving fighting as recently as May 1998 and numerous land mines were used by the Khmer Rouge in defending this strategic location against government forces.

SIEM REAP

For information on Siem Reap and the temples of Angkor, see those chapters.

KOMPONG CHHNANG

Kompong Chhnang is a tale of two cities, the ugly dockside seen by those travelling to Siem Reap by fast boat, and the old colonial quarter with its pleasant parks and handsome buildings. Connecting these very different parts is a long road lined with stilt houses and a maze of narrow walkways.

The town has nothing beyond atmosphere to offer the casual visitor, but for those with limited time who want a feel of provincial Cambodia, it makes an economical transit stop between Phnom Penh and Angkor.

Plans are afoot to redevelop the old cargo runway (used under the Khmer Rouge regime to fly in supplies from China for the 'self-sufficient' paradise), and turn Kompong Chhnang into something of a regional hub for trade. It may never happen, but if it does, expect some big changes.

Information
There are no banks in town, but phone and fax services are available at the post office in the colonial quarter.

Places to Stay & Eat
There are only a couple of hotels in town. The *Rithesen Hotel* is on the Tonlé Sap river and has singles/doubles for US$5/8, or with air-con for US$8/12. It is clean, but in the dirtier part of town, where the aromas can get pretty strong particularly when the river is low. The *Krong Dei Meas Guesthouse* is in the colonial sector just off the central park and has basic rooms with bathroom for US$5. Soldiers often stay over on their way back to the capital, so it can get noisy at night.

There are several small restaurants in either part of town. *The Mekong Restaurant*, near the Independence Monument, has a small but decent menu, including a sound offering of steak and chips, but the prices are high for such a small town. Better value and arguably with the better food is a *Khmer restaurant*, with no English name next to the Victory Monument. Most meals cost no more than US$1 to US$2.

There is also a western bar and restaurant called the *Half Way Pub & Grill* on the road to Pursat, which is run by a guy banking on the airfield being redeveloped. It could be a canny piece of speculation, but it could also be a spectacular flop.

Getting There & Away
Kompong Chhnang is 91km north of Phnom Penh on a reasonable, sealed road. Ho Wah Genting buses depart for and from Phnom Penh at 6.50, 9 and 11.30 am and 2 and 3.30 pm daily (5000r), and go past Udong; minibuses cost 4000r. Fast boats also make the trip, but are dear compared to the air-con buses. From Kompong Chhnang you can board the fast boat to Siem Reap, which comes through just after 8.30 am. Aim to pay about 30,000r, although they will probably demand more in US dollars.

PURSAT
Pursat sees very few tourists beyond those stopping for lunch on the road between Phnom Penh and Battambang. It looks a pretty dull place from National Hwy 5, but is actually quite pleasant once you wander along the banks of the river towards the better part of town. It will never attract many tourists, but is a useful overnight stop if you are travelling between the country's two major cities and want to explore the floating town of Kompong Luong on the Tonlé Sap lake, with its population of nearly 10,000, or the lush forests nearby in the Chuor Phnom Kravanh (Cardamom Mountains).

Information
There are no banks in town, but there are some phone and fax outlets near the market and a post office on the riverbank. The market was built by the province's governor, who now leases out the stalls at higher prices than in the near-abandoned old market. So why did everyone move, you ask. He called in the tanks and forced them out.

There is a tourism office behind all the government buildings that are located on the river's west bank near the island. The director is a helpful chap who knows the province well and has even written his own guidebook in Khmer called *Pursat and Picnics*.

Places to Stay & Eat
There is a good range of accommodation in Pursat as several NGOs operating in Pursat province use the town as their base. Prices are pretty uniform, with fan rooms costing US$5 and air-con rooms for US$10. The *Sereiroat Guesthouse*, a wooden building, is tucked away on a small side street. The *Orchidee Hotel*, on the west bank of the river,

is pretty popular with the expat community, while the nearby *New Tounsour Hotel* has similarly clean but larger rooms, particularly those in the new building. The best establishment in town is the *Vimean Sourkea Hotel*, also on the west bank of the river, but it charges no more than the competition.

There are several restaurants scattered across town. There is a new *restaurant* in the north of town on the river that does pretty good food, with prices as reasonable as 3000r a dish. It is a yellow building just past the barrage on the river.

If you cross the river on National Hwy 5 towards Phnom Penh and then turn immediately left along the river, there are a couple of *restaurants* about half a kilometre down the road. One overlooks the river, which makes it a nice place to eat in the late afternoon, and the other has pretty good food, the best in town according to some expats in Pursat. Another popular place is the *Reasmey Angkor Restaurant*, more commonly known as the Blue Restaurant. Out towards the train station is the *Lam Siv Eng Restaurant*.

Getting There & Away

In terms of time, Pursat is pretty much midway between Phnom Penh and Battambang, although in distance it is significantly nearer the latter. Minibuses (8000r) and pick-ups (10,000r inside, 4000r outside) go to Phnom Penh; share taxis (10,000r) and pick-ups (10,000r inside, 4000r outside) go to Battambang.

One train a day comes through Pursat, but it is only really worth considering to or from Battambang (1500r) to avoid the dreadful road. The longer stretch to Phnom Penh (3000r) is easier by road as the surface is reasonable. The train to Battambang leaves Phnom Penh at 6.30 am and comes through any time after about 1 pm, while the train from Battambang leaves at 6 am, arriving any time after 11 am.

AROUND PURSAT
The Tomb of Kleang Meung

Oknha Kleang Meung is a Khmer national hero who defeated the Thais in a celebrated battle in 1482. The old statue of Kleang

Meung now sits redundant in a shed, but the new gold one donated by Prince Ranariddh is quite impressive.

The tomb is about 5km out of town in the direction of Battambang, down a little road on the left after the bridge that marks the end of the tarmac.

Kompong Luong

The **floating town** of Kompong Luong on the Tonlé Sap lake is the most interesting place to visit in Pursat province. It is a town of as many as 10,000 inhabitants that is permanently afloat. It moves with the level of water in the lake, as recognised by one of the signposts on the road leading to it, which states Kompong Luong is maximum 7km, minimum 2km.

The town boasts pretty much all the facilities you would expect of a normal town except the ubiquitous cars and motorbikes, which comes as something of a relief. There are *floating restaurants*, schools, doctors and karaoke bars, and unlike in Venice the residents don't have to worry about sinking as everything has a boat as its base. There are plenty of places to stop for an ice coffee or a beer and just soak up the atmosphere of life on the water. There is not really anywhere to stay although if you want to get some photographs early in the morning or late in the afternoon you might try to arrange something with one of the nearby land-based villages.

The population of Kompong Luong is almost uniformly Vietnamese, so you may find the welcome slightly more subdued than in most rural Cambodian towns. This isn't so much a reflection of any latent hostility on the part of the Vietnamese, but rather a reflection of their ambiguous status in Cambodian society, which has taught them to be wary of outsiders. Massacres of Vietnamese villagers living around the Tonlé Sap lake by Khmer Rouge units were commonplace during the first half of the 1990s and even as late as 1998, more than 20 Vietnamese were killed in a village near the town of Kompong Chhnang.

Expect to pay about US$5 to charter a boat for an hour.

Getting There & Away Kompong Luong is between 35km and 40km north-east of Pursat depending on what time of year you visit. The easiest way to get there is to take a taxi or pick-up to Krakor for a couple of thousand riel and a moto from there to Kompong Luong for about the same price. Alternately engage the services of a moto driver in Pursat for about US$6 for the day. It takes about 1½ hours each way. The turn-off for Kompong Luong is in the town of Krakor. The cheapest way to get to Kompong Luong is by a combination of two re-morque-motos, one to Krakor and then another to the floating town.

NEAK LUONG

Neak Luong is the point at which travellers speeding between Phnom Penh and the Viet-namese border have to slow to a stop to cross the mighty Mekong River. The car ferry chugs back and forth giving children ample time to try to sell you strange looking insects and other unidentifiable food on sticks.

It rates a mention as one of the locations depicted in *The Killing Fields*. In 1975 it was heavily bombed by the US in an attempt to halt the Khmer Rouge advance on Phnom Penh. The intensive bombardment led to a horrendous number of civilian deaths.

It also acts as a gateway for a cheaper route into Vietnam. Take an air-con bus to Neak Luong for 4000r from the Psar Thmei (New Market) in Phnom Penh and pay the foot pas-senger toll (100r) to cross the Mekong on the ferry. Once on the other side arrange a share taxi to the border for about 8000r.

PREY VENG

Few travellers make it to Prey Veng as it is located on National Hwy 15 between Neak Luong and Kompong Cham, not really a road that visitors tend to use. It is, however, a pleasant enough backwater should you want to travel by an alternative route be-tween Phnom Penh and Kompong Cham. The town has a small museum that is rarely open and there is a pretty sorry zoo about 20km out of town on the road to Kompong Cham. There are a few decaying colonial structures around town and a few hotels to

choose from. The **Kessor Hotel** has basic rooms for US$5, while the **Chongpan Hotel** has a better location overlooking the river with smarter rooms for US$8/10 a single/double. Next door to the Chongpan Hotel is the unrelated **Chongpan Restaur-ant**, which also overlooks the river making it the most pleasurable place to have a meal.

The **Mittapheap Hotel** is arguably the town's best place to stay and has rooms with fan for US$5 and some with air-con for US$12. Across the road is the **Mit-tapheap Restaurant**, one of the town's best restaurants with good food and friendly staff. It is a couple of blocks back from the river, near the modern Khmer buildings housing the town's small museum and tourist office.

Getting There & Away

Prey Veng is just over 70km east of Phnom Penh and 83km south of Kompong Cham. The easiest way to get there from the capi-tal is to take an air-con bus from the Psar Thmei to Neak Luong for 4000r, cross on the ferry as a foot passenger (100r) and arrange a seat in a share taxi on to Prey Veng for about 2000r to 3000r. Minibuses and share taxis operate between Prey Veng and Kompong Cham for about 2000r and 4000r respectively.

SVAY RIENG

Svay Rieng is a quiet provincial capital that many travellers fly by when making the jour-ney between Phnom Penh and Ho Chi Minh City. It is much like Cambodia's other sleepy provincial capitals, but if you feel the urge to recharge the batteries between big nights out in Cambodia and Vietnam's liveliest cities, this is the most convenient place to do it.

Places to Stay & Eat

At the budget end, there are a couple of guesthouses to choose from with pretty basic rooms for rent for US$5 a night. The **Santepheap Guesthouse** and the **Samaki Guesthouse** are opposite each other and are the first places you come to when walking from the taxi stand near the market into the centre of town.

If you are prepared to spend more money, there are two hotels in town that offer air-con and TV. Overlooking the river, the *Vimean Monorom Hotel* and the long-running *Wai Ko Hotel*, complete with nightclub, offer fan rooms for US$5 and air-con rooms from US$10 to US$15. The Wai Ko Hotel's more expensive rooms come with a balcony overlooking the Vay Ko River.

Many of Svay Rieng's restaurants double as karaoke bars and discos by night, so pick your establishment carefully if you want to hold a conversation. The *Sereipheap Restaurant* has a prime location by the river, making it a good joint for a sunset supper. Other places near the river include the *Pich Restaurant* and the *Riverside Restaurant*, but the latter is really more of a nightclub after dark. The advantage of all these night spots is that you are not short of anything to do once you have finished eating. If your Khmer karaoke isn't really up to scratch, then you are probably best off heading to the Wai Ko Hotel's nightclub.

Getting There & Away

Share taxis for Svay Rieng leave from the other side of the Monivong Bridge at Psar Cbah Ambel (Cbah Ambel Market) in Phnom Penh. The cost is about 7000r per person if you can find one going all the way, but many taxis only go as far as Neak Luong to avoid paying the US$1 charge for the ferry across the Mekong River. It is easier and more comfortable to take an air-con bus from the Psar Thmei to Neak Luong for 4000r, cross the river by ferry as a foot passenger (100r) and arrange a share taxi on to Svay Rieng from the other side for about 4000r or so a person.

Travelling to Svay Rieng from Bavet, the Cambodian side of the border with Vietnam, may be more difficult as the taxi drivers simply won't believe you want to go there and generally prefer to wait for the more lucrative option of taking foreigners all the way to Phnom Penh. The best plan may be to stuff yourself into a taxi with some other tourists and ask to be dropped off at Svay Rieng. Expect to pay about US$1 for the privilege.

Taxis drop people off near the market in Svay Rieng, but surprisingly for a Cambodian town, this is not actually the centre of town. You need to head away from the market to get to the area of town where the hotels and restaurants are located.

North-East Cambodia

North-east Cambodia is the country's wild east, home to many ethnic minority groups known as *chunchiet* or *Khmer loeu* (upper Khmer), and on the stretch of the Mekong River between Kratie and Stung Treng, the last remaining freshwater Irrawaddy dolphins in Cambodia. The remote provinces of Mondulkiri and Ratanakiri, best visited from November to March, are home to some of Cambodia's most beautiful landscapes, and somewhere out there in the thick forests some rare mammals including tigers, leopards, elephants, and possibly even rhinoceroses and the country's national symbol, the *kouprey*, a type of wild cow unique to Cambodia.

It is one of the most inaccessible parts of the country and conditions vary widely between wet and dry seasons. Illegal logging is a major problem in provinces of the north-east, taking over from the rubber industry, which was once so important to the region, so it is important you are careful about waving cameras around in areas where the forest is being plundered.

Overland prices tend to be higher than elsewhere in the country as road conditions are so atrocious. Be warned that pick-up drivers are not afraid to leave without you if they don't like your price.

As overland travel opens up in Cambodia, it is possible to reach many of these places by a combination of boat and road. However, certain parts of the north-east are quite lawless so it is important to check the latest security situation before heading off into the middle of nowhere. You can visit Ratanakiri by land and be back in Phnom Penh in as little as a week if you move fast. With fortunate connections, Mondulkiri is more straightforward and a round trip could be done in as little as five days if you don't get stranded anywhere.

KRATIE

This small riverside town, pronounced Kra-*cheh*, is well preserved as it was spared war time bombing and was 'liberated' by the Khmer Rouge long before other parts of the country. You get some dramatic sunsets over the Mekong as it is on the east bank of the river and there are some very old **Khmer houses** on the edge of town. It is the best place in the country to see the rare Irra-waddy dolphins, which inhabit the Mekong River in ever diminishing numbers. It is also a handy overnight stop on the land route to Ratanakiri or an alternative stop on the way to or from Mondulkiri.

Information

There are no banks in town, but phones and faxes are available in offices near the market and at the post office. There is a tourism office by the river in the south of town.

Dolphin Watching

The freshwater Irrawaddy dolphin is an endangered species in Cambodia and some experts believe there may be as few as 60 left on stretches of the Mekong River north of Kratie. It is possible to see them about 15km north of the town on the road to Stung Treng, particularly during the dry season when water levels drop significantly – early in the morning or late afternoon seem to be the best times. It is best to go with a local moto driver as they know the best spots around the many tiny islands on this stretch of the river. You can arrange a boat to take you out on the water, from where you have an opportunity to view them at close quarters. Expect to pay about 30,000r to charter a small boat for an hour and about US$2 for a return moto ride.

Places to Stay & Eat

The cheapest places to stay in Kratie are the guesthouses along Rue Preah Sihanouk near the market. The *Vimean Tip Guesthouse* has basic rooms for US$2 while the *Hy Heng Ly Guesthouse* and its two nameless neighbours have rooms for 5000r to 10,000r, depending on who is renting the room and why. A little further along the road are three more basic places, the *Sok San Guesthouse*, the *Phnom Meas Guesthouse* and the *Nyta Guesthouse*, with similar prices. You won't have any trouble finding a cheap place to sleep in town.

There are a couple of established places in town that also have restaurants downstairs. On Rue Preah Soramrit, the *December 30 Guesthouse*, named after the town's liberation from the Khmer Rouge in 1978, has well-worn rooms for 10,000r. Nearby, the *Heng Heng Guesthouse* has fan rooms on the top floor for US$4 and rooms with fewer stairs to climb, TV and bathroom for US$7.

The newest hotel in town and also the most comfortable is the *Santhepheap Hotel* on Rue Preah Soramrit, which is owned by the same fellow that operates the Mekong Hotel in Kompong Cham. Spotless doubles with bathroom and fan cost US$5 and are at the rear of

MARTIN HARRIS

Morning and late afternoon are the best times to get a glimpse of the rare Irrawaddy dolphin, which inhabits the Mekong River.

AROUND CAMBODIA

the hotel. In the main building, doubles with air-con and TV are US$15. There are several karaoke rooms behind the hotel near the cheaper beds, so watch out for drunken chanting if the army is out on a bender.

The best restaurant in Kratie is the *Mekong Restaurant* next door to the December 30 Guesthouse. It has an English menu and the service is great at night, when you even get a selection of noodles brought out to choose from. It also serves what are probably the best French fries in Cambodia, if not Asia! Aside from the two other *restaurants* at the guesthouses, you are then left with the *market* during the day and a couple of nameless *restaurants* around the market area at night.

Entertainment

Surprisingly for such a small town, but perhaps unsurprisingly for Cambodia, Kratie has a disco that goes on until after midnight and, shock, horror, it has lights, so you can actually see who you are dancing with, not an altogether pleasant experience sometimes.

Getting There & Away

National Hwy 7 puts Kratie 343km northeast of Phnom Penh and 171km south of Stung Treng. By road from the capital it takes about eight to 10 hours and costs about US$5 inside a pick-up and about US$2 on the back. The road between Kompong Cham and Snuol is an absolute tragedy, something like a big dipper, log flume and bumper car combination. If your vehicle gives up the ghost, get on board another one quickly as the section of the road between Memot and Snuol is not always safe and bandit attacks occasionally occur.

There is a better route for those travelling by motorcycle or willing to shell out for a series of long moto rides and pick-ups. Take the river road north out of Kompong Cham as far as Stung Trong (no, not Stung Treng – that is way north of Kratie) and cross the Mekong on a small ferry before continuing up the east bank of the Mekong through Chhlong to Kratie. This is a very beautiful route through small rural villages, but can take from as little as five hours on a trail bike to 10 hours with bad connections on public transport. Still, anything is preferable to travelling out to Snuol on the highway from hell.

For details of the journey from Phnom Penh to Kompong Cham, see the Kompong Cham section earlier in this chapter.

The road north to Stung Treng is one of the least safe in the country as bandit attacks are frequent and some of the potholes are more like bunkers on a golf course. A number of travellers, however, are now using this route and pick-up trucks charge about 15,000r inside and about 10,000r in the back (six to eight hours), although you will have to bargain hard to get this price. *Double*

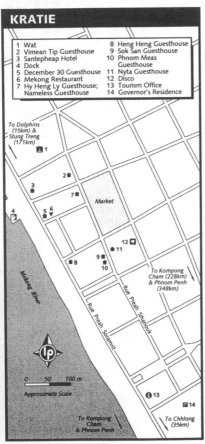

KRATIE

1	Wat
2	Vimean Tip Guesthouse
3	Santepheap Hotel
4	Dock
5	December 30 Guesthouse
6	Mekong Restaurant
7	Hy Heng Ly Guesthouse; Nameless Guesthouse
8	Heng Heng Guesthouse
9	Sok San Guesthouse
10	Phnom Meas Guesthouse
11	Nyta Guesthouse
12	Disco
13	Tourism Office
14	Governor's Residence

To Dolphins (15km) & Stung Treng (171km)

Market

Mekong River

To Kompong Cham (228km) & Phnom Penh (348km)

Rue Preah Sihanouk

Rue Preah Soramrit

0   50   100 m
Approximate Scale

To Kompong Cham & Phnom Penh

To Chhlong (35km)

check and check again current security conditions before setting out on this road.

Quicker and more comfortable are the fast boats to Phnom Penh (five hours; 30,000r). Boats leave Phnom Penh and Kratie at 7 am and stop at Kompong Cham; there are also slower boats to and from Kompong Cham (10,000r; four hours). In the wet season fast boats continue north to Stung Treng (30,000r; five hours). Departure times are irregular so ask at Kratie port. Slow boats also make the journey, but are tiresomely slow (15,000r; at least 24 hours).

MEMOT
This is a surprisingly large town set amid the rubber plantations of eastern Kompong Cham province. It sees very few visitors as there is little of interest here unless you work for Michelin. However, it is possible you might find yourself stuck here during the wet season if travelling between Phnom Penh and Mondulkiri or Kratie. There are a couple of very basic *guesthouses* and some good local *restaurants* near the market.

Pick-ups from Memot to Kompong Cham cost 10,000r in the cab and 8000r on the back; taxis charge 10,000r. From Memot to Snuol is the same price even though it is a much shorter distance, as security is pretty poor on this stretch of road.

SNUOL
This is another ends-of-the-earth town that you might find yourself stuck in when travelling upcountry during the wet season. A lot of travellers end up having at least one meal here as you tend to have to change vehicles when journeying between Mondulkiri and towns on the Mekong. If you do get stuck here the *Mittapheap Guesthouse* has simple rooms for 10,000r. There are also a few small *restaurants*, but you will need some Khmer language skills or a phrasebook if you hope to be fed.

Snuol is about 125km south-west of Mondulkiri and 135km east of Kompong Cham. It is only about 15km from the Vietnamese border. Pick-ups to Sen Monorom (15,000r inside, 10,000r outside; three to four hours) aren't all that regular. Pick-ups

also go to Chhlong via the new logging road, where the fast boats between Kompong Cham and Kratie stop (10,000r inside, 8000r outside; 1½ hours). The trip to Kompong Cham costs 20,000r in a taxi, the same in the cab of a pick-up and only 15,000r on the rear. To Kratie is about 10,000r.

STUNG TRENG
Just 50km south of Laos, Stung Treng is a real outpost town on the banks of the San River, just off the Mekong. Travellers heading between Kratie and Ratanakiri have to stop here for the night, but few hang around. The modern *Sekong Hotel* has rooms with fan and bathroom for US$10, or with air-con for US$20. The *Amatak Hotel* has prices more in line with provincial Cambodia, with basic rooms for US$5.

Getting There & Away
There are several flights a week to and from Stung Treng (US$45/90 one-way/return) with President Airlines and RAC. Pick-ups and jeeps travel the disgraceful road to Ban Lung in Ratanakiri (30,000r inside, 20,000r outside; seven to nine hours). The road is so bad that for most of the journey you will find drivers prefer to career through the jungle than take on the canyons. For details on the journey south by road or boat, see the Kratie and Kompong Cham sections earlier in this chapter and Getting There & Away in the Phnom Penh chapter.

BAN LUNG
Ban Lung is the provincial capital of Ratanakiri province and the best base from which to explore the natural attractions of the area. The name Ban Lung actually refers to the district, while the town is known as Labansiek. However, everyone calls the place Ban Lung. The town isn't that interesting, but the locals are extremely friendly and help make a visit a lively time. You can also ask around town about arranging an elephant ride in one of the surrounding villages.

Information
There are no banks in Ban Lung, but you can change US dollars into riel at jewellers

AROUND CAMBODIA

in the market in town. There is a post office on the road to Bokheo from where you can make international calls.

Places to Stay & Eat

One of the nicest places in town is the *Mountain II Guesthouse*, an old building with a breezy balcony; double rooms cost US$5. You get the sense that it was once the opulent home of a wealthy French rubber-plantation owner, but it now has a rather torpid feel to it. Owned by the same woman is the *Mountain Guesthouse*, near the airport, and rooms are the same price. Mrs Kim meets every plane that lands so she can take you to either establishment. The *Ban Lung Guesthouse* is the nearest to the airport and small air-con rooms cost US$10.

There are two hotels in town, the *Labansiek Hotel* and the *Ratanakhotel*, both of which have air-con rooms with bathroom for US$10. They are both near the central monument, although the Ratanakhotel has a slightly unfinished feel with wires and poles sticking out everywhere. It also has some hot fan rooms for US$5, but you'll probably end up sleeping on the roof if you opt for one of these in the heat of the dry season.

The best place to eat in town is the *Ratanakiri Restaurant*, also known as the American Restaurant, near the Mountain Guesthouse. Various foreign visitors have contributed to the menu, which claims to include Lobster Thermidor, although given the distance to the coast you may want to leave it alone. Naeh, the owner, is one of the friendliest restaurateurs in Cambodia. You can get cheap food at stalls near the *market*. The Labansiek Hotel's *restaurant* is expensive and the *Angkor Beer Restaurant* is pretty unfriendly: staff won't serve you if they can't be bothered.

Entertainment

On the road beyond the market are a couple of *nightclubs* that stay open until customers leave. They have the appearance of barns, but inside the atmosphere is a little more lively than some other provincial nightclubs around the country, and the lighting means you can actually see what is going on. Some of the moto drivers like drinking in these places at night, so keep an eye on their driving skills on the way home if you want to avoid running into a food stall.

Getting There & Away

RAC flies to Ban Lung from Phnom Penh several times a week and most flights go via Mondulkiri or Stung Treng, regardless of the published schedules; one-way/return costs US$55/100. President Airlines has three flights a week and costs the same. The road journey from Phnom Penh to Ratanakiri is an arduous three days and you must break it in Kratie and Stung Treng. However, between July and January you can make it in only two days as fast boats run between Phnom Penh and Stung Treng (60,000r; 10 hours). The road between Ban Lung and Stung Treng is hopeless, but pick-ups make the journey (30,000r inside, 20,000r outside; seven to nine hours).

BAN LUNG

To Voen Sai (35km) & Virachay National Park

Lake

Wat

To Lumphat (37km) & Stung Treng (165km)

To Boeng Yeak Loam (5km) & Bokheo (28km)

Market

Airport

Approximate Scale
0   100   200 m

1 Mountain II Guesthouse
2 Ratanakiri Restaurant
3 Banlung Guesthouse
4 Mountain Guesthouse
5 Royal Air Cambodge
6 Labansiek Hotel
7 Ratanakhotel
8 Post Office

AROUND CAMBODIA

There is no road linking Ratanakiri to Mondulkiri to the south. There is a road as far as Lumphat, but once you wobble across the Tonlé Srepok you are on a series of sandy ox-cart tracks until you reach Koh Nhek, about 80km south in northern Mondulkiri province. Some adventurous travellers are making this journey, but if you are considering it you should purchase some detailed maps of the region from the Psar Thmei in Phnom Penh and invest in a compass. With these accessories and a whole lot of water you can make it from Lumphat to Koh Nhek in one day on a 250cc motorbike.

Getting Around

Transport costs are higher in this province than other parts of the country. Motorbikes can be rented from Mrs Kim at the Mountain Guesthouse for about US$10 a day, or US$8 if you bargain. The Ratanakiri Restaurant sometimes hires out motorbikes for less than this. Otherwise negotiate to hire a moto for the day and sit back surveying the scenery. This will cost around US$8 a day and can be preferable to driving yourself about as you can be sure of finding all the waterfalls. If you are in a group and want to explore the province, then a Russian jeep might be the answer; you can hire them from near the market. These sturdy vehicles can carry about six people comfortably and cost from US$30 to US$50 a day, depending on where you want to go.

AROUND BAN LUNG

Boeng Yeak Loam is a circular, crater lake situated amid lush jungle. It is one of the most peaceful, beautiful locations Cambodia has to offer and the water is extremely clean with visibility of more than 5m. It is a great place to take a dip early in the morning or late in the afternoon. Entry is 1000r and there is a small centre nearby that has information on chunchiet in the province and on walks around the lake. It is 5km from Ban Lung. Turn right off the road to Bokheo at the statue of the chunchiet. Motos are available for US$1 return, but expect to pay more if you want the driver to wait around.

There are numerous **waterfalls** in the province, but many are inaccessible in the wet season and devoid of water in the dry season. The three most commonly visited are **Chaa Ong**, **Ka Tieng** and **Kinchaan**. It is best to hook up with a local moto driver to visit any of these as they are off the beaten track and can be difficult to find alone. If you are on your own motorcycle and having trouble finding the way, pick up a villager in the vicinity and they will guide you over the final stretch. The most spectacular of the three is Chaa Ong, as it is set in a jungle gorge and you are able to clamber behind the waterfall.

Located on the San River, **Voen Sai** is a pleasant little community including Chinese, Lao and Kreung villagers. Across the river is an old Chinese settlement dating back to 1700 and further downstream several Lao and **chunchiet villages**. You can cross the river for 500r or less. Voen Sai is also the gateway to **Virachay National Park**, the largest such park in Cambodia stretching east to Vietnam, north to Laos and west to Stung Treng. The park has not been fully explored and may be home to a number of larger mammals. Rangers also say there are **waterfalls**, some as high as 100m. Facilities are minimal, but if you contact the ranger post in town you may be able to arrange a walk in the area.

The old provincial capital of **Lumphat** is something of a ghost town these days thanks to US bombing. However, it is an embarkation point for trips on the Srepok River, depicted in the film *Apocalypse Now.*

The gem-mining town of **Bokheo** is pretty dull, but you may want to head out there to take a look at the mines, which are 10m-deep circular pits into which the miner descends. You can purchase cheap stones in and around the town, although you get the feeling you are being offered leftovers and the best stuff has disappeared elsewhere. Remember that if you manage to buy an uncut stone for next to nothing, you may end up having to pay quite a lot to have it cut. Bokheo is 28km east of Ban Lung on the road to Vietnam.

MONDULKIRI

Mondulkiri is another isolated forested province south of Ratanakiri, nestled against

Cambodia's eastern border with Vietnam. It really is another Cambodia, with scenery and a climate quite unlike anywhere else in the country. In the dry season it is a little like Wales in the UK, with sunshine; in the wet season like Tasmania in Australia, with dreadful roads. There are endless grassy hills and every here and there clumps of pines huddled together against the winds. At an average elevation of 800m, it can get quite chilly at night, so make sure you carry something warm.

It is the most sparsely populated province in the country and almost half the 30,000 inhabitants come from the Pnong minority group. Many other chunchiet make up the rest of the population, making Khmers very much a minority. The lack of people adds to something of a wild east atmosphere and there are certainly a lot of wild animals in the remoter parts of the province, including tigers, elephants, bears and leopards.

Getting around the province can be the hardest part of a visit here unless you have your own vehicle. Motos cost about US$10 a day, while a Russian jeep is between US$35 and US$50 a day depending on how far you want to go.

SEN MONOROM
Sen Monorom is the capital of the province and the only base from which to explore the province's surrounding attractions. It is a charming little community set among rolling hills and nearby are a number of chunchiet villages and picturesque waterfalls.

Information
Bring all the money you need with you as you are not going to be able to exchange any in this town. Prices are higher than in other parts of the country as everything has to be shipped in from Phnom Penh or Vietnam, so you should look at budgeting at least US$15 a day if you want to travel around a bit. Communications are also pretty much nonexistent.

There is a small tourist office in town near the lakes run by the ever helpful Sam Chin, who speaks excellent French and good English and can help to organise a Pnong guide for trekking or wildlife viewing. Another man

who knows the province very well is Long Vibol, an all-round Mr Fixit who runs a pharmacy in the market, is the town's dentist and wedding photographer and, of more relevance perhaps, is a tour guide with excellent English. He has also prepared a number of maps on some of the smaller communities around the province, which can be invaluable if you are planning some hardy travel.

Elephant Trekking
The village of Phulung, 7km north of Sen Monorom, is the place to arrange an elephant trek. The elephants are not kept in the village, so it is necessary to visit a day in advance to request they prepare the animals. Costs quickly mount as motos on the province's bad roads are expensive. The cost for a day of forest trekking is about 120,000r.

Long Vibol can help arrange trips at the village of **Pttang** not far from Sen Monorom. For those with less time, it is possible to arrange for the elephants to be brought to the village for a little joyride around the huts. The Pnong villagers will probably think you are mad, but the dramatic location of their community makes it a memorable experience. You will have to pay something to the village chief for the experience, about 30,000r or US$10 seems reasonable, which isn't much if there are a few of you.

Places to Stay & Eat
There isn't much choice in town, but the *Pech Kiri Guesthouse*, signposted at the airport, is excellent. It offers both bungalows with bathroom and cheaper rooms inside the main house. There is no electricity until 6 pm and no fans as the altitude takes care of night-time temperatures. The bungalows cost US$10 each, while rooms in the house with shared bathroom are US$5. Both prices include a breakfast of some of the tastiest baguettes in Cambodia and filtered Vietnamese coffee that will put hairs on your chest (prices come down if you are on your own). The rooms even have a sort of minibar with cans of soft drinks and bottles of water and, on request, crates of 333 Export Vietnamese beer, otherwise known as Ba Ba Ba. Madame Deu, the proprietor,

is quite a character and can tell you much about the area – quite a remarkable feat given she speaks absolutely no English.

There is another unmarked guesthouse near the Tourism Office known as the *Son Sann Guesthouse*, which has a fine setting overlooking the northern lake, but has higher prices than, and lacks the atmosphere of, the Pech Kiri. Singles/doubles cost US$6/12.

The restaurant scene is arguably even less advanced than the hotel scene. There are several cheap *stalls* around the market for lunch, but they don't last into the night. The *karaoke place* with the San Miguel sign next to the market can knock together some very good food, but it needs advance warning, particularly at night. It does a good loklak, and all the dishes are likely to come with chips unless you specify otherwise. Finally, the Pech Kiri offers meals that look a little overpriced at US$4 plus a dollar more for drinks, but the spread is quite incredible with plates and plates of food appearing as you eat. It is worth the splash at dinner.

Getting There & Away

RAC flies to Sen Monorom from Phnom Penh once a week. It costs US$50/100 one-way/return. There have been two flights a week in the past, but for now, should you choose to go by air, you will be going for a week.

To travel by road to Mondulkiri used to be a daunting experience, but it has become easier with the completion of a graded logging road from Chhlong, just south of Kratie, to Sen Monorom. It is pretty sad that to get Mondulkiri back on the overland map, Kratie province is going to lose a substantial part of its forest, but the only way things get done in Cambodia is if there is something in it for someone. Security is not always great on the more remote sections of the roads as bandit gangs are known to operate in eastern Kratie province. Check the latest situation before continuing beyond Snuol. If you are travelling by public transport you will encounter quite a few checkpoints and although you shouldn't be asked for money personally, the driver will have to pay something and an odd cigarette

might not go amiss. Travelling by motorbike, you should not be stopped at checkpoints, just smile, wave and proceed.

With the advent of the new logging road, there is now the enticing possibility of making it from Phnom Penh to Sen Monorom in just one day, quite unbelievable really when you look at the distance on the map and recollect the state of most of Cambodia's roads. Take one of the fast boats to Kratie as far as Chhlong (25,000r; 4½ hours), where the logging road begins. From Chhlong you can board a pick-up to Snuol (10,000r inside, 8000r outside; 1½ hours). From Snuol you can change pick-ups for the journey to Sen Monorom (15,000r inside, 10,000r outside; three to four hours). So for around US$10 you can leave Phnom Penh in the morning and wind up in Mondulkiri by late afternoon. It may be better to undertake this journey in a group as you can charter whole vehicles if there are slim pickings in Chhlong and Snuol later in the day.

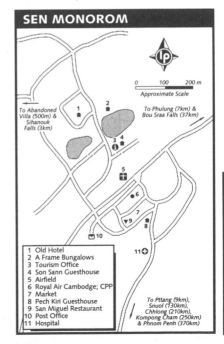

SEN MONOROM

0   100   200 m
Approximate Scale

To Abandoned Villa (500m) & Sihanouk Falls (3km)

To Phulung (7km) & Bou Sraa Falls (37km)

To Pttang (9km), Snuol (130km), Chhlong (210km), Kompong Cham (250km) & Phnom Penh (370km)

1 Old Hotel
2 A Frame Bungalows
3 Tourism Office
4 Son Sann Guesthouse
5 Airfield
6 Royal Air Cambodge; CPP
7 Market
8 Pech Kiri Guesthouse
9 San Miguel Restaurant
10 Post Office
11 Hospital

Heading to Mondulkiri from Kompong Cham, you first have to cross the Mekong River by ferry before boarding a pick-up for Snuol (20,000r inside, 15,000r outside; four to eight hours). The road to here is a heap of shit and is not all that secure. From Snuol you can arrange a share taxi or pick-up to Sen Monorom along the new logging road (15,000r inside, 10,000r outside; three to four hours).

Coming from Kratie, head to Snuol (10,000r), changing vehicles there to join the new logging road to Sen Monorom (six or seven hours in total).

Travelling by motorbike from Kratie, you can miss horrible National Hwy 7 altogether as there is a small trail south along the banks of the Mekong River to Chhlong. You have to cross several rivers by boat and clear one u-bend with some hard throttle, but the village scenery makes it a journey well worth doing. To Chhlong is as much as two hours, but once on the logging road, you can get to Sen Monorom, some 210km east, in as little as five hours.

AROUND SEN MONOROM
Sihanouk Falls

This small waterfall, named in honour of King Sihanouk, is attractively located in the forest about 5km from town. It is possible to swim in the pool at the bottom of the falls. Motos can run you out here for about US$2 round trip. Walking there, head straight on beyond the abandoned villa and when the trail eventually forks, take the left-hand side.

Bou Sraa Waterfalls

This double drop waterfall is an unforgiving journey of 37km from Sen Monorom, but it is quite impressive, the upper tier dropping some 20m and the lower tier 40m. To get to the bottom of the upper falls, take a left turn just before the road hits the river above the falls. To get to the bottom of the lower tier, you have to cross the river and take a left further down the track. A little way on is the Pnong village of Pichinda where you can pick up some very basic food.

Getting There & Away The 37km road between Bou Sraa and Sen Monorom is appalling, the bastard child of the devil himself! It is arguably the worst stretch of road in the country, and that's saying something. There are two large rivers to cross, three if you include the one at the falls, and several deep gullies. Most vehicles take about two hours to complete the journey, although trail bikes can do it a little quicker. To get there, you could hire a moto for the day or charter a Russian jeep between a group, neither of which is a cheap option. If you come on your own by motorcycle, be especially careful when crossing the river above the Bou Sraa Falls as the riverbed is as slippery as ice.

Other Places

Other attractions in the province include the **Dak Dam Waterfall** about 25km north-east of Sen Monorom and the gold mining districts in the centre of the province.

Language

The Khmer or Cambodian language is spoken by approximately nine million people in Cambodia, and is understood by many in bordering countries. Written Khmer is based on the ancient Brahmi script of southern India. Arguably one of the oldest languages in South-East Asia, Khmer inscriptions have been dated back to the 7th century AD. Although separate and distinct from its Thai, Lao and Burmese neighbours, Khmer shares with them the common roots of Sanskrit and Pali – a heritage of centuries of linguistic and cultural interaction and of their shared faith in Theravada Buddhism. More recently, many French words entered the Khmer language during the colonial period, especially medical and technical terms.

Unlike the languages of neighbouring countries, Khmer is non tonal, meaning that there are no special intonations of words that alter their meaning. This may be a relief for travellers in the region who have been frustrated in their attempts at tonal languages such as Thai, Vietnamese and Lao. However, the lack of tones is easily offset by the complexity of the Khmer pronunciation. There are 33 consonants, often paired in seemingly bizarre combinations, and some 24 vowels and diphthongs. Further complicating the language is the haphazard transliteration system left over from the days of French rule, which does not reflect accurate pronunciation of Khmer words by English speakers.

On the positive side, Khmer grammar is very simple. There are no verb conjugations or gender inflections, no endings for single or plural, masculine or feminine. Adding a few words changes sentence tense to past, present or future.

In any case, a bit of Khmer will go a long way – no matter how rough it is. The Khmers sincerely appreciate any effort to learn their language and are very supportive of visitors who give it even a half-hearted try. You'll find that as your skill and vocabulary increase, so does your social standing; people go out of their way to complement you, moto-taxi fares and prices at markets drop, and you may even win a few friends.

Though English is fast becoming Cambodia's dominant second language, the Khmer still cling to the Francophone pronunciation of the Roman alphabet and most foreign words. This is helpful to remember when spelling western words and names aloud; thus 'ay-bee-cee' becomes 'ah-bey-sey' and so on. French speakers will definitely have an advantage when addressing the older generation, as most educated Khmers studied French at some point during their schooling. Many household items retain their French names as well, especially those which were introduced to Cambodia by the French, such as *robine* (faucet) and *ampuol* (light bulb).

Recommend reading for those interested in further study of spoken and written Khmer are *Cambodian System of Writing and Beginning Reader*, *Modern Spoken Cambodian* and any other books by Frank Huffman.

Dialects

Although the Khmer language as spoken in Phnom Penh is generally intelligible to Khmers nationwide, there are several distinct dialects in other areas of the country. Most notably, the Khmer of Takeo province tend to modify or slur hard consonant/vowel combinations, especially those that contain 'r'; thus *bram* (five) becomes *pe-am*, *sraa* (alcohol) becomes *se-aa*, and *baraang* (French/foreigner) becomes *be-ang*. In Siem Reap, sharp-eared travellers will notice a very Lao sounding lilt to the local speech. Here, certain vowels are modified, such as *poan* (thousand), which becomes *peuan*, and *kh'sia* (pipe), which becomes *kh'seua*.

Transliteration

The transliteration system used in this chapter has been designed for basic communication rather than linguistic perfection.

Several Khmer vowels, however, have no English equivalent, thus they can only be approximated by English spellings. Other words are written as they are pronounced and not necessarily according to the actual vowels used in the words. (Khmer place names in this book will follow their common or standard spellings.)

Pronunciation

The pronunciations guide below covers the trickier parts of the transliteration system used in this chapter. It uses the Roman alphabet to give the closest equivalent to the sounds of the Khmer language. The best way to improve your pronunciation is to listen carefully to native speakers.

Vowels

Vowels and diphthongs with an 'h' at the end should be pronounced hard and aspirated (with a puff of air).

aa	as the 'a' in 'father'
i	as the 'i' in 'kit'
uh	as the 'u' in 'but'
ii	as the 'ee' in 'feet'
ei	a combination of 'uh' and 'ii' above, ie 'uh-ii'
eu	similar to the French *peuple*; try pronouncing 'oo' while keeping the lips spread flat rather than rounded
euh	as 'eu' above; pronounced short and hard
oh	as the 'o' in 'hose'; pronounced short and hard
ow	as in 'glow'
u	as the 'u' in 'flute'; pronounced short and hard
uu	as the 'oo' in 'zoo'
ua	as the 'ou' in 'tour'
uah	as 'ua' above; pronounced short and hard
aa-œ	a tough one with no English equivalent; like a combination of 'aa' and 'œ'. When placed between consonants it's often pronounced like 'ao'.
œ	as 'er' in 'her', but more open
eua	combination of 'eu' and 'a'
ia	as 'ee-ya', like 'beer' without the 'r'
e	as the 'a' in 'late'

ai	as the 'i' in 'side'
ae	as the 'a' in 'cat'
ay	as 'ai' above but slightly more nasal
ey	as in 'prey'
ao	as the 'ow' in 'cow'
av	no English equivalent; like a very nasal 'ao'. The final 'v' is not pronounced.
euv	no English equivalent; like a very nasal 'eu'. The final 'v' is not pronounced.
ohm	as the 'ome' in 'home'
am	as the 'um' in 'glum'
oam	a combination of 'o' and 'am'
a, ah	shorter and harder than 'aa' above
eah	combination of 'e' and 'ah'; pronounced short and hard
ih	as the 'ee' in 'teeth'; pronounced short and hard
eh	as the 'a' in 'date'; pronounced short and hard
awh	as the 'aw' in 'jaw'; pronounced short and hard
oah	a combination of 'o' and 'ah'; pronounced short and hard.
aw	as the 'aw' in 'jaw'

Consonants

Khmer uses some consonant combinations that may sound rather bizarre to the westerner's ear and be equally difficult for the western tongue, eg 'j-r' in *j'rook* (pig), or 'ch-ng' in *ch'ngain* (delicious). For ease of pronunciation such consonants are separated in this guide with an apostrophe.

k	as the 'g' in 'go'
kh	as the 'k' in 'kind'
ng	as in the final sound of the word 'sing'; a difficult sound for westerners to emulate. Practice by saying 'singing-nging-nging-nging' until you can say 'nging' clearly.
j	as in 'jump'
ch	as in 'cheese'
ny	as in the final syllable of 'onion', ie 'nyun'.
t	a hard, unaspirated 't' sound with no direct equivalent in English. Similar to the 't' in 'stand'.

th	as the 't' in 'two', never as the 'th' in 'thanks'.
p	a hard, unaspirated 'p' sound, as the final 'p' in 'puppy'
ph	as the 'p' in 'pond', never as 'ph' in 'phone'
r	as in 'rum', but hard and rolling, with the tongue flapping against the palate. In rapid conversation it is often omitted entirely.
w	as the 'w' in 'would'. Contrary to the common transliteration system, there is no equivalent to the English 'v' sound in Khmer.

Greetings & Civilities

Hello.
johm riab sua/ ជំរាបសួរ/សួស្ដី
sua s'dei
Goodbye.
lia suhn hao-y លាសិនហើយ
See you later.
juab kh'nia ជួបគ្នាថ្ងៃក្រោយ
th'ngay krao-y
Yes.
baat បាទ
(used by men)
jaa ចាស
(used by women)
No.
te ទេ
Please.
sohm សូម
Thank you.
aw kohn អរគុណ
You're welcome.
awt ei te/sohm អត់អីទេ/សូមអញ្ជើញ
anjœ-in
Excuse me/I'm sorry.
sohm toh សុំទោស
Pardon? (What did
you say?)
niak niyey thaa អ្នកនិយាយថាម៉េច?
mait?

Small Talk

Hi. How are you?
niak sohk sabaay te? អ្នកសុខសប្បាយទេ?

I'm fine.
kh'nyohm sohk sabaay ខ្ញុំសុខសប្បាយ
Where are you going?
niak teuv naa? អ្នកទៅណា?

(NB This is a very common question used when meeting people, even strangers; an exact answer is not necessary.)

What's your name?
niak ch'muah ei? អ្នកឈ្មោះអី?
My name is ...
kh'nyohm ch'muah ... ខ្ញុំឈ្មោះ ...
Where are you from?
niak mao pii prateh naa? អ្នកមកពីប្រទេសណា?
I'm from ...
kh'nyohm mao pii ... ខ្ញុំមកពី ...
I'm staying at ...
kh'nyohm snahk neuv ... ខ្ញុំស្នាក់នៅ ...
May I take your photo?
kh'nyohm aa-it thawt ruup niak baan te? ខ្ញុំអាចថតរូបអ្នកបានទេ?

Forms of Address

The Khmer language reflects the social standing of the speaker and subject through various personal pronouns and 'politeness words'. These range from the simple *baat* for men and *jaa* for women, placed at the end of a sentence, meaning 'yes' or 'I agree', to the very formal and archaic *Reachasahp* or 'Royal language', a separate vocabulary reserved for addressing the King and very high officials. Many of the pronouns are determined on the basis of the subject's age and sex in relation to the speaker. Foreigners are not expected to know all of these forms. The easiest and most general personal pronoun is *niak* (you), which may be used in most situations, with either sex. Men of your age and older may be called *lowk* (mister). Women of your age and older can be called *bawng srei* (older sister) or for more formal situations, *lowk srei* (Madam). *Bawng* is a good informal, neutral pronoun for men or women who are (or appear to be) older than you. For third person, male or female, singular or plural, the respectful form is *koat* and the common form is *ke*.

Language Difficulties

Does any one here speak English?
tii nih mian niak jeh phiasaa awngle te?
ទីនេះមានអ្នកចេះភាសាអង់គ្លេសទេ?

Do you understand?
niak yuhl te/niak s'dap baan te?
អ្នកយល់ទេ/អ្នកស្ដាប់បានទេ?

I understand.
kh'nyohm yuhl/kh'nyohm s'dap baan
ខ្ញុំយល់ /ខ្ញុំស្ដាប់បាន

I don't understand.
kh'nyohm muhn yuhl te/kh'nyohm s'dap muhn baan te
ខ្ញុំមិនយល់ទេ/ខ្ញុំស្ដាប់មិនបានទេ

How do you say ... in Khmer?
... kh'mai thaa mait?
... ខ្មែរថាម៉េច?

What does this mean?
nih mian nuh-y thaa mait?
នេះមានន័យថាម៉េច?

Please speak slowly.
sohm niyay yeut yeut
សូមនិយាយយឺតៗ

Please write that word down for me.
sohm sawse piak nu ao-y kh'nyohm
សូមសរសេរពាក្យនោះឲ្យខ្ញុំ

Please translate for me.
sohm bawk brai ao-y kh'nyohm
សូមបកប្រែឲ្យខ្ញុំ

What is this called?
nih ke hav thaa mait?
នេះគេហៅថាម៉េច?

Getting Around

Where is the ...?
... neuv ai naa?
... នៅឯណា?

bus station
kuhnlaing laan ch'nual
កន្លែងឡានឈ្នួល

bus stop
jamnawt laan ch'nual
ចំណតឡានឈ្នួល

train station
s'thaanii roht plœng
ស្ថានីយរថភ្លើង

airport
wial yohn hawh
វាលយន្តហោះ

What time does the ... leave?
... jein maong pohnmaan?
... ចេញម៉ោងប៉ុន្មាន?

bus	*laan ch'nual*	ឡានឈ្នួល
train	*roht plœng*	រថភ្លើង
plane	*yohn hawh/*	យន្តហោះ/
	k'pal hawh	កប៉ាល់ហោះ

What time does the last bus leave?
laan ch'nual johng krao-y jein teuv maong pohnmaan?
ឡានឈ្នួល ចុងក្រោយ ចេញទៅម៉ោងប៉ុន្មាន?

How can I get to ...?
phleuv naa teuv ..?
ផ្លូវណាទៅ ...?

Is it far?
wia neuv ch'ngaay te?
វានៅឆ្ងាយទេ?

Is it near?
wia neuv juht te?
វានៅជិតទេ?

Is it near here?
wia neuv juht nih te?
វានៅជិតនេះទេ?

Go straight ahead.
teuv trawng
ទៅត្រង់

Turn left ...
bawt ch'weng បត់ឆ្វេង

Turn right ...
bawt s'dam បត់ស្ដាំ

at the corner
neuv kait j'rohng នៅកាច់ជ្រុង
in front of
neuv khaang នៅខាងមុខ
mohk
next to
neuv joab នៅជាប់
behind
neuv khaang នៅខាងក្រោយ
krao-y
opposite
neuv tohl mohk នៅទល់មុខ

I want to get off (here)!
kh'nyohm jawng joh (tii nih)! ខ្ញុំចង់ចុះ (ទីនេះ)!

How much is it to ...?
teuv ... th'lay pohnmaan? ទៅ ... ថ្លៃប៉ុន្មាន?

That's too much.
th'lay pek ថ្លៃពេក

Please take me to ...
sohm juun kh'nyohm teuv ... សូមជូនខ្ញុំទៅ ...

this address
aadreh/aasayathaan nih អាស័យដ្ឋាននេះ

Here is fine, thank you.
chohp neuv tii nih kaw baan ឈប់នៅទីនេះក៏បាន

north	*khaang jæng*	ខាងជើង
south	*khaang d'bowng*	ខាងត្បូង
east	*khaang kaot*	ខាងកើត
west	*khaang leit*	ខាងលិច

Around Town

Where is a ...
... neuv ai naa? ... នៅឯណា?

bank	*th'niakia*	ធនាគារ
cinema	*rowng kohn*	រោងកុន
consulate	*kohng sul*	កុងស៊ុល
embassy	*s'thaantuut*	ស្ថានទូត
hospital	*mohntii paet*	មន្ទីរពេទ្យ

market	*p'saa*	ផ្សារ
museum	*saramohntii*	សារមន្ទី
park	*suan*	សួន
post office	*praisuhnii*	ប្រៃសណីយ
temple	*wawt*	វត្ត

police station
poh polih/s'thaanii nohkohbaal ប៉ុស្តប៉ូលីស/ស្ថានីយនគរបាល

public telephone
turasahp saathiaranah ទូរស័ព្ទសាធារណៈ

public toilet
bawngkohn saathiaranah បង្គន់សាធារណៈ

How far is the ...?
... ch'ngaay pohnmaan? ... ឆ្ងាយប៉ុន្មាន?

I want to see the ...
kh'nyohm jawng teuv mæl ... ខ្ញុំចង់ទៅមើល ...

I'm looking for the ...
kh'nyohm rohk ... ខ្ញុំរក ...

What time does it open?
wia baok maong pohnmaan? វាបើកម៉ោងប៉ុន្មាន?

What time does it close?
wia buht maong pohnmaan? វាបិទម៉ោងប៉ុន្មាន?

Is it still open?
wia neuv baok reu te? វានៅបើកឬទេ?

What ... is this?
... nih ch'muah ei? ... នេះឈ្មោះអ្វី?

I want to change ...
kh'nyohm jawng dow ... ខ្ញុំចង់ដូរ ...
US dollars
dolaa amerik ដុល្លាអាមេរិក

What is the exchange rate for US dollars?
muy dolaa dow baan pohnmaan?
ម្ងុយដុល្លាដូវបានប៉ុន្មាន?

Accommodation

Where is a ...?
... neuv ai naa?   ... នៅឯណា?
(cheap) hotel
sahnthaakia/   សណ្ឋាគារ/
ohtail thaok   អូតែល(ថោក)

I've already found a hotel.
kh'nyohm mian ohtail hao-y
ខ្ញុំមានអូតែលហើយ

I'm staying at ...
kh'nyohm snahk neuv ...
ខ្ញុំស្នាក់នៅ ...

Could you write down the address, please?
sohm sawse aasayathaan ao-y kh'nyohm
សូមសរសេរអាស័យដ្ឋានឱ្យខ្ញុំ

I'd like a room ...
kh'nyohm sohm bantohp ...
ខ្ញុំសុំបន្ទប់ ...
for one person
samruhp muy niak
សំរាប់មួយនាក់
for two people
samruhp pii niak
សំរាប់ពីរនាក់
with a bathroom
dail mian bantohp tuhk
ដែលមានបន្ទប់ទឹក
with a fan
dail mian dawnghahl
ដែលមានកង្ហារ
with a window
dail mian bawng-uit
ដែលមានបង្អួច

I'm going to stay for ...
kh'nyohm nuhng snahk tii nih ...
ខ្ញុំនឹងស្នាក់ទីនេះ ...

one day   *muy th'ngay*   មួយថ្ងៃ
one week   *muy aatuht*   មួយអាទិត្យ

Do you have a room?
niak mian bantohp tohmne te?
អ្នកមានបន្ទប់ទំនេទេ?
How much is it per day?
damlay muy th'ngay pohnmaan?
តំលៃមួយថ្ងៃប៉ុន្មាន?
Does the price include breakfast?
damlay bantohp khuht teang m'hohp pel pruhk reu?
តំលៃបន្ទប់គិតទាំងម្ហូបពេលព្រឹកឬ?
Can I see the room?
kh'nyohm aa-it mæl bantohp baan te?
ខ្ញុំអាចមើលបន្ទប់បានទេ?
I don't like this room.
kh'nyohm muhn johl juht bantohp nih te
ខ្ញុំមិនចូលចិត្តបន្ទប់នេះទេ
Do you have a better room?
niak mian bantohp l'aw jiang nih te?
អ្នកមានបន្ទប់ល្អជាងនេះទេ?
I'll take this room.
kh'nyohm yohk bantohp nih
ខ្ញុំយកបន្ទប់នេះ

Can I leave my things here until ...?
kh'nyohm aa-it ph'nyaa-œ tohk eiwuhn r'bawh kh'nyohm neuv tii nih dawl ... baan te?
ខ្ញុំអាចផ្ញើអីវ៉ាន់របស់ខ្ញុំនៅទីនេះដល់ ... បានទេ?
this afternoon   *l'ngiak nih*   ល្ងាចនេះ
this evening   *yohp nih*   យប់នេះ

Food

Where is a ...
... neuv ai naa?   ... នៅឯណា?
cheap restaurant
haang baay/   ហាងបាយថោក
resturaan thaok
restaurant
resturaan/   ភោជនីយដ្ឋាន
phowjuhniiyathaan
food stall
kuhnlaing luak   កន្លែងលក់ម្ហូប
m'howp
market
p'saa   ផ្សារ

I'm vegetarian. (I can't
eat meat.)
kh'nyohm tawm sait
ខ្ញុំតមសាច់

Not too spicy please.
sohm kohm twœ huhl pek
សូមកុំធ្វើហឹរពេក

No MSG please.
sohm kohm dahk bii jeng
សូមកុំដាក់បីុចេង

This is delicious.
nih ch'ngain nah
នេះឆ្ងាញ់ណាស់

Shopping

How much is it?
nih th'lay pohnmaan?
នេះថ្លៃប៉ុន្មាន?

That's too much.
th'lay pek
ថ្លៃពេក

I'll give you ...
kh'nyohm ao-y ...
ខ្ញុំឲ្យ ...

No more than ...
muhn lœh pii ...
មិនលើសពី ...

What's your best price?
niak dait pohnmaan?
អ្នកដាច់ប៉ុន្មាន?

Health

Where is a ...
... neuv ai naa?   ... នៅឯណា?
dentist
paet th'mein   ពេទ្យធ្មេញ
doctor
kruu paet   គ្រូពេទ្យ
hospital
mohntrii paet   មន្ទីរពេទ្យ
pharmacy
kuhnlaing luak   កន្លែងលក់ថ្នាំ/
th'nam/
ohsawt s'thaan   ឱសថស្ថាន

I'm ill.
kh'nyohm cheu   ខ្ញុំឈឺ

My ... hurts.
... r'bawh kh'nyohm cheu
... របស់ខ្ញុំឈឺ

I feel nauseous.
kh'nyohm jawng k'uat
ខ្ញុំចង់ក្អួត

I feel weak.
kh'nyohm awh kamlahng
ខ្ញុំអស់កំលាំង

I keep vomiting.
kh'nyohm k'uat j'raa-œn
ខ្ញុំក្អួតច្រើន

I feel dizzy.
kh'nyohm wuhl mohk
ខ្ញុំវិលមុខ

I'm having trouble breathing.
kh'nyohm pi baak dawk dawnghaom
ខ្ញុំពិបាកដកដង្ហើម

I'm allergic to ...
kh'nyohm muhn treuv thiat ...
ខ្ញុំមិនត្រូវធាតុ ...
penicillin
penicillin   ប៉េនីស៊ីលីន
antibiotics
awntiibiowtik   អង់ទីបីយោទិក

I need medicine for ...
kh'nyohm treuv kaa th'nam samruhp ...
ខ្ញុំត្រូវការថ្នាំសំរាប់ ...
diarrhoea
rowk joh riak   រោគចុះរាក
dysentery
rowk mual   រោគមូល
fever
krohn/k'dav   គ្រុន/ក្តៅខ្លួន
kh'luan
pain
cheu   ឈឺ

antiseptic
th'nam samlahp   ថ្នាំសំលាប់មេរោគ
me rowk
aspirin
parasetamol   ប៉ារ៉ាសេតាម៉ូល
codeine
codiin   ខូឌីន

o

quinine		
kiiniin	គីនីន	
sleeping pills		
th'nam ng'nguy dek	ថ្នាំងងុយដេក	
condoms		
sraom ahnaamai	ស្រោមអនាម័យ	
medicine		
th'nam	ថ្នាំ	
mosquito repellent		
th'nam kaa pia muh	ថ្នាំការពារមូស	
razor blade		
kambuht kao pohk moat	កាំបិតកោរពុកមាត់	
sanitary napkins		
samlei ahnaamai	សំឡីអនាម័យ	
shampoo		
sabuu kawk sawk	សាប៊ូកក់សក់	
shaving cream		
kraim samruhp kao pohk moat	ក្រែមសំរាប់កោរពុកមាត់	
sunblock cream		
kraim kaa pia pohnleu th'ngay	ក្រែមការពារពន្លឺថ្ងៃ	
toilet paper		
krawdah ahnaamai	ក្រដាស់អនាម័យ	

Time & Date

What time is it?
eileuv nih maong pohnmaan?
តើឥឡូវនេះម៉ោងប៉ុន្មាន?

in the morning		
pel pruhk	ពេលព្រឹក	
in the afternoon		
pel r'sial	ពេលរសៀល	
in the evening		
pel l'ngiat	ពេលល្ងាច	
at night		
pel yohp	ពេលយប់	
today		
th'ngay nih	ថ្ងៃនេះ	
tomorrow		
th'ngay s'aik	ថ្ងៃស្អែក	
yesterday		
m'suhl mein	ម្សិលមិញ	
Monday		
th'ngay jahn	ថ្ងៃចន្ទ	

Tuesday		
th'ngay ahngkia	ថ្ងៃអង្គារ	
Wednesday		
th'ngay poht	ថ្ងៃពុធ	
Thursday		
th'ngay prohoah	ថ្ងៃព្រហស្បតិ៍	
Friday		
th'ngay sohk	ថ្ងៃសុក្រ	
Saturday		
th'ngay sav	ថ្ងៃសៅរ៍	
Sunday		
th'ngay aatuht	ថ្ងៃអាទិត្យ	

Numbers & Amounts

Khmers count in increments of five. Thus, after reaching the number five *(bram)*, the cycle begins again with the addition of one, ie 'five-one' *(bram muy)*, 'five-two' *(bram pii)* and so on to 10, which begins a new cycle. This system is a bit awkward at first (for example, 18, which has three parts: 10, five and three) but with practice it can be mastered.

You may be confused by a colloquial form of counting that reverses the word order for numbers between 10 and 20 and separates the two words with *duhn: pii duhn dawp* for 12, *bei duhn dawp* for 13, *bram buan duhn dawp* for 19 and so on. This form is often used in markets, so listen keenly.

1	*muy*	មួយ
2	*pii*	ពីរ
3	*bei*	បី
4	*buan*	បួន
5	*bram*	ប្រាំ
6	*bram muy*	ប្រាំមួយ
7	*bram pii/puhl*	ប្រាំពីរ
8	*bram bei*	ប្រាំបី
9	*bram buan*	ប្រាំបួន
10	*dawp*	ដប់
11	*dawp muy*	ដប់មួយ
12	*dawp pii*	ដប់ពីរ
16	*dawp bram muy*	ដប់ប្រាំមួយ

20	*m'phei*	ម្ភៃ
21	*m'phei muy*	ម្ភៃមួយ
30	*saamsuhp*	សាមសិប
40	*saisuhp*	សែសិប
100	*muy roy*	មួយរយ
1000	*muy poan*	មួយពាន់
one million	*muy lian*	មួយលាន
1st	*tii muy*	ទីមួយ
2nd	*tii pii*	ទីពីរ
3rd	*tii bei*	ទីបី
4th	*tii buan*	ទីបួន
10th	*tii dawp*	ទីដប់

Emergencies

Help!
juay kh'nyohm phawng!
ជួយខ្ញុំផង!

It's an emergency!
nih jia reuang bawntoan!
នេះជារឿងបន្ទាន់!

Call a doctor!
juay hav kruu paet mao!
ជួយហៅគ្រូពេទ្យមក!

Call the police!
juay hav polih mao!
ជួយហៅប៉ូលីសមក!

Could you help me please?
niak aa-it juay kh'nyohm baan te?
អ្នកអាចជួយខ្ញុំបានទេ?

Could I please use the telephone?
kh'nyohm braa-œ turasahp baan te?
ខ្ញុំប្រើទូរស័ព្ទបានទេ?

I wish to contact my embassy/consulate.
*kh'nyohm jawng hav s'thaantuut/
kohngsuhl r'bawh prawteh kh'nyohm*
ខ្ញុំចង់ហៅស្ថានទូត/កុងស៊ុលរបស់ប្រទេសខ្ញុំ

I've been robbed.
kh'nyohm treuv jao plawn
ខ្ញុំត្រូវចោរប្លន់។

Stop!
chohp!
ឈប់!

Watch out!
prawyaht!
ប្រយ័ត្ន!

Is this path safe to walk on?
*phleuv nih mian sohwatthaphiap dai
reu te?*
ផ្លូវនេះមានសុវត្ថិភាពដែរឬទេ?

Are there any land mines in this area?
neuv m'dohm nih mian miin reu te?
នៅម្តុំនេះមានមីនឬទេ?

toilets
bawngkohn
បង្គន់

Where are the toilets?
bawngkohn neuv ai naa?
បង្គន់នៅឯណា?

Glossary

apsara – heavenly nymph
ASEAN – Association of Southeast Asian Nations
Avalokiteshvara – the Buddha of Compassion and the inspiration for *Jayavarman VII's* Angkor Thom

baray – reservoir
bas-relief – a form of sculpture in which the figures or carvings project only slightly from the background
boeng – lake

chunchiet – hill tribes
CCB – Cambodian Commercial Bank
CCC – Cooperation Committee for Cambodia
CPP – Cambodian People's Party
cyclo – pedicab or bicycle rickshaw

devaraja – cult of the god king, established by *Jayavarman II,* where the monarch has universal power

FCC – Foreign Correspondents' Club
FUNCINPEC – National United Front for an Independent, Neutral, Peaceful and Co-operative Cambodia

garuda – mythical half man, half bird

Hinayana – a school of Buddhism (see *Theravada*)
Hun Sen – Cambodia's prime minister

Jayavarman II – the king (ruled 802-50) who established the cult of the god king, kicking off a period of amazing architectural productivity, which resulted in the extraordinary temples of Angkor
Jayavarman VII –the king (ruled 1181-1201) who drove the Chams out of Cambodia before embarking on an ambitious construction program, of which the walled city of Angkor Thom was part

Kampuchea – the name Cambodians use for their country; it is associated with the bloody rule of the Khmer Rouge, which insisted that the outside world use the name Democratic Kampuchea from 1975 to 1979
Khmer Krom – ethnic Khmers living in Vietnam
Khmer Rouge – a revolutionary organisation that seized power in 1975 and implemented a brutal social restructuring, resulting in the suffering and death of millions of Cambodians for the following four years
King Norodom Sihanouk – King, film director and constant presence in Cambodian politics
krama – scarves

lingam – phallic totem

Mahayana – school of Buddhism (also known as the northern school) that built upon and extended the early Buddhist teachings
moto – small motorcycles with drivers; a common form of transport in Cambodia
Mt Meru – the mythical dwelling place of the Hindu god Shiva
MPTC – Ministry of Post & Telecommunications

naga – mythical serpent, often multi-headed; a symbol used extensively in Angkorian architecture
NGO – non-governmental organisation

Pali – ancient Indian language that, along with Sanskrit, is the root of modern Khmer
Party of Democratic Kampuchea – the political party of the Khmer Rouge
phlauv – local term for street used in Phnom Penh; abbreviated to ph
phnom – mountain
Pol Pot – the former leader of the Khmer Rouge who is roundly blamed for the suffering and deaths of millions of Cambodians under a radical social experiment from 1975 to 1979; also known as Saloth Sar
Prince Norodom Ranariddh – son of King Sihanouk and leader of FUNCINPEC
psar – market

RAC – Royal Air Cambodge
Ramayana – an epic Hindu poem composed around 300BC featuring the mythical Rama-chandra, the incarnation of the god Vishnu
remorque-kang – a trailer pulled by a bicycle
remorque-moto – a trailer pulled by a motorcycle
RCAF – Royal Cambodian Armed Forces

Sangkum Reastr Niyum – People's Socialist Community; a national movement, led by King Sihanouk, that ruled the country during the 1950s and 60s
Sanskrit – ancient Hindu language that, along with Pali, is the root of modern Khmer language
SNC – Supreme National Council
STI – sexually transmitted infections
Suryavarman II – the king (ruled 1112-52) responsible for the building of Angkor Wat and for expanding and unifying the Khmer empire

Theravada – a school of Buddhism (also known as the southern school or Hinayana Buddhism) found in Myanmar (Burma), Thailand, Laos and Cambodia; this school confined itself to the early Buddhist teachings rather than an expanded doctrine
tikalok – like a fruit smoothie, often very sweet and, if an egg is added, frothy

UNDP – United Nations Development Programme
UNESCO – United Nations Educational Scientific and Cultural Organization
UNHCR – United Nations High Commissioner for Refugees
UNTAC – United Nations Transitional Authority in Cambodia

vihara – temple sanctuary

WHO – World Health Organization

Year Zero – the Khmer Rouge proclaimed 1975, the year it seized power, Year Zero; currency was abolished, postal services halted and Cambodia was cut off from the rest of the world as part of a radical and brutal social experiment

Acknowledgments

THANKS

Many thanks to the travellers who used the last edition and wrote to us with helpful hints, useful advice and interesting anecdotes:

S Adlington, J Alan, Dean Anderson, Richard Astley, Jane Bartlett, Kirk Benson, James Robert Bierman, Oda Bogger, Francis Brannigan, Thomas Brecelic, Bryan & Helen, Andrew Brouwer, Gabriella Brusadelli, Mary Ann Buchanan, Ian Butler Eduardo, Will Carless, Cloda Cassidy, Vien Chom, Eric Chu, Ken Chuah, Kong Sun Chun, Nermin Colak, Tui Cordemans, Brian Cornah, Sam Cornah, Robin Crompton, Kate Davey, David & Lucy, Fabiana Dimase, Francis Dix, Julian Doorey, Alexandra Dorrie, Dacia Ezekiel.

Anne Falconnier, Abby Fateman, Frank Feliciano, Hanne Finholt, Hilary Frater, Kevin Garvey, Walter Genenger, Spencer George, A Golden, Martin Gray, Christiane Habich, Caul Haney, David Harcombe, James Harpur, Frances Hayes, Michael Hayes, Rolf Herrmann, John Hitchcock, Heinz Hogelsberger, Robert Hooton, Kylie Horsfall, John Hryniuk, Mathieu Jobin, Owen Jones, Stuart Jones, Idsert Joukes, Ken Kaliher, Peter Kapec, Jeffrey Kaye, Jonathon Keigan, Lidee Khmer Guest, Sako Klinker, Karin Kostel, Jim Krische, Kam Lam, Sean Lawson, Christophe Le Cornu, Marie Lesaicherre, Peter Leth, Wolfgang Liebe, Francis Lim, Nick Linnane, Cofe Linsbauer, Dr WK Loftus, Philip & Wendy Lomax, Gabriel Loos, Ragne Low, David Mackertich, Madi Maclean, Dave Marini, N Marsh, Cardellini Martino, Richard McIntosh, Lucy McKinley, Sunil S Mehta, Ophir Michaeli, T&T Millage, Laurence Monnier, Judy Moore, George Horey Morres, Joanne Morrison, Troy Neatte, Steve Newcomer, Jan Nowicki, Michael Nugent, Nick O'Connell, Yildiray Odemis.

James Parsons, Robert Patterson, Dave Pearsell, Arnaldo Pellini, Piergiorgio Pescali, Markus Phillip, Lucy Pike, John Power, Janet Preston, Robyn Preston, Christoph Pulster, Kim Baldwin Radford, Tom & Liza Redston, H Rose, David Rostron, Sam Rowland, Rip Russell, Antti Saarela, Thomas Saftich, Yutaka Saida, John Salmon, Mark Savige, Nicki & Steffen Scheunemann, Jochen J Schnell, Rachael Scott, Mike Searson, Roy Sharma, Nancy Shilepsky, Wendy Silva, Say Sisakith, Jady Smith, Krzysztof Sobkowski, Oliver Sprinz, Marc Stoeckli, Orazio Strazzeri, Ryan Taylor, Anne-Marie Thepaut, Brant Thompson, JM Thomson, Phil Ting, Gilad Ulman, Olaf van den Boom, Mario Van Hecke, Monique van Wijnbergen, Mogens Vejtorp, Erwin Vruggink, Dick Warren, Jennifer West, Ric Wilson, Christine & Michael Wong, Michael Wong, Andy Wright, Jane Zhang.

LONELY PLANET

Phrasebooks

Lonely Planet phrasebooks are packed with essential words and phrases to help travellers communicate with the locals. With colour tabs for quick reference, an extensive vocabulary and use of script, these handy pocket-sized language guides cover day-to-day travel situations.

- handy pocket-sized books
- easy to understand Pronunciation chapter
- clear & comprehensive Grammar chapter
- romanisation alongside script to allow ease of pronunciation
- script throughout so users can point to phrases for every situation
- full of cultural information and tips for the traveller

'... vital for a real DIY spirit and attitude in language learning'
– *Backpacker*

'the phrasebooks have good cultural backgrounders and offer solid advice for challenging situations in remote locations'
– *San Francisco Examiner*

Arabic (Egyptian) • Arabic (Moroccan) • Australian *(Australian English, Aboriginal and Torres Strait languages)* • Baltic States *(Estonian, Latvian, Lithuanian)* • Bengali • Brazilian • British • Burmese • Cantonese • Central Asia (Uyghur, Uzbek, Kyrghiz, Kazak, Pashto, Tadjik • Central Europe *(Czech, French, German, Hungarian, Italian, Slovak)* • Eastern Europe *(Bulgarian, Czech, Hungarian, Polish, Romanian, Slovak)* • Ethiopian (Amharic) • Fijian • French • German • Greek • Hebrew • Hill Tribes • Hindi & Urdu • Indonesian • Italian • Japanese • Korean • Lao • Latin American Spanish • Malay • Mandarin • Mediterranean Europe *(Albanian, Croatian, Greek, Italian, Macedonian, Maltese, Serbian, Slovene)* • Mongolian • Nepali • Pidgin • Pilipino (Tagalog) • Quechua • Russian • Scandinavian Europe *(Danish, Finnish, Icelandic, Norwegian, Swedish)* • South-East Asia *(Burmese, Indonesian, Khmer, Lao, Malay, Tagalog Pilipino, Thai, Vietnamese)* • South Pacific Languages • Spanish (Castilian) *(also includes Catalan, Galician and Basque)* • Sri Lanka • Swahili • Thai • Tibetan • Turkish • Ukrainian • USA *(US English, Vernacular, Native American languages, Hawaiian)* • Vietnamese • Western Europe *(Basque, Catalan, Dutch, French, German, Greek, Irish, Italian, Portuguese, Scottish Gaelic, Spanish (Castilian), Welsh)*

Lonely Planet Journeys

JOURNEYS is a unique collection of travel writing – published by the company that understands travel better than anyone else. It is a series for anyone who has ever experienced – or dreamed of – the magical moment when they encountered a strange culture or saw a place for the first time. They are tales to read while you're planning a trip, while you're on the road or while you're in an armchair in front of a fire.

These outstanding titles explore our planet through the eyes of a diverse group of international writers. JOURNEYS books catch the spirit of a place, illuminate a culture, recount a crazy adventure or introduce a fascinating way of life. They always entertain, and always enrich the experience of travel.

LOST JAPAN
Alex Kerr

Exploring rarely visited temples and shrines, studying calligraphy, talking with Kabuki actors: Alex Kerr draws on more than thirty years of personal experience in presenting this backstage tour of a Japan that outsiders rarely glimpse.

'one of the finest books about Japan written in decades' – *Insight Japan*

ISLANDS IN THE CLOUDS
Travels in the Highlands of New Guinea
Isabella Tree

Isabella Tree travels through the remote and beautiful highlands of Papua New Guinea and Irian Jaya – one of the most extraordinary and dangerous regions on the planet – with a Highlander who introduces her to his intriguing and complex world, changing rapidly as it collides with modern technology.

'a gifted writer and reporter with a lively style . . . she reports on her journeys with compassion and insight' – *Los Angeles Times*

A SEASON IN HEAVEN
True Tales from the Road to Kathmandu
David Tomory

In Iran and Afghanistan, in Rishikesh and Goa, in ashrams, mountain villages and dubious hotels, a generation of young people got hip, got busted, lost their luggage, and sometimes found themselves. From confusion to contentment, from dope to dysentery, A Season in Heaven presents the true stories of travellers who hit the hippie trail in the late 1960s.

Only available in Canada and the USA

SHOPPING FOR BUDDHAS
Jeff Greenwald

In his obsessive search for the perfect Buddha statue in the backstreets of Kathmandu, Jeff Greenwald discovers more than he bargained for. Politics, religion and serious shopping collide in this witty account of an enlightening visit to Nepal.

'Greenwald's quest reveals more about modern Nepal . . . than writings that take themselves much more seriously' – *Chicago Tribune*

LONELY PLANET

Lonely Planet Travel Atlases

onely Planet has long been famous for the number and quality of its guidebook maps. Now we've gone one step further and produced a handy companion series: Lonely Planet travel atlases – maps of a country produced in book form.

Unlike other maps, which look good but lead travellers astray, our travel atlases have been researched on the road by Lonely Planet's experienced team of writers. All details are carefully checked to ensure the atlas corresponds with the equivalent Lonely Planet guidebook.

- full-colour throughout
- maps researched and checked by Lonely Planet authors
- place names correspond with Lonely Planet guidebooks
- no confusing spelling differences
- legend and travelling information in English, French, German, Japanese and Spanish
- size: 230 x 160 mm

Available now: Chile & Easter Island ● Egypt ● India & Bangladesh ● Israel & the Palestinian Territories ● Jordan, Syria & Lebanon ● Kenya ● Laos ● Portugal ● South Africa, Lesotho & Swaziland ● Thailand ● Turkey ● Vietnam ● Zimbabwe, Botswana & Namibia

Lonely Planet TV Series & Videos

onely Planet travel guides have been brought to life on television screens around the world. Like our guides, the programs are based on the joy of independent travel and look honestly at some of the most exciting, picturesque and frustrating places in the world. Each show is presented by one of three travellers from Australia, England or the USA and combines an innovative mixture of video, Super-8 film, atmospheric soundscapes and original music.

Videos of each episode – containing additional footage not shown on television – are available from good book and video shops, but the availability of individual videos varies with regional screening schedules.

Video destinations include: Alaska ● American Rockies ● Argentina ● Australia – The South-East ● Baja California & the Copper Canyon ● Brazil ● Central Asia ● Chile & Easter Island ● Corsica, Sicily & Sardinia – The Mediterranean Islands ● East Africa (Tanzania & Zanzibar) ● Cuba ● Ecuador & the Galapagos Islands ● Ethiopia ● Greenland & Iceland ● Hungary & Romania ● Indonesia ● Israel & the Sinai Desert ● Jamaica ● Japan ● La Ruta Maya ● London ● The Middle East (Syria, Jordan & Lebanon) ● Morocco ● New York City ● Northern Spain ● North India ● Outback Australia ● Pacific Islands (Fiji, Solomon Islands & Vanuatu) ● Pakistan ● Peru ● The Philippines ● South Africa & Lesotho ● South India ● South West China ● South West USA ● Trekking in Uganda & Congo ● Turkey ● Vietnam ● West Africa ● Zimbabwe, Botswana & Namibia

The Lonely Planet TV series is produced by: Pilot Productions
The Old Studio
18 Middle Row
London W10 5AT, UK

LONELY PLANET

Guides by Region

Lonely Planet is known worldwide for publishing practical, reliable and nononsense travel information in our guides and on our Web site. The Lonely Planet list covers just about every accessible part of the world. Currently there are thirteen series: travel guides, shoestring guides, walking guides, city guides, phrasebooks, audio packs, city maps, travel atlases, diving & snorkeling guides, restaurant guides, first-time travel guides, healthy travel and travel literature.

AFRICA Africa on a shoestring ● Africa – the South ● Arabic (Egyptian) phrasebook ● Arabic (Moroccan) phrasebook ● Cairo ● Cape Town ● Cape Town city map● Central Africa ● East Africa ● Egypt ● Egypt travel atlas ● Ethiopian (Amharic) phrasebook ● The Gambia & Senegal ● Healthy Travel Africa ● Kenya ● Kenya travel atlas ● Malawi, Mozambique & Zambia ● Morocco ● North Africa ● South Africa, Lesotho & Swaziland ● South Africa, Lesotho & Swaziland travel atlas ● Swahili phrasebook ● Tanzania, Zanzibar & Pemba ● Trekking in East Africa ● Tunisia ● West Africa ● Zimbabwe, Botswana & Namibia ● Zimbabwe, Botswana & Namibia travel atlas
Travel Literature: The Rainbird: A Central African Journey ● Songs to an African Sunset: A Zimbabwean Story ● Mali Blues: Traveling to an African Beat

AUSTRALIA & THE PACIFIC Auckland ● Australia ● Australian phrasebook ● Bushwalking in Australia ● Bushwalking in Papua New Guinea ● Fiji ● Fijian phrasebook ● Healthy Travel Australia, NZ and the Pacific ● Islands of Australia's Great Barrier Reef ● Melbourne ● Melbourne city map ● Micronesia ● New Caledonia ● New South Wales & the ACT ● New Zealand ● Northern Territory ● Outback Australia ● Out To Eat – Melbourne ● Out to Eat – Sydney ● Papua New Guinea ● Pidgin phrasebook ● Queensland ● Rarotonga & the Cook Islands ● Samoa ● Solomon Islands ● South Australia ● South Pacific Languages phrasebook ● Sydney ● Sydney city map ● Sydney Condensed ● Tahiti & French Polynesia ● Tasmania ● Tonga ● Tramping in New Zealand ● Vanuatu ● Victoria ● Western Australia
Travel Literature: Islands in the Clouds ● Kiwi Tracks: A New Zealand Journey ● Sean & David's Long Drive

CENTRAL AMERICA & THE CARIBBEAN Bahamas, Turks & Caicos ● Bermuda ● Central America on a shoestring ● Costa Rica ● Cuba ● Dominican Republic & Haiti ● Eastern Caribbean ● Guatemala, Belize & Yucatán: La Ruta Maya ● Jamaica ● Mexico ● Mexico City ● Panama ● Puerto Rico
Travel Literature: Green Dreams: Travels in Central America

EUROPE Amsterdam ● Amsterdam city map ● Andalucía ● Austria ● Baltic States phrasebook ● Barcelona ● Berlin ● Berlin city map ● Britain ● British phrasebook ● Brussels, Bruges & Antwerp ● Budapest city map ● Canary Islands ● Central Europe ● Central Europe phrasebook ● Corsica ● Croatia ● Czech & Slovak Republics ● Denmark ● Dublin ● Eastern Europe ● Eastern Europe phrasebook ● Edinburgh ● Estonia, Latvia & Lithuania ● Europe on a shoestring ● Finland ● France ● French phrasebook ● Germany ● German phrasebook ● Greece ● Greek Islands ● Greek phrasebook ● Hungary ● Iceland, Greenland & the Faroe Islands ● Ireland ● Italian phrasebook ● Italy ● Krakow ● Lisbon ● London ● London city map ● London Condensed ● Mediterranean Europe ● Mediterranean Europe phrasebook ● Norway ● Paris ● Paris city map ● Poland ● Portugal ● Portugal travel atlas ● Prague ● Prague city map ● Provence & the Côte d'Azur ● Romania & Moldova ● Rome ● Russia, Ukraine & Belarus ● Russian phrasebook ● Scandinavian & Baltic Europe ● Scandinavian Europe phrasebook ● Scotland ● Slovenia ● Spain ● Spanish phrasebook ● St Petersburg ● Switzerland ● Trekking in Spain ● Ukrainian phrasebook ● Vienna ● Walking in Britain ● Walking in Ireland ● Walking in Italy ● Walking in Spain ● Walking in Switzerland ● Western Europe ● Western Europe phrasebook
Travel Literature: The Olive Grove: Travels in Greece

INDIAN SUBCONTINENT Bangladesh ● Bengali phrasebook ● Bhutan ● Delhi ● Goa ● Hindi & Urdu phrasebook ● India ● India & Bangladesh travel atlas ● Indian Himalaya ● Karakoram Highway ● Kerala ● Mumbai (Bombay) ● Nepal ● Nepali phrasebook ● Pakistan ● Rajasthan ● Read This First: Asia & India ● South India ● Sri Lanka ● Sri Lanka phrasebook ● Trekking in the Indian Himalaya ● Trekking in the Karakoram & Hindukush ● Trekking in the Nepal Himalaya
Travel Literature: In Rajasthan ● Shopping for Buddhas

LONELY PLANET

Mail Order

Lonely Planet products are distributed worldwide. They are also available by mail order from Lonely Planet, so if you have difficulty finding a title please write to us. North and South American residents should write to 150 Linden St, Oakland, CA 94607, USA; European and African residents should write to 10a Spring Place, London NW5 3BH, UK; and residents of other countries to PO Box 617, Hawthorn, Victoria 3122, Australia.

ISLANDS OF THE INDIAN OCEAN Madagascar & Comoros ● Maldives ● Mauritius, Réunion & Seychelles

MIDDLE EAST & CENTRAL ASIA Arab Gulf States ● Central Asia ● Central Asia phrasebook ● Hebrew phrasebook ● Iran ● Israel & the Palestinian Territories ● Israel & the Palestinian Territories travel atlas ● Istanbul ● Istanbul to Cairo ● Jerusalem ● Jordan & Syria ● Jordan, Syria & Lebanon travel atlas ● Lebanon ● Middle East on a shoestring ● Syria ● Turkey ● Turkey travel atlas ● Turkish phrasebook ● Yemen
Travel Literature: The Gates of Damascus ● Kingdom of the Film Stars: Journey into Jordan

NORTH AMERICA Alaska ● Backpacking in Alaska ● Baja California ● California & Nevada ● Canada ● Chicago ● Chicago city map ● Deep South ● Florida ● Hawaii ● Honolulu ● Las Vegas ● Los Angeles ● Miami ● New England ● New Orleans ● New York City ● New York city map ● New York, New Jersey & Pennsylvania ● Pacific Northwest USA ● Puerto Rico ● Rocky Mountain ● San Francisco ● San Francisco city map ● Seattle ● Southwest USA ● Texas ● USA ● USA phrasebook ● Vancouver ● Washington, DC & the Capital Region ● Washington DC city map
Travel Literature: Drive Thru America

NORTH-EAST ASIA Beijing ● Cantonese phrasebook ● China ● Hong Kong ● Hong Kong city map ● Hong Kong, Macau & Guangzhou ● Japan ● Japanese phrasebook ● Japanese audio pack ● Korea ● Korean phrasebook ● Kyoto ● Mandarin phrasebook ● Mongolia ● Mongolian phrasebook ● North-East Asia on a shoestring ● Seoul ● South-West China ● Taiwan ● Tibet ● Tibetan phrasebook ● Tokyo
Travel Literature: Lost Japan

SOUTH AMERICA Argentina, Uruguay & Paraguay ● Bolivia ● Brazil ● Brazilian phrasebook ● Buenos Aires ● Chile & Easter Island ● Chile & Easter Island travel atlas ● Colombia ● Ecuador & the Galapagos Islands ● Healthy Travel Central & South America ● Latin American Spanish phrasebook ● Peru ● Quechua phrasebook ● Rio de Janeiro ● Rio de Janeiro city map ● South America on a shoestring ● Trekking in the Patagonian Andes ● Venezuela
Travel Literature: Full Circle: A South American Journey

SOUTH-EAST ASIA Bali & Lombok ● Bangkok ● Bangkok city map ● Burmese phrasebook ● Cambodia ● Hanoi ● Healthy Travel Asia & India ● Hill Tribes phrasebook ● Ho Chi Minh City ● Indonesia ● Indonesia's Eastern Islands ● Indonesian phrasebook ● Indonesian audio pack ● Jakarta ● Java ● Laos ● Lao phrasebook ● Laos travel atlas ● Malay phrasebook ● Malaysia, Singapore & Brunei ● Myanmar (Burma) ● Philippines ● Pilipino (Tagalog) phrasebook ● Singapore ● South-East Asia on a shoestring ● South-East Asia phrasebook ● Thailand ● Thailand's Islands & Beaches ● Thailand travel atlas ● Thai phrasebook ● Thai audio pack ● Vietnam ● Vietnamese phrasebook ● Vietnam travel atlas

ALSO AVAILABLE: Antarctica ● The Arctic ● Brief Encounters: Stories of Love, Sex & Travel ● Chasing Rickshaws ● Lonely Planet Unpacked ● Not the Only Planet: Travel Stories from Science Fiction ● Sacred India ● Travel with Children ● Traveller's Tales

LONELY PLANET

Lonely Planet Online

W hether you've just begun planning your next trip, or you're chasing down specific info on currency regulations or visa requirements, check out Lonely Planet Online for up-to-the-minute travel information.

As well as miniguides to more than 250 destinations, you'll find maps, photos, travel news, health and visa updates, travel advisories and discussion of the ecological and political issues you need to be aware of as you travel. You'll also find timely upgrades to popular guidebooks that you can print out and stick in the back of your book.

There's an online travellers' forum (The Thorn Tree) where you can share your experience of life on the road, meet travel companions and ask other travellers for their recommendations and advice.

There's also a complete and up-to-date list of all Lonely Planet travel products including travel guides, diving and snorkeling guides, phrasebooks, atlases, travel literature and videos, and a simple online ordering facility if you can't find the book you want elsewhere.

Lonely Planet Diving & Snorkeling Guides

B eautifully illustrated with full-colour photos throughout, Lonely Planet's Pisces books explore the world's best diving and snorkeling areas and prepare divers for what to expect when they get there, both topside and underwater.

Dive sites are described in detail with specifics on depths, visibility, level of difficulty, special conditions, underwater photography tips and common and unusual marine life present. You'll also find practical logistical information and coverage on topside activities and attractions, sections on diving health and safety, plus listings for diving services, live-aboards, dive resorts and tourist offices.

LONELY PLANET

FREE Lonely Planet Newsletters

We love hearing from you and think you'd like to hear from us.

Planet Talk

Our FREE quarterly printed newsletter is full of tips from travellers and anecdotes from Lonely Planet guidebook authors. Every issue is packed with up-to-date travel news and advice, and includes:

- a postcard from Lonely Planet co-founder Tony Wheeler
- a swag of mail from travellers
- a look at life on the road through the eyes of a Lonely Planet author
- topical health advice
- prizes for the best travel yarn
- news about forthcoming Lonely Planet events
- a complete list of Lonely Planet books and other titles

To join our mailing list, residents of the UK, Europe and Africa can email us at go@lonelyplanet.co.uk; residents of North and South America can email us at info@lonelyplanet.com; the rest of the world can email us at talk2us@lonelyplanet.com.au, or contact any Lonely Planet office.

Comet

Our FREE monthly email newsletter brings you all the latest travel news, features, interviews, competitions, destination ideas, travellers' tips & tales, Q&As, raging debates and related links. Find out what's new on the Lonely Planet Web site and which books are about to hit the shelves.

Subscribe from your desktop: www.lonelyplanet.com/comet

Index

Text

Bold indicates maps.

Boxed Text

MAP LEGEND

CITY ROUTES

Freeway .... Freeway	==== ...... Unsealed Road
Highway .... Primary Road	.... One Way Street
Road ...... Secondary Road	.... Pedestrian Street
Street .... Street	.... Stepped Street
Lane .... Lane	⇥== .... Tunnel
.... On/Off Ramp	.... Footbridge

REGIONAL ROUTES

.... Tollway, Freeway
.... Primary Road
...... Secondary Road
.... Minor Road

BOUNDARIES

.... International
.... State
.... Disputed
.... Fortified Wall

HYDROGRAPHY

.... River, Creek	Dry Lake; Salt Lake
.... Canal	Spring; Rapids
.... Lake	Waterfalls

TRANSPORT ROUTES & STATIONS

.... Train	.... Ferry
... Underground Train	..... Walking Trail
.... Metro	.... Walking Tour
.... Tramway	.... Path
... Cable Car, Chairlift	.... Pier or Jetty

AREA FEATURES

.... Building	.... Market	.... Beach
.... Park, Gardens	.... Sports Ground	.... Cemetery

.... Campus
.... Plaza

POPULATION SYMBOLS

CAPITAL .... National Capital	**CITY** .... City	Village .... Village
CAPITAL .... State Capital	Town .... Town	.... Urban Area

MAP SYMBOLS

.... Place to Stay	.... Place to Eat

| .... Point of Interest |

Airfield, Airport	.... Embassy	.... Museum	..... Shopping Centre
.... Bank	.... Golf Course	.... National Park	...... Swimming Pool
.... Border Crossing	.... Hospital	.... Palace	.... Synagogue
Bus Stop, Bus Terminal	.... Internet Cafe	... Parking, Taxi Rank	.... Telephone
.... Cave	.... Lookout	.... Police Station	.... Temple, Pagoda
.... Church	.... Monument	.... Post Office	.. Tourist Information
.... Cinema	.... Mosque	.... Pub or Bar	.... Zoo

Note: not all symbols displayed above appear in this book

LONELY PLANET OFFICES

Australia
PO Box 617, Hawthorn, Victoria 3122
☎ 03 9819 1877 fax 03 9819 6459
email: talk2us@lonelyplanet.com.au

USA
150 Linden St, Oakland, CA 94607
☎ 510 893 8555 TOLL FREE: 800 275 8555
fax 510 893 8572
email: info@lonelyplanet.com

UK
10a Spring Place, London NW5 3BH
☎ 020 7428 4800 fax 020 7428 4828
email: go@lonelyplanet.co.uk

France
1 rue du Dahomey, 75011 Paris
☎ 01 55 25 33 00 fax 01 55 25 33 01
email: bip@lonelyplanet.fr
www.lonelyplanet.fr

World Wide Web: www.lonelyplanet.com *or* AOL keyword: lp
Lonely Planet Images: lpi@lonelyplanet.com.au